ULRIKA

JONSSON

HONEST

SIDGWICK & JACKSON

First published 2002 by Sidgwick & Jackson
an imprint of Pan Macmillan Ltd
Pan Macmillan, 20 New Wharf Road, London N1 9RR
Basingstoke and Oxford
Associated companies throughout the world
www.panmacmillan.com

ISBN 0 283 07367 5

3 5 7 9 8 6 4 2

A CIP catalogue record for this book is available from
the British Library.

Typeset by SetSystems Ltd, Saffron Walden, Essex
Printed and bound in Great Britain by
Mackays of Chatham plc, Chatham, Kent

To Cameron and Bo

*Remember, if the worst comes to the worst,
being screwed up can sometimes
make you more interesting.*

A woman is like a tea bag.
It's not until she's in hot water that
you realize how strong she is.

CONTENTS

ACKNOWLEDGEMENTS

This book is also dedicated to my mother and the memory of my father, without whom I would simply not have been possible.

A big thanks to Pan Macmillan for telling me I can write, but an even greater thank you to my editor at Sidgwick & Jackson, wise Gordon Wise, who sometimes told me I couldn't. Without his advice, guidance and flair this book would have been even worser.

I want to thank my close family for their support, patience and kindness, shown to me at times when I may not have been too gorgeous.

Equally, I have been overwhelmed by the public response I seem to have generated over the years. The kindness and generosity and empathy of those who have written or spoken to me in the street does not go unappreciated. Thank you, so very much.

My friends, who I'm sure would appreciate anonymity, have been true, best and honest. I love you all very much.

The closest of these is Melanie. Meeting you was one of the best things that ever happened to me. I feel so close to you and am eternally grateful to you for your understanding, patience, support and ridiculous hearing. At times my journey has been hard but your unfailing strength has made it easier. I'm here for you, too.

John, your presence in my life has not only been enriching, but it has also been the best thing since flapjacks from the Handmade Flapjack Company. Your intelligence, wit, understanding and support have kept me afloat when I thought I would drown. You're a beautiful person – thank you for Cameron.

I'd like to extend my gratitude to my nanny, Michelle, whose enthusiasm and flexibility is second to none – bar one major hiccup (page 403). We love you lots!

Without the support, care and expertise of the cardiac team at Guy's Hospital, and in particular Bo's outreach nurse, Catie, we wouldn't have got through the last two years.

Thanks to lovely Saab for keeping me safely and fantastically mobile. My professional appearance is predominantly courtesy of two hard-working, patient and loving people: Amanda Monk and Gary Cockerill. Thanks for being on board. And without my therapist, surgeon, beautician and accountant I would not be standing so taut!

Thanks to my celebrity friends, of which there are at least – oh, I don't know – two or three. You know who you are. Or were.

Lastly – Cameron, you are truly the greatest little man and Bo, you are truly the best whistler and a blessing in disguise. I love you both more than anything. Without you life is not worth living.

La-La Land,
Berkshire,
2002

INTRODUCTION

I have been married, divorced, faithful and unfaithful. I have battled with depression and enjoyed moments of bliss. I have had an abortion, I have been raped and I have stripteased. I have told black lies and white lies. I have loved myself and loathed myself. I have surrendered my body and soul for two other lives . . . my children's.

Throughout my life, my exterior and my interior have done battle – not just on account of being born one nationality and living quite another, or indeed of having parents at opposing ends of the personality spectrum, but also on account of having lived my life very publicly for some fourteen years. At the age of thirty-two what had surfaced was a crisis of persona. The public person I read about had no relevance for the private person I lived with. I had endured the insecurity of an unstable childhood, and subjected those around me and myself to a private life in the public domain, but had failed to have the courage to believe and trust in myself and, despite having borne adult responsibility early on, failed to mature in the sense of becoming spiritually confident.

I was born in Sweden – the country that practically invented political correctness, off the back of a powerful women's movement and an overwhelming immigrant population. Where railway carriages are hypoallergenic and liquor is queued for at state-run outlets; a nation where true poverty does not exist, thanks to a social security system to die for and where everyone is some sort of middle class. This is a country where women hold their own and real men stay at home practising submission.

I grew up as part of the newly created 'non-smoking generation', for whom everything was recycled and recyclable, and who only flushed the toilet when absolutely necessary. Sweden is a nation that tends towards the functional, rarely the aesthetic. Its people are natural in their appearance and in their approach. Their reputation across the world as sex-mad naturists sits a little uneasy with them. However, nudity itself does come as easy to the Swedes as talking about the weather does to the English. In Sweden, breasts are an acceptable part of the body – oh, and incidentally, the pussy is known as a mouse.

This was in stark contrast to what I encountered in England upon my arrival in June 1979. Since then I have been anglicized, moralized and hypnotized by this beautiful country. I feel Swedish in England and fantastically English in Sweden. But one thing is not transient, and that is my soul. Well and truly grounded in Sweden, it is free, born out of free spirits and a naturalness so common in my fellow countrymen.

This is not the story of an abused childhood, even of a sensational childhood by any means, but when I started to write this book I wanted to go back and look at what in my life has contributed towards the person I am today. I have found in myself surprising insecurities, volatile vulnerability and unstable strength, and I wanted in some way to attribute them. It is not meant to be a book about the quality of my parents; my feelings and my impressions may differ from theirs, but certain experiences have undoubtedly left their mark and helped shape the person I have been and to some extent still am. My hope is that armed with this knowledge, I can better understand my past actions and reactions.

HUGO WAS A GIRL

'Hugo was a girl, daughter to Bo and Gun Jonsson', read the announcement of my birth on 16 August 1967. Which, with hindsight, wasn't strictly true. I was born a girl – true – but for the most part brought up a boy. And therein lies the essence of the two people who occupy Eva Ulrika Jonsson. My father had jokingly suggested the name Hugo early on in the pregnancy, and, finding it not to my mother's taste, had taunted her with it constantly – it wasn't as though he was actually keen on it himself. But unfortunately for him she grew quite attached to the name and, as the birth loomed, my father was praying for a girl, if only to avoid having a Hugo for a son. My beginnings were further complicated by my mother choosing Eva as my first name, but always calling me Ulrika.

At 9lb 11oz it was obvious, upon my very arrival, that I was never likely to do justice to a tutu. I apparently enjoyed my mother's womb so much that I outstayed my welcome . . . by three weeks. After my delayed birth, my mother was stitched and re-stitched without anaesthetic, an experience which must in some way contribute towards her feelings for me.

So there I lay in my cot, the largest baby to be born in that hospital for some time; overripe, covered in thick bluey black hair, content in my fatness; with a teenage mother and a father who had missed my birth on account of a bicycle puncture. My mother grew up overnight as a direct result of her new-found responsibility. My father, however, did not. Ever.

Bo Folke Christer Jonsson, the son of an international opera singer and a pianist mother, had placed himself in the very comfortable occupational seat of driving instructor by the age of twenty-four. With the exception of the occasional middle-aged or geriatric learner, his custom consisted mainly of eighteen-year-olds, of which at least half would be female and ripe for the picking.

Of average height, slender features, sporting a heady quiff and a Kirk Douglas dimple, my father, with his charm, wit and relaxed manner, secured his place in many a young woman's heart and loins. My mother, a well-groomed, flirtatious, vivacious secretary, daughter of a foreman and an office worker, and on the very threshold of life itself, was no exception. After successfully manoeuvring a hill during one lesson, she was promised a date. Little did this redhead know that she was thus embarking upon a radically changed future. Some time after, she was in the club.

My first home was a bedsit on the Skälby estate, twenty kilometres north of Stockholm. Despite being a fundamentally contented baby, once my dislike of my mother's breast had been established, I was probably not a symbol of the young, carefree future my mother had hoped for. I restricted her tremendously. Staying at home in a tiny bedsit for the first five months, with only fellow mums to talk to, began to suffocate her. She needed to return to work both for financial reasons and for the sake of her faculties. She was nineteen and didn't need to be obsessively ambitious to have set her sights higher than a fourth-floor bedsit and an overweight toddler.

So both my parents worked, my mother as a secretary and my father at the driving school. As a result, when I was one year old we could afford to rent a ground-floor, two-bedroom flat in nearby Häggvik. We even had a small terrace, and I had the luxury of my own room. My joy was complete when my parents decided to get a dog. Frida was a Boston terrier, the cutest thing. It was in this place that I can truly say my life began.

Klasrovägen 45a was in one of six blocks of flats on a very pleasant and green estate. This was no council estate, but a classic example of Scandinavian social progress: a housing association sub-

town. We were lower-middle-class, with the front of our flat look-ing out on the adjacent upper-middle-class development, whose inhabitants owned their own houses and had large gardens. The back stared vacantly out onto another block of similar abodes. But what stood between the two blocks was what was to become my saviour, my torment, my sparring and kissing ground and the reason for my chubby, grubby fingers: the playground.

*

Oddly enough, one of my earliest memories has me sleeping in the cabin of my dad's home-built motor boat. I remember the lapping of the water against the hull, and the soft, gentle rocking, lulling me to sleep. Yet it is the memory of a child whose father spent most of his time away from the family building that boat or training at the local sports club, or absent for any number of reasons. My father's absences, his white lies, infidelity, hedonism and committed unreliability were eventually to be his downfall.

His relaxed, carefree manner chalked my mother's cheese. I suspect my dad's wit lifted him out of many domestic shit holes. He regularly 'forgot' dinner dates with the in-laws, much to my mother's despair, but he would ultimately either waltz in and win everyone over with a prank, or affectionately repent with the words, 'You know how I am,' and my mother would forgive him. He even excused an affair on the same vacuous grounds. But it was hard to stay angry with a man who had such an ability to break down barriers with humour and charm.

I would hear my mother nag and raise her voice occasionally. It was the voice of a frustrated woman. But I also remember her laughter. It was strong, bordering on harsh, and would eventually dissolve into giggles and tears, or alternately crescendo into an almost screech. She was always rather glamorous-looking for her age. Her strict make-up routine fascinated me. I will never forget how she would lay it all out on tissue paper on the kitchen table and grimace in the mirror as she proceeded with her transformation. I remember a little pot with a black lid, which contained powder to be applied to her eyelashes prior to the mascara. I remember the purple and burgundy eyeshadows and the tube of rouge that brought her cheeks to life. Just as my dad didn't really need a drink to make him funny, my mother's face did not really require any paint. She was a natural beauty, but the fashion in those days required thick, hard lines and paler lips. And the application of this paint made her seem more alive, kinder and friendlier, somehow.

From what very little my mother has subsequently told me of her life together with my father, it emerges that she spent a lot of her time chasing around, with me in tow, looking for him. A beautiful, organized and increasingly impatient young mother, she embraced her maternal tasks with all the practicality and matter-of-fact efficiency that made her such an able office worker. Yet in her haste and desire to get everything sorted out and move swiftly along to the next thing, physical tenderness was often sacrificed. She applied cream to my face with all the dexterity of a boxer; combed my hair roughly; and held me in a firm headlock to clean my teeth.

My father, on the other hand, was gentle in his movements, unhurried and unrushed. There was almost a feeling of him living in slow motion, so relaxed was his demeanour – something which no doubt stood him in good stead in a nerve-racking profession. The word impatient was one he didn't understand. In fact, the only thing it appeared my parents had in common, apart from me, was a sense of humour and a lively social life.

As I grew up there were parties galore. My parents' social circle was made up of members of the boat club (the only religious dedication in our household), a couple of my dad's colleagues, a woman my mother had met on the train and my auntie Mona. Despite money being tight, a bring-a-bottle policy ensured happy drink- and smoke-filled parties, and in progressive Scandinavian fashion, it was never suggested that children might not be in attendance. I must have been no older than six then, and the experience stood me in good stead: I was always very excited at the prospect of crisps and nuts being left out on tables, and the promise of a friend to play with for the duration. The only times I can remember anything untoward happening was when my father broke his big toe kicking a stone – which had looked remarkably like a football at the time, and when my mother, who became loud and carefree under the influence, ate all the blueberries I had laboriously picked that day. Apart from that, and the time I went on the run with my friend Sanna, these were happy times.

I never met Sanna's black father, but her white mother was my mother's closest friend. She was also briefly a communist, which proved irresistible to my mum, who promptly became a fully paid-up member of the Party. My impressionable mother had up until now preferred to socialize rather than be a socialist, and the only party she had attended was not of the kind she would encounter at a communist gathering. I was frequently dragged along to rallies and demos, shouting slogans such as: 'What does Nixon say? Nixon says peace. What does Nixon do? Nixon keeps on bombing!' I had no idea who Nixon was except that my mother was very angry with him, and I had a very limited knowledge of communism. But then I was only six.

In between communist rallies and wild seventies parties, I managed to fit in daily visits to the local crèche. My first childcare institution was a short train ride away. The ten-minute walk to the railway station seemed to take hours, despite my mother's daily attempts to reduce it to forty-five seconds. If this journey had been part of our lives for more than two years, I would now be typing with only one hand. Such was the power of her march, my mother would be in possession of the other, arm, socket and all.

At the crèche they took children from two months up to school age, which in Sweden is seven. Activities ranged from gardening, arts and crafts and picking raisins off a table, to cutting my friends' hair with blunt scissors, running away and having sex. Oh, and we did have the occasional outing.

Yes, indeed: kindergarten is where I first had a bit of hanky-panky. One of the other girls and I used to get naked with one of the boys under one of the beds used for afternoon sleeps. I do recall his name, but I'll spare him the blushes 'cos his winky was only dinky. But he knew where to put it, and whilst I'm not convinced there was actual penetration, I do remember lying on top of him and feeling extremely good. So good, in fact, that I proudly rushed home to tell my communist mother, who laughed her head off as I mispronounced the word 'fuck'. I've often wondered if I lost my virginity then or if it was in Marbella eleven years later . . . that occasion was, sadly, not as pleasurable.

*

Life on our estate was good. The housing association from which we rented provided a fridge and cooker for each flat and a never-ending supply of hot water. I should know. One day I was determined to challenge the system by taking six baths and four showers. It was true, it was never-ending! But communal washing machines and drying rooms were situated in a building at the top of the estate. You could reserve a machine by attaching a small padlock bearing your personal housing-association number to a grid of hooks marked with the days of the week. My mother sighed and moaned when up there because she could never find a suitable time slot. She, alongside much of the rest of Sweden, was at work from eight in the morning until six at night, and had to fight for the over-subscribed washing times.

I, on the other hand, loved it. When my mother eventually left us, I did the washing. I used to look at the different powders people were using and try to smell the difference between them. There were lots of interesting boxes of powder; ours was the economy packet without any logos or pictures. But what I loved most about that place were the rooms where you hung your laundry to dry. The smell of the laundry, together with the warmth and the hum of the machines, was comforting and irresistible. I used to run between the sheets and the clothes – dancing and pirouetting, allowing the sheets to sweep across my face, over the top of my head, and then fall down my back. The heat was so reassuring and slightly dangerous. I often dreamed of being locked in there to see how long I would last, but also to see if anyone would notice I was gone.

My father, though unreliable, was extremely practical. What was lacking in his head on account of being expelled from school at the age of fourteen, he more than made up for with his hands. He was incredibly artistic and would often draw, paint murals or indulge in his love of photography. He would also decorate, build or mend. And all this with a Prince cigarette hanging out of the left side of his mouth, or secured between his fingers. There was something reassuring about the smell when he was working or watching TV. However, when it made its way into the car, I felt quite nauseous. My mother smoked heavily, too.

Our living room was a confusion of green – three different greens on each of three walls. The room was dominated by three gigantic windows. These 1960s monstrosities had stone window sills, which played host to several sad, insecure houseplants and cacti. These were my windows on the world: I loved to lean on the cold sills and stare out at the silent playground, on falling snow, or at the screwed-up faces of the women carrying home the shopping. Then one day, quite out of the blue and without provocation, I balanced on one arm of the sofa and, to an audience of four or five outside, took my clothes off, piece by piece. I also insisted on bending over and showing off my every orifice. Some years later it caused me no end of embarrassment as the spectators would insist on recalling the event, calling to me about it from across the street.

My parents' love of green made its way into my room, where I endured a heavy khaki check for too many years. All my friends were allowed to choose their wallpaper, but mine kept its depressing dark tones. My room had a window under which I slept on a red-stained pine bed. On my seventh birthday I got a brown pine writing desk, which was my pride and joy. I had a long mirror, and my walls were plastered with my untypically girly passion: horses.

Just outside my room was a narrow hallway leading to the kitchen with grey MDF fitted wardrobes. Off the hallway lay first a separate toilet and further along a small bathroom. One night I went to the toilet and after locking the door found that I couldn't get out. I called, but my parents slept on, unaware that their most precious commodity was in trouble. Maybe this was a sign that I wasn't so precious. Or maybe God was just giving me a helping hand on the narrow road to claustrophobia. I've never been good in confined spaces since.

Our kitchen, being Swedish, was naturally very practical – although somewhat depressing with its grey units and frail-looking white handles. Once again, a large window was the dominant feature. My parents' bedroom led off to the right in a riot of red and orange. Not the most calming choice of colours for the marriage bower, I would have thought. It was dominated by their two single beds, pushed together, and had a glass door that opened out onto our tiny, but significant, terrace. It gave me quick access to the playground and my pool of friends, and a couple of flower beds encouraged my love for planting and growing things.

There was a mad man next door but one, the son of a very fat couple. All the children were terrified of him, as his behaviour was unpredictable – once he tried to strangle our dog. A couple of doors down lived a wonderful Polish lady called Genia. She had a small white poodle that always stank of piss, but I forgave her as she let me play with her fibre-optic lamp, which was truly magical. And just a bit further up lived my soon-to-be first boyfriend, who was overweight and rough – a sign of things to come for me – but his parents had a chandelier in their living room, which I thought was the height of luxury. His father was an alcoholic, and it was in his mother's bathroom that I first smelled Elnett hairspray. An unforgettable smell.

So that was my early, early life. Parents with different priorities, who lived at two different speeds, moving increasingly in differing directions – one building boats, the other building a family. One with a wicked sense of humour and one with a growing element of seriousness. One happy with his lot, the other hoping there was more to life than an estate and an untamed husband.

LICKING LAMP-POSTS

I cannot say that there was any one particular moment when I sensed that things were going wrong between my parents. I was too young to understand. There were arguments and fights, never physical, but extremely vocal, followed shortly by my father moving out for a while. When they fought it was mainly in the evenings and at night-time. I would be in my room in the dark, guessing blindly at what was going on. I heard talk of a *skilsmässa*, or divorce, which I did not understand at all. But as I spun the word round and round in my head and chopped it in half, I thought the last bit sounded like *mössa*, which in Swedish means 'hat'. So I felt this must be a positive thing, that they would probably both wear hats for a while, until things got better.

Things, however, did not get better. My father ultimately moved out to a bedsit on a nearby estate, where both my mum and I would visit him. There appeared to be no animosity between them. They were civil towards each other. My mum's mum, my *mormor*, even helped my dad out with curtains and odd bits of furniture. My dad was able to carry on with life pretty much as before. He was able to look after himself very well, even if his methods were sometimes unusual. On one occasion when I may even have stayed with him, I woke up in the morning to find him in the shower. Beside him was a pile of shirts, and he was actually wearing one as he showered. This was my dad's way of washing clothes, far from conventional, but practical somehow.

My mother met a new man. He had a flat in Stockholm, which

we often visited. I didn't understand him. He always seemed angry and was, in fact, mad-bordering-on-violent. One unhappy holiday to Rhodes (where my arms got so sunburnt that they erupted in blisters the size of yoghurt pots) and several smashed plates later, my mother ended the relationship and took up with my father again. The reunion was brief, and by the time I turned eight my mother had gone.

She was, however, around for my first year at school. I can still recall her standing by the sink with her back to me, saying, 'Who's a big girl starting school, then?' and I remember feeling extremely proud.

Prior to the commencement of school, each pupil was issued a list of classmates, complete with addresses and telephone numbers, and the name of the form teacher. I only recognized two names on the list – 'Åse', with whom I often played at the boat club, and myself. Åse had not been a great friend of mine – there was something frail about her that unnerved me – but as I was standing on the threshold of an exciting new, frightening world, she suddenly qualified.

Already, at seven, my life had gone full circle. The school I was about to attend was back in Skälby, across town where we had originally lived in the bedsit. Then, sometime during my first school year, my mother left. I vaguely remember her talking on the phone to someone in English and showing me a photo of a kind-looking man with a beard who had apparently come to Stockholm for a business meeting some time before. When she spoke on the phone to him, she was always laughing and smiling, which made me happy too. She would positively beam as she came off the phone. I cannot for the life of me recall the day she left, nor if I understood what was going on, which with hindsight was perhaps a good thing. I was too young to question.

So, as my mother left for a new life in Holland with Michael, the kind-faced Englishman in the photo, I carried on my life with my father in our little flat.

My father was no disciplinarian. He had, as a child, broken every rule, so had low expectations of me. He treated me like the boy I suspect he had so longed for and we did almost everything together. At weekends and non-school times, Frida and I went everywhere with my father: football training in summer and *bandy* training in winter (a traditional Swedish game that's a bit like English land hockey on ice); building boats; messing with cars; plane spotting; visiting army surplus outlets; watching military parades; eyeing up women. Just the kinds of things a healthy young girl of eight should be doing. So whilst my friends were choosing new clothes for their collections of Barbies, I could be found, head under bonnet, changing the oil in a Fiat Mirafiori.

Building boats was more than a hobby for my father: it was a lifetime's passion. He had initially been a lover of fast motorboats, but when he discovered sailing the fire in his heart was truly lit. When I was about nine he embarked on his biggest project ever – building his own yacht. Over the next few years he put absolutely everything into it, from the sweat on his brow to the skin of his hands; his every anxiety, his every spare moment and everything, if anything, that was in his bank account. It really was quite a remarkable feat. It was called a Rapier 28, and I remember vividly how he unfolded the drawings in my grandfather's garage and studied them for hours in silence. I looked on in silence out of respect. It was as if we were looking at a 3,000-year-old document revealing the whereabouts of some long-lost treasure. The following day he began to flatten a small area of my grandparents' garden in preparation for the shed he would erect to house his holy creation. Then I felt honoured to be in attendance. But over the next three or so years, excessive familiarity with this building site and its meaning began to signal boredom and frustration for me.

I played on my own in my grandparents' garden for hours on end. My dad was too engrossed in his project to speak to me and his parents rarely spoke anyway. Farfar, my grandfather, was once a formidable international opera singer, but was by then very much retired. He spent most of his time banished to the cellar of the house by his wife – my *farmor* – sucking raspberry sweets, puffing on cigarillos and humming classical tunes. Farmor freaked me a little as she wore a wig, with the longest, thinnest grey hair underneath. She was small and rather humpbacked. Quite a cold woman, she was extremely miserly – tight even with food. Whilst Farfar kept himself to himself, Farmor constantly moaned about her backache, ensuring my father did every little errand for her. I had the feeling I irritated her somewhat, so whenever I was around I spent most of my time outside, and would only occasionally sneak in to use the toilet or have a gentle tinkle on the piano in their living room.

My father was the eldest of three children. I was close to my uncle Pettan but not my auntie Agnetha. She was rarely around, but her daughter Carina, my cousin, became my friend. Carina, Frida, a budgie called Stumpen, a stray tomcat and the mouse I usually kept were my powerful allies. Mice were cheap and replaceable pets, but I still wept openly as my father's carelessness managed to kill three of them in quick succession. Later I even lost my darling budgie – my father had left the cage open overnight, and Stumpen had an untimely collision with one of our fantastically large windows. These incidents tended to lower my father in my estimation for a bit, although he would always have me believe I was the stupid one.

Stumpen was replaced with a frigid, petrified budgie who hated being handled and could take hours to be persuaded back into the cage. The pets were, however, my responsibility and I cared for them religiously. And this despite learning, as a result of having fifty-four needles stuck in my back on a visit to hospital, that I was allergic to furry animals. There was never any suggestion we would get rid of any of our animals, and nor would I have agreed. I adored the biggest offender, Frida, and was quite prepared to suffer for her sake the permanent nasal congestion, itchy, red swollen eyes and painful eczema in the folds of my arms and legs that had initally prompted the hospital visit. It was a relief to my family, apparently, that we had finally discovered what it was that made me so unwell, but not much relief for me, as I spent the evenings bathing my bleeding arms and legs in astringents, and for the most part 'guessing' what food tasted like on account of being constantly bunged up. Even once

I knew what was good for me, I would not leave the dog alone; I was determined to ignore advice and carry on as I wanted.

So, without siblings, the animals became my family, and I cared for them with the love and efficiency of a mother. I instinctively fostered my father, too. But I also felt a distinct lack of protection for myself, and hence invented an older brother, Peter, to whom I often spoke, whenever he wasn't away doing military service.

*

In my third year at school, some of us joined a new class. My new classmates were very conservative and to all intents and purposes well-behaved, well-dressed and bright. Little did we newcomers realize that the class had a well-established pecking order that was nigh on impossible to penetrate. At the top of the tree were the Johnson twins, who were, unsurprisingly, blonde, but also desperately pretty; then came their fifth wheel, Lotta, with rather piggish features. Another girl, Marianne, was lovely, but unusually tall and quite large. Clabbe was the King of the Jungle and had strikingly good features; his sidekick, Jarri, was the half-Finnish son of an alcoholic. The rest of us were very alike in being unremarkable. But I made friends easily, predominantly due to my insatiable desire to please. After all, as part of the non-smoking generation popularity and approval were the only addictions available to me.

The boys in the class were a minority, but being a tomboy myself, I felt I inflated their numbers by one. Deep down my loyalty was quite torn between the sexes. I enjoyed the roughness of the boys, both physically and psychologically; but I was equally tempted by the girls' role-playing games. Living with a dad who treated you like a boy meant giving as good as you got. He made me strong physically and my body often made up for what I perhaps lacked in genuine courage. I suppose bruises up and down a little girl's arms could have been a cause for concern, but in my case they were genuinely sustained from play-fighting with 90 kg of father.

Between school finishing and my dad coming home I was still obliged to go to a childminder. Her name was Dagmar and she lived with her husband and two of her three children in what seemed to me a large house, right across the road from us. She was incredibly strict, in an admirable, no-nonsense kind of a way. Her husband's pastime was hunting and his silences scared me; I figured that a man who knew how to operate a gun deserved to be feared. But my two or three years with Dagmar provided me with some much-sought-after stability and normality, the novelty of routine, and at least one good meal a day – a nutritious afternoon snack, which changed daily, all of which had to be eaten up whether you liked it or not. She used to force us to play outside, regardless of the weather, which in winter was harsh with few hours of daylight. Her loud speeches about the virtues of fresh air didn't always cut it with the eight-year-old standing on her porch unable to move in $-23°$ C.

Dagmar also cared for a baby, a toddler and a boy my age, Niklas. We often played together with Dagmar's youngest son and always had to help out at mealtimes or with the little ones. Dagmar was strict on manners and we weren't allowed to run the taps whilst washing our hands, as this wasted water, as did flushing the toilet unnecessarily. The TV was never on. Instead our creative needs were met in the form of various art and craft projects including knitting, sewing, crocheting and papier mâché. It was the start of a lifetime's pastime for me, knitting.

To comfort me further Dagmar kept a very full fridge and also introduced me to a series of books, called *Kotten's backvända 'b'n*, about a little girl aged about eight who lived with her father as her mother had moved to Holland, and who kept getting her b's and d's mixed up. It was a relief to me that my mother wasn't the only one who liked Holland.

Four of us girls gradually joined forces on our daily walk to and from school. Åsa and Åse lived on the same estate as I did, and Annette, just spitting distance away in a big house. The girls were quite different from me, all from strong, solid families, but we did all share a certain insanity which often had us laughing until we positively exploded. I alternated best friends with Åsa and Annette. Never Åse. For the most part the group was strong, except on one occasion when I was frozen out on account of 'hitting too hard' when we messed around. I took the point, but it was difficult to temper my blows given what I was used to doing to my father. A boy in my class once stared at me for too long so I flattened him. He was taken to hospital for stitches.

The only other time the group found fault with me was when they complained about being able to see my father walking around our flat naked from where they lived. This was not something that had ever bothered me, but well, if it was an issue for my friends . . . I took it up with him. He laughed loudly and to my shame proceeded to run around the flat stitchless, swivelling his hips to the maximum so that his penis went around like a Ferris wheel, then bending over for his finale to split his bum cheeks with his hands to expose the heart of his anus. 'There!' he shouted with great satisfaction, and walked away. And that was my dad.

Otherwise, the four of us were great together. We all had different characters but I was the one willing to do anything to secure their friendships. This meant winning the competition for walking the furthest with snot hanging out of my nose and saliva hanging from my chin; scrumping forbidden apples; and using my dad's phone as the headquarters for our ritual abuse of random phone numbers. But, blessed with the same dose of intelligence and luck as the man who had fertilized my mother's egg, I remained blissfully unaware that the man whose number we were dialling to torture him daily lived only two doors away. This came to my attention one unfortunate evening, when the man, nervous, broken and dishevelled, knocked on our door and informed my dad that his neurosis was a direct result of relentless, abusive phone calls made from my father's address. He had spent a fortune having them traced. My father apologized unreservedly and assured the lost man that he was not the perpetrator, but that he had a good idea who might be. He assured the man that the bill would be paid by me and out of my friends' pocket money. Then he took his coat and went out to work on the boat.

I felt stupid. But it wasn't the only stupid thing I did. On one occasion I decided it would be a good idea to see what would happen if I let a stray cat loose in our home. It was not a pretty sight. When I put it down, both the cat and our dog went bananas and the cat left claw marks all the way down my legs. My father's car had dual controls. Once, whilst he was driving at 70 kmh, I decided to try out the brakes. Another time, my father had laboriously written out a team sheet for the sports club with a red felt-tip pen. I asked if I could look at the sheet, and he said fine, but not to get it wet as the ink wasn't permanent. So I took it out in the rain, just to check.

It is also a well-known fact, in Sweden, that lamp-posts get very cold in the winter and that freezing metal should not be touched, let alone licked, as you can either get stuck or get a freeze burn. Well, I just had to try it. Don't ever tell me I shouldn't do something, because I will always want to find out for myself. Well, the time I licked a lamp-post in winter, I found out a lot about lamp-posts at close range, and for some time, too. It took three friends to breathe warm air on me in order to loosen my tongue's grip on the pole. Boy, was my tongue sore.

MY FATHER
AND OTHER ANIMALS

To say I was no oil painting would not be to exaggerate. As soon as my second lot of teeth came through, my mouth looked as if someone had stood some distance away and simply thrown my teeth in. I was proud of my bottom teeth, even though they slightly crossed over. But my top front teeth became the bane of my life. They stuck out at such an angle that I could comfortably fit my thumb between the top and bottom rows with my teeth clenched. Whenever I smiled in those days, I used my lower lip to conceal my top tusks. And my father used them for focusing his camera whenever he was preparing to take a shot. I was skinny and grubby for the most part and likened my nose to a freckled potato. I had short, very blonde hair, because my father preferred girls with short hair. My ears were pierced, from the age of six, but this still didn't stop people asking my dad how old the boy was at the turnstiles when we went to the football.

Both my father and I were fervent football fans and would go along to local matches, as well as to see Hammarby, one of three Stockholm teams, play. I would take the train into town to meet my father and my uncle Pettan, hiding my team scarf inside my jacket so as not to attract attention from the opposition's fans. Once at the match, my dad would have me on my feet, whilst everyone else remained seated, shouting out abuse along the lines of 'The referee is blind!', which was always met with laughter.

I adored football. I loved the smell, the feel and the excitement
of a football match. Nothing quite compares. In the years I had my
dad to myself, a particular treat would be going to games or watching
the sports news every Sunday night together. My dad played the
football pools and we would eagerly await the results. He often let
me help predict wins, losses and scores. It was at this time that I
chose a team to support from the second half of the pools coupon –
the English Division One. I nearly picked Arsenal, because I thought
it sounded like 'arsehole' (funny how you always learn the swear
words in a foreign language before any grammar), but eventually
plumped for Manchester United for no specific reason. I was nine
have been a loyal supporter ever since, contrary to popular opinion.

At our local sports club, my father did a mean line in commen-
tating, even getting himself into the local papers for his wicked
humour. I was his hanger-on, if at times a bit lost – and there was
nowhere else for me to go. I became so much a part of my father
that, as if I was a parasite, he did at times forget about me. Like the
time after football practice when I had to wait for him in the
changing rooms. I felt embarrassed by the presence of so many nude
middle-aged men, a thought one might relish today, but didn't dare
to show it. Eventually one of my dad's fellow players pointed me
out, and my dad said it was OK to go and wait outside.

Running his own driving school inevitably meant long, irregular
hours for my father. On a normal workday, if he wasn't working on
the boat, he would be out of the flat by six in the morning – his first
lesson was at seven o'clock. On the five or so days a week he was
building the boat, he would leave me in a deep sleep in his bedroom.
I often shared with him from about half past four in the morning. I
would lie next to him and dig my feet under his covers, winding and
twisting them around his legs. I loved to feel the weight of his limbs
on me. It made me feel secure; it anchored me somehow. He would
rarely return much before seven thirty in the evening; if he was
working on the boat, he would not be through the door before half
past nine. So not much time to play happy families.

At the age of nine I was given the keys to the city. It was a coming of age, something I had been waiting for impatiently for some years: I officially became a latch-key kid. Whilst the key to our flat had hung around my neck on a piece of black bias binding since I was seven, I was now able to bypass Dagmar's house after school and open the front door to further independence. Latch-key kids are the norm in a country where most women have jobs and careers. Most of my friends' mums worked part-time or were at home, so to some extent I was the exception and presumably in breach of the law. But running a household, looking after my dad and being in possession of my own set of keys brought about in me a kind of maturity which would not manifest itself in my friends for a good five or six years yet. But the flip side for a child who grows up too quickly is the persistent desire to be childish long into adulthood. Eventually there have to be moments of madness, hedonism and immaturity.

I loved my friends, but I frequently found myself engaged in conversation with their mothers. I often opted for the kitchen rather than my friends' rooms: there was both food and stability there. I loved the fact that they cooked and baked, and in my mind pictured myself in their shoes. Their dedication, patience and care warmed me greatly. I longed for something similar. Food in our home was hard to find. We had a larder full of tins dating back to happier times and a fridge with nothing to refrigerate. Surprisingly for a man who loved to eat and was fast becoming a larger version of his former self, food was an afterthought for my father. He couldn't cook, so he made sure we habitually hung around other people's houses long enough to be offered a meal. If we didn't succeed, we went to the hot-dog kiosk or desperately tried to rustle up something out of nothing at home. Ninety-five per cent of my diet consisted of sandwiches, hot dogs or hamburgers and the occasional injection of cold ravioli straight from the tin. School provided the remaining five per cent. In fact, Frida ate better than I did. Twice a day my father would fry her a hamburger in a bun and serve her in the kitchen. Or I would when he wasn't around. Vegetables never made an appearance, except in the form of tinned tomatoes when my dad cooked pork chops with rice. When that happened, I knew there was a new girlfriend on the scene, so that particular menu was met with as much trepidation as it was with hunger.

When we went food shopping at OBS!, the local hypermarket, my dad would dig deep in the bargain bins, juggle cans and eggs, and break large cucumbers over my head. We would mess around, role play and be generally totally daft. I could see the other bored children looking on with envy. When I pleaded for food items he said we didn't need, he would make a quick escape down to the DIY and sailing-supplies section, his ulterior motive for the trip.

I also grew to share my father's love for very varied music. He liked to live in a world loud with music. We often had Manfred Mann, Little Eva or the Beach Boys blaring through the flat. Or I would wake up with a start to the sound of his cornet accompanying the Grand March from *Aïda*. Other times would see us whistling to Verdi's other works. Our whistling was nothing short of an art form: there were high notes to be reached, twists and turns accomplished, anticipation and gesticulation provided. My father would always manage the crescendos in between puffing on his cigarette. I, on the other hand, often collapsed into giggles before the finale. I subsequently learned that he taught himself to read music and play the cornet and other instruments. He never had a lesson in his life. On my ninth birthday he bought me a guitar and I started lessons which lasted until my departure for England three years later.

*

There may not have been much continuity to my life with my dad, but although he tended towards the neglectful and hedonistic, there was one aspect of him which offered some regularity: he was pedantic. The flat had to be tidy and clean – everything in its place. Whatever I hadn't achieved in the day, he would often take care of in the middle of the night. I would wake up in the early hours to the sound of the vacuum cleaner or the tap running. He would get a bee in his bonnet about cleaning at *precisely* that time. It just had to be done. Whenever we went shopping the items had to be placed in bags in a particular order, so as to make most efficient use of space and make unpacking easier. I wasn't allowed to brush my hair in the hallway because I'd get hair on the carpet. Everything had to be practical and functional and 'just so' and he had an incredible ability to make me feel stupid when I didn't apply his policies, or when I showed any sign of sloppiness.

Communication with my father for the most part was in the form of notes left on the kitchen table. Scrap pieces of paper would incorrectly notify me of when he would next be home. He could tell the time and he wore a watch but was incapable of adhering to any sort of time commitment – ironic considering his insistence on shipshapeness in other areas. We rarely spoke about school. He was never able to attend an event and could only just force himself on a couple of occasions to turn up for parents' evening. Late. We talked mainly sports results, which army surplus to visit next, or the current state of the flat.

If I spoke of my mum he would nod, at the same time as forbidding me to phone her to ask for money for clothes. I did phone her, though. Often. And missed her greatly. So, I suspect, did my dad. He pretended to get on with life, and he had supported her in her decision to leave, but any man who repaints the entire kitchen with the help of his daughter in order to entice his loved one back has not totally moved on. I remember him telling me to ask my mum to bring her hairdryer with her on her next visit, so she wouldn't have to go back for it. I made up some cock-and-bull story about us not having one. But she still arrived without it.

Despite his failed, pathetic, unacknowledged efforts to win my mother back, my father maintained a small harem of women, charmed by his wealth of personality and humour (well, it certainly couldn't have been suavity, sophistication or money they were attracted to). Every woman who darkened our doorstep was a product of his driving school. And they were many. Often running con-currently.

The first girl I remember was a sweet, chubby-faced, dark-haired eighteen-year-old called Lilian. She was kind to me and loved our dog Frida. My father's manner of wooing was flattering, if not a little unusual. He offered an initiation meal; a sailing boat for dirty weekends; a self-proclaimed terrific performance in bed; a dog who performed tricks at the drop of a hat and an independent, self-maintained tomboy who also performed tricks. If this didn't prove irresistible, there was always the line about his wife having left him. Alone with the kid. In fact, given that Frida and I would regularly accompany my father to work, we were often part of the charm offensive from the very outset.

He had a fantastic ability to make girls feel wanted and desired, by adding fun, special touches to the relationship. He was incredibly thoughtful, attentive and imaginative. Thrifty and practical, he was able to do all this without really spending much money – and in Sweden, he had the most stunning geographical backdrops at his disposal. He would be smitten every time and fall deeply in love. I now think he must have enjoyed the pursuit more than the endurance of any relationship, because there was never an announcement of the end of one – simply the start of another, the presence of a new arrival in his bed, followed by some throwaway introduction.

At times this put me in a difficult position on the phone or at the front door. One might be sneaking out the back, as another knocked at the front. One might phone whilst another was involved in some bedroom gymnastics. I was never quite sure what to say or how best to lie, and was regularly blamed for ballsing things up. What I eventually learnt was that my father simply couldn't bear to do the nasty bit, the finishing. He was a man of peace, not of conflict, which meant that he bottled out, failed to return phone calls and left the girls to draw their own conclusions. Sometimes with the help of a slip-up from me.

There was Lilian, Ann, Kerstin, Nina and Harriet, to name but a few, colourfully sprinkled with the occasional one-night stand. The common denominators they all shared seemed to be large breasts or a passion for nature. Both appealed to my dad and were easy for him to deal with. He had a boat for sailing the seas, and two hands cupped and willing.

There seemed to be a different set of rules when a girl was on the scene. For a start, they were allowed to brush their hair in the hallway, and I would be banished to sleep in my own bed. It also became impossible for me to attract my father's attention. Believe me, I tried. I went through a period when on three occasions I faked my own suicide, leaving a blood-stained knife in the hallway and hiding in his wardrobe. Initially I think he was shocked, if not a little bemused by the ketchup on the knife, but by the third time he simply walked through the door and shouted, 'You can come out now!' A couple of times I ran away. But he just seemed annoyed when I came back. Another time I pretended to be a burglar trying to break into his bedroom, which he was sharing at the time. Each time I simply became a greater irritant and each time he failed to get this little nine-year-old's desperate and ridiculous message. Even the time when I called a taxi for his Finnish one-night stand, in the pathetic belief that she would actually leave.

Naturally, I felt in the way and unwanted, but this was somehow contradicted by the fact that my father and whoever would go about their business regardless of my presence anyway. I don't know how many times I was forced to witness noisy, lively sexual acts. The absence of discretion was a constant feature, whether it was in the boat I was sharing with them, on the living-room floor, in his bed or in a bed immediately next to me. I knew what they were doing and I hated it. I hated the noises, the smell and the fact that these girls were able to give my dad pleasure in a way I couldn't. I hated them for that and hated him for letting them. I found it dirty and disgusting and casual and I never associated it with an act of love. And the high volume of pornographic material by my father's bedside did nothing to contribute to any amorous image. *Au contraire.*

At about this time, briefly, I began to feel important. As evidenced by my bedroom, horses were an obsession, and my father was delighted to discover, through a girl who attended his driving school, a weekend horse-riding camp a couple of hours away. This was to be his saviour. For my part, I couldn't believe my luck – and

I couldn't believe how thoughtful my father was being. He was actually paying for me to go horse riding. I was deeply flattered. The feeling was fleeting, however, for when it came to pick-up time, he was usually two to three hours late, girlfriend in tow, and both smelling of sex. Wrapped up in each other, they hardly heard my account of my adventures. I realized my weekends had been a banishment after all.

I knew I couldn't count on my dad, but somehow never gave up hope. I would set myself up for the fall time and time again, with ever renewed enthusiasm. The only times I was rewarded was when he, Frida and I would go out sailing together around the nearby archipelago, setting anchor at his boat club's island. Our arrival was always signalled by my father playing a short fanfare on his cornet, followed at nine o'clock in the evening by Last Post, performed from the highest point on the island. Everyone would respond by taking down their flags from their boats for the night.

He would spend the days chatting to his friends, fixing bits on the boat or generally messing around on the island. I would escape with some of the other children into the depths of the forest, go swimming or, when it rained, seek cover in other people's boats to play cards.

Evening barbecues were always a feature, and every night I would look longingly at the mothers who had prepared chicken salad, coleslaw and macaroni for their indifferent children. Sometimes I would hang around unnecessarily in the hope pity would extend to an invitation for dinner. If not, a hot dog and ketchup waited near my mildly intoxicated father, who would be the group's entertainment for the evening. He would play practical jokes or his cornet or tell funny stories – sometimes crossing the boundaries of what might be considered decent behaviour. When he wasn't taking the piss out of someone else, there were always tales of my clumsiness and stupidity. Or he would boast about how independent I was; how he could leave me alone and not worry about me; how I looked after him, the flat and myself. And I would laugh. Because everyone else did.

AN EXTENDED FAMILY

Two important people happened to me at about the age of nine. The first was my new form teacher, Ann-Charlotte Markman; the second, a beautiful, long-haired, doe-eyed 22-year-old I found sitting in our living room one Friday afternoon. She was called Berit. She continues to have a massive impact on my life.

My new form teacher was a patient, modern, understanding mother of three. As a teacher she was fair and likeable, and commanded respect from her colleagues. She would have to tell you her impressions of me herself, but I suspect she saw a scruffy, dirty, noisy, independent little soul, with her domestic circumstances written all over her. It was she who made my father attend a parents' meeting, and she used the opportunity to ask him a few questions. To his credit, he admitted he did struggle to be around for me at times. She suggested I could stay with her if he was ever pushed – which it turned out he was, on at least two occasions. I just stayed the night, but I did get to feel the warmth and security of a loving family. I hasten to add that this did not mean I became teacher's pet. On the contrary, Ann-Charlotte's fairness meant that she was even quite hard on me, presumably to get the best from me. A couple of years later, when I had made my decision to join my mother for a new life in England, she spoke to my mother before I left, piled my arms high with books on my new country of residence and talked to the class about it. Ann-Charlotte and I shared the same birthday and are still in touch to this day.

Berit was a skinny bird with the most incredibly long eyelashes.

That was my first impression of her. The second was her warm smile and perfect teeth and the way she made eye contact with me and listened to what I had to say. Not surprising perhaps, when I found out that she worked with children professionally, and often difficult ones.

She came as a shock to my father and a pleasant surprise to me. She had just come out of a turbulent relationship and I think she saw my father as a saviour – the calm after the storm. Berit seemed to move in pretty immediately and to my astonishment I didn't seem to mind. She included me in activities and conversations, for a start, would sometimes even side with me against my father, and gradually introduced some structure into my life. Before I knew it I had a bedtime, negotiated in the utterly neutral, diplomatic and fair way only Swedes know how to do. We even had discussions about things that may or may not be good for me. *And* there was food in the house, because someone had finally rejected sandwiches in lieu of proper meals.

I did, no doubt, have my moments with Berit. I was probably awkward, needy, resentful, angry and complicated at times. But she didn't give up on me or push me aside. She tackled me head on, confronted me and talked to me. At first I thought this was weird, but gradually I began to sense strength in the new boundaries, and felt my way forward in a new way. The application of structure to our lives was something my father subtly rejected. He found all the sensibility and respect for individuals a little too much. It irritated him, because it implicitly questioned his way of doing things, and put a pressure on his life that he had up until now avoided.

Berit was a solid, dependable person, despite having grown up in insecure surroundings herself. She took my dad's word for it when he told her he was in love with her and those words called out to her breeding instincts. From what little I could gather, Berit and my father seemed to have a good relationship. There were more heated discussions in the flat than I remember with anyone before, but they now represented constructive debates, and were probably the natural result of the introduction of a more structured, normal lifestyle where there had been none. And what's good for an unkempt nine-year-old is not necessarily desired by her hedonistic 34-year-old father. The straw that broke the camel's back came in the form of a positive pregnancy test . . .

Berit had alerted me to this possibility by drawing my attention to her swollen breasts and a most complicated list of dates, which she called 'a menstrual cycle'. Whilst slightly confused by this, I did respond with an abundance of delight and enthusiasm to the prospect of having a sibling, and a family. The joy was short-lived, however. I remember standing in the hallway as Berit walked up to my father in the kitchen, threw her arms around him and imparted her delirious news. It was met by silence. Followed swiftly by the closing of the door. Perhaps they want to celebrate alone, I thought. But as I walked away I felt deep inside that there was something distinctly uncelebratory about his reaction.

I don't know what went on in his head at the time – he never said, not then, and not since. However, a conclusion had to be drawn from the fact that Berit's bags were packed shortly after and she found herself a one-bedroom flat in the next town. I missed her terribly.

I never asked questions. The environment was not conducive to openness of that kind, and I think I somehow feared my father. He got so angry when I tried to get his attention; he seemed irritated by my presence; he dismissed me so readily. Yet I was always so impressed by him: he was the standard by which I would measure everything. And in the absence of a permanent maternal influence, there really was no alternative. Especially since the one I was beginning to grow attached to was now walking out the door, bearing inside her the only potential for a family unit that I could hope for.

Berit stayed in touch. I don't know how often she spoke to my father, but we spoke every day, and carried on our relationship as if, somehow, nothing had happened. One of the most beautiful things she did for me was to keep me involved in the pregnancy. Bit by bit I saw her body change, learnt new biological facts and shared with her the wonder of a book called *A Child is Born*, by the pioneering

Swedish medical and scientific photographer, Lennart Nilsson. It takes the reader on a fantastic journey from conception to birth with the help of colour photography from inside the womb. No book had ever had an impact on me in the way that book had, and nothing has since. To this day it rests by my bedside and I introduce it to all newly pregnant women I know. At about that time I was able to acknowledge some form of maternal instinct within me. And it was then that I saw myself with a child or more children. I would be a mother one day, I thought. But in that vision, I saw no partner.

Throughout Berit's pregnancy my father continued to see other women. At one point he was seeing Nina, with the big breasts, and she was to know nothing about Berit and the impending birth. One day when Berit came to see me while my dad was out, Nina phoned. Now, I liked Nina. But I also liked Berit. I couldn't be seen to like both, and I wasn't sure where my true loyalties lay. So I kept my voice low as I spoke to Nina on the phone, I didn't want to sound too nice, and I lied when she asked what I was doing. But Berit knew about Nina, and she asked to speak to her. Suddenly my loyalties were split three ways. Berit took the phone, and I ran for cover.

Within half an hour Nina was sitting on the sofa in our living room, next to a bulging Berit. Like two women scorned they sat and awaited my father's return. And waited. And waited. I, meanwhile, paced the hallway nervously, praying for divine intervention. But God, it seemed, was just not hearing me! For as I prayed, I heard my father's car pull up outside. But then, just as I was becoming flushed and agitated, I heard him pull away again – he'd seen Nina's car.

And there you have the coward that was my father. The ladies were denied their confrontation and left, deflated. But not I. I took the rap. It had been *my* fault, of course. The torture of split loyalties, not wishing to let anyone down, of not quite knowing where the boundaries lie has stayed with me ever since those days. I learned well from my father; a fear of confrontation and sense of cowardice has ruled my personality to a large extent. It took me a long time to learn the actual lesson. I have tried in recent years to improve my ability to prioritize and to be a little braver.

When Berit's waters eventually broke, she sent me to the shop for sanitary towels. I had a sleepover at a friend's that night and my father also missed the birth – he was in the throws of his own birthday party and in no fit state to attend. On 28 May 1977, my beautiful sister Linda Annette Olsson was born, taking her mother's surname. I spent as much time with them as possible, kissing the little angel's feet with delight on every visit. I was nearly ten.

My father naturally fell in love with Linda, and whilst Berit had to tell him how a father should behave (he'd not picked much up the first time around), he did enjoy looking after her now and then, with my help. He was definitely proud of her.

*

Parts of my school holidays, and even the odd weekend, were spent in Holland with my mother and new 'stepfather', Michael. I experienced something completely different on my visits there.

When she left us, my mother moved into Michael's terraced house in the suburbs of Amsterdam. I would travel to my mother's by plane on my own, qualifying up to the age of twelve as an 'unaccompanied minor', after which the airlines leave you to find your own way around the airport. I only nearly missed a plane once, on account of the staff forgetting about the little Swede in the corner with the passport around her neck. It was a slightly nerve-racking method of getting from parent A to parent B.

The house in Amsterdam was nothing amazing, except that it had an upstairs and a bathroom with walls decorated entirely in foil – very seventies, but I thought it was dead posh. Michael and my mum were very much in love, and he used to drive me crazy with his constant public displays of affection for her. His kissing and hugging her annoyed me no end. And he knew it.

He was, however, an extremely kind-hearted man. When I visited, there would be family sightseeing or educational visits. At

all times he would talk to me – and in English – filling my mind
with elaborate stories or pieces of history. I understood what little I
could – even if I was trying not to listen – and he had me captivated.
When we went for long walks in the flat Dutch countryside (which
I'd defy any nine-year-old not to find dreary), he would turn them
into spectacles of song and dance as he recited lyrics and performed
movements from musicals past. There wasn't a word in the
dictionary about which he didn't know a song. No one had ever paid
me this much attention and I found it deeply uncomfortable. It was
annoying. I didn't want to like him.

My mother was a secretary for Cinema International Corporation, and Michael worked in the same building as an executive in
the Dutch offices of the film company MCA. When they went to
work – they couldn't take every day off when I was there – I was
left alone in the house, the size of which quite daunted me, so I filled
the days with trips to the local shops or riding around on a bike. If
Mum and Michael were redecorating, they would leave me some
paint and a brush and I would happily exercise my practical skills.
Sometimes at weekends Michael and I would decorate together. We
became 'Cyril and Norman, the decorating men'. And we would
sing. Together.

On other occasions I would spend the day with Michael on my
own, whilst my mother would put on skirts and high-heeled boots
and go to the office (she was still incredibly beautiful and very
glamorous, I thought). Hard to imagine many executives taking
the day off for a defensive tomboy, to take her to the beach, to the
funfair, trampolining or horse riding. But he did – not that I always
appreciated it. On one occasion, which we both recall and laugh
about now, I sobbed while clutching my pocket-size dictionary,
pleading with him to 'åking, to my mother'. 'Åka' is Swedish for
'drive' – in my upset and panic I'd swapped the languages around.

Michael was a very well-travelled, well-read individual. He had
lived in Australia, France and Italy; he looked after himself and
had learned to cook. He had studied hard at school and had loved
nothing better than reading under the covers with a torch after lights

out. He was brought up in the harshness of working-class Burnley, Lancashire, at the beginning of the Second World War, and his upbringing had been far from privileged. He was also eleven years older than my 28-year-old mum.

My new stepfather became a far more consistent influence than anything I was experiencing in Sweden. What's more, he had an incredible ability to make you feel special. On one birthday he spent the day cooking for us, had large gladioli delivered to the house *and* took me to the Amsterdam premiere of *Grease*. But this was all in such sharp contrast to my humble, frayed and disorientated life in Sweden that I think I reacted to it: what I knew in Sweden felt safe, although in fact the opposite was probably true. There was a huge element in this of wanting my mum back where I still thought she belonged, but the passion that really gripped me was jealousy – of the love she had for Michael. Despite Michael's massive efforts, I felt left out. And the truth is, not by him, but by her. I needed more from her – reassurance, affection, affirmation and emotion. An expression of her pain at being apart from me. Reassurance that everything would be all right. But I never felt that. Her evident happiness with her new life I saw as a direct rejection of my old life with her – and ultimately of me. So I think this is why I gave Michael a rough ride. Many children do in these situations: if security is lacking from the biological parent, the child has no alternative but to feel rejection and react defensively. Some children have the tools with which to make themselves heard; the rest of us, especially if steeped in insecurity and lacking in confidence, fail to do so and act nonsensically.

From Holland we would often drive to France or Belgium for the weekend, camping or sightseeing. On these trips Michael would continue 'Educating Ulrika', and I now know how fortunate I am to have shared in these experiences. Books and history went hand in hand with food and culture. I tried food I had never dreamed of tasting, ordered by him in a language I never dreamed I would ultimately converse in best. He even threw in a bit of French for good measure.

The 'new' family unit was completed by Michael's parents, Winnie and George, who often visited from England in the summer. They were the loveliest people I had ever met, taking me under their wings and treating me not only like their own grandchild, but like a grandchild should be treated. How unlike the chill and distance of my father's parents. But my loyalty to my father prevented me from getting *too* immersed in this way of life.

The night before I would travel back to Sweden, it was an unwritten rule that I should be allowed to sleep in my mother's bed. I always looked forward to it. I was, however, always left with the impression that she didn't. Her bedroom was always freezing cold on account of her sleeping with the window wide open. I always hoped we would snuggle down together to share the relatively new experience, to me, of a feather-down duvet, but cuddling wasn't my mother's strength. Of course, it wasn't as though I would lie still for more than ten seconds. But whichever way, if I wasn't asked to go back to my bedroom, we would end up sleeping poles apart, defeating the object of the exercise.

EDUCATING ULRIKA

Sometime before my twelfth birthday, I vaguely recall my mother mentioning that she was moving on to England with Michael as a result of him getting promoted to a job based there. She was applying make-up in the foil-clad bathroom, and casually put it to me that I might like to come along too. She further explained that I was now getting to an age when I would need my mother for things a father couldn't help me with. I wasn't entirely sure what she was talking about, but I walked away feeling deeply flattered and excited . . . until I thought about my father. Mum said I should think about the suggestion, and whichever decision I made, not feel bad either way. She had obviously spoken to my father about it, because he rather unhelpfully *also* told me not to feel bad either way. I expressed my concern for my father's welfare should I leave, to both of them. I couldn't understand who would look after him if I wasn't there. But I was desperate not to let my mother down, despite not knowing what to expect if I did go with her.

I talked to my friends about the fact that I might be moving to England, and it seemed to them to be utterly the coolest thing in the world – London was, in our opinion, the centre of the universe. And as if we were living in East Berlin, I was under the impression that I should get out while I could. So, if I'm brutally honest, it was not I who made the decision to join my mother in a new country; it was made for me by my friends, who thought it would be quite revolutionary. Thus both friends and relatives looked upon me with admiration and excitement. I felt proud of 'my' decision, as if I was about to embark on a great adventure – which indeed I was.

I decided to give the announcement of my choice on the phone to my mother a proper build-up. 'I've decided not . . . [long pause] . . . to stay in Sweden,' I exclaimed, in great anticipation of a joyous reply. But my momentous, life-changing decision was all too swiftly absorbed, so keen was she to move on and talk about something else – always in a hurry for the next thing. So fickle was I that even as I put down the phone, I began to regret my decision. I didn't feel appreciated, or longed for, after all.

Nevertheless, arrangements were made for me to fly to my new life in England on 19 June 1979, to be followed some weeks later by my father with a car packed with my belongings. I said my farewells to friends, relations and the various animals sharing my home at the time, and set off with a sense of excitement, trepidation and the knowledge that I could always return.

*

My new home was dramatically different from my father's suburban flat. I entered a vast red-bricked Georgian house in the small Buckinghamshire village of Farnham Common. The house had huge rooms and high ceilings, and a garden that filled three-quarters of an acre, which I promptly described in a letter to my dad as a 'queen's garden'. To my absolute disbelief it had an outdoor swimming pool. My new world seemed one of luxury. The room I was given was decorated in a Laura Ashley print, a little too feminine for the tomboy in jeans, but it seemed bigger than half our Skälby bedsit. And we were shortly to take delivery of a double bed – for me!

The house was beautiful, so beautiful you could practically lose yourself in it. My mother had even inherited a cleaner with the house, Lilian, who was something of a fifties throwback. I struck up a friendship of sorts with her, whilst Mum and Mike went to work in Uxbridge. I spent the days swimming, drawing and writing, awaiting the imminent arrival of my father with a car full of my things. It was glorious, until the day my mother announced I would be starting school. I had been in England for two weeks.

I was to attend the last fortnight of the English school year, then return in the autumn and do the final year of middle school, despite being almost twelve already. (A fortnight was deemed not sufficient to determine what sort of school I should go on to.) This meant I was older than everyone in my class – in some cases by more than a year. My mother accompanied me to my first day at Farnham Common Middle School, where she spoke briefly to the headmaster, who promptly placed me in Mrs Bolingbroke's class. And there I sat, with everyone staring and mispronouncing my name, which usually ended up as 'Orrika', 'Eureka' or 'Ollrika'.

To my relief we had to wear uniform. This meant I no longer had to worry about choosing something to wear each morning from the undernourished, badly coordinated wardrobe I had brought with me from Sweden. Clothes had never been anything but a necessity in my dad's household, so it was a comfort to know I would look the same as the other kids, for a change. In all the time I lived with my father he bought me only one pair of trousers and a deeply unfashionable denim waistcoat. In nearly four years. (My mother would replenish my wardrobe whenever she could.) But despite believing that we would all look the same in uniform at school in England, it became clear that there were very distinct class differences. You could always make out the better-uniformed kids. And I was now one of them.

So, I saw out the last two weeks of term in a new school, in a new country, speaking a new language. The first break time, I found myself standing in the centre of an overwhelmingly curious crowd of schoolchildren who were firing questions at me, pointing at me and touching my hair. I didn't just feel foreign, I felt alien.

My English improved daily. It had to – it was sink or swim. I also gradually adjusted to an under-funded education system where you shared books with friends and where repairs to the school were left incomplete. Where the food was diabolical, but where serious discipline instilled a respect for the teachers and where the children were allowed chocolate at morning break. I also worked out that a private swimming pool is a guarantee of many new friends.

Eventually my father drove down to stay with us from Sweden, bringing with him my all-important trinkets and things. He stayed a week or so, driving my mother insane with his beer drinking and cornet playing until four in the morning. He was, however, still able to make her laugh. There was no bad atmosphere between my triangle of parents, and certainly not between Michael and my father. They got on very well despite being entirely different creatures. My father was not jealous, and Michael far from feeling threatened.

I spent the beginning of that summer playing badminton with my dad, fixing things around the new house and washing cars. Not much change there, then. When it was time for him to leave I had a pain inside me which was so difficult to heal that I cried and cried for days. I found it so hard to be without him; regardless of his near apathy as a father, we had an understanding that often did not require words. We liked doing the same things; we laughed at the same things; were able to be ridiculous together; could clown around and seize the day. In truth, I didn't really know my mother. She had a sense of humour, but it didn't come out to play often enough. She seemed much more serious, more proper, and remote at a time when I had to get used to a whole new lifestyle. And while I had, of course, missed my mother every time I had left her to return to Sweden, that pain seemed temporary.

My feelings for Michael required something other than the feelings I had for my father; the two people were so completely different. Michael showed concern and acted upon it. He was disciplined and a disciplinarian and clearly felt he was in charge of the household. But he also had time for me and developed in me an absolute passion for cooking, something which must have lain dormant during my culinary barren years in Sweden, where it simply had not had the facilities nor the encouragement to evolve. He taught me with discipline and experience about diet, and the flair and imagination of his cooking captivated me. I would then experiment with great success, producing cakes, puddings and savoury dishes alike on a weekly basis. With Michael's encouragement, I finally found something I was good at.

Michael was a man of morals and I knew deep in my heart I liked him and loved him. Yes, there were rules and regulations, but he had the ability to personalize things too, for instance by never forgetting birthdays – making them days to remember for ever – by making you get excited about life itself. Finally I was leaving behind me those days in Sweden when I had woken up on my birthday only to find a scribbled note from my father to say he was working on the boat. Not to mention, of course, the times he forgot my birthday completely.

Michael took the trouble to arrange a holiday that first summer I moved to England. He had me believe we were flying to Paris for the weekend and promised I could have something I had always dreamed of – breakfast in a hotel room. But even then he succeeded in surprising me: at the airport I actually found myself getting on a plane to Tunisia. I was twelve years old, and I was going to Africa!

*

The friendships I had made that summer helped ease the burden of starting the new school year in September 1979. Halfway through the term I was chosen to play Prince Charming in the school's panto, *Cinderella*. I guess the teachers took one look at my bow legs in a skirt and knew I was made for the part. Tracy Salter was my Cinderella. She was fantastic and despite my singing and goofy teeth she still talks to me today. Looking back, I guess it was some kind of an achievement to have a lead role in a play in a foreign language just months after arriving. But that's the beauty of kids: when needs must, they do.

By contrast with my summer idyll, the beginning of the next term, brought me some of the most miserable experiences of my early years in England. For no apparent reason, or so it seemed, I became subject to an intense bullying campaign. My crime remained undisclosed to me, but overnight I found myself frozen out of my circle of new friends. Break time and lunch time became never-ending periods of darkness, loneliness and fear. No one would talk to me or come near me – and if they did, it was with a barrage of insults and taunts. At break, I sought refuge with my back up against a wall at one end of the playground. Meals were spent alone. And class times were spent avoiding eye contact with anyone and attempting to drown out the laughter and whispering that went on behind my back. It was inexplicable, and beyond painful. I asked no questions, made no attempts to regain friendships for fear of further rejection. Sometimes the pain and fear were so intense that it felt as if I couldn't breathe. Only very, very occasionally I allowed the emotion in me to surface and I would find a quiet corner of the cloakroom and weep. Then I began to question myself – what was wrong with me? And I too began to dislike myself. I never told my mum; I never told a teacher. And something inside me was beginning to tell me I deserved it.

I was, of course, the ideal victim for this. I was an insecure but lively and colourful contributor in class, seeking approval. I cared greatly what people thought about me and I would happily submit in order to win over friends. Somehow the spirit that had got me through years alone with my father, and which had seen me through so many contrary situations before, now refused to surface. A lack of pride and self-confidence handed me on a plate to the aggressors – some of whom, I'm sure, were not quite sure why they themselves were involved.

It was a dark period that seemed to take for ever to lift, but somehow it did. I guess it had run its course and burnt itself out like these pointless childhood things often do. At the end of that school year I found I could not only breathe again, but had also won an award for the best-kept diary on a school trip to Brittany (a credit to my newly acquired English language skills), not to mention passing the twelve-plus exam, which secured me my escape to Burnham Grammar School. Michael and my mother were extremely proud, and gave me a handsome cheque and an oil-painting set. I banked the cheque and started painting.

*

Throughout my early years in England my loyalty remained to Sweden, but when my mother and Michael married in August 1981 a stamp was placed in my Swedish passport giving me 'leave to stay in the United Kingdom for an indefinite period'. At that time, however, I certainly didn't feel I would stay in Britain for ever. My heart and soul were still in Sweden and I firmly remained a foreigner on these shores. I still found England a little impractical, illogical and old-fashioned, although with hindsight I was slowly developing a very deep love for a generous, welcoming and hospitable nation – which had a fantastic slapstick sense of humour and, what's more, commercials on TV.

By now my circumstances had reversed. I would visit my father during Easter and summer holidays, leaving behind a disciplined and structured life. But I found leaving Sweden again increasingly difficult and a year or so later I decided to move back for good. I missed and worried about my father so terribly, and I could no longer bear the days of mourning every time I returned to England. I missed my little sister Linda, too. The death of our dog Frida shortly after my move away and the death of my father's father some months after that further contributed to this feeling of displacement. My father said he was happy to take me back, and I wanted to be allowed to look after him again. And if truth be told, I felt that I was still not very close to my mother, and daily life with Michael was turning out to be very different from when I was newly arrived or the times I had just been a visitor. I felt sure my mother would understand, but she burst into tears and stormed out of the room, asking if it was because I thought Berit would be a better mother. The question was unexpected, and hung heavy in the air. I didn't really understand it. I didn't think of either of my parents as either good or bad. My mother wasn't a 'bad mother' in my books.

The issue was about me wanting to be back with my father, where I felt I could be put to better use, rather than being surplus to requirements in her organized household.

I stayed. And the battle of loyalties continued inside.

*

Then life in England changed. To my absolute delight and joy my mother gave birth to a gorgeous baby boy on 20 March 1982. They called him Kristian Michael George Brodie. I was coming up to fifteen years old. Kristian became the light of my life. I spent virtually every waking hour with him – my mother found she had her own built-in Scandinavian au pair, and this one didn't require payment as Kristian's smiles were worth more than all the meatballs in Sweden.

Up until this point my number one priority had been schoolwork. Michael was proving to be quite tough. He insisted that I spend any spare moment studying, and I never managed to develop any form of negotiating technique with him. Further, I found I had no direct access to my mother: everything would be decided by Michael, and it was his way or no way. As a result I was not allowed much time with friends. There was no going to the cinema or popping into town and school discos were, for the most part, a no-no. It was, to say the least, frustrating.

But Kristian was allowed to become my new project. I certainly did not object: I was totally in love with him, and would rush in after school and relieve my mother of him and care for him until I had rocked him to sleep to the sounds of John Lennon's 'Woman'. This is not to say that Michael did not remain obsessed with exams and results, in which he had himself excelled. As I approached my O levels, it virtually became impossible for me even to go to the toilet without him questioning why I wasn't studying. Had he not cracked the whip quite so hard, I would have enjoyed my work far more. And I'm sure I'd have benefited from some of the extra-curricular activities in which my friends were indulging. Besides, this was a time of crucial development, of becoming a young woman with that monthly friend, a time of gaining maturity. Michael's argument was that he was trying to protect me from the world outside, and that if I allowed him to show me the way I would thank him when I was older. Right then, I'd leave the room feeling lost, helpless and angry. My mother chose never to get involved, and I'm afraid I began to dislike Michael very much. His regime was making me a social recluse, and making me want to bolt because the barn doors were so firmly shut.

My term work was rarely reflected in my exam results, except in languages and literature. In exams, like so many young people, I would fall apart. I lost concentration, was overwhelmed by nerves, and eventually my mind would become distracted. I often found myself in a different world; dreaming, imagining, fast forwarding, doing anything but tackling the paper in front of me. The silence in the exam hall even unnerved me – it was all that I could do to stop myself from standing up and screaming, or laughing loudly, or maybe even singing.

I did, however, excel in languages and the arts. I could see the point in learning French and German, whereas sciences were slowly becoming the death of me. Chemistry seemed to be series of letters added together to make longer sequences of letters. Physics was an alien language and in biology the only thing I truly understood was how the eye worked. In history I saw the virtues of Marxism, until I learnt about fascism, at which stage I decided that politics never truly worked on a practical level and all politicians were vain fools. Maths became the bane of my life. I needed it at O level for entry into university, but despite extra tutorials on Sunday mornings, nothing would stick. If there is such a thing as mathematics dyslexia, then I have a severe form of it. My eyes glazed over, I became sleepy and my mind would only question why on earth I was being forced to study this. And I have yet to apply Pythagoras' theorem in daily life.

I got on well with the teachers in general. Despite my respect for authority, I continued to make lively and humorous contributions in the classroom. It was as if I wanted to break the rigidity of school life and try to establish a more relaxed and human approach. This meant I was in the line of fire whenever the teachers suspected foul play, even when I was utterly innocent, and I consequently saw the interior of the headmaster's office more than once, for totally the wrong reasons.

Despite my reasonable popularity, in the second year I found myself the victim of more bullying. I had stayed well clear of the instigator of the previous hate campaign, who had come to Burnham Grammar too, but I soon found myself arriving in classrooms where slurs had been patterned on the blackboard, such as 'slag', 'tart' and their antithesis, 'frigid'. Added to this were comments about my late development in the breast department. The contradictory nature of the insults reassured me that they were without substance, but that was of little comfort. Apparently I was tight and had no tits.

The latter was certainly true: I was a late developer. My period did not make an appearance until I was fourteen, despite daily prayers that it should come sooner. My bosom was like a couple of paracetamols on an ironing board. I had had very little boy experience. Yes, at fourteen I had snogged, but no one had attempted to lead me any further astray. Only one friend stood by me throughout this war of nerves. She was a true friend who showed remarkable courage in the face of prejudice. That friend was Joy.

Much in life at that time was not enjoyable. School life was stressful, academically and personally. I couldn't and didn't confide in my mother. I struggled to determine her moods after school each day and could never decipher if I was their cause. She would fail to acknowledge me as I walked through the door and then see her silence right through to the evening. It made me feel nervous and disliked, diminishing any potential confidence I might be acquiring. I never understood it and tried to counteract these moods with more helpfulness and 'people pleasing'. My mother had Kristian's needs to attend to, in which I helped her hugely, but in short I hated that period in my life. Any spare time away from the family was spent in my room listening to music and writing down thoughts and dreams of another life. Teenagers are notorious for their awkwardness, and in many respects I was no exception. And I felt doubly plagued by the bullying at school and the lack of communication with my mother. I also struggled to have any of my emotional needs met at that time; Michael had no respect or time for my friends, they were often ignored and their messages left abandoned, and anything outside school was considered a waste of time. Make-up was forbidden and boys were not only frowned upon but violently discouraged. With one exception – my darling brother Kristian, who would be promptly delivered to my bed at six thirty in the morning at weekends. A welcome but tiring sight.

*

But it wasn't all bad. Mike was working for the film studio Universal, and throughout my early teens I would regularly attend film premieres with him and my mum. Because of his job, Mike would often be in the line-up on the occasions when members of the royal family were in attendance. At one of these premieres, I think it must have been an Indiana Jones one, I was introduced to Mr Spielberg himself. He asked me if I was an actress. 'No,' I replied, 'but I'd like to be.' (How many times must he have heard that?) Well, he said, you go on the stage here, then come make movies with me. Steven Spielberg said that. *To me*. What I was not aware of was that he was contemplating doing a remake of Peter Pan, and when my mum and Michael met up with him at the Deauville Film Festival the following autumn they were asked if I would be available for a screen test. 'No,' said my mum, apparently, 'she's studying for her O levels.' So that was that. And she didn't tell me until long afterwards. Which was nice.

But I must say, when my period made its eventual appearance, my mother was what any teenage girl could have hoped for. She was incredibly open, bought the relevant accessories and was very sympathetic. She also took great interest in my appearance, trying to develop some kind of taste in this scruffy teenager. She introduced me to the virtues of moisturizing, and tried to drum into me the joys and results of a beauty regime. In that way she was a fantastic

mother. I had always admired her taste in clothes and believed I had
one of the most beautiful mothers in the world. Everyone who laid
eyes on her would immediately comment on her looks.

I began to grow my hair long, after years of sporting a boyish
cut. My mother took me to a dentist to whip two teeth out, in order
for my front teeth to be pushed back into a more vertical position.
My brace hurt like hell. At the worst of times I was in severe pain,
and at the best of times I could only manage to pass soup through
my mouth. Not only was it painful, but it was a social taboo. So
after years of making my lower lip cover my upper teeth when I
was smiling, I now couldn't smile at all. On top of which I had the
delight of taking the brace out every so often to pick off bits of food
that had attached itself to it. But to wear or not to wear when kissing
boys? That was the question.

In between school and studying, my life was richly scattered
with holidays to destinations I could only have dreamt of. Every
school holiday we went away, and sometimes I was even taken out
of school in order to go. We travelled Europe, America, and Africa,
as well as enjoying some of the beauty this country has to offer. On
my sixteenth birthday we were in Los Angeles for a month, house-
and cat-sitting for one of Michael's bosses. It was a stunning home
and we were told to take care. But if I wasn't licking lamp-posts in
Sweden, I was bouncing beach balls down a sweeping staircase in LA
– and shattering a valuable chandelier in so doing. However, the
holiday was memorable not only for that. David Bowie, of whom I
was a great fan, had just made *Merry Christmas, Mr Lawrence* for
Universal. My friends were green with envy to learn that not only
had I gone to see him in concert for my birthday, but we'd been
invited to meet him at a small reception. When we were introduced
and had our photo taken together, I was overwhelmed.

We often travelled with Club Med, and it being a French
company I was supposed to use the opportunity to practise my
language skills. Supposed to. And the travel opportunities Michael
made possible for me, like the cooking, did help open the door to my
mind, which had been closeted in Sweden for so long. I would never

have experienced any of these things had I remained with my father. Michael was smart, quick, confident, and had the ability to make even the dullest of things sound interesting. As my father had showed me to use my hands and be practical, Michael was now encouraging me to use my head, challenging me at every opportunity. He also had a great sense of humour. He frequently laughed at me, at times when I didn't feel it was appropriate, but I often found myself dissolving into laughter myself when I saw the humour of it all. Michael was a man striving for the best and nothing but the best for his family. Our tough times aside, I am grateful to him.

RITES OF PASSAGE

My first boyfriend, in spite of disapproval at home, was probably Kevin. I was fifteen. He was a fairly tough member of a gang called 'the Dorney Boys' (after a neighbouring village), and therein lay the immediate attraction. He was rather rough round the edges, but really quite sweet. He was at my school and lived about twenty minutes away, as well as supporting Manchester United. Oh, and he smoked. Of course, I would not have gone near anything resembling a cigarette. Not only would Michael have killed me with his bare hands, but it just didn't appeal to me in the slightest.

Tobacco breath aside, Kevin and I did the usual snogging, and he was the first guy to ever turn me on. It was with him I performed my foreplay initiation, in someone's steamy Burnham bedroom on one of the days I had been allowed out. It was awkward and kind of messy and quite, quite exhilarating. I didn't mind him messing with my bits, but found it a little embarrassing getting to grips with his genitalia, especially as his premature ejaculations were a source of pride for him and a cause of concern for me.

At this age I still had no intention or even desire of having sexual intercourse. I was happy with a quick slap and a tickle in a dodgy corner somewhere, but thoughts of anything else just hadn't entered my mind. Whenever I babysat for Kristian I was never allowed to have anyone around, because Michael thought I might get tempted, but nothing could have been further from my mind. I was scared.

I passed seven O levels in the summer of 1984. One A grade, three B's and three C's, plus an Advanced O level in German. I failed maths and biology – no surprises there. My mother was very proud and we were all delighted I could stay on at school to take my A levels in English, French and German. At about this time I started working in our local library for three hours every Saturday morning. Although I struggled to stay quiet during my work hours, I thoroughly enjoyed the independence the job signified.

I had by then managed to fall for a boy in the upper sixth, who was by far the most handsome in the school. Yes, Robert was to become a big love of mine. We courted and even petted heavily, as I was by now guaranteed one night out a week. I felt sure I would sleep with him: things were heading in that direction. But then I remember some clever dick telling me that the first time with someone is always awkward and, if it goes wrong, it can mark the end of an otherwise good relationship. So, as I didn't want to do anything to jeopardize being with Robert, I set about losing my virginity elsewhere. On holiday with my parents – by this time I was seventeen – I flirted with a man; eventually we snogged, and I knew it would simply be a matter of time before he would ask me to go with him, and I knew I would say yes. I just wanted it over and done with. When the time came, we found us a corner of the hotel's crèche at midnight, and he laid me down on the floor and did his funky thing. It was painful and embarrassing, and he stole a litre of milk from the kids' fridge on the way out. Michael had been out looking for me within the compounds of the resort all night and was not happy to see me. I bet he hadn't thought of looking in the kids' club. That was Marbella 1984.

Life carried on pretty much as normal. The usual squabbles at home. Me feeling I needed my own space, but knowing that I still had one more year of school to complete, and my most important exams yet to come. I was going to apply for university, and felt resolute that I should not have a boyfriend for my last year of school. For my eighteenth birthday my mum and Mike completely surprised me with my own car. He was a red Fiat Panda, and I decided to call him Rupert. I loved him to pieces and looked after him very well indeed. Robert and I had gone our separate ways, not as a result of the Marbella incident, which he is only just now reading about, but because he took up a place at college in Portsmouth. We did sleep together. But probably only once. Or twice.

In the beginning of 1985 my mother fell, unexpectedly, pregnant again. It was a surprise to her and a delight to me. On 21 September she gave birth to Kelly Maria Kristina, who gave us all cause for concern as she would not feed properly. It turned out she was born with a cleft palate. She had fortunately escaped a hare lip, but due to her condition she suffered continual colic and irritation. She was the prettiest little thing, but with sad, tear-filled eyes at all times. We all took it in turns to walk around with her as she rarely settled, until my mother employed a dear old lady to help her. She adored Kelly as much as we did, and we called her simply Nanny.

I suppose it was inevitable that I would meet someone who took my fancy in my final year at school despite vowing I wouldn't. He was Tony, he was two years older and working, and I fell in love for the very first time. Now, Tony was very handsome, although pretty useless romantically. But sexually there was no problem. I went on the Pill, and I remember making love to him believing I would never, ever, ever make love to another man in my entire life. How nearly true.

Naturally my parents' concern about my studies increased as my desire for them decreased. Tony and I felt we couldn't concentrate on anything apart from each other. But I was still allowed out only one night a week, when I would end up driving Tony and me from pub to pub; he had a car but no licence. We also went on a skiing trip together with my savings and some parental subsidy. Michael, of course, didn't like him, and during one of Tony's visits asked when 'that fucker' was going to leave. Lesson number one for parents: the more you disapprove, the more we love.

Our relationship was strong enough for Tony to accompany me to Sweden the following summer to go sailing with my dad. They got on like a house on fire. They both liked a drink. Or two.

*

I had studied hard for my A levels, but only managed to achieve three D's. My mother rejoiced. She had thought I was going to fail them all. I had also sometime in the sixth form applied to go to the Central School of Speech and Drama in London, believing I was destined for a career on the stage. I was called back for a second audition, but failed to earn a place.

But my A level results did secure me a place at Goldsmiths College, London, to spend the next four years studying French and drama. However, after eleven or twelve years of the discipline and, to me, claustrophobia of studying, my brain was drying up and needed a change of fluid if it was going to function at all. It made sense to take a year out. It was my mother's suggestion that I started looking into doing a secretarial course, her reasoning being that as a prospective actress I would spend ninety per cent of my time unemployed, and secretarial skills would give me a means of making money. A great tip, well intended, but I'd have welcomed a little more faith in my acting ability. Whatever – she was right.

But even before I had further qualifications, I got paid. I found a job in a London office as general dogsbody until I took up residence in Oxford to start a private secretarial course at St Aldate's College, Oxford. Digs consisted of my own room in a flat with five other girls. Rachel was from a well-to-do family in St Albans; Juliet from more humble beginnings in the West Country; Tracy was a hippie from somewhere; Nadine's parents were based in Jakarta; and Emma was a virgin from Canada. We shared one bathroom and one toilet, which made for an interesting year. It wasn't long before I gave up queuing for the bath in the mornings, and resorted to scraping together enough twenty-pence pieces for a shower in the communal hallway three flights down. A couple of the girls had never experienced self-sufficiency up until then, and it showed. Before too long it became necessary to create a cleaning rota, although it proved virtually impossible to implement.

We all got on surprisingly well. However, my phobia for noise, other than my own, was further enhanced by the fact that Tracy's half of her room was directly below mine, and her bedroom gymnastics kept me awake more than I liked.

My parents gave me twenty pounds a week to live on and I had enough money saved to rent a bike to get around for the first term. I surprised myself with my dedication to the course. I did not go out once in the first term. I would stay in and complete my homework, then watch some black-and-white TV. Without an aerial. Part of the evening's entertainment was working out what it was I was watching. And as far as the homework went, I had found something I enjoyed and was very good at.

My relationship with Tony continued – only thanks to me, mind. Every Friday night I loaded up Rupert, my Panda, and drove back to Farnham Common – to help out at home, and to see him. I finally negotiated with my parents that I would spend one night with Tony and one night at home. But this one-way street meant that we gradually grew apart. And it began to feel as if he was moving too slowly for me. There had been a time when, as a sixth-former, I had been quite impressed to have a boyfriend with a job, but with my new-found independence I was no longer excited by this.

In my second term of college I had to walk everywhere. I'd overspent on my Access card. My main friend was a girl called Liz, from Cardiff. She really was the only one with whom I had anything in common – most of the other girls were there because their wealthy parents hoped that, after failing school, St Aldate's would prime them to get a half-decent job. The majority of the girls seemed to be thick, but wealthy, whereas I saw myself as intelligent, but drastically poverty stricken. Liz and I would get together to bitch about the other girls and to try to scrape together enough money for a Marks & Spencer sandwich at lunch time. M&S was an ill-afforded luxury; I lived mainly on rice, pulses and vegetables.

Sometime during the last term of St Aldate's I checked out of my relationship with Tony. I was feeling ready for a little more worldly exposure. Despite his heartbreak, tears and devastation, this lady was not for turning, and soon I wasn't missing him at all. Amazing how you can be so in love with someone and see nothing in the future that could make you change your mind. Then, suddenly, you look at the same person, and you cannot comprehend what it was you saw in the first place. Love was scary and seemingly transitory.

As the end of term approached, and I was clearly one of the brighter girls at the college, with pretty much top grades in everything secretarial, I came to the conclusion that I did not wish to go on to study at Goldsmiths. I wanted to spread my wings and fly beyond educational institutions and twenty pounds a week. All the girls were applying for jobs and most, if not all, had secured places at the Foreign Office or in the City of London. But these left me cold. I was looking hard for a secretarial post in TV or the film industry, but to little avail. I sat a secretarial test on a manual typewriter at the BBC and failed miserably – I had only ever practised on electric. I knew then, in my heart of hearts, that if the kudos of working for the BBC meant familiarizing myself with a manual typewriter, I would never work for them. So dedicated was I. Besides, a job at the Beeb would only have paid about five and a half thousand pounds a year, whereas the City would offer around eight. And for that, quite frankly, dear Aunty could keep her archaic office equipment.

The closest things I could get to TV or film were poorly paid, oversubscribed ad agency jobs. I went for several interviews and was offered every job I applied for. I remember in particular the man who raised his eyebrows with delight as he discovered I was Swedish. What was he expecting – a blow job whilst taking shorthand? I left in disgust. However, none of the jobs really appealed, or made economic sense. Then one day I saw on the notice board at college an agency advertising a junior secretarial post for the managing director of a 'breakfast television' company. I tore the notice down and rushed to the nearest call box. The lady at the other end didn't seem to understand how right I would be for this job, and said reluctantly that she would send them my CV, but that they would take a week or so to get back to her. This was a worry: I was fast running out of time. I had the very real potential of leaving college jobless, for no time was allowed off for interviews during the final two exam weeks. But the next morning she had heard back – and they were interested in an interview.

I knew nothing of breakfast television, still a novelty in Britain, so I tuned into Anne Diamond and Nick Owen on *Good Morning Britain*, my prospective employer's flagship programme, for the following two days. I had been briefed about my potential boss, a colourful, extrovert Australian who was also director of programmes. His name was Bruce Gyngell, and I was specifically asked to pronounce his name correctly. It went round and round my head a thousand times a day – Gyngell – hard first 'g', soft second one. Let's see how he copes with 'Ulrika', I thought.

At St Aldate's we were encouraged to wear navy skirts, blazers and tights for interviews. That was too ladylike for me and I would have none of it. The others might want to look forty before their time, but not I. So I prepared for the interview as I had done for the others by washing my hair, applying no make-up and putting on a yellow blouse, a beige skirt, no tights and tan shoes.

Good Morning Britain, which had started in 1983, had completely revolutionized the Brits' idea of morning television – to such extent as it had existed. It waved goodbye to the stiff, dull, navy blue presenting of the BBC and welcomed instead a warm, colourful, informal style of presenting, featuring news alongside entertainment. Its theme was one of 'eternal summer', and it aimed itself firmly at the families of Britain, and in particular its housewives and kids.

Like its programming, TV-am's landmark premises at Camden Lock were rather wacky. The building had not only been a large two-storey car park in a former life, but it boasted large, highly unattractive eggcups jutting out along the roof line – to denote 'breakfast'. The offices were open plan and colourful, in keeping with the set in the studio, and there was one central staircase. I found this a relief. If I got a job there, at least there would be no risk of the claustrophobia attacks I had been prone to since my childhood.

I was greeted by the personnel officer and a lady in her fifties

who was Mr Gyngell's (hard first 'g', soft second one) senior
secretary and alongside whom I would hopefully be working. After
an intense role-playing interview to see how I would deal with this
situation and that, I was invited to meet the man himself.

I was eager. Eager to meet him. Eager to have the job.

Mr Gyngell (hard first 'g', soft second one) welcomed me into
his office overlooking the canal, wearing a pink shirt and tie. He was
a tall man with handsome, fine features and long fingers. His eyes
were big and brown, and he had a slightly freckled and moled face
from excessive sun. Relaxed and friendly, he sat himself at the head
of his boardroom table and pulled out a chair near him for me. He
talked to me a little about TV-am and asked me what I really wanted
to do, because he couldn't believe I would want to be a secretary all
my life. I explained that I had originally wanted to do something
dramatic, but the opportunity hadn't yet presented itself. He suggested the job was mine, and that it would be good for me to get my
foot in the door and take it from there.

I felt complete. I had just landed myself a dream job working for
one of the top men in TV, but to cap that, it commanded a salary
of nine thousand pounds a year and five weeks holiday. My cup
runneth over, methought, and I was due to start immediately after
my exams.

KICKING CORGIS

On Monday 6 July 1987 I became a working girl. I moved back home and started to commute by train and tube to North London. The daily trip from Buckinghamshire felt long and exhausting, but worth every minute. I learnt that my new boss had been dubbed 'the Pink Panther' by the press due to his love of pink and insistence that all presenters wear bright colours on screen. I would, when I could, wear a pink blouse, but stuck mainly to yellow or white. Black was a definite no-no. Bruce detested black and it was potentially a sackable offence to arrive dressed for a funeral. Shame, I loved black. Blondes look great in it.

As soon as I started at TV-am things moved very quickly. Christabel, Bruce's senior secretary, was utterly kind and patient. She showed me around and filled me in on who was who and what was what. It seemed a wonderful place to work. With the offices so open, everyone could see everyone and there was a tremendous feeling of light and space. Not to mention the splashes of colour Bruce insisted on, not just on screen, but off.

On my second day a letter landed on my desk. It was a short note inviting me to a ball that coming Saturday, and the note was signed James Baker. I had to ask Christabel what it was all about – I was not sure who he was, and I had certainly never attended a ball. I'd apparently met James the day before. He worked in the kids' programming department, and was, according to her, extremely kind, respectful and trustworthy. I called him on his extension and accepted, once we had agreed there would be no strings attached. He said he would pick me up at 5.30 p.m. on Saturday.

At this point, I was still struggling a little with my femininity. It was a personal battle for me to wear a skirt every day for work, but nothing else seemed proper. Skirts made me feel uncomfortable and severely restricted. Not to mention, of course, that I hated my bow legs which sprouted out underneath. My hair was long, but for the most part tied back, so as not to feel too feminine. I was of average build, but was fast developing childbearing hips.

So I was looking forward to Saturday night with as much trepidation as excitement – and what's more, I managed to lose my purse with my week's money and credit card two days before. True to his word, James turned up in his Peugeot, a little early. He suggested we could get changed at a friend's in Windsor, despite the Riverbank Ball taking place in Henley. I had borrowed a silk cocktail dress from my mother and had, for a change, applied a little maquillage.

As we arrived in Windsor, he drove surprisingly close to the Castle. As I was about to point out to him that he couldn't get any closer without being arrested, we actually passed through the gates and drove right into the massive courtyard. I was silenced. I didn't quite know what was going on. James then kindly explained that HRH the Prince Edward was a long-standing friend of his, and we were attending the ball with him.

As we got out of the car, we were directed to the gardens, in which corgis and a few royals roamed. On closer inspection I discovered that the couple to be found lounging there were none other than HRH the Duke and HRH the Duchess of York. Edward and a girl called Georgia welcomed us. Too late to become nervous, I just went with the flow. The Duke of York sneered at me and asked what I did for a living, then sneered at that too. His wife, on the other hand, was full of laughter and kindness. The dogs, which snaked around our feet or were too old to move, seemed as unpopular with the others as with me.

When the time came to change I was allocated a room with an

en suite, and even a maid who helped to tie the bow at the back of my little number. Then we set off for Henley with detectives in tow. Edward's date for the night was Georgia May, who was jolly and lovely at the same time, but I actually sat next to His Royal Highness at the dinner. I thought he was very nice, and I enjoyed myself so much that it wasn't until six o'clock in the morning that I found myself inviting James back to my parents' for a bowl of cereal. On Monday morning he sent me flowers.

James and I became friends, and close ones, quite quickly. I thought he was simply the most fantastic person I had ever met: kind, thoughtful, intelligent, stylish, practical – everything. The following Wednesday he asked me to the theatre with 'Ed'. This time we met his princely friend at Buckingham Palace. The name of HRH's escort on that occasion escapes me, and her personality did too. We didn't chat much. Further, I cannot for the life of me remember what it was we went to see, but Toyah Wilcox was in it. This time we were all in one car – the detective drove; Edward was in the front; I was directly behind him with Miss Personality to my right and James to her right.

As we pulled up outside the theatre, Edward and I must have got out at the same time and, lo and behold, the unexpected happened. As I walked up alongside him, but not particularly near him, a photographer jumped out of nowhere and flashes started going off. It all happened so quickly, but the detective immediately knocked the snapper off his feet. We went inside, said nothing about it, and afterwards all returned to BP for 'supper'.

As I went to catch my train to work the following morning, I nearly jumped out of my skin. There on the front page of the *Daily Mail* was a picture of me, in my stripy skirt and top, alongside HRH. I was stunned; flabbergasted; filled with disbelief. I immediately bought a copy, of course, and was impressed that they had got my name right, but horrified that they said I was eighteen. I was nineteen years old, for goodness sake.

Outside TV-am waited a photographer. Inside waited the press office. They showered me with questions and requests: should they issue a press release or not? What exactly happened? And was I really seeing him? I was confused until James pulled me to one side and explained that the press would now not leave any stones unturned and would be likely to phone day and night in order to try to get something out of me. He ordered me to say 'no comment' to absolutely everything and not to buckle under pressure. This was a world away from my first encounter with the press, when I was just five and had been pictured in a story about kindergarten allotments in one of Sweden's daily nationals. Back then, I hadn't even been asked to comment.

So, what had originally started out as a fun evening at the theatre was now turning into something much more dramatic. James told me Edward wanted a word on the old blower, and would I oblige? Sure, I said. Edward very kindly just wanted to check if I was all right and he apologized profusely for causing all this trouble. He offered help or support should I need it. How kind, I thought. But little did I realize that the worst was still to come.

Before I knew it my father was on the phone from Sweden, panicking because he had not been able to get hold of me. What was all this about 'some Prince Andrew'? 'Edward,' I said. 'Oh, right,' he said. 'Well, I've just invited some of the journalists standing on my doorstep in for a beer and I've shown them pictures of you as a kid. Would you believe it, hey?' Oh yes, I thought, I would.

When I went home that evening there was a posse outside my mum's house, who persisted in bothering my parents throughout the weekend. They'd got a scoop out of my school friend Tracy's mum: I had worked for her as a Saturday assistant in the local library. They'd even found Tony. Everyone was panicking. So I hid inside my parents' house for the weekend while they fought off the offending parasites. Every time I did come into contact with any of them I simply said hurriedly, 'No comment.' I wasn't quite sure what exactly this meant to me or to them, because they still refused to go away and for my part there was nothing to say 'no comment' about.

James remained a great support, and tried to explain to me the intricacies of the press, but I continued to feel unsettled by the speed at which they worked, and the depths to which they would go to obtain an iota of information. A friend's boyfriend, who was a photographer and who had a year or so before taken some photos of me for his portfolio, had even sold the fully clothed pictures to the *Daily Mail*, which ran them under the headline 'The Prince and the Showgirl'. Apparently my sense of fun and my clowning around were what had attracted Edward to me. Poor Edward, we had only met twice, and we were now apparently having a public romance.

So by the time I turned twenty a few weeks later, I was as well known throughout the TV-am building as Anne Diamond herself – and further limelight was beckoning. The children's department, the *Wide Awake Club*, was looking for a new co-presenter. Bruce, who was a firm believer in internal promotion and who had not that long before had a conversation with me about spreading my wings eventually, suggested I audition. This is bizarre, I thought. I've only worked here three weeks and in that time I've dined with a Prince, made a whole new circle of friends, and am being told to audition for another job. Encouraged by James, who worked in the department as an occasional presenter, I looked at the script. The audition required reading autocue, telling a story, performing an interview with someone, and three minutes of whatever you could to best sell yourself. I chose to play my guitar and sing a song in Swedish. Looking back, I cannot for the life of me imagine what I thought I was doing, apart from frightening the children I was supposed to entertain with my guitar playing.

Nobody got the job from all the auditionees. However, I couldn't fail to notice a letter sent to Bruce – it was my duty to read memos addressed to my boss – from Nick Wilson, the man in charge of the kids' programming, It said that one other girl and I had rated very high on his list, and he wouldn't hesitate to employ me under different circumstances. Perhaps he meant without the singing . . .

I had alerted TV-am upon my appointment that I had booked a holiday, a glorious two-week package holiday in Crete. It was booked in the throes of my relationship with Tony, but as we had parted ways my friend Liz took his place. It was, needless to say, a retsina-and-bazuki-playing-filled fortnight, with Liz believing she could walk on water one night, and me throwing up the next. We drank, ate nothing and sunbathed.

Upon my return we met at Buckingham Palace for dinner again – James, Edward, Georgia and myself. By now, James and I knew to bring our own wine, as Edward was not the most adventurous in that department. We'd sat through enough meals with Liebfraumilch and Blue Nun as our fellow guests. So, we brought our own Laurent-Perrier rosé champagne, introduced him to Deacon Blue and were served dinner in his apartment by men clad in black wearing white gloves. I didn't feel one way or the other about the royals, as the Swedish royal family tends to be very down-to-earth and accessible, and I generally felt able to be myself, but it was a million miles from anything I had experienced before and sometimes I really didn't have a clue what they were talking about, but we had fun and HRH was always very welcoming. He was, of course, deeply in love with Georgia, who unlike me spoke his language. But she was a lively, posh girl from a Catholic family, and therefore, James explained, not a marriage option. I thought this was sad. They were great together. Not that that stopped me accepting a solo invitation to accompany HRH to hear the brilliant Danish comic pianist Victor Borge play at the Royal Festival Hall. My dad and I had been fans of his, and he didn't disappoint – nor did we attract any press attention. I'm sure I was only invited because someone let him down last minute. Little would my father and I – or perhaps even Edward – have dreamed that one day, a decade later, I myself would host a whole Swedish classical music evening for Radio 2 at Birmingham's Symphony Hall. That night I actually met opera legends Jussi Björling and Elisabeth Söderström, who had both sung with my grandfather. It was an honour to be in their presence, and not so much a job as an experience to treasure.

The following week I began to feel exhausted and ended up taking two days off work with tonsillitis, something which would always affect me whenever I became run down. I was prescribed penicillin, but by the Sunday we had to call the doctor out as I was unable to swallow at all: my mouth was full of blisters and a migraine occupied my head heavily. It turned out I had streptococcus and glandular fever. With hindsight I guess this was inevitable. The past few months had been non-stop work and fun, and commuting three hours every day was beginning to take its toll.

For anyone who hasn't suffered from glandular fever, I can tell you it is one of the most debilitating of sicknesses there is. Exhaustion hijacks your body like there is no tomorrow. No matter how much rest or sleep you get, it is never enough. Walking up the stairs leaves you puffing for air and stumbling into bed. I was transformed from a lively twenty-year-old into a crippled ninety-year-old. For most of the time I could not even muster the energy to speak. My mum tried to stuff me with vitamins and great food, but while I could just about manage *Neighbours* twice a day, food was for the most part beyond me. When Edward drove out with Georgia to visit me and offer me some homeopathic pills my mother nearly had a fit cleaning the house before they arrived.

Work kept asking when I might be back, and I remember thinking that I didn't even have the energy to walk down to the village without having to sleep for four or five hours, let alone commute into London. When ten days into my sick leave there was a horrific fire at King's Cross Underground station, which I passed through every morning and every night when I changed tube lines on my way to and from work, I watched the TV in horror and counted my blessings.

In order to make my life a little easier upon my return to work, one of Michael's oldest friends and former colleagues offered to rent me a room in his flat in Earls Court for a while. I jumped at the chance, although I still wasn't well enough to go back to the office on the day planned. Had I returned that Monday in November, I would have seen quite a different TV-am – a TV-am without programmes, a station that was about to change television as we knew it for ever, and that would ultimately change my life for ever, too.

CROSSING THE LINE

The Association of Cinematographic, Television and Allied Technicians supplied virtually all TV-am's technical staff. After a long-running dispute, which was industry-wide, Bruce had decided to take a stand. The ACTT threatened to strike; if they did, said Bruce, he'd lock them out. He would allow staff a three-month period in which to come back without the union, but after that they would be sacked. It was a brave and highly controversial stand, and repercussions were felt throughout television.

Bruce had a very clear vision of right and wrong, but was often equally capable of changing his mind. On this issue, however, he felt crystal clear. ACTT members were amongst the highest earners in the industry due to their right to massive overtime payments and a strict work to rule. They basically had the industry by the balls. Technicians such as cameramen and sparks – lighting operators or electricians – were often required to work odd hours in order to cover breaking news stories, and could consequently claim crippling salaries. One cameraman had reportedly been able to claim around £70,000 overtime whilst covering the Zeebrugge ferry disaster.

Britain was at this point under the strong influence of one Margaret Thatcher and it was no secret that Bruce was a dedicated follower. I had been requested at times to take down dictation for letters to Downing Street, and it was with her support that Bruce faced the union's hold on the industry head-on. No one had hitherto thought it possible to do so and succeed.

Having literally no experience of anything political (the anti-

Vietnam War activism of my toddler years aside), oblivious to the existence of Radio 4 or a broadsheet newspaper, I hadn't got a clue what might happen. As soon as I returned, I was asked by Bruce whether I would be willing, on top of my secretarial duties, to come in before dawn and make a valuable contribution to the running of the breakfast station. He also made it quite clear that my job would not be in jeopardy if I refused. To Miss Clueless, Naïve and Totally Impressionable it sounded exciting – and I offered to 'help out' whenever I could. And it was an 'all hands to the pump' situation.

Technician-less, TV-am was barely able to transmit cartoons for its three hours and twenty-five minutes of transmission time. But thanks to the few members of the management who had technical experience, the *œuvres* of Warner Bros and Walt Disney were transmitted non-stop between 6.00 and 9.25 a.m. every morning. However, Bruce knew that the Independent Broadcasting Authority's patience and tolerance of such transmissions was limited; before too long it would require TV-am to resume its news and current-affairs output.

Under Bruce's direction, members of staff were introduced to technical equipment on the studio floor, told how to point a camera and focus, and how to roll the autocue rhythmically for the presenters. On the first day one of the secretaries actually fainted with the fear and stress of it all as she attempted to operate a camera. The presenters, predominantly members of the National Union of Journalists, were encouraged by their union not to partake in any broadcasts, but since they themselves were not in dispute with TV-am, they were obliged to fulfil their contracts.

As it became clear that Bruce refused to recognize the ACTT within the realms of TV-am, a few technicians did reluctantly begin to trickle back to work. Like the rest of us, they suffered verbal and sometimes even physical abuse as they crossed the forecourt picket line. A dozen or so members kept a fire burning outside day and night, while inside secretaries operated cameras and executives cued commercials. I was given the role of running the autocue. Nowadays this process is performed with a computer, but in 1987 you had to print off a long, narrow roll of paper with the script on it and feed it through a machine. It was a minor nightmare and I forget how many times I ended up rolling the script backwards.

The main presenters at TV-am at the time were Anne Diamond – the queen bee – Nick Owen, Mike Morris, Richard Keys and Gordon Honeycombe, who read the news. Gordon, like so many others, was as deeply irritated by the dispute as by having to work with a bunch of amateurs who didn't know which end of a camera was the lens. I was instructed to roll autocue for him every morning as he read the news. It was a complicated process that involved cutting and pasting the roll of paper during the news bulletin as and when the news stories changed. On one occasion he was so frustrated with my inefficiency he reduced me to tears. Rude bastard.

TV-am put us out-of-towners up in a nearby hotel, in order to ease the burden of getting up at 3.30 a.m. to get things rolling at the studio. Some two or three weeks into the 'lockout' we were pretty much back on track with transmissions, in between long episodes of 1960s *Batman*, which boosted the station's ratings tenfold and kept the advertisers happy. Once we'd signed off at 9.25, we'd have a post-mortem where non-technical staff would be thanked by Bruce for their continued support, and where questions would be raised as to why we'd faded to black on three occasions that morning, or why the commercials had run late, or failed to appear, or why the camera was focusing on a wall instead of on Anne Diamond's lovely face. Bruce had taken it upon himself to direct the shows, with the ever-faithful Christabel by his side as his production assistant. He had directed programmes in his early television days in Australia, but in his fifty-ninth year he was not quite as sharp as he thought he was. Christabel tended to take the rap for his mistakes, despite being right ninety-nine times out of a hundred. Bruce was a vivacious character and in command of some of the most colourful language I have ever heard. He meant nothing by it, though, and we had to keep that in the back of our minds at all times. Sometimes he would even make you laugh with his swings and turns.

After the post-mortem we would return to our day jobs, with

myself and Christabel continuing the dialogue with Downing Street and Mrs T, as well as accepting messages of support from fellow independent TV stations. Often we would work a twelve-hour day without a break, proving as a result that an independent television station could survive without the presence of an ACTT shop within it. For the industry as a whole, this was to come to mean that management was no longer required to respect any work to rule, nor to regulate working hours, travel arrangements or anything which might contribute towards the welfare of a technical member of staff. The immediate result was that with anyone now able to call themselves, say, a cameraman – no longer being required to have a union-stipulated training – the floodgates were open for anyone to come and work in an industry which had, until then, adhered to strict rules of professionalism. For better or worse, a seemingly irremovable union had been toppled. Margaret was delighted.

*

By this time, James and I had grown apart a little, predominantly on account of me working every hour God sent but also because I was not sure I wanted our strong friendship to develop into anything more. After James left TV-am for another job, I was introduced to someone who can only be referred to as a charming bastard. He was handsome and, it turned out, wealthy – but I wasn't particularly interested in that. The best thing he did for me was to introduce me to the nicest crowd of people you are ever likely to meet, and despite him starting to mess me around two weeks into our relationship, I decided to join his friends for a New Year's celebration away together, to be remembered for gales of laughter, copious amounts of alcohol and gorgeous countryside.

So 1987 ended with me still holding down a two-part job while dating a man who could behave both arrogantly and with obsessive jealousy on a regular basis in between being witty and attentive. He was initially eager enough for me to befriend his crowd, but then would snap at or even slap me when I greeted them with the warmth and joviality with which they welcomed me. He became completely unreasonable when he felt he was no longer in control of the situation.

The first time he slapped me I was shocked. The two times after that I lashed back, in a show of defiance, but also because I began to resent him. The significance of his actions was beyond me then, but, I wanted him to know at least that I wouldn't take it lying down. His verbal bullying, however, extended itself to the bedroom. It would be true to say that I had not yet had a considerate lover. My experience was that sex was an act principally for the enjoyment of the man, and so I remained most of the time on my back thinking of England. Or Sweden. The relationship was pretty on and off during this period.

Although more and more people became available to take over our technical positions on the studio floor, it was often our responsibility to train them up. One day I had had to place myself in Mr Honeycombe's chair to pretend to read the news while a new girl practised the autocue. As I sat there Bruce must have walked past, for in the post-mortem meeting that morning he suggested, in front of everyone, that since I looked good on screen, would I like to be trained up as a stand-in weather girl? Personally I couldn't have imagined anything more boring, but TV-am's weather girl at the time, Trish Williamson, was pregnant and would shortly be going on leave. So, I said 'yes' and was passed into Miss Williamson's care. It seemed she found my elevation from secretary to potential weather girl too swift for her own liking, and made no attempt to hide it. I didn't care. I wasn't interested in the weather, but thought it would be rude to turn down Bruce's invitation. So myself and another secretary, whom Miss Williamson *did* like, followed her round the London Weather Centre a few times, read up about climate change and practised writing daily reports. I learnt about cumulus and nimbus, high pressures and occluded fronts.

On 17 February 1988 every member of the ACTT at TV-am who was not back at work received a letter through the post terminating their employment. Their time had run out. The forecourt reception that morning was at its least welcoming, objects and abuse were hurled at us. Bruce had been successful in his attempt to rid the industry of the ludicrous union rules. But on 19 March he paid the price, and had a heart attack.

Over the previous six months, Bruce had moved from being my hero for employing me in the first place, to becoming a man I respected, loved and admired tremendously. He was an extrovert: a gregarious character who loved people and life. He was a family man, who was able to appreciate the beauty of women at a distance. He was confident and he had his own way of doing things which often raised eyebrows in a country where being loving towards strangers can be considered a madness. He was generous to a fault. Strikers apart, I saw how time and time again he paid for holidays and gifts for staff. He was warm, friendly and well meaning. When Bruce insisted on presenters wearing bright colours in order to radiate eternal summer into people's living rooms, staff tittered quietly. When he wanted to turn the open-plan newsroom into green jungle, they thought he was mad. When he insisted on the use of only fresh orange juice in the canteen and ceramic serving dishes instead of stainless steel, they thought him ludicrous. But these were the people who readily accepted his gifts, donations and kindness.

However, as one of his secretaries I had also the pleasure of seeing the other side of Bruce. The side which would expect special-strength vitamin C powder to appear at the click of his fingers; who would pass you in the mornings without as much as a hello; who would dictate a letter to the IBA whilst jumping on his office trampoline and who would order a BMW for his wife without test driving it, and then decide *he* didn't like it. He was a stickler for dietary requirements – after years of living on rich hotel and restaurant food, he'd decided to take the macrobiotic route, insisting on various potions being constantly available in his office, and adopting a new fad at the blink of an eye. But while he didn't drink alcohol or coffee, he would be the first to nick a chocolate from your desk while you were gone. He was not a bully, but he did keep me on my toes. Despite achieving 130 wpm shorthand, I was damned if

I could read back anything I had taken down from an Aussie who would mumble, shout or simply change his mind three times in the middle of a sentence. He never intimidated me, even if he was in a foul mood – I always felt there was a reason for his mood swings. Besides, fifty per cent of the time we had him eating out of our hands and laughing.

I was devastated by the news of his heart attack, and immediately thought of his family – I wasn't sure if people survived. I couldn't imagine a TV-am without him, although there was a growing feeling others immediately around him weren't being quite as loyal.

Sometime before Bruce was taken ill, I had written him a letter expressing my excitement at the changes within TV-am as a result of the strike, and in the television industry as a whole. I wasn't sure the whole weather thing would lead anywhere, as there was a chilly north-easterly wind blowing from Miss Williamson, but I thought my chances would be better if I was trained properly in the business of television. I asked him if there might be an opening on the news desk as an assistant or something similar. Bruce suggested I turn my attention to the director of news and current affairs, a northerner called Bill Ludford. But Bill was not really entirely in Bruce's camp – he thought him a little too unconventional – and I was told that at that time there was no opening. So I plodded away with my rain reports and continued trailing Trish. The worry was that I had actually started to become fascinated by the weather, and was even buying books on the subject.

One morning I discovered that the other 'potential weather girl' had actually been auditioned. Without my champion around, I wondered if I had been deliberately ignored. Christabel pushed me to approach Mr Ludford about it. He conceded that I should be given a fair crack, although given that I had no support, no help and no guidance, I wasn't really. Anyway, he threw an audition my way. I was pretty appalling. In fact, I was clueless. But so was the other girl. She, however, got the job.

*

I had been slowly developing a curious attraction for one of the main presenters at TV-am – no, not Mike Morris, Richard Keys. After a few casual chats at work we began to meet for lunch or morning coffee, and he looked out for me in a way my charmer wouldn't have known how. This was a friendship that was a world apart from all that. Richard was extremely respectful and on top of this he was married, which in my books was a big 'no-no' for anything other than friendship. Strange how the charmer hadn't been a definite 'no-no' after the first time he slapped me – well, there you go.

Richard admired me and cared for me in a deep way, which put me off immediately as I didn't have the maturity to understand it. Perhaps he saw me suffer sadness and unhappiness at the hands of the charming bastard and wanted to support me, somehow. What he said was that he thought one day I would make a great presenter. I thought he was being ridiculous.

Then one day, out of the blue, I had a phone call from an old TV-am honcho, who was now working for an independent production company. He had been commissioned to put together a pilot for Swedish TV and needed a native presenter. For some reason, out of all the Swedish people in London television, he thought of me. I was delighted, and duly set about to translate the script and polish up my Swedish.

The shoot was in a shoebox studio, and I did a mediocre job. In the building at the same time was a male presenter who had just finished recording something for another company, and he wasted no time in striking up conversation in the foyer as I was leaving. I thought him a little too persistent, particularly as he insisted in following me to the tube station, but when he handed me his number with an invitation to a party that coming Sunday, I felt slightly exhilarated by his energy and his good looks.

I phoned him the next day for directions, and said I would be bringing a girlfriend. I'd had a date fixed with the charmer, but here was the perfect opportunity to jump ship and 'forget' our rendez-vous. I guess I'd come over with a touch of my dad . . .

The party was swinging that Sunday, and with the help of

generous liquid hospitality, my girlfriend and I had a fantastic time. By the time I called the charmer to tell him I was sorry I hadn't been in touch, I thought it was extremely funny to tell him I had instead chosen to go to the moon. He was not amused, and had he been there I would no doubt have had a slap.

The presenter and I got on well. We snogged a bit before I went home and we agreed we would go to the pictures together the following Tuesday.

That day was to change me profoundly. The presenter turned up at my hotel room with flowers, and I was touched. The television was on, and as I was getting my handbag together for the date he started petting. We kissed a bit, but I was quite keen to get going so as not to miss the film, and tried lightly to dissuade him. He ignored me, by now kissing me quite hard and starting to touch my breasts and around my bum. I had been fully dressed when he arrived, but now he was slowly, yet brusquely, pulling at my clothing, despite my increasingly persistent objections. I pulled away, only for him to pull me back towards him until he eventually pushed me onto the bed.

I landed on my back and remember saying out loud, 'No, no, don't.' This was the first point at which I began to feel fear. I felt that I had somehow lost control of him and that I didn't have the power to stop him. I panicked and raised my voice, attempting to wriggle out of his reach and repeating, 'No! No! No!' In what seemed to be no time at all he had my trousers off and he was tugging at my knickers. This was crazy, I thought. *Surely* he is going to stop. Can't he hear me? But just as that was going round in my head he inserted himself inside me with all the force of his big body. The words I was shouting made no noise as they left my lips; I was breathing, I knew that, but no words were coming out any more. All that I could do was beat with my fists on his back and kick a little with my legs. He ignored me, continuing to kiss me hard. I did not reciprocate, and instead turned my head from side to side as it lay trapped between his head and the bed.

Once he had deposited his load inside me, he climbed off me and started talking as if nothing had happened, pulling up his trousers. I remember lying very still, not even able to pull up my underwear. He urged me to get myself together so we could get going. I remember the sound of his voice so vividly at that point – although he was talking to himself: I was in no state to reply. Eventually I managed the words, 'I think I will just stay here,' as I curled myself in a ball on the covers of the bed. He didn't seem bothered and said we should talk later. I had been raped.

*

I lay there for the rest of the evening feeling very sore down below, even feeling sore around my mouth where he had kissed me so forcefully. My legs ached from remonstrating, and my head was confused. That night I awoke with pains in my lower tummy and an unstoppable desire to wee. Every time I did so I was in unbelievable amounts of pain. By three o'clock I decided to call into work to explain I would not be in that morning to roll the autocue – I was bleeding by then, and I didn't sleep any further. I didn't know what to do.

At nine thirty I phoned Christabel to say I thought I had severe cystitis. I was walking as if I had been riding a horse all night or taking part in a major porno movie – which couldn't have been further from the truth. She arranged an appointment with the company doctor, who prescribed antibiotics, and I went back to the hotel room barely able to stand up, let alone walk. In the after-noon I spoke to my mum and said that I needed to come home. To my surprise and relief Michael offered to come and pick me up. All he knew was that I had cystitis.

That night the pain increased and no amount of pain relief made any difference. By the morning my mother resolved to take me straight to Wexham Park Hospital where I collapsed upon arrival. I vaguely remember being scanned, being asked if I could be pregnant and how long I had been in pain, but I couldn't bring myself to tell them what had actually happened to me. I felt ashamed and dirty.

I was finally administered enough painkillers to allow me to drift off to sleep.

When I woke up they said I was bruised inside and that my bladder and urinary tract were infected and had taken a bit of a beating. I was given stronger antibiotics for that, but nothing for the shock in my head. I couldn't even bring myself to confide in my mother.

I remained in hospital for four days, sharing a ward with women who had recently had hysterectomies and were pissing in bags. Severely weakened, it took an age to learn how to get back on my feet. My mother visited me daily and took me for slow, gentle walks around the grounds of the hospital after a couple of days. Richard visited and was deeply angered by what I confided in him. James visited, too.

Back at my mother's I continued to suffer from pains in my lower regions, which even the tablets failed to reach. While it was depressing to find myself back at home with my parents once again, it was certainly a welcome respite from the hotel. I was still very shaken. Eventually I plucked up the courage to tell my mother. I had been a little fearful that she might not sympathize, but I was relieved to discover that she was of course appalled. She wanted me to do something about it, but I couldn't see involving the police would result in anything more than my word against his. Having invited him up to the room in the first place and having kissed him at the party was hardly going to stand me in good stead. The only thing I had was the record of my hospital stay, but I didn't know what they would make of that. Besides, my understanding of rape was the kind of act women walking home late at night were forced to endure by a stranger. I was scared, was the truth. Scared of him, scared of what had happened to me and scared of having sex again.

The incident had further compounded in me the sentiment that sex was for the enjoyment of the male only. I hadn't up until that point had a tremendous amount of pleasure from it myself. My attitude to sex dated back to my days as unwilling voyeur of my father's acts and the sight of the pornography by his bedside. I felt it was dirty and was very uncomfortable about it. This experience did nothing to help change my mind. I was now even more self-conscious about sex than ever.

A week later I returned to the scene of the crime to pick up my belongings, only to find a dozen or so messages from the hotel reception telling me the presenter had called. I saw he had even sent flowers.

*

Although very affected by the incident, I returned to work and resolved to channel my emotions into something positive: buying a flat. I had real conviction about this; I would never forget the incident, but I would harden my resolve and move forward – to a position of independence. It was May 1988 and the property market was going bananas – things were moving so fast people were offering for places without even viewing them. I did my homework: went to a hundred different mortgage lenders, talked to a thousand estate agents until, after much cogitating, exasperating and calculating Michael agreed to come and look at some properties with me. He was never going to be won around easily, but I had worked out that I could afford a £30,000 mortgage, and he might like to invest some £50,000.

I found a flat in Maida Vale that my stepfather approved of, although he liked to keep me on my toes, threatening to pull the plug the night before we were due to exchange. Time apart had in general meant less conflict, and I believed that if we could achieve this one thing together, we might be able to live in even greater harmony. So when on 29 July 1988 I became the part owner of a tiny one-bedroom flat it felt utterly delicious and I started to decorate immediately. All those years of painting and sanding with my dad, of tiling and grouting with Michael, were now, finally, going to be put to good use. Right then, Flat 3, 146 Shirland Road was the most exciting thing to happen to me all my life.

The charmer still stayed in touch once in a while, assuming, I presume, that I still gave a fuck. And then one day in June as I came into work and walked up the central staircase, I glanced down to my right at the hubbub at the bottom. The star guest that morning was Frank Stallone, Sly's brother.

No great shakes. But he had spotted me too, and called to ask me to attend a film premiere with him that evening. I obliged, flattered, but more importantly because I had no reason to say no. We had a very pleasant evening, despite the fact that I discovered he curled his eyelashes with eyelash curlers, and we even had a bit of a snog, but I was too scared to take things further. He asked me to return to Hollywood with him, because I seemed so sweet and natural. I agreed, naturally. No, of course not – and I never heard from him again. In fact, it would be a long time before I would take things any further with any man.

At work I was more or less back to regular secretarial duties – no more 3.30 a.m. starts – and with Bruce firmly back at the helm. He had been sorely missed and ignored doctor's orders to take it easier. The man just simply didn't have it in him.

Through a friend of my stepfather's I heard that a London-based company broadcasting to Sweden, Denmark and Norway on cable was looking for Swedes with British work permits. I met their director of programmes in her office, which ironically looked directly over TV-am's Camden Lock offices. When I was asked if I had any presenting experience, I told her about my weather audition for the company over the road. Her eyes lit up: they were also looking for a weather girl. Irony of ironies.

After a second interview I was offered the job of production assistant, which I later learned in their set-up really meant runner or gofer. Now, I didn't actually want to leave TV-am. I had been so utterly comfortable there; but it was only the best *first* job anyone in the world could have wished for. While I was a good secretary, I felt the need for more stimulation, another challenge, new territory. Here was an opportunity to stop messing around with auditions and get on with learning about TV production as a whole. I didn't care what I had to do; I just wanted to learn.

I handed in my notice to Bruce rather nervously. I'd been with him just over a year, but in some respects I had done well to last that long. Bruce said he was sad to see me go, but knew that it was inevitable, and even took me out to dinner with his family the night I left.

TV3, my new employer, ran a small Scandinavian ship in modern offices with only about thirty employees. The man in charge, who styled himself president of the company – despite its modest size – was a small stocky Jewish chap with an endearing soft spot for me. So disorganized were they when I joined that I had to type up my own contract. My salary had now gone up to a handsome £10,000 a year. And within the first weeks of working for them, they had me doing a screen test for the weather. They had a sponsor for the spot, Goodyear Tyres, but no weather girl. They were so desperate that I think the only criterion was that I spoke Swedish. So, by some strange twist of fate I was destined by the autumn of 1988 to present weather bulletins in Swedish from a makeshift studio in England for transmission in Scandinavia. And that was just my lunch hour. For the rest of the time I worked in the offices – organizing, typing, booking presenters and props for other productions, and making strong coffee for the Swedes.

I was still meeting up with HRH from time to time, but nothing resembling regularly. He would phone out of the blue and invite me to Windsor for a picnic or BP for dinner, for the most part with detectives in attendance. Yes, there were generally three of us in that relationship and I wasn't sure what to make of it all. Yes, I liked him. Yes, we laughed and talked about most things, and I like to think I made him laugh too, even if it was only by telling him about scraping the bird shit off my windscreen that morning, or about how people in the real world have to do things like change plugs. And on one occasion after dinner at Windsor, we kissed. On another occasion, some months later, we did a little more. In fact, we did nigh on the full works – but absolutely not quite. So, the answer is no, I didn't sleep with HRH. And no, there is nothing particularly gay about him at all.

*

Despite my defection, I kept in touch with my former colleagues at TV-am, meeting up after work whenever we could. Richard Keys arranged for me to have my first professional publicity photographs done by Harry Ormescher, renowned for his Page 3 work. I kept my top on though, smiling sweetly with an umbrella sticking out the back of my head.

Back in Sweden, my broadcasts generated interest on two levels. Firstly, my Swedish, which had been neglected for some time, was the cause of much hilarity. My father was highly amused and would phone me to tell me what had made him laugh that week. Secondly, the Swedish press had not been slow in picking up on the fact that the girl who did the weather on TV3 was the same girl who had dated the English Prince Edward. One newspaper requested an interview and, without confirming or denying the state of my relationship with HRH, I had let my guard down enough to give away details of when and how we would occasionally meet up. When the story was printed in Sweden, the English papers went crazy. Within no time at all photographers and journalists had the TV3 offices surrounded. They phoned, knocked, followed and hunted. I felt such an utter idiot. I had been stupid, naive, nice and too generous. I had to call Edward and apologize, but he was cool about it. My boss, on the other hand, was over the moon. He believed he had a star on his hands.

For Christmas, TV3 decided to indulge Scandinavia's children in a little Disney advent calendar drama of their own making. I ran around maniacally getting props together, arranging schedules and even drawing up budgets. There were so few of us there that one of the producers had to take the main part – that of the postman – although thankfully the rest were played by 'real' Disney actors dressed in character costume. We had a week's shoot at a studio in the West End, during which I would rush back to Camden Town every lunch time to record my weather report.

My main job for the production was to look after the props and keep track of the hundreds and hundreds of children's letters we had pinned to the walls of the set. I was also involved in some of the scriptwriting and rehearsals. It was a busy week, with very early starts and late finishes, and there was little time to attend to anything else. But one thing did not escape my notice, and that was the man working on camera two. He wore big lace-up boots and had a nice profile.

During the course of that week I managed to make some inroads towards the gentleman and his colleagues. We talked about lots of things, including TV-am and how life was now for the majority of technicians. He was nice, a little inquisitive, but I could always brush him off by being busy, busy, busy . . .

On the last day, as I was making my mad dash back for my weather routine, he followed me out of the studios, tripped and fell at my feet. He excused himself and after straightening himself up asked gently whether he might have the opportunity to photograph me for his portfolio. He had started out as a photographer, and maintained a strong interest in photographic work. He would under- stand if I said no, but would be grateful if I would consider it. I smiled. I thought he was so sweet, so terribly genuine – and quite handsome, too. I took his number and said I would be in touch.

While I had no desire to be photographed further, by him or anyone else, I decided he was gorgeous enough for a phone call. So it was that a week or so after the production had ended John Turnbull and I met for a date.

I was quite fed up with men by this stage, but the Turnbull was really refreshing. He was quietly spoken, but witty and sarcastic. What's more, he drove a VW Golf, which was my favourite of all the cars my father had ever driven. At the end of a respectable drink, he asked whether I would like to accompany him to his company's Christmas do that coming Saturday. With TV3's Christmas dinner the night before, I agreed, deciding to make one hell of a weekend of it.

I behaved with appalling naivety towards drink at my company's Christmas party, mixing wine, champagne, schnapps, brandy and beer. My finale was a champagne cocktail. I have never been so ill from alcohol in my entire life, and barely made it up the stairs to my third-floor flat, where I struggled to fit a key in the three keyholes that suddenly appeared on the door. I crawled up the small internal staircase and made it just in time to say hello to God on the great white telephone. I was so violently ill I couldn't move and, being alone, I could easily have choked to death or swallowed my tongue. Sometime the following day, whilst still rejecting a diet of dry crackers, I phoned the Turnbull to cancel my attendance from that evening's proceedings. Like any good girl, I said I had food poisoning. It was a white lie. Only one word was untrue.

The Turnbull sounded very disappointed and decided that he would come by my place on his way out to see if I had improved. No chance, I thought, you haven't seen me. I managed to clean the bathroom up before he came, but did nothing about my appearance in an attempt to frighten him off. The glorious man only turned up with a bouquet of red roses and the numbers 1, 4 and 6 to attach to my outside door, as there were none. He saw how terrible I looked, but encouraged me to get changed. Which, despite still wishing to throw up, I did. And spent the whole evening at his company's do sipping carrot soup and aggressively rejecting offers of alcohol, to people's offence and surprise. We had our first kiss on New Year's Eve.

I felt comfortable with John in a way I had never felt with anyone ever before. He had a sharp wit and continually made fun of me, which I enjoyed as I have always had a great ability to laugh at myself – I didn't take myself seriously for one second. But John did. And we talked about everything. He treated me with the utmost respect. It made me feel very together. I was soon introduced to the rest of his family – his parents and three older brothers. They, too, were wonderful people – honest, genuine, kind, respectful, welcoming. I felt truly at home whenever we visited them. In truth John had the kind of stable background and family I had longed for all my life. Their relationships were based on a common union, respect and a deep love. I fell in love.

*

Working for a TV station in one country and being transmitted in another is quite a peculiar experience. You rarely get feedback, you have no idea how you are fitting with the audience and you feel isolated. The news team at TV3 of which I was now part – at lunch times at least – consisted of Swedish, Danish and Norwegian journalists of a high calibre. All the presenters, regardless of nationality, would broadcast in their mother tongue, working on the theory that the languages are not dissimilar and share some common words, so that everyone would understand at least something.

I remained the apple of my boss's eye and was to be part of the new 'live' evening broadcasts about to start in May. The station decided to give its news output a serious, new push by not just investing in new wardrobes for everyone, but also hiring a major news presenter from Swedish state TV. Up until now, I had been doing my own make-up for the bulletins, and put on whatever I had in my wardrobe at the time. Now, they wanted heavy make-up and strictly dark clothes. A million miles away from Bruce's vision across the road.

Then one day I had a phone call from Nick Myers, one of the programme directors at TV-am, asking me what I was up to. When I told him, he asked me to send a tape over. Well, I walked over with a VHS myself and handed it straight to Bruce, who unfortunately was in the kind of mood that made people cower and walk in the opposite direction. But I knew I had to place the tape into his hand and no other, and so I played deaf and blind to his temperament. A couple of weeks later Nick Myers called me back to say that Bruce hadn't understood 'a fucking thing' I said on the tape, but would I be interested in coming in for a screen test? I requested the morning off work and went in.

Having spent the past six months or so standing in front of a chromakeyed map (a blank blue cloth in fact, but with a small TV monitor at eye level in the corner showing the map and yourself in front of it so you knew what to indicate) and an unmanned camera, I had developed a technique and even some style. I was no longer petrified by the camera; I had got used to wearing plain clothes and had learnt to control the movement of my left arm so as not to confuse or frighten the viewer; and I actually knew and believed in what I was talking about. Rather than the stuttering rabbit caught in the headlights of my last test, TV-am now saw a presenter who was comfortable, at ease and distracted by nothing.

They wanted me.

Nick Myers booked me as stand-in for their then weather presenter Carol Dooley, a cute, spiky-haired Irish girl, the week commencing 8 May while she was on holiday. But I knew that no way would I be allowed to take time off work at TV3 a week after the relaunch of their news. So I decided to attempt to do both jobs. While TV-am required an alarm call at 3.30 a.m., and my last bulletin at TV3 was at 11 p.m., it would be worth it. Even if it didn't lead to anything further, I would at least have placed myself on screen in the country in which I actually lived.

I had several bosses at TV3. There was 'El Presidente', and he had a couple of deputies. I told him my exciting proposal straight away. He was delighted for me and said I would have to take the matter up with the head of news, but he made me promise that if I got permission, this week's work was not a screen test for a permanent job at TV-am. Of course not, I interjected, with my fingers crossed behind my back.

One boss said I wasn't allowed. The other said I could do it as long as I could cope with both schedules. Convinced it was meant to be, I went out and bought myself lots of relaxing body products to prepare for the week of no sleep, along with five relatively cheap, but bright, outfits to wear for Britain.

On the first day, Richard presented the first hour, so I was in safe hands, and the rest of the morning went well, with the other presenters treating me generously and kindly. The reception from the public was good, too. To say that the comments that came in to the station's duty log were positive would be an understatement. I felt relaxed, content and as if I was enjoying every minute of it. It felt natural to me. I felt at home.

MORNING HAS BROKEN

On my second day at TV-am I was asked to take part in a press call, to draw attention to my presence there, apparently. A dozen photographers asked me to dip my feet in the Lock at Camden whilst sipping a make-believe cocktail. 'It was sunny and so was the gorgeous smile on the face of TV-am's weather girl' or something along those lines, read the headlines. I just did what I was told. Shortly after, Jeff Berliner, another programme director, pulled me into his office and on behalf of TV-am offered me the job permanently. I was quietly overjoyed. This is what I had hoped for, but had never dreamed might actually happen.

The rest of that punishing week continued. At two thirty in the morning I'd leave John in bed asleep, wash my hair and take myself off to Camden Lock, driving the same route I had taken so many times before as a secretary. Once the make-up department had caked me in make-up and styled my hair, I'd make my way into the studio, this time as a presenter, not rolling autocue. After we finished there was time for a couple of hours' kip before I was due back across the road at 2 p.m., where the 7 p.m. bulletin had to be assembled. After the eleven o'clock one I rushed home for a couple more hours' sleep, in anticipation of my alarm sounding again at two thirty.

When the week was over, I was exhausted and exhilarated. John very kindly arranged for us to go away for the weekend to allow me to recharge my batteries. It was lovely, but became a bit of a blur due to my tiredness. But we talked a lot that weekend about the future. John was delighted I had been offered the job and wholeheartedly supported me. TV-am wanted me to start in just over a month's time. I was only required to give TV3 one month's notice, on top of which I was owed lots of holiday. I had also been holding down two jobs with them for nine months without a salary rise, and they had yet to ask me to sign a contract. I wrote my boss explaining that I had been offered an opportunity at TV-am, but that I would, of course, work out my notice, expressing gratitude for everything he and the team had brought me. He took one second to read it before exploding. I was quite petrified. He cursed me, he cursed TV-am, he cursed the world, and then he cursed me again. I remember sitting on a chair in the middle of the room, wringing my hands nervously as I watched him race around his office. At one stage he eyeballed me, threatening to sue me, to sue TV-am, and saying he would personally see to it that I would never work in TV again. Ever. Oh, and I was very seriously in breach of my contract. My boss even called in his deputy to tell me so. After a long pause, the deputy quietly and reluctantly had to point out that I hadn't signed a contract yet. I was made to leave the office.

Not sure what to do, I went into the newsroom as before to start working for the evening's bulletin. The head of news followed me and told me I was banned from going on air – I would not be presenting that night's bulletin. I was left sitting on a chair with nothing to do, except to wonder at how dramatically different the beginning of this week was in comparison to the elation of the last. By the tenth day of just sitting there my good friend Gunilla, one of the news directors, pleaded that I might be allowed to leave. For good. That day.

And I was.

*

As a result of the whole experience I suffered a bout of anxiety attacks, which physically manifested themselves as excruciating pains in my solar plexus. Only with time and John's support and reassurance was I able to pick myself up again. We planned some time away before I would start working again.

John had by now more or less moved in with me in Maida Vale, and I thought the holiday would be a good break from the cramped flat we shared. Our relationship was very easy and reasonably uncomplicated; we respected each other and rarely argued. But while we were away, as if part of me felt I was having it too good, I began to question things. I began to feel unsure, but I wasn't sure what about. I may have been the louder one in the relationship, but John was by far the stronger, more solid. Was it that I was uncomfortable with all the unfamiliar affection, care and attention I was receiving? In any event, when we returned I told him I thought we should cool it a little, although as soon as I said it, I started missing him.

Richard Keys was by now becoming a bit of a mentor. He asked if I wanted him to act as my agent, for any work that might come in once I started back on screen. It seemed to make sense: I didn't know anyone else, and wouldn't have known whom to trust. Richard's motive wasn't a money-making one; it was genuine and considered. And he had knowledge and experience of the business from both sides, which would be invaluable.

Well, Richard was right. Work started to come in. There were photographic shoots, show pilots and personal appearances, and thankfully I was able to hand the requests to someone who would guide me through them. I began to be recognized out on the street – people greeted me with enthusiasm, kindness and occasionally wolf whistles. I felt embarrassed by the attention and tried to laugh it off; I knew I didn't deserve it. I felt slightly awkward when I was asked for an autograph, thinking it a little silly, but obliging respectfully. I certainly didn't lap the fame up.

My mum was delighted with my success. Michael too, I guess, although he sneered at my newly doubled salary, claiming I should have negotiated more. All I knew was that I had been able to pay off my overdraft. TV-am also sent me out shopping with a lady from the wardrobe department to buy lovely, bright clothes, which pleased my mother no end, especially since they were the kind of suits and jackets an older generation might be wearing – shoulder pads, collars, that kind of thing. She had spent a lifetime looking at me in black, or in jeans. My father was also pleased and proud, but said he missed my appearances on TV in Sweden, as they had made him laugh so.

And the *Good Morning Britain* weather was only the start of it. I was actually sent to Sweden to shoot a holiday programme, and fronted a career and education advice line called 'Success 89', which involved interviewing celebrities and experts in various fields. Doing more than my 'slot' taught me how to keep tightly to times on a live show, and coordinate a lot of information being thrown at you at in a short time. And it was thought that I showed potential, because I was offered a television journalism course, run by the Independent Television Association, at TV-am's expense. My new employers felt it was important for me to have the right grounding for future presenting work with them. It was a show of faith on their part which I eventually repaid by collapsing with laughter during one of my weather reports. Harry Enfield had come on TV-am to promote his new comedy series, which had started the night before. It was very funny and as they handed over to me for the weather I was asked what I thought of the clip. I had no time to think about what I was saying. My reply came: 'I enjoyed that – but not as much as I did last night.' The studio broke into giggles and I was left helplessly weeping with laughter by the weather board. The incident has been shown on *It'll Be All Right on the Night* too many times.

But I was also clearly seen as a pretty face too: the fiftieth anniversary of the outbreak of the Second World War saw me modelling the various uniforms of the ladies who had helped the war effort.

*

The atmosphere at TV-am was very good considering we were all constantly knackered. The girls, Lorraine Kelly, Lisa Aziz, Maya Even and myself, would joke daily about how the punishing hours we were keeping were hammering our sex lives. None of us seemed to have the energy or inclination, or indeed, find the right time for it. All presenters were supposed to have every seventh week off, to rest and recuperate, but for nine months my schedules never seemed to allow for this. I wasn't complaining – I loved what I was doing – but it did mean that as soon as I did have any time off, I caught every bug and sickness going.

My television journalism tutor, Miss Sue Lloyd-Roberts, was a highly respected journalist who seemed to object quietly to having a blonde floozy in her class. The majority of trainees came from hard-news ITN, and the three of us from TV-am felt as though we were fairly dismissively treated – although as it happened we all did a fantastic job. The course itself involved electronic news gathering, interviewing and studio presentation, law, police and local government, politics and industrial reporting, as well as various editorial exercises.

To complete the final stage, we had to put together a programme incorporating all the aspects that the course had covered. This basically involved cutting together the stories we had shot and reported on as projects into a news bulletin. I had shot a couple of stories, but my main one covered the growing number of homeless on the streets of London. I ventured down to a very hostile Waterloo, where two days prior a German news crew had been badly beaten up, and managed to entice one of the many homeless to speak to me. Due to exhaustion I didn't feel that positive about my achievements, but I knew it was all good experience. However, my course work was very good, except for my written law exam, and anything with a political aspect, which I simply failed to grasp. So when the course finally came to an end in April 1990 I was overwhelmed to discover that my bosses at TV-am had been told that my news story was the best covered. Not one iota of me had any desire to continue further into the field of journalism. But I did agree to host a weekly review of events on Sunday mornings called *Good Morning Moments*. Memorable, I'm sure.

The press maintained a strong and steady interest in me and my career, and I even continued to do bits of publicity in Sweden, whenever asked. I became the cover girl of many glamorous magazines such as *Woman's Own* and *TV Times*. I probably even fronted

Knitting Weekly, if there is such a thing. This was considered by our press office to be the kind of material our viewers would read, and therefore we should be in it as regularly as possible. I was never really in a position to say no, so simply did everything and anything requested. I don't know if it was this willingness that sparked rumours that I had my eye on the main presenting job at TV-am, following in the footsteps of the glorious Anne Diamond. I was described as ambitious, ruthless and a serious contender for the post. Nothing could have been further from the truth! With so much additional work at the station, and still enjoying my weather slot tremendously, I had no intention of placing my arse on that sofa: I would remain standing, thank you. And as far as my career outside TV-am went, Richard and I really had no long-term plan. I simply did whatever was thrown at me, with the permission of TV-am, of course.

TV-am had the right to control my image on screen – that is to say, what I wore, my make-up and hair styles. I was contractually obliged to not bring the station into disrepute outside working hours and in, and would always require permission for a haircut. It seemed a relatively small price to pay for doing the job of a lifetime and getting paid for it. But they drove a hard bargain at TV-am and my salary was way below everyone else's, in spite of having double the workload. I was still just considered 'a secretary made good'.

Speaking of image, I did find that I had to put myself on a Weight Watchers diet as the hips-growing programme I'd devised for myself was going a bit too well. I lost about a stone. And since Bruce insisted that we looked radiant and colourful on screen, he actually arranged for us all to have free sunbeds at a salon in Mayfair – the start of a lifetime's passion.

At Easter, which saw my first week off in a long time, John and I went to Rome to visit his brother Paul and girlfriend Francesca. We'd been once before and fallen totally in love with the city. This time, though, another love was to bloom. On 20 April, John proposed marriage by scribbling a note to me: would I go to Mexico with him? This was our code for a long-term, marriage-like commitment, in the way you send people to Coventry when you're pissed off with them. I had always been a girl who claimed I would never marry, feeling strongly that it was of little significance in a world filled with divorce. I would always joke that John would never get me in a church – but I realized he already had, both when his brother had married and on our visit to Il Vaticano. I found I didn't hesitate in saying 'Yes'.

And there it was. I was twenty-two and I was going to get married.

*

Despite feeling that John was so definitely the right person for me on account of his kindness, stability, and consideration, I felt reluctant and a little scared by my reply. I began to panic a little and said we should keep it under our hats before making any announcements. I would imagine these feelings are not uncommon with newly engaged couples. You wonder how it will change things.

However, by the following weekend I was bursting with excitement to tell mum and Michael. My mother, who was a great fan of John's, was extremely happy for us. Michael, on the other hand, played the role of the grim reaper, telling John he must be out of his mind, and that I would bring him a lifetime of misery. Which was nice.

Unfazed, as soon as we had decided on a short engagement and an intimate wedding I launched myself into wedding fever. By the end of May I was in possession of a nine-diamond-studded white gold engagement ring designed by John, and TV-am made an announcement to the press. We would marry on 29 September 1990. It was going to be a year of weddings, with two good friends marrying in May and my colleague Lisa Aziz in June. It was very exciting – almost as exciting as the World Cup, which had me glued to the TV at every spare moment.

Bruce was delighted I was getting married, but proceeded to appal me by saying he would pay for the wedding himself. I objected strongly: I wanted to be beholden to no one. Yes, Mum and Michael had hosted an engagement party for us in June to take the place of a BIG white wedding, but what Bruce was suggesting was something quite different. In his eyes I was one of the daughters of TV-am, and he saw this as the perfect opportunity to cover the event on screen and even offer a wedding dress by my designer as a competition prize! I was horrified. I lied, telling him no filming was allowed in the church. Get the vicar on the phone, he shouted. Trust me, I pleaded. Get me God on the phone then, he retorted. So Bruce. I didn't want to seem ungrateful, but I couldn't possibly take part in what he was suggesting. It was one of the few battles I won with Bruce.

Naturally I wanted my father to attend and I thought I would have both my half-sisters and half-brother as bridesmaids and attendants. But when I suggested this to my mother, she went cold. She did not understand why I would want my father at the wedding, when Michael had been the one who brought me up. In my mind I had imagined the two men sharing the walk up the aisle between them, and saw no problem in inviting my thirteen-year-old sister over. My mother was adamant. She said, plainly, if he comes, I won't.

I couldn't believe what I was hearing. But I lacked the strength to tell her to not be ridiculous, or to simply tell her to like it or lump it. Instead I took a cowardly way out, not wishing to rock the boat or disturb the peace, and phoned my father to tell him that he wouldn't be welcomed by certain people. It was an unbelievably hard thing to do, and all because I couldn't bear further ructions between my mother and myself. My father took it very badly, despite me trying to convince him that the wedding was going to be so small it would be virtually invisible. The irony was that Michael had no problem with my father attending.

John couldn't bear to see me so upset by the dilemma, especially when my father had phoned me in tears asking me what I would do if he simply turned up anyway. My husband-to-be took it upon himself to go in person to see my mother and ask her to reconsider, and to think of me instead of herself. She refused.

Truly, it is about the only thing in life I wish I had not done. I'd stood up to Bruce so as not to lose sight of whose wedding it was, but had still sold out to what someone else thought was right.

We decided to allow *Hello!* magazine to have the pictures of our wedding day, without any money changing hands. Having no press agent at the time, except the staff in the TV-am press office, I felt more comfortable telling them what pictures they could have and taking no money for it, rather than them believing they could run the day at a price. Little did I realize I could have done both.

On 29 September 1990 at eleven o'clock I married John Gordon Turnbull in front of twenty-five people in St Giles' Church in Stoke Poges. The world's press waited outside and all got their snap of the happy couple leaving the church for a lunch at a secret destination. I hadn't even dared to tell our thirteen lunch guests where the reception was in case the press found out, but we had no trouble from them at Le Manoir aux Quat' Saisons. The day was disastrous weather-wise, with lashing rain and grey skies, but they say that is supposed to bring you luck.

ULRIKA-ON-THE-MOVE

Mr and Mrs Turnbull returned from two magnificent weeks' honeymoon in the Seychelles, where we nearly drowned after capsizing a catamaran we had taken out for a sail, and launched back into work with a vengeance. Even while we were away I was unable to shake my early-morning starts from my system, my body insisting on waking me up at the crack of dawn. John's work took him away from home at least three nights a week, commuting the length and breadth of the country to cover sports events, operas or rock concerts. Given my ludicrous working hours, we were unable to establish any form of social life. We simply worked hard, and on days off would walk the countryside or indulge in home improvements. Early nights were the order of the day, and nights out were limited to maybe one or two a month, if that.

Having grown my hair for my wedding, the tomboy in me wanted a shorter style immediately after. I had to seek permission from TV-am and Bruce's reaction was reluctant if not forbidding, but after a month I was the proud owner of a shoulder-length bob. Apart from that, 1991 brought no major changes to TV-am except that the management was knee-deep in new franchise strategies. The lovely Margaret Thatcher, TV-am's friend, had introduced a policy before her resignation on 22 November 1990 that meant independent television franchises would be granted to the highest bidders. Some form of quality control would also be stipulated, but no one knew quite in what shape or form. The TV-am board, confident in its close links to Downing Street, was determined to secure another ten years of broadcasting when the renewals came up in the following year.

Outside in the greater world, we had all followed with trepidation the threats and actions of Saddam Hussein. His invasion of Kuwait brought to our attention not only that area of the world, but the potential threat it might have on us all and our futures. On 17 January, as I put myself into a taxi at 4 a.m. to go to work, the driver didn't hesitate in telling me that we had, overnight, gone to war against Iraq. I felt very nervous. I was not quite sure what a war in the nineties would bring.

TV-am suddenly rose to the challenge of offering a hard-news and current-affairs service, with experts and politicians being dragged in from all corners of the universe to take part in its transmissions. There was a tremendous sense of excitement and drama as we watched night-vision footage emerging on our screens. But deep in our stomachs, too, there was fear.

By contrast, my contribution to the war effort was to present a daytime game show for the BBC, called *Who's Bluffing Who?* – and to be honest none of us was really sure. The concept was so utterly confusing it had the producers and the studio audience baffled into silence in every show. It was exhausting, taking up a further ten hours on top of my already six-hour working day. Richard had great enthusiasm for the show, but he was about the only one. It went largely unnoticed in the daytime schedule of the greatest broadcasting corporation in the world.

Against a backdrop of war and game shows, John and I were growing increasingly frustrated by life in the big city. Both of us longed to wake up to the sounds of birdsong, rather than car alarms and loud music. We decided that with my boosted salary and the extra work I was taking on, we could afford ourselves a place in the country. Besides, the flat was really not big enough for two. And with ever-increasing feelings of broodiness, I was determined we would have a place big enough for four or five little monkeys. After excitedly looking around the commutable areas of Berkshire and Buckinghamshire we found ourselves a Victorian cottage in a village near where I had grown up.

Media-wise I was important enough to have an accountant, launch a ship in Sweden and briefly be agony aunt on TV-am's new kids' feature, 'Backchat'. As I flew to Liverpool to cover the Grand National I resolved to change agents. I needed more help with prioritizing than I was getting with Richard, and I think we'd outgrown each other. People outside the business tend not to know what an agent actually does. It is imperative you find someone who completely understands you and your needs; who can share the direction in which you are going and who can instinctively feel their way forward with you. It is a little like finding someone to go on a long trip with and knowing you both speak the same language and that you will grow tired neither of each other nor of each other's intentions.

As if by chance, a journalist I had been interviewed by a couple of times mentioned that he knew someone who would love to get their hands on me, professionally at least. Melanie Cantor was an experienced publicist who felt she could take me a step further on my journey. Our first meeting didn't start too well. I had suggested we meet for lunch at a place called Raoul's in my native Maida Vale. As more and more time passed while I sat there waiting at the table, it became increasingly clear that she wasn't going to turn up. Little did I know that next door but one, at Raoul's café, sat Melanie slowly concluding I wasn't going to turn up either. Thankfully, she took the initiative of asking if there was another place with a similar name. I had no idea what she looked like, but when an incredibly well-groomed, pretty woman of five foot and a whisper marched in I knew it had to be her. We laughed at the misunderstanding and have not looked back since. That was eleven years ago. I think we've done all right. Richard wasn't too sad to see me go, and was probably secretly quite relieved.

*

At the beginning of that summer TV-am had developed another project for me: 'Ulrika-on-the-Move'. This had one express intention: it was to show the Independent Television Association that TV-am was truly committed to its regional output, ahead of its submission of the franchise bid. Someone had the brilliant idea of me presenting my weather reports from a different location every morning. I was to start with a week's tour of Northern Ireland, followed by Scotland and then Wales. I thought it was a brilliant idea and promptly went out to buy brightly coloured weatherproofs. It was June after all.

We toured Northern Ireland, starting at the spectacular Giant's Causeway. It was exhausting but everyone we came across was unbelievably welcoming and helpful. On the last day we were at Enniskillen, preparing our usual travelogue to wrap round the live report. Throughout the transmission was the annoying and persistent sound of a military helicopter circling above us. Unbeknownst to us, there was an IRA funeral later that morning in the town, so the military helicopter was there to try to offer us some protection. With a live broadcast, we were evidently a sitting target. Nice to know, boys.

After Ireland came Scotland, with a day in-between at home to wash and re-pack. Inverness was followed by Loch Ness, Dundee, and the riding festival at Selkirk in the Borders, where I had to mount a horse called Willy. Then, after another twenty-four more hours at home, I was off to North Wales for a tour stretching from Betws-y-Coed to Hay-on-Wye. As a PR coup for TV-am the trip worked a treat. Everywhere we went people gathered in droves to speak to us live on telly. They brought banners, gifts, their sense of humour and sometimes the inbred members of their families. I had the most brilliant producer, Teresa Poole; a fab make-up artist, Simon Jay; and Lorraine Kelly's other half, Stevie, on camera. Together we laughed our way from location to location, struggling with our constant states of jet lag and attempting to catch forty winks whenever we could.

When I returned it was to our new marital home in gorgeous Berkshire. We had swapped the cramped one-bedroom flat, which remained unsold (and somewhat unsellable given the property market crash), for a four-bedroom semi with a small garden. I could hardly contain my excitement as I opened the door to what was essentially a Tardis. However, the excitement had to be put on ice, because twenty-four hours later I was due up north for the Liverpool Festival and John was heading for Wimbledon.

Our paths crossed rarely and we had to steal moments together like thieves in the night as one came home and the other left. But it was exciting that work was going well for both of us, and the cottage was a project in common. The house needed a lot of work doing to it but despite now being better equipped financially, we seemed determined to do most of the work ourselves. There were ceilings to come down, a staircase to put in and floorboards to be laid. While John carried on working, whether it was opera at Covent Garden or covering a G7 meeting, I bought a sewing machine and gave my skills as a seamstress a long overdue airing, running up curtains, pelmets, seat covers and anything else that would make the house look homely.

The one time we did work together it was a joy. Not only did it mean we got to spend more than twenty-four hours in the course of a week together – and that included sleeping time – but we complemented each other professionally. John is the antithesis of me, calm, studious and concentrated to my bubbly, lively, distracted and slightly manic. We enjoyed a whole seven days down in Torquay as part of my tour of the seaside resorts of Great Britain, before John left for a cycling commitment with Channel 4 and I headed for Great Yarmouth.

As we were flying back from Newcastle (where I'd gone straight on from my seaside specials to host the third year of TV-am's career-advice segment, now 'Success 91'), the warning signs that a punishing schedule and erratic lifestyle were taking their toll began to flare up. After three days of bad stomach pains and a pounding headache John rushed me into our local hospital, bent double and throwing up. While my discomfort was stabilized with a little help from an injection of pethidine in my bum, all I could do was lie in bed and think about how I would get to Blackpool for Monday's transmission. The doctors, despite being unable to tell me what was wrong with me, told me I was going nowhere. At TV-am, being absent from work was nigh on illegal, death's door notwithstanding. So my numbed stomach pain was overlaid with guilt, concern and angst – even though I was allowed a week off to try and recover. My mother, bless her, wept with worry as she blamed the poor diet I had had as a young child. Little did we realize how right she was.

To cap it all, three wisdom teeth had arrived in my mouth without a prior reservation. There was no room at the inn and they needed to be taken out. So serious was my condition that one specialist had to explain the risk of 'post-operative paraesthaesia' to a somewhat baffled me. Due to the complex root development of one of the teeth around a nerve, there was as much as a fifty per cent chance of being left with no sensation in my lower lip, whatsoever. Leaving aside for a second the complexities of kissing with a lip I had no control over, I considered the potential of dribbling without knowing it, or even remnants of food going unnoticed on my chin for days on end. It was not a pretty prospect. I mean, how many dribbling presenters do you know? Still, I knew I had to take the risk.

So, it was amidst toothache, a possible ulcer, press interviews, heavy DIY, my first wedding anniversary and the occasional platonic lunch with HRH that I awaited with the rest of the team news of the result of the renewal of TV-am's broadcasting franchise. The station had prepared itself for safe passage into a further ten years of broadcasting by hiring specialists, consultants, legal eagles and media wizards. Bruce felt confident, and so presumably did the rest of the board, that they would easily fulfil the quality threshold required; the only uncertainty was the amount they could bid – the franchise was going to be awarded to the highest bidder, after all.

16 October 1991 was the day. As we came into work that morning you could cut the atmosphere with a knife. Granted, waitresses were decking out the lobby area with champagne glasses and filling buckets with ice and pink bubbly, but there was also the unspoken fear of redundancies. As soon as the show was over we

presenters locked ourselves away while everyone else attempted to shuffle papers in an inane attempt at occupying the hour or so we had to wait. Bruce closeted himself in his office with the other directors, closed curtains and a fax machine about to spew out the final decision, worth its weight in gold. But before Bruce had a chance to hear the pulsating of the paper coming out of the machine, I remember letting out a shriek of horror. There, on an ITN News special, came the announcement on a rolling script across the screen that the losers were TV-am, TVS, TSW and Thames. The reverberation was felt like a 7 on the Richter scale as the news swept through the building, like only devastating news can, leaving secretaries tearful, journalists confused, researchers nervous. People were gathering in clusters and others ran like mice from the farmer's wife.

I wasn't rendered speechless. On the contrary. But the words I was full of refused to form themselves into comprehensible sentences. After regaining my composure I wanted to steal a second with Bruce to express my disappointment, but also to express my love for this great man who had given his life and soul to something which by now had a shelf life of only fourteen months. As I fought my way to him, Carol Thatcher, one of the station's guest reporters, could be heard screaming across the office, 'Mummy's on the phone!' Without hesitation, Bruce let me go and ran in her direction. Well, I didn't have to be political editor to work out that she was bound to be phoning to offer her apologies. Yes, she, who had watched and condoned Bruce's crushing of the technical union; she who had waited for someone like him to have the courage to do what she was unable to; and yes, she who had passed the legislation in the first place to allow the 'purchase' of television franchises to proceed in a less sophisticated way than at a local antiques auction. And she was. She wept as she gave Bruce her condolences.

As it turned out TV-am had been way out of its depth, offering only £14.3 million in comparison to its rival, who offered £36.4 million. That rival was GMTV. Bruce went on the record to say it was a travesty. And to a huge extent he was right.

THE ULTIMATE CHALLENGE

With the passing of the franchise battle, everyone's attention turned to future employers and career shifts, and none more so than mine. My fellow presenters at the station were employees, which meant they were entitled to substantial redundancies. Unlike me. As a freelance presenter, TV-am had little, if any, obligation towards me and I realized that it made no sense to stay until the bitter end in the expectation that something would fall out of the sky for me, or that indeed I would receive an inflated leaving present. So, as well as promotional, publicity, and corporate work outside of TV-am, I was busy compiling a showreel of all the work I had done for the station, in a feeble attempt at impressing someone. I carried on with my sewing machine and my paint brush at home, went to Sweden to launch an aeroplane and spent that Christmas at home with John, on our own. I even thought it was now safe to cut my hair, but Bruce's response to my much shorter bob was a reading of the riot act *and* the Ten Commandments, plus a memo stating that I was in breach of my contract. Always a nice eye for details, our Bruce.

One job that came through in the New Year was a pilot for a new show for the BBC, to be called *Out on a Limb*. It was a celebrity challenge, filmed down in Bath, where I was paired up with the Welsh comedian Max Boyce. We were racing against the likes of Keith Chegwin, Suzanne Dando and Paul Coia, to complete a series of challenges. We had to be photographed sitting on potties in a shop window by a vicar; sing the Marseillaise in a public building; and re-enact the death of Julius Caesar at the Roman Baths in the city centre. I was unbelievably competitive (Melanie's instructions to me had been that I should show them what a good sport I was . . .), and after schlepping a slightly overweight Max halfway round Bath and nearly crashing the Toyota Previa I insisted I drove, we were the first to make it back to the wonderful Lucknam Park to claim our prize. I rushed into the lobby, dazed and confused, clutching Polaroids of evidence and followed by an exhausted crew, only to realize something was up. There in the reception was Noel Edmonds. The whole thing had been a set-up. I had just won myself a Crinkley Bottom *House Party* 'Gotcha Oscar'!

Not content with just one award that week, I was shortly to receive another – one for which I had been runner-up for the past two years. I had won the much coveted, highly controversial 1992 Rear of the Year, which was interesting bearing in mind no one ever saw my arse except my husband. Interviews and a photocall followed in return for which the sponsors gave my 'womanly' size-twelve behind a pair of jeans. Hoorah!

But the most exciting clothing proposition came in the form of the Grattan mail-order catalogue, which for two weeks' work was prepared to pay me the same as I was earning at TV-am in a year. At the meeting with them I kicked Melanie under the table good and hard as we held our breaths in a vain attempt at remaining dignified. Once we left we virtually pissed ourselves with excitement and danced like thirteen-year-olds at a bar mitzvah.

To celebrate I had an endoscopy, when they force a tube with a camera on the end of it down your gullet, in an attempt to get to the bottom of my stomach condition. I enjoyed it tremendously, as I had decided to couple it with a severe case of cystitis on the same day. I don't believe I have ever felt so good. Surviving that must have given me the fortitude to commit to a pantomime in Crawley that coming Christmas. Bold as brass I was. But what was really about to change things was a meeting in early April with London Weekend Television.

I was told they had a programme idea they wanted to put to me. I was all ears. An American format, it involved a group of extremely fit, muscly men and women who would take on members of the public in series of innovative games. It would be a 'David and Goliath' kind of thing. I was still listening. The games would engage aggressor and defender on rings suspended from the ceiling; or would have them compete over a climbing wall. OK, I thought, a bit wild, but I'm with you. Or, said the producer/director, they would simply try to beat the hell out of each other on podiums with giant cotton buds. No, I thought, you've lost me now – that will never take off. The producer was Nigel Lythgoe, and the show was going to be called *Gladiators*.

Being a woman of no integrity, a slave to my career and a whore to television, I naturally accepted the job without hesitation. We pretended to hesitate, Melanie and I, but it was going to be a Saturday-night show and there are only so many high pressures and low pressures a girl could get excited about. And I was to co-host with a footballer called John Fashanu.

At this stage I still required permission from Bruce before I took on another project (let alone cut my hair), but Melanie and I had come to the conclusion that with this and a few other little pies I had my fingers in, I could probably take a chance and leave TV-am before the franchise ran out in December. Sounds like I was jumping ship, and in many respects I was. But what the hell, the others had life jackets. I had to swim for my life.

Bruce, surprisingly enough given that it was so soon after our Vidal Sassoon encounter, was very understanding. He agreed that I could leave around the time my contract was up anyway, which would have been June, but asked if I would stay on a little extra had they not found a replacement by then. Of course I would, I said, as we kissed and made up, once again, before skipping out of his office knowing that finally my three-thirty alarm calls were coming to an end.

*

I was not quite prepared for what I encountered as I stepped into Birmingham's National Indoor Arena that first day. Armed only with histories of two score contenders and pages and pages of game rules – not to forget a list of the most inspiring names for our aggressors – I entered an arena filled with smoke, rocking with music and scattered with muscle-bound He-man-like creatures (and that was only the women). I was taken aback. A crew of hundreds were darting around fixing, lifting, creating, shouting and laughing. Production staff were waving bits of paper, issuing passes and directing runners and gofers left and right.

In the midst of it all stood my producer and director, Nigel. He was a slight man with dance-like movements and a cigarette in the corner of his mouth as he clapped and jeered to make Fash and me feel welcome. He looked hassled, troubled and deeply engrossed. He spoke so quickly I was hardly able to take in any of his briefing about contenders, rules, games, music, direction, shots, prize money. It didn't stop. Fash looked at me blankly. I stared back vacantly. But before we knew it Nigel had us whisked away to the cupboards that were to be our dressing rooms.

Nine programmes had been commissioned, of which six would be preliminaries, followed by two semi-finals and a final. The prize was around £2,000 cash and an off-road vehicle I think. Fash's and my job was to explain the games on camera to the audience at home, and to interview contenders and Gladiators alike before and after each game.

It seemed the Gladis had already bonded and established their own pecking order, headed by a jet-black giant who would only answer to the name of 'Shadow'. Fash and I were still struggling to put a face to the twelve gladiatorial names we had learnt by heart. Well, one of us had, anyway. The girls seemed pleasant enough and the boys were, well, just huge. They were all as excited as little children who are about to be let loose at the funfair. Nigel talked to us at 100 mph about the show he had been living, breathing and making love to for the past few months. He positively oozed *Gladiators*, and it positively oozed with his vision. And his vision was something neither Fash nor I could possibly imagine. He explained how we would record two shows concurrently, with 'quick change' rooms for us to swap outfits. Each game would be recorded four times, once for each sex and once for each show. He was going to cut this into that; put that music over this; use graphics to show the other; and light this in that special way. For my part I focused on getting to know the contenders.

The Warriors, Wolves and Phoenixes of this world were unknowns, but behaved as though they were stars already made. Even more unknown, however, were those who were foolhardy enough to challenge them. I studied the information supplied about them intently, going through it with a fine-tooth comb, and then spent fifteen to twenty minutes speaking to each and every one of them. Our scriptwriter, a delightful man called Colin Edmonds, had prepared clever comments for me to put to them when we came to recording. To be frank, the suggested comments were a little old-fashioned and twee for me – more in the style of Bob Monkhouse than a vibrant Swede well versed in matters meteorological. Now, whilst Bob and I might share a love for sunbeds, that's where the similarities end. But Colin was kind, thorough and in other ways inspiring, and we were actually able to have a bit of a laugh. Fash had seemingly no ability to concentrate for more than ten minutes and we often lost him halfway through a sentence, when his mobile would sound or he would decide to change the subject completely. We both had long scripts to learn for our PTCs (pieces to camera); although I was used to working without autocue they did mean homework for me, and they proved a real problem for Fash. I tried to talk him through them, abbreviate and cut them down, but nothing could get round the fact that we would have to stand in front of an enormous arena audience and recite those scripts. Neither of us really relished the prospect.

I had two further concerns. Nigel had decided I should go for a sporty look, donning bright leotard tops and black leggings. Well, there was nothing particularly sporty about my pear-shaped figure and I was dreading the thought of drawing attention to my breasts, which had over the years grown into Gala melons. Further, he had come up with the suggestion that I should, in between pieces to camera, run into the depths of the audience and interview members of families who were there to support their loved ones. Even fully clothed, this would not have appealed in the slightest. Dressed like Wonderwoman with implants, I felt self-conscious, exposed and naked. However, it would not do to start rejecting suggestions so early on, so I put my head down and got on with it.

When the day finally came for our first recording, everyone was nervous and the 'giant stars' were no exception. Tickets to view the recording inside the arena were free, but I think we only managed to drum up an audience of about 1,000 (the arena could hold 8,000). It looked sad and somewhat unmomentous, but a relief, too, for my footballing other half and myself. I had learnt my script, even understood my role, but had yet to grasp how the whole show would cut together. Fash and I would step out into the arena, welcome the audience, explain the show, then rush backstage, change, then do it all over again. And so it would continue until late into the night. When it came to me snaking my way through our little audience, I was variously jeered, cheered, stared at and had my arse pinched – all a delight for someone who was already painfully self-conscious. Nigel loved it. I had to tell him I hated it, and gradually he understood it wasn't really working.

I had briefed my contenders of the questions I would put to them at their introduction. I then had some of the Gladiators telling *me* how they wanted me to interview them – what they wanted to say, how they wanted to say it, how they wished to come across. I tried to persuade them that a sense of spontaneity might result in greater excitement. They looked at me blankly. I think the word was too long – certainly for the boys. The girls for the most part were sweet and friendly and more together; they had a fairly good idea what was required of them and focused on the task. A couple of them shone. It was no secret that most of the men on the production team fancied the former gymnast, 'Jet'; and 'Lightning', who was originally only a stand-by, impressed Nigel so much with her gymnastic flips and acrobatics that she was given more of the limelight. On the boys' side, 'Shadow' was the biggest and the blackest, and – as I fast discovered – a man of very few words. Whenever I went to interview him, he said nothing other than 'Ultimate Challenge'. 'Warrior' too was humungous and made no apologies for it, but had at least a wicked sense of humour; then there was 'Wolf', for whom Nigel had already carved out a 'nasty' character. My instant favourites were 'Saracen', a black fireman who was relaxed enough to take it all in his stride, and 'Cobra' who, not dissimilarly to Norman Wisdom, was about the only one who had the ability to laugh at himself.

Recording was generally purgatory. Fash's failure to grasp his pieces to camera made for long retakes, which I have to say he dealt with admirably. We both tried to help each other. Having been trained in live television, I rarely got my links wrong – in fact, I would only give myself one take. However, when it came to the interviewing, Nigel would come flying out of the room from where he was directing the show to tut, complain or remark on the words used and their tone or inference. I had never worked with people who had indulged me in any way, and Nigel was no exception. His first words to me had been, 'I won't be pandering to you and filling you with compliments.' Well, that was true. However, a few kind words of encouragement for two lost souls wouldn't have gone amiss. Instead, he would often rush up to us in front of everyone and gasp, 'What the fuck was that all about?' or 'What the fuck were you saying that for?' The tot of whisky Fash and I consumed pre-show did little to rid me of my ongoing sense of awkwardness and embarrassment. And on top of it all we were both struggling to maintain a hold on which show it was we were actually recording, with the constant changes and recording games out of sequence. By the end of that first shooting day we ran out of time before reaching the deciding 'Eliminator' round, calling it a day at 11 p.m. The contenders would have to hold on to their anticipation until the following evening. I returned to a hotel full of lumbering and pent-up Gladis, and fell into bed utterly exhausted but unable to sleep.

The two weeks continued with more of the same. Neither Fash nor I behaved like prima donnas: we just worked hard and kept our heads down. But just as our heads fell lower than they ever had done before, our live spectator audience grew, day by day. And not only did it increase, but people actually got caught up in the excitement, grasping the audience participation element of a show on a massive scale – they arrived with banners; in look-alike outfits; with autograph books; and with giant foam hands to wave. What's more, when the first show went out in October it may have received a mixed welcome from critics, but the viewers voted with their arses. They stayed put and watched it. Then, for the first time, I finally saw what Nigel had been on about. I understood his vision, shared his excitement and lived his dream. Even so, when filming the first series of *Gladiators* came to a close with the inevitable crew wrap party, both Fash and I thanked our lucky stars that we were still alive, and I saved a dance for lovely Nigel.

*

I returned to TV-am for a final week. My last day was tinged only with the slightest sadness: it was in truth much longed for and above all else, much needed. The day was filled with flowers, champagne, farewells and my darling husband John shooting the whole thing with his camera. I felt released and ready to move on – which I promptly did by flying first class to Los Angeles for my first Grattan assignment. I could barely contain myself, it felt so extravagant. The week's shoot actually turned out to be extremely hectic and tiring, and by the time I managed to sneak in a morning's sunbathing, I'd come to the conclusion that photo sessions and modelling were about more than being a pretty face. They were about fussing, tedium *and* a pretty face.

When I arrived back home, jet lag and an ingrained early-morning habit aside, I was a woman in her element. I spent the days pottering around our lovely little house, clearing, changing things, and adding to what was fast becoming a home. I loved my garden. I'd taken it on myself, rain or shine, in order to have a release mechanism, and mugged up on books about gardening and advice from my father-in-law. Out there, I would not only physically exhaust myself, but would also psychologically escape to a world where I had no name or recognition, free of frills and spills, and without demands or ambition. I thoroughly loved it.

Not to say that I was done with putting myself about a bit, by any means. A girl's gotta work, after all. Some do *Playboy*. I did Playtex. They basically make comfortable underwear, and my job was to make it look sexy. Thanks to make-up and hair reconstruction, some moody lighting and a provocative but respectable pose, we got a great result. When the pictures came out, everyone was quite taken aback. I had always been seen as the 'safe' girl next door, and I was now portraying a lady of the night. The press couldn't believe it. They talked about my new 'image', how I had changed and what a little minx I was turning out to be. Trouble was, I didn't feel an inch minx-like. I did feel like the 'safe' girl next door. I maintained that this was just another side to me, as opposed to a 'new' one.

Inside was a different story. Every month I became a woman possessed. Possessed by the devil called PMS. I became more than irritable, but also quite aggressive and very down. I needed something rather stronger than the evening primrose oil I was consuming at a rate of knots. Then I cricked my neck doing aerobics. I made an appointment to see my doctor and was rather disappointed to end up with a locum. His name was Dr Mark Broomfield and I want to thank him for the following. After chatting briefly about my neck he turned his attention to my notes and the on-going saga of my probable ulcer. He asked how it was, and I replied as usual, that I kept on taking my acid-killing tablets at night, but was resigned to living with it. He then told me about some trials that had been going on down in Cornwall, which had shown that such conditions often developed at a young age due to bacteria in the stomach. The revolutionary treatment was a long course of antibiotics. My eyes only vaguely lit up for fear of another disappointment, but I accepted the prescription with gratitude, and left hoping for the best. Well, it was a slightly complicated treatment, but I stuck to it. I had to take two sets of antibiotics concurrently – one for two weeks, and the other for four. One set could not be combined with any yeasty foods, and the other should not be taken with any dairy products. So for a month I avoided bread and dairy products, and not only lost a lot of weight, but was also finally cured of my daily bouts of acid indigestion, heartburn and belching. So thank you, Dr Broomfield. I haven't had a day's indigestion since – except during pregnancy. This really transformed my life: I was no longer in seemingly untreatable pain, and I was able to eat what I wanted. And drinking a glass of wine was no longer like pouring fuel on a fire. Thank you, thank you, thank you, kind sir.

With my new stomach I was able to start living like most other people, and finally could save my husband the embarrassment of my loud, public and very vulgar belching. Perhaps that is why he worked away such a lot . . . who knows?

This also meant I was in tip-top shape for my next challenge: pantomime in Crawley, Sussex, with Brian Cant (of *Playaway* fame) and the lovely Ross King (of all sorts of fame). Despite having committed some ten months before rehearsals began in early December, as the start date approached, I found myself feeling increasingly reluctant. But I was top of the bill. Cinderella in *Cinderella*.

Everyone in the cast, including our director, the same Mr Cant, made me feel very welcome, but nothing could disguise the fact that I was a panto virgin. Last time I had taken part in this show was in the last year of middle school, and then I had been the Prince. And the only other times I had trodden the boards were Christmas plays at secondary school – a wench in *As You Like It* and a whore in *A Comedy of Errors*. Seems to be a connection, but can't think what.

This time was more serious, however. I was being paid. Just about. And it became quite clear on or around the first day that I was going to hate it. For a start I had to commute two hours, there and back, every day. Secondly, I wasn't particularly keen on the singing bits (pretty fundamental really). Thirdly, fourthly and fifthly, it was damned hard work. Now, Ms Jonsson ain't averse to a bit of hard work. But only of the kind she enjoys. And she weren't enjoying this.

I rehearsed well with Ross, my Buttons, who was nothing short of superb. He was talented, experienced and incredibly generous in showing me the ropes with such patience that I got through my first and last pantomime experience without putting my head in the microwave. My prince, Philip Day, had even been in the Royal Shakespeare Company, another true professional – except he couldn't remember his lines, and had me in stitches. Everyone else was working their butts off too, all for the love of the theatre, which in turn was admirable. I just wasn't loving the theatre the same way. This lady was brought up in live television, and used to doing everything just once. But in truth it might have had more to do with the fact that all the bits I thought were great, our beloved director cut. And as he himself was playing the role of Baron Hardup, he thought fit to expand his own role a bit. But we did manage to have a right laugh when Brian Cant wasn't looking. And it wasn't me who changed the spelling of his name on his dressing-room door.

*

On 31 December I attended the funeral of TV-am. I went on air with presenters past and present to pay my respects and give my thanks and gratitude to the company and the station which had been the making of me. Many former colleagues were moving on to pastures new; others mumbled about the quality of life without obligations. I felt optimistic too, for myself; *Gladiators* was fast becoming the success it deserved to be and I couldn't have been busier if I had tried. However, it didn't stop me looking back with a tinge of longing at the spot on the set where I had stood religiously every morning, bringing sunshine and rain into people's living rooms.

INFIDELITY

The only fantastic thing about the beginning of 1993 was that panto would shortly be over. Back at home I was becoming more accustomed to not working every day. I would have pockets of intense work, like a Grattan shoot in Palm Springs, or no work at all. There was never a good balance. It didn't bother me too much, as I filled any time off with working on the house, or burying myself in the garden.

February saw a corporate presentation on behalf of Coca-Cola. You may have heard of them. Big organization, nice drink. I was to host a presentation at Disneyland Paris – or EuroDisney, as it was called then – to their European managers for a new venture called 'Coca-Cola is the Music'. I had been given a script, in English and French, linking music and dance performances throughout the evening. We rehearsed one whole, full, long, mother of a day, time and time again. By ten or eleven at night we were all totally shattered, and the script was sounding outrageously repetitive and uninspiring. I suggested a few changes here and there, as you do when you are the messenger and the message isn't actually very exciting. My points were noted and by the following morning they had decided to scrap the entire show and write another, which would involve me and my enthusiasm a little more. Now, let me tell you, when you are doing a job, TV or corporate, big or small, paid for or not, as a performer you can easily become slightly unnerved by a last-minute change of plan. This was more than last minute, and more than just a change of plan. I sat myself down with the PR company and helped rewrite the script of a show that didn't now exist. We had less than one full rehearsal, and as the main host, I had almost to feel my way forward in the dark. Bilingually. But the performance, song and dance included, was a success, by their standards. Everyone got a pat on the back and a large drink of Coke. And I got some more experience.

Corporate jobs were becoming a distinct feature in my professional life. They were a good earner and for the most part better than you anticipated. I was still in the habit of adding up my earnings as I went along, in order that I wouldn't worry too much about John's and my future. John was very good at accepting that I was by now the main breadwinner. We actually lived quite frugally, though, and sometimes I would even go so far as to say we were a little hard on ourselves. I think we could have afforded to loosen our belts a little. But I truly respected John's judgements and admired his ability to cope with the reversal of financial roles.

London Weekend Television was so encouraged by the success of *Gladiators* that it decided to hire Wembley Arena for a series of live shows. We did five shows over three days in the same vein as the TV ones, but without the stopping and starting and without two nervous presenters. By now, Fash and I had decided to grab the bull by the horns and sock it to them. I thoroughly enjoyed it. I thrived on the word 'live' – it gave me a buzz like no other. A buzz that comes with knowing there is no going back, you have to get it right first time around, and anything can happen. That is when I am at my best: under the greatest pressure.

Perhaps this was one reason why I kept thinking it might be time to add a baby into the equation as well. I had never lost that passionate desire, ever since my sister Linda was born. John suggested we wait a while, and give my career a bit more of a chance. He *did* want a child, I knew that – we had discussed it long before we were even married – but the time wasn't right for us, in his opinion. Well, it had been right for me for nearly sixteen years, but this was a partnership and I respected, reluctantly, his point of view.

What was also becoming increasingly apparent to me was that

despite the absence of a job that required early nights and early starts, we still didn't have any social life together. I was at home more, and readily available to go out or have friends over. John, on the other hand, was still restricted by his job and his constant travelling. This, in turn, meant he had no way of guaranteeing his presence in the event of us ever being invited out. I tried hard to stimulate some form of social anything, and John was willing, but unable. As a result I either ended up going to things without him, or for the most part not going out at all.

*

When I arrived in Birmingham in June to tape the second series of *Gladiators*, I was a significantly more confident young woman, less tired, less unwell and a freer spirit. As usual I left John behind, racing around Britain, covering Wimbledon, *Question Time* and anything else that needed televising. He came up to visit for a night and to watch one of the recordings. Bit of a busman's holiday, bless him, but whilst he made the effort so we could see each other, I had always felt more comfortable keeping work and private life separate.

What happened up in Birmingham that June will be hard for me to articulate as it was something so unexpected, so quick and so disastrous. It was the start of something inside me, which would not be quick to go away. I was about to embark on something extra-marital.

Wherever I worked, whenever I worked, I had the highest regard for the technical staff. Not only because I was married to one, but because although the star of the show is often perceived to be the one in front of the camera, the real champions are the ones behind it. They often work longer hours, in less comfortable conditions and with considerably less recognition. I would often talk to them, laugh, joke and generally mess around. I am not an outrageous flirt, but I do enjoy a good banter. This year at *Gladiators* was to be no exception.

I had developed a better relationship with the lovely Nigel, and we could by now argue or flirt, depending on our moods. He was marginally more relaxed, though still manic by all intents, and felt reassured enough by the success of the first series to be a little more accessible. Fifteen programmes had been commissioned, plus a celebrity show. With two shows to record a day over a three-week period, our schedule was pretty taxing. Further, the recognition the Gladiators themselves had received over the past twelve months had not failed to go to their heads. Despite being small fry in the big world of television, they were turning up in new convertible cars and expensive clothes and with big ideas. They remained friendly, but there was a scent in the air that smelt ever so slightly of arrogance. A couple of new additions to the team wanting a slice of the action were made to form an orderly queue behind the rest. They were a strange breed to me. I admired their ability and discipline to create the bodies they sported, but found it hard to come to terms with the amount of time they could dedicate to themselves, their look, their tan and the mirror. They sunbedded with disturbing regularity (even our black Gladiators) and applied the foulest fake tan (even our black Gladiators). Eventually the hotel had to start charging them for the sheets, which became heavily soiled from the lotions they used. They were obsessively fussy eaters and demanded special diets of chicken fillets, omelettes with no yolk, bananas, and mountains of pasta . . . and that was just the girls. I renewed acquaintance with them all, in particular my favourites, but for the most part kept to my room at night, watching TV and writing new lines. Fash, too, retreated, filling his time with various business ventures of his own, but we continued to work well together and he could always make me laugh. If I was feeling sociable, I tended to hang out more with our delightful team of cheerleaders, who entertained our growing audience in the arena for hours on end while we set things up. They were the prettiest, fittest, funniest bunch of girls, and I both loved and respected them.

Now, it came to pass that our wrap party had to come before the end of the last show, on the Thursday before our Sunday finish (with, thankfully, a day off on the Friday), because as soon as we stopped recording, our riggers and crew would have to go straight into laboriously de-rigging the entire spectacle. The party was nothing grand. A few sausage rolls, lots of drink and a busy dance floor. Nigel very generously made a speech thanking everyone, and Fash and I both received flowers and champagne. I hadn't partied for a long, long time – probably for some four or five years – so I fully entered into the spirit of things. Ladies, there is nothing quite like a bloody good dance, even if you yourself are coordinatedly challenged and find yourself surrounded by twenty-year-old dancers; after all, what the body can do, the mind doesn't worry about.

But, there, that night, on the dance floor, I found myself dancing opposite one of the cameramen. The dance was not a slow one, we were not touching each other, but when I looked at his lips a fire started within me that almost made me forget who I was. I wanted to get so close to him, I wanted to kiss him so long and hard, and if it hadn't been for one of the other girls dragging me back to the Hyatt Regency, I would have lost complete control of my intoxicated senses.

Back at the hotel, people were gathering in someone's room, scrambling madly for the minibar and room service. When gradually they began to leave I could see through the ghastly net curtains that the sun was beginning to rise. There were only three of us left. It was time to go to bed, but I wanted to play. I wanted to stay awake, have another dance, go out for a picnic in the early morning sunshine – I remained intoxicated by the alcohol and my colleague on the dance floor. Reluctantly, I returned rather noisily to my room where I gave birth to a great idea. It was four o'clock in the morning and I picked up the phone. Amazing how when one is pleasantly inebriated, one expects the rest of the world to be too, or at least be delighted to hear from you. I dialled the number of the neighbouring hotel and asked to be put through to my colleague, Phil Piotrowski.

Oddly for four in the morning, he picked up the phone and put it down again without as much as a 'hello'. I smiled to myself, and called back. This time he answered with a thick, slow voice. I asked him to guess who it was, but he didn't seem to be in the mood. Funny, that. When we had formally introduced ourselves and he had got over his surprise wake-up call, we chatted for, oh, a couple of hours. I cannot remember what we found to talk about, but what I did know was that I wanted to kiss him, and I was allowing this desire to rule me. He had planned to spend his day off with friends, and I had a costume fitting in Birmingham at lunch time to prepare for my next Grattan shoot. We agreed we would speak at the end of the day.

So it was with only three hours' sleep and a dehydrated head and body that I greeted my friends from Grattan, who proceeded to make me do the worst thing in the world on that particular day – bend myself in half to try clothes on. I managed to stop myself from introducing them to what I had been drinking the night before, but only just, and decided that lunch and a sleep would be a very good idea.

When Phil called me to say he was back, I suggested we meet – although he would have to exercise some subtlety and come to my hotel, rather than meet at the one all the technical staff were assigned to. He did. When he came into my room I talked nervously and obsessively for some time. My mind was nowhere to be found: I seemed to be there, but somewhere else at the same time. After quite a while, I finally got to kiss those lips and yes, they stirred up the fire deep inside me which was suddenly so big, so alive and so unquenchable that I felt dizzy. I blotted out the existence of anything else in my world, except those lips, those lips, and that fire. I became blinded by the kissing, sucked in by the backdraught and engulfed by my hunger. My light head refused to entertain any thought that might lead to reasoning. I wasn't beyond stopping myself; I just did not want to. Physically, I had no desire to pull back. Instead I just kept stoking that damn fire. After long hours of intense kissing and rolling around fully clothed on my hotel bed – which I had not long since shared with my husband – we decided that he should leave, in spite of ourselves. It was one of the hardest things to do and it still remains a mystery to me how were both capable of not taking things any further.

When he had left, I was too energized to sleep. The thought of it all set me alight, again and again. In my obvious state of insanity I knew that this was infidelity. That no matter how much I turned it over and over in my head, I had crossed the line. But then my mind would be blurred by optimistic thoughts that this was surely only a one-off experience, and that kissing was, perhaps, after all, in some genuine way, just possibly not really infidelity. At all. But I knew that I was afflicted; tainted; knew that my mind had disconnected from my body and that as long as I had no power to extinguish the fire, I was left powerless to its influence.

A few hours later it was time to get over to the arena. Still, I had the energy of a long-distance runner – it seemed relentless. I behaved as normal, whilst my brain was going over and over the previous night's encounter. And of it I remembered only one conversation, which was Phil's shock and disbelief that I had kissed only John over the past five years, that there had never been anyone else. Perhaps because I had slipped into what I had done with such ease. Perhaps because infidelity, which had never previously crossed my mind for one second, was, in fact, so commonplace to others. On that basis, something inside me told me briefly, very briefly, that I had done well to last so long, but that now, *now*, I must not allow it to go any further. Yet in the absence of any other drug in my life, ever, this was truly temptation in its rawest form.

My secret tryst would remain undiscovered by those around me unless I allowed my behaviour to betray me. And once I had kicked myself hard enough and slapped myself across the face a few times to alert myself to my professional duties, I was indeed able to get my words out, in the right order, and forge ahead.

Phil came to see me again that night once we had finished working. Once again we kept our clothes on. Once again I seemed powerless to resist the devil that had taken up residence in my head and my lower abdomen. And once again it was hard to let each other go, but we did. For the last time.

The following day when we finished filming Phil left me a note on which he had scribbled his number. Clearly maladjusted, I reasoned with great conviction that as long as I had his number I

would not call him. Had I left without his number, the 'what ifs'
might possess me to my dying day. This was the right thing to do.
Take his number and don't call. But as I drove home from Birmingham, with every mile between myself and the city a longing and a
hollow slowly replaced the fire's flicker.

I arrived back home to a welcoming husband who understood I
was tired and who went out of his way, as ever, to see that my needs
were met. But I was changed. I was gripped by a silence that
imprisoned me and distanced him. I had physically brought myself
back, but spiritually I had stayed away. John had no idea; no idea
how to bring me back; and no idea what possessed me. And there I
sat, opposite my best friend, the husband I loved so much and who
cared for me so deeply – there I sat with my soiled hands, my scarlet
lips and my untidy head – and I, too, had no idea how to bring me
back from the wilderness of a captured heart.

REHEATING THE SOUFFLÉ

I continued to be troubled that coming week – John would have had to be deaf, dumb and blind to miss it. And he didn't. I snuck out of the house a few times to call the number I wasn't going to call from the local payphone. I had to. I needed to hear the voice of my co-conspirator, to find some form of comfort or reasoning to counteract the madness in my head. But instead of feeling reassured, I became like an addict desperately scrambling for her next dose. Unable to acknowledge anything in my immediate vicinity, I was searching for something that didn't exist. I couldn't touch or feel the thing I was seeking, because, quite simply, I didn't really know what it was. Still, the only thing it felt like was a fire which was engulfing me, suffocating me and stopping me eating.

At the beginning of the week I had to do a job and I had arranged with Phil that he would pick me up afterwards and take me home, so I would at least see him briefly. That, I thought, would do it. I wouldn't need to see him again. And John was working. So, we met and talked during the journey back to my sleepy little village, kissed goodbye and he left. The meeting, quite naturally, only served to intensify my confusion. And I couldn't wait to see him again.

John and I would always talk in the rare instances when something was causing friction between us. But what virus had got me now? I wanted desperately to tell him of my predicament, of my sin, of my distracted thoughts, but I simply couldn't bring myself to. I had turned to him countless times before for advice, comfort, arguments, and now, now that I needed him most of all, I was unable to look him in the eye and open my mouth. My honesty would have killed him, I felt sure of that, so instead I let my deception kill me. Slowly. I had no choice but to stay silent, weeping, and whispering, 'It's me, it's me!' When John refused to let me take responsibility for whatever it was that was affecting me so profoundly, it sickened me to my belly and I would weep, repeating, 'You don't understand. You don't understand.' And he didn't.

The following week John was away covering the Open Golf in Kent while I had a couple of jobs to do as well as getting myself ready for a trip to Arizona with Grattan. On the Tuesday I was due to meet Melanie for lunch. I had never really talked to her about anything other than professional engagements – for that I had always turned to John. But now I had no John. Well, I had a John, but I had no courage, or sense of right and wrong. As Melanie sat herself down opposite me, asking, 'How are you, then?' I remember replying, 'I think I left something behind in Birmingham.' During the course of the lunch I opened the sluice gates of my heart and head. I failed to put any food past my lips and simply stirred it around the plate, over and over again, although a couple of glasses of wine washed down the bitterness of my words. She listened. She understood, as much as she could, but of course she could not do for me what I needed to do for myself. And she could not offer me any reassurances, conclusions or undertakings.

I knew I needed more time to think. I told John – who himself was still away – that after Arizona I needed to get away for a while, on my own, and would meet up with my family who would be on holiday in Mexico. This was all about as out of character as things could get, but he took it on the chin. Not that he didn't try to talk me out of it, saying he didn't understand me. I didn't want him to talk me out of it, because I didn't understand me either.

So I packed a large suitcase whilst consuming my daily diet of a bottle and a half of Chardonnay and a chocolate flapjack made by the Handmade Flapjack Company. On this I had now been surviving for two weeks, and it was beginning to show. The night before I set off, I took Melanie to the premiere of *Jurassic Park*. I looked skinny and tanned and got completely plastered at the after-party. I was really not fit to travel the following morning.

In Arizona the adrenalin guaranteed a slightly hyper and marginally manic performance, if there is such a thing. I didn't get tired, I couldn't sleep; I laughed like a woman possessed and wanted an alcoholic drink in my hand whenever possible. Thank God the team working on the shoot were so professional. Most days I managed to speak to Phil, who was also abroad working, which kept me fuelled and dazed at the same time. The distance and intimacy between us were tantalizing.

Then, unexpectedly, John called to say he was joining me for the first half of my two-week Mexican 'retreat'. He thought it would be a lovely surprise. I panicked. Hadn't he understood I wanted to be alone? How could I reject such an admirable attempt at 'help' from someone who so desperately wanted to find the tools to mend this broken 'something'. What's more, I wasn't going to be in Mexico; I would still be in La-La Land.

That first week in Mexico, John brought not only gifts, but memories of a life to which I felt I no longer belonged. He continued to offer me encouragement, strength and confidence but I remained untouchable, cocooned in my own reality. When he left I felt relieved. I have no idea what he felt. I wanted to be alone – very alone, I didn't even really want to be with Mum and Mike and the kids. I went for long walks on the beach, played tennis, and lost myself in the depths of the pool. I read, thought and drank. And reached no conclusion whatsoever. Except that I wanted to kiss those lips one more time.

Once home, extra-marital life proved a stronger influence on me than anything else. Soon, I was no longer battling with the inevitable: the writing was on the wall. I was going to go the whole way. No more stopping at second base. So while John remained away working, Phil and I grasped each other and the opportunity to take things to the point of no return. After that my fate was sealed; I was in deeper than I had ever thought possible. And I found it was exactly where I wanted to be. I had made this happen, and like a ship ripping through rough waters, I was beyond comprehending the risk of destroying my own fabric – not to mention that of others – as I sailed on regardless. I was in a world where there was only room for one. I didn't think beyond my moments with Phil. I didn't plan a life with him or a life without John – it wasn't about planning. I lived in my now – regardless of anyone else's personal hell.

When John returned from work a day or so after my full-blown infidelity I was walking confirmation that things were a long way off normal. I'd so shocked myself that all I could do was weep with my mouth firmly closed. Everywhere I stared, there were blank walls, with no pattern, form or direction. I didn't want John around, but couldn't say so. He desperately tried to coax an explanation from me, and as I wept on and the words were all but slipping off the tip of my tongue, I resolved I would allow myself until the morning to confirm my desire to tell all.

The morning in question I was due to fly up north for a job and decided to stay at Melanie's that night to give both John and me the space it seemed only I needed. He agreed. But I had no intention of staying with Melanie: the druggie in me scrambled for yet another fix, and I made my way to Phil's.

That night the most awful thing happened. As we lay in a desperate and unresolved state, the phone rang. Phil handed it to me. It was John. Having decided to search for clues to my condition himself, he had come across notes of thoughts I had written, alongside Phil's number. They had encountered each other professionally in the past, both being cameramen, but were by no means close friends. I flew into a predictable panic, and remember only the words 'At least he knows now', coming from Phil's lips. This did nothing, nothing to comfort me. I didn't deserve comfort. I deserved hanging. The news was out. What now?

I returned home the following morning, after a wakeful night, to an empty house. John had packed and left.

As if I had needed a further injection of adrenalin – as if! I was now positively burning up with fear, trepidation, guilt and pain, only temporarily relieved by alcohol and bewilderment. I had always known I would not be able to keep a secret of this magnitude, and to all intents and purposes, the way I had been behaving made no secret of it. My only wish was that I had had the strength to tell John myself. And I hadn't. My window of opportunity had long since passed.

I told my mother everything. She was supportive and sympathetic, but above all saddened. I stayed with her for a few days, but although she was a good listener, I was pretty much beyond help. And I went out riding in an attempt to rid myself of some of the adrenalin and Chardonnay running through my veins – I was still the nervous daily consumer of one flapjack and a bottle and a half of the alcoholic grape juice, and losing weight by the second.

Any attempts to reach John were denied me. In the days before mobiles, all I could do was leave unreturned messages wherever I could. I wanted to speak to him, yet I had no idea what I might say. 'Sorry' was a little vacant, weak and tardy. My birthday came and was just passing when I managed to locate him at his parents'. We didn't say much, but we agreed to meet and talk. Yet, in my heart of hearts I knew it was too soon. I was still severely afflicted; I still had the fever and was incapable of taking any cure.

John insisted on living away from me, which was probably for the best, although I did take it upon myself to drive to his parents' in Kent to see him. We talked, even smiled a little together. I missed his company, but was still unable to open myself to him. I remained impenetrable.

By the time I went up to Edinburgh a week later to do a job and meet up with Phil, who was also working up there, I had at least admitted to myself that I was having an affair. But I still wasn't feeling any better – even if infatuated and hostage to a physical experience that required few words.

Back in London I met up with Phil a further couple of times. One Sunday morning we strolled the length of the King's Road in Chelsea. Whilst it felt highly unnatural in our state of physical closeness, I remember asking him to not show me any affection in public. Which was difficult – for us both. I also remember seeing a photographer at a great distance snapping away. I reacted, but felt unsure. I was naive enough to wonder whether we were the subjects of his intentions. And naive enough to think that the King's Road was a world where no one knew me.

*

The following Friday morning, 3 September, Phil called me early to say that someone had alerted him to a picture of us together in the *Today* newspaper. I felt sick and horrified. I was even more horrified when I saw that in the newspaper I was credited as walking 'romantically with my husband, John Turnbull'. Shit! Everyone knows that's not John, I thought. While I was briefly grateful for the sloppy journalism, I knew, without doubt, it wouldn't last.

By 6 p.m. I had half a dozen journalists banging insistently on my front door, as if they had finally found the fugitive and had come to arrest me. I must have answered that door a hundred times, until eventually I couldn't face it any more and just paced the three square feet of my study floor. I was genuinely rocked. I cowered and managed to arrange for my mother to come and pick me up and take me to her place.

They followed. They phoned, they knocked, they spied – and they did not relent. My mother and Mike gave no comment but struggled to keep them away. I was petrified. I had lost control of myself, of my marriage and now of everything around me. Melanie was inundated. She was, unlike me, a woman of great integrity and honesty and whilst she was attempting to keep the sharks at bay she insisted on a strict code of absolute honesty between us. There was nothing false or manufactured about her, she knew the system but would not enter into games with the press and kept a guarded but true line of communication with them. She wanted to protect both John and me, yet had to warn us what an enormous story this was turning out to be.

I had no John and I lived dangerously close to the road and the distance between the kerb and our front door was exactly one car length. I could not remain in a house where lenses from the street could penetrate uncurtained windows and where my voice inside could be deciphered outside. I had no protection save the two-inch thickness of my front door. I came out in a cold sweat and shakes every time there was a knock at the door or the phone rang. I'd find myself losing control of my senses and coordination in the short step outside to my little Fiat Panda. My neighbours, too, were hard hit – accosted, interrogated, pursued; but thankfully had the fearlessness to attempt to move the hacks and their cars on. Despite feeling utterly displaced and completely compromised, I had no choice but to leave the home I loved so much – the place that had brought me such comfort and reassurance over the past few years. I hurriedly packed a bag for Hampstead, where Melanie lived. It was unnerving to be denied your place of refuge when you needed it most.

John, too, was being pursued, but was, thanks to colleagues and a low profile, able to escape predominantly unscathed. Phil was not so lucky. He was hounded, persistently photographed and generally obstructed. He remained defiant, in spite of being offered huge amounts of money to tell, sorry, *sell* his side of the story. But the press needed someone's version and with no luck in the three main camps they turned their attention elsewhere.

On Friday 10 September, exactly one week after the story had broken, the *Daily Express* ran an interview with Phil's ex-girlfriend. I had understood that they were separated but still living together for financial reasons. But according to the piece, they were deeply in love and I had stolen her Phil. I had, apparently, been ruthless, ambitious, flirtatious and all the other words one might expect to hear from a woman scorned. I wasn't angry, but I knew this would do nothing to make the story go away. Now, it would run and run. Despite the venom directed towards me, I couldn't really feel any worse than I did. And her story ultimately meant that love had a price tag on it.

For my part, I was asked to co-host *The Big Breakfast* with Chris Evans for a week. It was a request that had been made off the back of my 'marital troubles' – I was high profile and that's what they needed. It was a distraction and it was a job – both of which I needed.

Cheeky buggers had also asked Phil to operate camera for that week only, but he sensibly declined – this funfair didn't need another spectacle.

At the same time, my ongoing desperate silent pleas for help had not gone unnoticed by Melanie. Since I didn't know where to turn, she suggested I seek professional help. To begin with I rejected this, on the basis that no one knew my marriage better than John and me, so how could anyone else possibly guide us? But within no time my desperation and displacement became so overwhelming that by Thursday 16th I had an appointment with a psychotherapist called Renee in London.

I was apprehensive and reluctant, to say the least, but after weeping fifteen minutes into my hour, it didn't need a genius to work out I had a lot to resolve. And as I walked out of her office, I felt vulnerable for the first time in months – I felt touchable, raw, exposed, alone and incontrovertibly confused.

Two days later I went back and agreed that I would accompany her on the long journey she would take me on. She was a large, older lady – a diabetic who walked uneasily. She was gentle; she talked little, instead listening and calmly guiding me through the wilderness that was my life. She wanted to connect the pockets of uncertainty within it and help me understand. She wanted to enter the world of my childhood, which I immediately felt was unnecessary and insignificant. But she persisted gently. And every time I opened my book to her, I wept. With every page we turned came a self-deprecating conclusion – a rejection or a volatile aggression. I didn't understand. She worked mysteriously.

She talked of the confusion, fear and unsettledness I must have felt as a child – how evident my lack of confidence was and how readily I would put myself down. She wondered whether it all stemmed from an absent-minded father and absent mother. And whether my father's constant disappointments and dismissive nature had helped feed this inferiority within me. I told her I always felt stupid; that I feared rejection and fought my own corner fiercely as a result. How I refused to allow myself to feel sorry for 'me', or to feel that I deserved to have any feelings of self-pity. She suspected I had missed my mother more than I allowed myself credit for and that when I failed to 'connect' with her when I moved in with her, that in turn was another disappointment. How I had battled for the affection of my parents and was so eager to please them, at all costs. And how, in my parents' lives there was always someone else other than me. A partner, who would invariably take preference.

And there was more. More to do with the relationships I had formed: with the kinds of men I had chosen and why I had behaved the way I had with John. I talked in general terms and in specific ones. Of the morning of my wedding when I wanted a cuddle from my mother and was denied it; of when she had once asked me to leave the house so she, Mike and the children could have some 'family time' together; how my father was never at home and hadn't been there when I had walked home across town from babysitting at four in the morning when I was only nine. The situations she drew my attention to had gone largely unnoticed by me. I had accepted them as part of life and had never considered questioning anything. And still there was more.

I told John I was seeing a therapist, which he thought was a very positive step, and I decided I should stop seeing Phil, which would have to be a positive step. It was hard. I had really fallen for him, but I was also plummeting down a large hole of insanity with so much to cope with in my head that I felt it was for the best. Phil understood. He felt pretty messed up too.

By the time our wedding anniversary came around in September, John and I had already met up a few more times. Tentatively, we decided to go out for lunch. And gradually, as I progressed with my appointments with Renee – becoming dependent on my once-a-week hour with her – John started to move back in. We really talked about things. A friend of his had made the suggestion that our situation depended on whether we could 'reheat the souffle'. And we both hoped we could. I never once made excuses for what I had put him through. I cried with pain and sadness, but I took full responsibility. And it became evident to me that my soul required someone with the kind of empathy, intelligence, foresight and patience that only John had. And that he, too, in spite of it all, still wanted me.

But I remained a tortured soul and felt nowhere near being healed as I had two issues running alongside each other: my marriage and my relationship with my parents. Both were hard to reconcile, and each required my undivided attention. But the saddest thing for me was that when I finally found the strength to take up the subject with my mother, she once again dismissed me without hesitation. I tried to ask her how she felt when she had left me, and more to the point, how she had been able to do it in the first place. She replied that she wasn't sorry she had done it and if she were to have her time again, she would do the same. Subject closed. With that kind of snub I got no answers to my questions, because my questions would not even be heard. I got nowhere. She had unnerved me again. And again I had failed to get close to her; to see her vulnerable; to have her acknowledge my feelings – and maybe even need me. Was it really irretrievable? But I could not advance from the level she was keeping us at. All she would give away was that she felt trapped in Sweden and needed to get out. I felt she had done it at all costs and left me with the man she hadn't been able to trust, couldn't rely on and had lost respect for. But she would not answer me and remained defiant. I also confronted my father about my sadness at his absence during my childhood and it took a lot for me to say the things I wanted to him to hear. But hear he did. And he wept on the phone as he condeded that he had had no idea that was how I felt.

John had the grace and dignity to affirm that he would not be using my infidelity as a stick to beat me with at regular intervals: we'd leave blame outside on the doorstep. He saw our most recent experience as part of the 'for better, for worse' vow and believed that we could move on. We also discussed my burning desire to have a child and what role that might have played in my downfall. Throughout our rapprochement we still had to dodge the press. John would often park his car somewhere else and then jump over the fence into our back garden in order to avoid the doorsteppers. We did pretty low-profile things, but never stopped looking over our shoulders. On one occasion when John did park the car outside the house, it was broken into and a few personal things stolen. This was followed two days later by a phone call to his company's offices from someone apparently from DVLA wanting to confirm who the car belonged to.

Throughout this troubled time, the newspapers continued to make substantial financial offers through Melanie for my own personal version of events. But I was nowhere near ready to talk. I was embarrassed and still felt awkward about the whole public/private experience. However, even without saying anything, the coverage continued: seemingly every day the papers had a story, or at least a line, about my problems, about John or about Phil. What had gone wrong with TV's golden girl? What was happening now? Would she get back with her husband? Would she return to her lover? Would he speak? It was tiring, disturbing and frustrating, to say the least. As the pressure intensified we struggled to keep the hacks away.

I abhorred the idea of 'selling a story'. I didn't want money for a piece of my life. But I was now walking a tightrope between the public and the private, and every day less and less seemed private. Although I had allowed elements of my personal life into the public domain during my formative years in TV, it was high time to claw it back. Damage limitation was the order of the day – why should this mean playing by the rules in a game I really did not want to play? John felt similarly, but did point out that in the past enough other people had been selling newspapers off my name; if I could call the shots I would have an opportunity to set the record straight, dispel any gossip and untruths, and give an approved version of these most awkward events. I couldn't believe what I was hearing. John had grown to hate the press as much as I had over the period, but I conceded that maybe he had a point. And what's more, once the story had been told, all the other newspapers would go away. We decided to do it. After establishing a decent line of communication with the *Daily Mirror*, as it was then, and with Melanie strongly stipulating what I would and what I would never talk about, an offer was put on the table.

There was just one person I also wanted to keep in the picture – Phil. He had been so strong to reject the press's financial rewards for a piece of his action and had kept his mouth so tightly closed that I felt the least he deserved was to know what I was doing and what I intended to say. He agreed it was probably for the best, and he 'approved' my intended words.

So I had long, heavy interviews with the *Daily Mirror*'s Anton Antonowicz, and the gorgeous Brian Moody took some twee, soulful photos of me looking slightly forlorn. He helped put me at ease, during what was an uncertain time in uncharted territory. However, I was far from home and dry. If one newspaper secures a major news or showbiz story, the others will do everything to put out what is called a 'spoiler'. In others words, they will attempt to do one better than their competitor by securing a different angle from someone close to the subject, which might even reveal a completely different outcome. The *Mirror*, therefore, was keen as mustard to keep under wraps the fact that it had secured my story until the first edition was published. But it proved nigh on impossible and by the end of the week the *Sun* had cottoned on. A friend who ought to remain nameless but who is often known as Richard Keys called me to say that he had been approached with the suggestion that I had slept my way to the top. I was flabbergasted. If only it had been true, then I might have been a little more relaxed about it. But it wasn't, and if that went into print, trying to convince millions otherwise would be next to impossible. I had been with John before I had hit 'the big time' and had been with no one else, other than Phil, since. But according to my friend, they were trying to rake up all sorts of exes and men who would be glad to speak. 'They've just offered me £50,000 to say I slept with you,' he said when he called, clearly highly amused by the very thought of it. 'And what did you say?' I asked. 'Well, Ulrika, £50,000 is a lot of money . . .' Needless to say, he never did go to the papers. The games they were prepared to play left me speechless. I worried about my decision to 'sell' my own story, but genuinely felt that I had been cornered. The press had put me in a position where I had little choice, and now that I had opted for damage limitation, other newspapers would try to bring me down.

My story went out for three days running, and despite having copy approval I subjected myself and others to headlines such as, 'I won't confirm I slept with Prince Edward, but I won't deny it either'. I couldn't wait for the three days to pass.

FORTY-ONE WEEKS

Once the dust had settled and the press attention began to relent, John and I both resolved to reclaim all the wonderful aspects of our marriage. In them we would find the strength to reunite. It felt calm, sensible and above all right.

We both made time for each other. John took more time off work, which enabled us to have more social time together – and we were even able to meet up with friends on a semi-regular basis. And together, we decided secretly and at last to try for a baby.

We were both so relieved to be rid of the atmosphere that had clouded our lives for those few months that there was a renewed enthusiasm about us. I knew I had done the right thing to keep my marriage. John truly is a wonderful person to have by your side, and given my ongoing complicated parental set-up, was certainly the most stable person in my life. Soon we felt very together – so much so that we decided to invite my dad, Linda and Berit down for a family Christmas.

Shortly before Christmas, I was called to a meeting with Sir Christopher Bland, chairman of London Weekend Television. I had no idea what it was about – but work, I hoped! I was wrong. Sir Christopher, whom I had never previously had the good fortune to meet, wanted me to walk the Channel Tunnel. For his charity, Queen Charlotte's Hospital. Of course I will, sir. Thank you for asking me. (I reckoned any other reply could have amounted to professional suicide.) So I set about training for a 31-mile underground walk from France to England due to take place in the New Year. Not much pressure, then.

One meeting I didn't make before Christmas descended was my appointment with Renee. I never saw her again. In January 1994 she was taken ill and she died a couple of months later. My work with her, like so many other things in my life, was left unfinished.

John helped me train for my charitable challenge by accompanying me on six-, ten- and twenty-mile walks every second day or so. I became quite obsessed with my challenge and insisted on measuring the distance of anything, everywhere, every day. I was also able to persuade my mum to come out training with me. She was rather envious of my task: as a self-confessed fitness freak, she exercised every day. When I set off at the end of January to fly the Grattan flag again – this time in Palm Springs – I packed my training gear, should there be an hour off for an encounter with a treadmill. But there was something rather depressing about leaving: I could feel the start of period pains down below. It ended up being a stressful shoot dogged by bad weather and a cold that seemed to be afflicting us all. I was working with the same German team as before, and it felt strange imagining myself in the state I had been when I saw them six months before. I was exhausted for the whole trip – the cold, period pains and an inability to conquer jet lag were taking their toll.

By the time I returned home to John my period was four days overdue. Unheard of. I was regular as clockwork. But with the persistent pains I knew I couldn't be pregnant. John, however, had more confidence and insisted I did a test. Which I had to ask him to buy, just in case someone saw me buying a pregnancy test kit in Boots. It was abundantly pink. It was positive. I was expecting. And according to my pregnancy book, which had stood on the shelf for some years waiting for this very moment, we were going to be parents around 11 October that year.

To be honest, I was so shocked and remained so pessimistic that I refused to believe it. But my doctor explained that the 'period' pains I was feeling were due to my body not yet producing enough pregnancy hormones to cope with the changes that had started. They would fade in time, I was told. Whatever, I soon started feeling sick and my breasts were as tender as overripe peaches, but hard as stones. And the doctor told me I must not attempt a 31-mile walk whilst pregnant. Whoops! The charity walk was a fortnight away.

The charity greeted my cancellation with great disappointment, although it was all that I could do to not throw up all over them when I told them the news. Little did they know the real reason why, despite my impeccable preparation, I had been certified 'unfit'. In order not to have to share the news with the world before it was wise to do so, I'd been issued a doctor's certificate stating that I'd sustained an injury.

Early on Saturday 12 February 'Le Walk' kicked off from the French side. I made my way down to Dover full of nausea and disappointment and by late evening little heads and feet were emerging from the huge tunnel. And there I was able to greet my stand in. My mother. I was proud of her and grateful to her, and she was excited too, mainly because she got to kiss Richard Branson on the cheek at the finish line. She was brilliant, so fit and so keen. I felt quite envious, and sick.

We managed to keep news of my pregnancy quiet for twelve weeks. I would have preferred it to remain a secret for longer than that, but what I want and what I get are two different things. So it was a shock on the day of my twelve-week scan to open my front door to a bunch of journalists who congratulated me on my forth-coming event. We made no comment, and they followed us in their cars, and even into the local hospital. John and I had to quickly call around all the people we hadn't told before we issued a press statement, or they would have read about it in the papers. The leak could have come from a number of sources – someone spotting medical records perhaps, or my over-generous-with-his-mouth father. We will never know.

When I finally stopped feeling sick after three and a half months – yes! – it was a huge relief. I began burying myself in the mountain of pregnancy books I'd now bought, and revelled in my expanding waistline and growing breasts. Although neither John nor I knew the truth, whenever I patted my belly it was with the presumption that I was carrying a boy.

That Easter *Gladiators* graced Wembley Arena once more. I still felt distracted and queasy and tired, but the show, whilst remaining nail-bitingly exciting, almost ran itself by now and everyone knew what was required of them, so Fash and I actually enjoyed ourselves. By now *Gladiators* fever had swept the nation and taken no prisoners. It was a show popular with young and old alike, and it stirred up excitement and tension in even the most reluctant spectator. It had everything – rock 'n' roll, virtually naked bodies, action, humour and silliness – who could ask for more?

Other work continued to flow – presenting here and there, the great honour of being awarded 'Spectacle Wearer of the Year' alongside Mr Motivator – but it seemed that post-affair my name had not remained as intact in certain quarters as we had hoped. Grattan was one employer who had been a little thrown by the amount of publicity surrounding my extra-marital activities, but they were soon positively having kittens at the prospect of having to photograph me pregnant. Personally, I thought it was a great opportunity for them to produce an exciting maternity range of clothes, as I was fast running out of clothes that would fit comfortably around my belly and thighs, not to mention my augmenting 36FF bust. Instead, I found myself hiding my pregnancy, and it felt almost shameful.

But others were remarkably less easy to put off. In my sixteenth week of pregnancy I was actually asked to take part in *The Good Sex Guide* for TV. Given that I'd grown myself a floppy watermelon around my stomach, I couldn't help but laugh solidly throughout the performance. What's more, shortly after that I was taken off to Barbados to front a 'dangerous sports' video. Again we managed to hide my growing bump and I managed to avoid the helicopter trip and the submarine – a pregnant woman with claustrophobia is not every producer's dream. Jobs like that are a little like going through the motions – the motions of recorded television. There are no interviews, no interaction and no live element – and hence they are not, for me, the greatest challenge in the world. But apart from feeling a little ungainly – oh, and the flight out, during which the producer, sitting in steerage, got so drunk that the airline staff had to restrain him thinking he might be an obsessive fan of mine – it was all great.

I found my twenty-week scan fascinating. I actually felt humbled by the little creature I was carrying and it was moving to watch 'him' move about inside of me. 'Him' was still a guess; John had decided he didn't want to know the sex, so I thought it best not to find out. I couldn't trust myself. But I felt very confident that it was a little man-child and was enormously relieved when the sonographer saw everything she needed to. So we took away Polaroids of our child's upper body only and I clung to them with tears in my eyes, eventually managing to tear one out of my hand to give to my mum.

The other resolutions we'd made were also holding fast. In keeping with our 'new' relationship, John and I were making every effort to spend time together and to support one another. However, a holiday in a Tuscan hilltop hotel full of Germans fast turned into an uncomfortable experience – although not because of the state of our marriage. My litany of woes was hardly unreasonable: I was getting bigger by the day; my bra didn't fit; the roads were long and winding and I suffer from car sickness; the heat was unbearable and we had no air conditioning in the car or the room; the pool at the hotel was unheated and being 'in the club' meant that I wasn't able to enjoy the fine wines of the area. Not the most fun person to be with, but then that's the sort of thing you have to put up with if you're my husband. Amazing John stayed. But apart from all that the holiday was a success.

So I was finally awaiting the child I had so longed for, and with John I felt secure, safe, calm, myself and loved. I felt for him a deep love based on this security and safety, and I felt calm in the knowledge that he would never leave me. The past had never left me, though. I thought of what I had done every day – the anxiety, the stress, the pain it had caused and all for no gain whatsoever. I looked at other people who appeared in love and felt, perhaps, that what I felt for John was deeper than that, more structured, more practical and more sensible. It wasn't a whimsical feeling, based on infatuation. It felt serious and solid and nicely predictable.

*

By the time *Gladiators* hit its third series it was one of the most popular light-entertainment programmes on TV. Despite being pregnant I was allowed to present the show alongside Fash, who wasn't, but not without a fight. Nigel had always wanted me to host the show, but naturally, as men tend to be when women are pregnant, he was worried. Despite feeling fit and energetic and with a medical to prove it, there was concern about my stamina, and most of all about insurance. Nobody seemed to be quite sure if I could be covered. And did LWT really want to take the risk? After desperately trying to convince them to relax about it and that I would be absolutely fine, a compromise was reached. LWT insisted on employing a midwife, the wonderful Sue Ensor, to accompany me on and around the set at all times – to find me a chair to sit on between takes, and generally keep check on me. I thought this was rather endearing and agreed without hesitation – if it meant I could carry on working. I felt determined that as long as my huge, varicosed legs could carry me and my humungous breasts, I should be allowed to work. (And by the way, that wasn't the only part that was varicosed. Ever heard of the vulva? Thankfully it wasn't on view, but not from want of trying.)

The Gladiators themselves were much as usual, complaining of their own punishing schedules and making known their many and varied star needs. They even had to have their own set of bodyguards taking them to and from the arena, for fear of ten-year-olds throwing themselves at their feet. Fash and I, on the other hand, were left to make our own way, despite me being six months pregnant. Most of those who hadn't become star-struck with themselves by the first or second series had crossed the river by this stage. Weekly personal appearances and thousands of screaming fans had spoiled them. Looking at the way some of them behaved – arrogant, over-confident, and highly ambitious – was a bit like watching a newly-formed band quibble over who was going to go solo.

They also moaned about the money they were being paid and how, understandably, they felt restricted by LWT's strict rules of ownership. *Gladiators* was now big business – and big business owned by LWT. Without their express permission the Gladis themselves could undertake no work whatsoever. And certainly not without the company taking a huge cut. It was a source of much anger and frustration among the muscly people, and Nigel was fast having a revolution on his hands. The Gladis were taking themselves very seriously and quickly losing sight of reality. They even organized meetings to voice their predicament, not unlike a union about to go on strike. I never got involved in any issues off the arena floor, and simply carried on admiring their courage on the rings, up the wall or in the duel.

Once again, there were a few new additions to the muscly team. One was the cutest young Yorkshire lad, James Crossley, who answered to the manly name of 'Hunter'.

Despite the tension, the series went remarkably well and I was able to fulfil what was asked of me, whilst wearing large flowing clothes not dissimilar to Claire Rayner's wardrobe. I was, however, asked not to present their 'Ashes' shows (England's Gladiators v Australia's), which apparently would have put me under too much pressure. I let that one go without a fight. Couldn't be bothered. Anyway, I was still dining out on the fact that Sweden had drawn in a match against Brazil in the World Cup. Not bad for a practical nation. When it came to football I always had enthusiasm and loyalty, at least.

Being in Birmingham brought memories of the previous year flooding back, and I found I had an overwhelming desire to speak to Phil. He wasn't on the show any more, so I'd have to phone him at home. I felt it was the wrong thing to do, but knew equally that I wouldn't feel at peace until I heard his voice. We had not spoken since the previous October. He was kind and polite and congratulated me on my pregnancy – something, he said, he felt was inevitable. He knew more about me than I did, I thought. He said he was happy and was living with an aerobics instructor. When I asked him what he now thought about everything that had happened, he simply replied that he must have been crazy to think he could ever have had me. I wasn't completely sure what he meant: I felt that he could so easily have had me. But in different circumstances. Perhaps that was what he meant. When I put down the phone I momentarily missed that passion I had once felt for him. And felt a million miles away from it.

*

I felt highly unattractive during my pregnancy, but was so completely and utterly focused on the forthcoming event that I didn't care what I looked like. And I think it showed. As well as becoming inevitably large, I also became frumpy. But in my mind all that was important was the welfare of my baby and anything else just fell by the wayside. Despite heartburn, I was eating for Sweden and England combined and was by now the size of a small semi-detached. And talking of houses, we had our kitchen ripped out to make way for a new conservatory-kitchen. Despite this, I found things to eat and places to prepare food. I should have had shares in Sara Lee and Ribena. I would polish off a Danish Pecan Pie with Häagen-Dazs in record time and wash it down with three litres of anything sweet and wet. Sweet. Not salty.

John and I were under some obligation to attend Queen Charlotte's Ball at the Grosvenor House Hotel in celebration of the charity for which my mother had walked the Channel. My mother and Mike went too. By now my face was the size and shape of a basketball. It was hard to hide, and also hard to smile with all the fat around my mouth. Now, balls are not my scene. The thought of getting all dressed up to sit next to a bunch of people you do not know leaves me cold. For this one it was a struggle finding anything to wear in the first place, and my swollen feet meant I had to invest in a quaint, comfortable, cheap pair of shoes. With bows on the front. Hot and constantly bothered and tired and large, I did manage to catch sight of Sir Christopher Bland, and felt it would be the polite thing to show my face and introduce my mother. When he turned around, I said, 'hello', and he stared vacantly at me for some time and then blurted, 'Should I know you from somewhere?' Which was nice. Next time he wants someone to walk thirty-one miles for him, I'll remember to give him Carol Vorderman's number.

*

Five of us in my antenatal class were expecting babies within two weeks of each other. Twelve days before my due date, three of the girls had already given birth. 11 October came and went and my friend Diane also gave birth. The waiting game started to get boring. John was working away a lot, but stayed in touch constantly in anticipation of any signs. I found it hard, despite my size, to sit around and do nothing. I kept on the move – tidying, sorting, moving things around and cleaning. On the following Sunday I felt it was time to clear out the airing cupboard. This involved ladders, lifting, shifting and hot flushes. John was away covering the snooker championships, for his sins, and only came home very late.

Reading about births can sometimes be a bit of a drag, for while there is no textbook birth where absolutely everything goes marvellously, as all mothers know, certain things remain the same. Contractions, waters, pain, blood, sweat and tears. Not necessarily in that order. So I will attempt not to give minutiae.

As with every night, I was up several times for a pee. But at four o'clock in the morning I discovered a significant amount of blood in my underpants. I almost panicked, but resolved to stay calm. I ran into the bedroom, trying to raise the dead, but John was so exhausted he couldn't move. I rang the labour ward and they didn't sound unduly worried, which worried me. But if I was concerned, I should come in, they said. I packed my bag and managed, just, to wake the mummy lying in my bed, unaware he was about to become a daddy. As we drove to hospital in the dark I was full of anticipation, excitement and nerves. I had spent so much of my life in the presence of babies, but now that I was expecting my own, I felt clueless, fearful, naive and the whole thing was even slightly surreal.

A firm, jokey midwife and the long stream of doctors who came in to 'visit' me asked to see the contents of my underpants. Honestly! Some people's hobbies baffle me! But I was unable to add to their collection as I had left them in the laundry at home. Which seemed like the normal thing to do. According to the monitor I was hooked up to, my contractions weren't many and weren't strong. So there I lay in the biggest anticipation, with my big bump and my big arse on a big bed with my exhausted husband by my side with nothing big happening at all. Several hours and several cups of tea later I had to let the midwife go off shift, and was disappointed to be moved up to the antenatal ward. I had been antenatal for months and now I wanted to be labour. But my baby had different ideas.

John even went home for a while and my mum came to visit, sitting by my side urging the baby to come out. But to no avail. The day passed slowly and I had no further bleeding. When my wonderful obstetrician, Mr Bill Tingey – a humorous, no-nonsense kind of a guy – popped his head around the door and, after frisking me like a security guard, talked of letting me go home, I pleaded with him to let me stay. My baby was six days overdue and remembering that I myself had only popped out three weeks after my due date, I was damned if I was leaving this hospital with the little blighter still inside me. My pleading paid off and Mr Tingey said he'd be back later that night to see if he could get things started. Not the first time I've wanted to hear a man tell me that!

I either lay there or paced the ward while watching woman after woman progress in labour and be taken downstairs for her grand finale. It became disconcerting. I felt left out and rather envious. But my little monkey was showing no further signs of departure.

When Mr Tingey returned at about half past nine, I heard, 'Don't let him give you the gel,' being mumbled by one of the midwives under her breath. 'It's like dynamite.' Oh, I said, as Mr Tingey extracted his hand from my tunnel of love. Oh.

'I'm going to give you the gel,' he announced. 'That should get things going – it's like dynamite.'

Oh, I said. I wasn't sure I liked dynamite, but I was willing to give it a go under the circumstances. In any event I was hoping a thing called a TENS machine would help relieve any associated pain. Once again he inserted his hand into my honeymoon passage and confidently lubricated it. Thank God for small hands. And an obstetrician who keeps you amused at all times to minimize the loss of dignity. So, there I lay with my TENS machine strapped to my lower back and dynamite up my nunnie, watching *The Good Sex Guide*, which just happened to be on the telly right then. Oddly enough, sex was the last thing on my mind.

Just when I thought the dynamite must have lost its oomph somewhere, I was suddenly gripped by the most intense tightenings around my abdomen. The pains took my breath away and I was overwhelmed to the extent that I was unable to remain lying. Or standing. Or sitting. Or, indeed, in any position. I identified the pain as an extreme version of the period pains I had suffered since the age of fourteen, but this was of no comfort. I was beyond help and whilst I pleaded with the Lord above for assistance, it appeared he, too, was watching *The Good Sex Guide* and didn't hear me. It was recommended I took a hot bath to relieve the pain, which didn't sound terribly medical in my books. I needed help – not a fucking bath. I did, however, have one. Of sorts. I was in and out of it, having something akin to physical fits in between. Had John not been with me I would probably have drowned.

At least something was happening though, I thought. But apparently not. A further intrusion in my downstairs revealed I was showing no signs of dilation. I was tight as an arsehole. Maybe they were checking in the wrong place . . .

After nearly three hours of excruciating pain and acrobatics from a woman who had completely lost control of her body, I requested some pain relief – which at last got me whisked down to the labour ward. But there they explained that as long as I wasn't dilating they were not keen to give me the epidural – I wasn't considered to be in labour just yet. OK, whatever, whatever, just give me SOME-THING! And so they did. And it was wonderful. I cannot remember what it was called, but for a woman who had still never experienced recreational drugs of any kind, it seemed just marvellous. After having rain danced my way around the antenatal ward for some hours, I was now floating around a labour room. There were suddenly three clocks on the wall; I had two husbands and not a care in the world. I was delirious. At that point I may have drifted off a little – into a whole new world – and John was told to go home for some kip.

By the following morning the effects of the dynamite had worn off and whilst I was still contracting, I was still showing few signs of dilating. *Plus ça change* . . . Then jolly Mr Tingey came in, like Little Bo Peep, with a hook in his hand and requested I lie back and think of 'nice things', while he broke my waters. One tiny prick, and the waters fell. And fell, and fell . . . Not only was I an immobile, huge lump who had been prodded, pushed and interfered with (admittedly without objection, bearing in mind the greater good), but I was now incontinent, too.

I was supposedly now guaranteed to be privy to some action in the 'labour' department. Yeah, right. Not this chick. My baby liked his home with or without fluid, and showed no further signs of making an appearance. By midday it was decided they would start to induce me. That would get things going for sure. I immediately requested a visit from a nice anaesthetist who might like to stick a needle and some fluid into my spinal cord. They would see if they could find one on duty.

My mum had come in early that morning and was highly encouraged by my request for drugs. She was a firm disbeliever in drug-free births and championed my cause. My mother had evidently not stayed in Sweden long enough to develop her any earth-birthy-type habits: Drug me up and whip it out! was her motto. So, an epidural went in, just after one o'clock that afternoon, and I was rendered completely immobile from my navel down. As a whale, I was well and truly beached.

When John finally turned up again – a little later than I had anticipated, but he had been knackered – he had actually missed nothing except me wetting myself. Together we watched the monitors, my drip and the lovely midwife, who had thankfully returned on shift. She was from Iran and her name was Marie Robertson, but she answered to Robbie. She was a delight – easy-going, sympathetic and brimming with 'dahlink' and 'sweetie'. I felt comfortable in her care and now confident somehow, although I simply had to let everything inside me take its course.

Unfortunately, however, by four o'clock that afternoon things were still not taking their course. I remained only a few centimetres dilated, which was the gravest disappointment of all time. I was exhausted. After yet another examination of my nether regions, one of the doctors threatened that if there was no change by six o'clock, they would 'have to get the knives out'. In order to avoid any misunderstanding, I asked him to expand on his comments, where-upon he explained that they would have to perform a Caesarean. I had, up until that point, not cared quite how the baby came out, as long as it was unharmed and healthy. But now, as I lay there on the threshold of a potential Caesarean I knew I didn't want it to be cut out of me. The idea was frightening and I reckoned risky. I knew I wanted to go to every length to have the baby normally. 'Don't worry, dahlink,' reassured Robbie, 'it won't come to that. We will still have this baby vaaaginally.' And with those words I concentrated my mind on a little more dilation.

Thankfully by 6 p.m., and four top-ups of anaesthetic later, I was finally opening up. At least that's what Robbie told me after her head emerged from betwixt my legs. 7 cm. Hoorah! *And* I couldn't feel a thing. By nine o'clock Robbie kept asking if I had an urge to push. I felt no such urge, but lied, rather successfully. I was beginning to feel discomfort down there as the latest anaesthetic was petering out, but most of my pain was actually coming from underneath the ribs on my right. The baby's legs or feet – or something – were lodged under my ribs and it was stopping my natural breathing and causing me pain. Then, as if from nowhere, Robbie howled with delight – 'I can see the head, I can see the head! Do you want to see the head?' and before I had a chance to say 'I don't think so,' she had placed a mirror between my legs and urged me to sit forward. Ladies and gentlemen, it was not a sight to behold. Suffice to say it looked not unlike a coconut between two fillet steaks.

Enough. That was all I needed. Just get this thing out. And with three pushes I did. After the third push I thought my head was going to explode, but instead out popped a little miracle. I looked down at this huge, long, screaming creature and exclaimed, 'It's got a winky!' And with that I became a mother and John a father. At exactly 9.30 p.m. I had given birth to Cameron Oskar George Turnbull and in my disorientation, relief and exhaustion I managed to find the sanity of mind to ask how much my son weighed. '9 lb 11½ oz,' came the reply. 'No! No!' I objected, 'the baby, how much does the baby weigh?' I have no idea, to this day, what it was I thought they were weighing . . .

He was a big baby and as they handed him to me I looked at him, overawed and bemused, and asked him softly, 'Who are you, then?' But my time holding him was to be short-lived. Within a minute or so I had to hand him to John. I was going to be sick.

The next moments passed in a blur. Doctors came rushing in, there was a hushed tone and some state of emergency. I was made to lie flat on my back as they tended to me. I had haemorrhaged. It was bad. Bad enough for them to be concerned and consider a transfusion, but in the end I was stitched up and allowed to be reunited with my own little monkey.

CHARMERON

I slept with my darling Cameron, named after the dastardly character in my favourite radio drama, *The Archers*, for which I had developed a penchant since leaving TV-am, but I was weakened greatly by the experience of labour. I had lost a lot of blood and was severely anaemic and as a result was forced to stay in hospital longer than I had anticipated. My beautiful little boy, who took a day or so to open his eyes, was content, but heavy. I struggled to lift him and felt frail and faint. He had been put on my breast as soon as he was born and I persisted with the breastfeeding despite the excruciating pain in my breasts and belly. My undercarriage looked more like a patchwork quilt by now and it was a struggle to even wee. Forget what they tell you about the magical experience of childbirth: the whole experience had been undignified and painful, messy and rather awkward, but I didn't care in the slightest. I felt so strongly about this little creature I had had a hand in creating, and nothing could take away the awe I felt and the love which ached so in my heart for him.

I had decided to pay for a private amenities room in my NHS hospital for practical reasons. It would not have been beyond the press to make their way into the ward for a quick snap of mother and child. And for the bargain price of thirty pounds or so per night, it did more than buy peace of mind. My room was filled with flowers from friends, family, colleagues, and TV execs too. I felt slightly humbled by that. When it finally came to going home, after five days in hospital and a further investigation by Mr Tingey's hand, I actually felt reluctant. I was weepy and frightened and wanted the nurses to come home with me.

When I opened the door to what was now our *family* home there were even more flowers and John had kept the house immaculate. But I was scared. I was scared of the responsibility, scared of my exhaustion and almost scared of my little son. For someone who had always acted with great confidence around children and babies, this was a new and uncomfortable sensation. John was, as always, reassuring. And together, somehow, we fumbled through our first week of parenthood. And then our second. And then our third.

Cameron, or Baby Blue, as I called him, after the Van Morrison song, 'It's all over now, Baby Blue', supped well at my huge breasts, but slept little. He was a happy baby. He loved his mummy and he loved his daddy, but he loved his mummy just slightly more because she was made of the white stuff. He slept in bed with us, next to me, and I was overwhelmed by the closeness and intimacy. He smelt so wonderful – his breath was sweet like honey and his eyes big and beautiful. He had long fingers and a long body and thick black hair on his head. I was completely seduced by him: he became my little obsession.

I thrived on my time with him despite being physically drained by anaemia. I slept when I could, with him, and adored being at home with him. I cared nothing for the world outside. I felt so content and harmonious, complete and fulfilled. I adored him. I was so involved in him and this new way of life that I struggled to enter the outside world again. Not only was it a practical nightmare taking a newborn out, but I really just wanted to stay at home. When I did start to venture out with Cameron, on at least one occasion we were snapped by photographers hoping to sell their picture to a newspaper. I didn't really mind, just felt it was a little underhand. However, when Cameron was five weeks old I did do an interview with Richard Barber for *OK!* magazine, which served several purposes. The press interest in me had increased since my extra-marital affair; an interview and beautiful pictures would, in those days, be circulated to them all by the magazine (in order to publicize the issue) and would therefore deal with everyone in one fell swoop and on my terms. I had, very reluctantly, entered the ring where personal is made public, and there is always a desire for the conclusion to a story. To that end the interview also covered the experience of infidelity in a marriage and surviving it. It went along the lines of: Look at you now, you've managed to overcome infidelity and now you even have a son. It was a nice, sympathetic piece, and I think it showed that it is possible to move beyond terrible emotional experiences. Cameron, John and I were photographed alongside the words from the interview. But as far as I was concerned, this was not about me. As I was having the photographs taken I could think of nothing else but Cameron. My words were irrelevant and meaningless. He was all that mattered, and I was there because I wanted to be with him. I had no urge inside me, in the slightest, to be apart from him for a second. Ever.

John was fantastic, and with my time being completely swallowed up by the little monkey, he even had to learn to cook, and rose to the challenge. He doted on Cameron, and helped out whenever he could – which wasn't too often in the early days, as Cameron was constantly on the breast. But as he grew and developed, they spent more and more time together, bonding with tremendous intensity.

We spent Cameron's first Christmas with mum, Michael, Kristian and Kelly as I was too exhausted to entertain a turkey myself. A few days later the Vikings descended on us in the form of my dad, Berit and Linda. They all fell in love with Cameron, too – it was impossible not to, even if he still didn't sleep much. My father always jokingly referred to him as Charmeron. I was lucky if he napped for two half-hours a day. Christmas, of course, did nothing to change the fact that I was still the size of a house.

When in early January I flew up to Liverpool to appear on *This Morning*, with the gorgeous Richard and his Judy, in order to promote Tommy's Campaign, a charity for research into premature births and birth defects, I took Cameron with me. I also appeared on Lorraine Kelly's morning show talking on the same subject. Lorraine is lovely, always has been since we both started out with TV-am, and probably always will be. She, like me, couldn't stand the fuss and bother of make-up and clothes shopping, preferring to lounge around the studios in leggings and a rather archaic pair of floppy slippers. She sometimes even kept them on whilst on air. Nowadays, she remains the queen of breakfast TV, and is also my neighbour.

So, slowly, very slowly, I was being eased back into the routine of work. But I remained reluctant. I wasn't the sort of working mother that craved it. I just wanted to be at home with my little dream come true. I actually became slightly fearful of work. It meant having to organize leaving Cameron (which I hated), or take him with me but be distracted from him. I didn't want to miss a second of the joy and happiness the wonderment of him brought, and I couldn't bear even a moment of not seeing his face, smelling his skin and touching him. But other realities beckoned, whether I wanted them or not. I felt under pressure and almost resentful, but I needed to get over it. Grattan was waiting just around the corner, and taking my current non-negotiable moods and necessities into consideration, generously agreed that our new season's shoot would take place at a house down on the Kent coast at Rye. John's wonderful parents even came along to help look after my darling son. The shoot went well despite me being outrageously uptight and wanting to cry all the time, and the fact that as soon as I heard Cameron's little cry or whimper in the next room, my heart would leap.

On the shoot, a friend and member of the Grattan team was in the throes of an extra-marital affair, so much so that the gentleman in question even joined us for dinner one night after work. My friend seemed so happy and excited, and I remember feeling mildly jealous. I myself could recall those feelings of passion, stolen moments and excitement to the point of suffocation. Not that I wanted to swap my life for hers, not for one second, and I couldn't forget either how uncomfortable I had been with the deceit. But I still remembered those feelings of passion. Boy, I remembered them.

It was not until Cameron was just four months old that I had to leave him for a whole day to do a show in Manchester. Emotions

Clockwise from top left: Shotgun wedding. April 1967. My gorgeous mum
(before the gold cap went) and my 25-year-old balding father.

Gun Jonsson. Nineteen and a mum already.

On the road with my dad. The lettering on the car is his own artwork.

Showing my knickers - again!

Clockwise from top left: Frida and me. You couldn't stop a pig in a passage with those pins.

My glamorous mum on one of her visits to Sweden from Holland, 1977.

Goofy of Sweden (aged ten).

Asleep with Stumpen.

My dad building his first boat, Emma.

Clockwise from top left: Playing a lady of the night in 'The Comedy of Errors', aged fifteen, Burnham Grammar School.

Meeting David Bowie on my sixteenth birthday in Los Angeles, 1983.

Michael and me on my twenty-first birthday, August 1988.

Six months after I arrived in England I played Prince Charming in the school panto (on the left in the carriage).

My first publicity picture.
Lovely hair. So understated.
(Harry Ormescher)

On screen at TV-am, 1989.
Shoulderpads were all the rage!

Dancing the night away in a
tartan creation at a TV-am
bash, alongside the enigmatic
Bruce Gyngell; the dignified
Lisa Aziz and the Scottish
Lorraine Kelly.

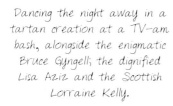

From the front page of the
'Daily Mail', 27th July 1987.
'Now you're famous,' Mum said.
The last thing I wanted was
to be famous by association.
(Bill Cross)

Backstage at the first series of 'Gladiators'.
I look petrified.

As bloody Cinderella in panto
in Crawley. I wanted to be
an ugly sister.

With some of my favourite
Gladiators (clockwise from left:
Saracen, Trojan and Cobra).
(LWT)

John and I, with Raymond Blanc on our
wedding day, 29 September 1990.

On my wedding night.
What have I done? (Kidding!)

My beautiful mother and
Mormor (my Swedish grandmother)
on my wedding day.

My dad and I out sailing.

My wonderful sister Linda.
At her school-leaving, 1996.

The second boat my father built,
Aquavit. Aptly named.

My gorgeous brother Kristian and
lovely sister Kelly.

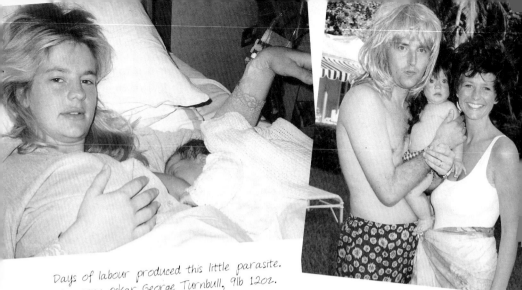

Days of labour produced this little parasite. Cameron Oskar George Turnbull, 9lb 12oz.

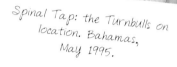

Spinal Tap: the Turnbulls on location. Bahamas, May 1995.

My beautiful boy cooling off in the sink.

My dear friend Jennifer and Cameron on holiday in Indonesia, February 1999.

Cameron with my lovely Nana, Christmas 1994. Winnie was my English grandmother and she loved me like I was one of her own.

On location for Comic Relief with my dear friend Richard Wilson. The Cliff, Barbados, 1999.

On location in downtown LA with my dear friend Charles Worthington, 1997.

'The Pajama Game', Birmingham, 1999.
Richard Adler, Simon Callow, Doris Day, Graham Bickley and Mrs Adler.

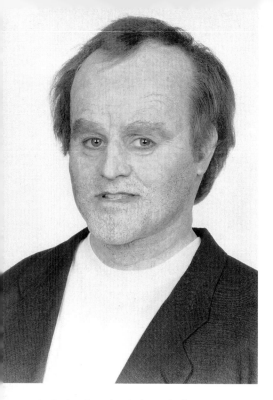

As Phil Collins for 'It's Ulrika'. (BBC)

And as Cher. (BBC)

With my dear friend
Mike Edgar in Dublin for
Heineken Hot Press Rock
Awards, 1999.

Snapped with Phil Piotrowski
on the King's Road.

James Crossley, aka Hunter.

That fateful night in
Paris, World Cup
1998. With Stan,
Richard Wilson and
Ewan McGregor.

With Markus in the Maldives,
February 2000.

With Cameron (and Bo) five minutes before I left
for hospital, November 2000.

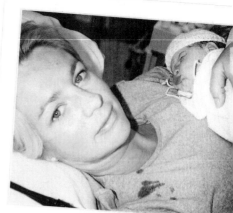

Ten minutes with my darling Bo before they to
her away, November 2000.

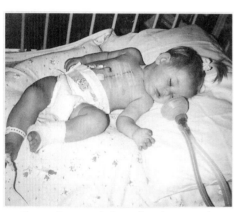

Bo on the second day after her second
operation, Guy's Hospital,
11 September 2001.

Bo with Jim (aka Vic Reeves).

The Swedes have landed
(from left to right: Berit, Linda's boyfriend
Andreas, Linda, me and Bo).

aside, it was to be complicated further by that little accessory every breastfeeding mother carries with her in the absence of her baby: the breast pump. My tits ached like crazy and I spent most of the time in my dressing room. Expressing. Like a cow. And when I phoned John – on the first mobile that I owned – all I could hear was Cameron crying in the background and Michael's mother, Winnie, saying that he wouldn't take the milk. I had expressed milk for him, but he wouldn't take it. Not unless it was actually coming from my breast. I felt devastated and couldn't wait to get back.

Looking back, we appeared to have had no intention of dealing with the subject of childcare – or at least I didn't. When the *Gladiators* live shows came round – which that year were held in Sheffield – John had to take time off work and accompany me. There were going to be six shows over four days and I was having kittens about the whole thing. Once again I would have to don my 'work hat' and leave my 'mummy hat' at home, or at least in the hotel suite, and the thought stabbed me deep in my stomach. As a result, I was probably a less enthusiastic host than previously.

No sooner had we come home, but my mother phoned with the devastating news that Nana, Michael's mother and my 'English grandmother', had died suddenly. It was horrible. I kept shouting 'No! No! No!', trying to undo my mother's words. Winnie had been the most lovely, charming, funny, young-hearted, warm person I had got to know when I'd first visited England. Everyone loved her – she was a ray of sunshine, a lover of life and food alike; she was always laughing and had great energy for a woman of her age. She truly was one of a kind. I had dealt with the death of three grandparents already. All three of my 'grandfathers' – two Swedish and Nana's husband George. I had been saddened by their deaths, but could not quite come to grips with the fact that I would never laugh with Nana again.

Then something came along which, although parading under the title of 'work', was actually, hopefully, going to be quite good fun. John and I had long been fans of Reeves and Mortimer and would catch them on Channel 4 whenever we could. It was John who brought them to my attention, and I have never looked back. So I was already a massive fan when they asked me to take part in a one-off quiz show called *Shooting Stars*, with the kings of comedy as hosts and myself on one of the teams. It was to be a quiz with serious questions from the 1960s, interspersed with their wacky comedy. I agreed, but did not honestly enjoy it. The show didn't seem to work, mixing the serious with their inherent madness. However, when the BBC, for their sins, decided to commission a series of six programmes, I once again agreed to take part as team captain, because they promised me it would be nothing like the pilot. They took out the serious questions and simply added more mad, alternative 'Reeves and Mortimer' stuff. Vic (who will from now on be referred to as Jim, as this is his real name) and Bob were the hosts. Mark Lamarr was my fellow team captain and a funny-looking fellow called Matt Lucas would play the part of 'George Dawes', who kept the scores.

I was flattered and delighted to be working with two of my heroes, although I still found it unbearable to be without Cameron. But if you have to go to work and you can go to work and laugh, then you are a lucky man. Or woman. So that is exactly what I did. I sat in my chair on the set, taking the point-scoring a little too seriously, and laughing like a drain for hours on end.

The boys were just the funniest things. Bob was a grubby little man (by his own admission), with incredible attention to detail. How he and Jim came up with their ideas and comments remains a mystery to me to this day – there is no getting into their heads. Bob's humour was particularly infantile and slapstick. He would generally centre it around human body parts, sex or shameful piss-taking. But guests on the programme would rarely complain. We all just sat in awe of these outrageous performers.

Jim, on the other hand, played things maturely off-screen, if not on. He is a marvellous artist in his own right, with the mind of an intellectual – albeit an intellectual who one day decided to half bury a car on his property down in Kent. It was, he said, art. He had grand ideas and an insatiable desire for knowledge. Quirks, however, abounded. Once on our way to a photo session he phoned in advance to request an apple to be ready on a doily for his arrival. When I asked him why, he replied that he simply wanted to see if they would do it. And, as would be expected in the world of showbiz, an apple on a doily on a plate was handed to him within two minutes of his arrival. Together, the boys would flirt and take the piss out of me and I forgave them anything, because the Swede in me saw us as equals. I just gave as good as I got – if sometimes in a slightly unladylike fashion. I was after all a boy at heart too.

Mark Lamarr and I did not instantly bond, but he was civil. Again, he was incredibly bright and talked seriously and non-stop about music, films or women. I have never known anyone to attract as many girls as Mark. And it was later to become a small hiccup in his relationship with Jim, as they would both tout for the same women.

Matt Lucas, on the other hand, was not only very friendly, but a true 'actor'. He, too, was artistic and, quite rightly, took his role as George incredibly seriously. He became a cult figure within what was fast becoming a cult show. I took my father along for one of the recordings. He had a great sense of humour but I wasn't sure he would 'get' Reeves and Mortimer. I think on that occasion I was asked if I could wipe the fake snow off a car windscreen with my arse. My father laughed like a madman in the audience and when I asked him what about, he said he wasn't sure. But that was Reeves and Mortimer for you. You were never quite sure why you were laughing, sometimes it was just them, sometimes it was a walk, a voice, a move or an expression, like, 'You wouldn't let it lie!' The source of their inspiration was, and remains, their enigma. But I don't care. They are the DBs.

We carried on recording the shows over a period of three weeks, during which I also took part in a commercial with Cameron for Sainsbury's, promoting their new parent-friendly services. It was actually even more nerve-racking working with my son than without him. I was so concerned he would be unhappy or uncomfortable that I was constantly on tenterhooks. But as usual he was as good as gold, despite the takes and re-takes. I hadn't given serious thought to any consequences of bringing Cameron into the public eye. But felt, instead, that the project was appropriate and PC and I wanted to be part of something which would improve parent-friendliness. Above and beyond that I had no intention of pushing him into the limelight.

A week or so before I slipped off to Birmingham for the new *Gladiators* series, an event seemingly destined to punctuate my life annually for evermore, I remember standing with John at my cousin Catherine's wedding thinking how content I was. Yes, the fourth series was going to be an entirely different challenge for me; I was going to have to face the fact that I would have to juggle work away from home, and be away from my son for one or two nights at a time. But John and I had managed to arrange a mix-and-match babysitting schedule for the three-week period. My mum would help; so would John's parents; and so would John. Between the lot of us we would find a way to care for the nearly ten-month-old Baby Blue. Not that this stopped me crying my bloody eyes out as I left him behind and made my way north as fast as I reluctantly could.

Once again, that year, people had changed. Some were new arrivals. Some had got bigger. Some had got cockier. And some had developed an even greater love of themselves. As I entered the full-on work arena once more, my breasts slightly deflated by the lack of milk in them and my hips and arse even smaller, I was forced to shut myself away from the life I'd carved out at home. But I was too emotionally charged not to feel a longing for my child and to carry on working as if nothing had changed. That's called being pro-fessional – and I wasn't very good at it. Yet I would simply have to learn to block out the longing the second I stepped inside the National Indoor Arena. Once I was back at the hotel, I knew their excellent Chardonnay would soften the blow.

Hard as I found it to concentrate on work, I disciplined myself to call and check on Cameron only a few times a day. Actually, I couldn't bear to hear him in the background – and was always fearful that I'd call while he was crying. When that happened I'd find it hard to not rush home. But my mum was very reassuring, telling me how happy he was and how lovely he was being. It gave me confidence. Perhaps this would work.

This was also my first proper time away from John in a year. And looking back I realize something. I had utterly, willingly dedicated myself exclusively to my son for some seven months and loved every sleep-deprived, exhausted minute of it. I had been more than a dedicated mother. I had immersed myself in motherhood and oozed it from every pore. But as I had buried myself in my son, if I had dared be deeply honest with myself at that time, I would have seen that I had neglected my role as a wife and a lover.

Needless to say I felt less cumbersome that year than I had the last, and whilst I probably wasn't as slim as I had been pre-pregnancy, I was feeling reasonably lithe. As a woman, I now had the best of both worlds: for the first time in almost a couple of years I felt more like I used to – for a start, normal clothes were fitting me – but having had a child had also given me confidence in a way nothing else ever had. I felt real. However, it was important to occupy every single second up there in order to avoid my mind straying into child-longing territory. I worked hard and knew, too, that I might have to play hard in order to busy myself. Quite a challenge after three years of keeping myself to myself – except of course for the time when I kept myself to someone else, but that you already know about.

I could pretend I don't know what happened next and when it happened, but that wouldn't be strictly true. I do remember walking into the arena for the first time that year and being greeted by Gladis here, crew there, production staff, whoever. And I do remember walking past the famous 'Wall' when a couple of the boys were practising, and feeling a friendly kiss hello on my forehead from the Gladiator we had to call Hunter. He had grown a year older and a little cuter and I remember it making my heart skip a little beat. I didn't know why.

From that moment on I noticed him wherever I went. It's a little like considering buying a Saab and finding that every car you see on the road is a Saab. When something is in your mind, it seems it is also everywhere else. So, already, I wasn't thinking straight. Or indeed thinking at all.

There must have continued to be brief, harmless flirtations between myself and the young man, and in a very straightforward way it made me feel womanly again. Wanted. Desired, I guess. I'm not sure if he intended anything by it, but it was beginning to become clear that the devil in me was still in residence.

I tore home on my day off and would travel back the following evening in time for the next day's recording. One night some of the team were going to the cinema and I thought I would make the effort, too, in the full knowledge he would be there. I tore back up to Birmingham on an empty stomach and bumped into the Huntsman in the hotel lobby. They were just leaving. I decided I wouldn't go, and told him he 'owed me one'. Not sure how that worked, and nor did he probably, but there it was – the gauntlet had been laid down.

We worked the following day and I felt that I was no longer accidentally bumping into this big lump of muscle from Yorkshire. By now, we were subconsciously seeking each other out. There was a frisson between us and it was becoming unavoidable. What's more, I was feeding it and so was he. There were no words. Just looks, glances, brushing past each other.

What in this world was I thinking of? Had I not already caused enough pain and destruction? Had I not been given a second chance by singularly the man I most respected in the world? Had I not mothered a child by this man less than ten months ago? What *was* the matter with me? Well, I can tell you I thought none of these things. I was obsessed with occupying myself, at all costs, and it seems that I was prepared to let sanity and reality slip through my fingers like sand. I moved to another planet, where nothing has happened, and nothing will happen, but where you live only for the now. Where nothing else exists except for you, you, you.

I was still self-possessed enough to make it home on another day off to do an interview with Deborah Ross from the *Daily Mail*, to promote *Gladiators*. I would give an interview, talk about life, my life and my mistakes, and people would read it and consequently watch the show. Apparently. It was a full-on interview and she was a tough interrogator – she would let nothing go. Inevitably we talked about my childhood, my marriage troubles and the state of things today. I was honest, as I tend to be in interviews. I had spent the past year or so living with my infidelity and the fallout thereof. I had never blamed my infidelity on the experiences in my childhood. But I had learnt that certain experiences contribute towards making you the person you are. I took full responsibility for my actions – it was nothing I was forced to do. She wanted to talk about my mother and her role in my 'downfall'. I found it hard. I wanted to say that I got on really well with my mother and that we had a very close relationship; that I had overcome my lack of understanding for her and she for me, but it wasn't the truth. I loved my mother. I knew that. But I still remained unable to reconcile the differences between us; including the reasons why and how she left when I was young. I didn't express all these things – I simply talked 'around' them. I had learnt to be on my guard, and I knew Ms Ross was an intelligent woman. And as I sat there talking about how my personal life had quickly been rebuilt and filled with the joy of my first child, I was, in actual fact, on the threshold, once again, of infidelity. I sat there and talked joy, peace and happiness, all the while consumed by something poisonous once again, the poison of a devil I knew only too well. And yet, I did nothing to halt it.

A couple of days later John came up to Birmingham with my lovely little boy and my father, who was visiting from Sweden. My father doted on Cameron. He thought he was the coolest thing since getting pissed. I think he was the son my father had always wanted, and it was heart-warming to see them together. They stayed a few nights. I had booked my dad into the room next door to mine and he played with the minibar and the TV like a child in a toy shop. There was a crew party one night and I didn't want to go, but John insisted. I didn't want to go because I knew where my eyes would be directed. And they were.

By then we still had seven international shows and one celebrity one to record, and there was only one week left of madness. In some respects it was a relief when John and Cameron finally left. And not because I wanted to pursue my extra-curricular activities, but because I wasn't able to give my son and husband my undivided attention. When they did leave, however, I found it impossible to deny the inevitable. There was going to be a union of myself and the Huntsman. There was going to be a meeting of bodies. We both felt it. But I was not seduced by him. He didn't go all out to hunt me down. I went for him. We snogged and messed around as if I was a single woman with no other life but the there and then. As if I wasn't a mother, a wife and decent human being. And as I reoffended I knew there would be no going back. Ever. This was it. My position as wife was no longer tenable.

There was not a single inkling in my mind that I would remain married to John for any longer than it would take me to tell him. I knew there would be no way I could stay member of a club in which I would go on breaking the rules. There was just something that kept me from adhering to them. I couldn't spend the rest of John's and my life fancying other men. It simply wasn't right. I knew it and soon John too would have to know. Whatever it was that had made me stray in the first place, two years prior, was clearly still in me. I hadn't exorcized all my ghosts. When I'd gone through my first rebellion against my marriage and then had to face my fucked-up relationship with my parents, I had allowed the latter to take precedence and the former to become my security, safety net and platform. I had been so busy concentrating on the controversies of an awkward childhood, puberty and adulthood that I had allowed myself to just slip back into the comfortable arms of someone who cared for the whole of me, who could understand when I didn't, and who could guide me when the darkness fell. But I hadn't actually worked the marriage side through for *me*. John was the person I had looked to for help in surviving the two, but really he could only be there to support me on the one. And now, I was cruelly turning my back on him. I was denying him a life with me, which was all he wanted. But seemingly it wasn't what I ultimately wanted.

So what do I say about John? He was either too much or not enough. He gave me what I think made up ninety per cent of a good relationship. And I was now about to leave him in search of a volatile ten per cent. I was going to leave him in search of capturing that fire in my belly, a life of unpredictability and possibly of vulnerability. But to me, there was no other way. In my mind I felt a little like a murderer who had failed to be convicted after his first offence and was now committing another in the full knowledge that he would be going down anyway. Defeatist. Improper. Indecent. Crude. Vulgar. Inexcusable. Weak and dangerous.

And there was our son. My beautiful, beautiful boy who loved his daddy so much and whose daddy loved him to bits. I was about to tear their world apart – all to my own end. I couldn't think about whether John and I would be amicable, the word didn't enter my head. All I knew was that I had to do it. I couldn't live like this and I didn't want to and perhaps I had discovered that I didn't need to, too. Cameron would be well cared for by both of us. But Cameron would remain with me, without a doubt. I would never give him up – over my dead body. There was no question in my mind about *that*. And there was also no question that, as much as I dreaded it, this time I would have to speak to John. I wasn't looking for a way around it this time. I would take whichever hard road I would have to. That was very, very clear in my mind.

IT'S ALL OVER NOW, BABY BLUE

My state of health had different ideas, however. Towards the end of the run I usually became run down and exhausted, but this time the hard schedule and the mad dashes home to see Cameron combined to contribute to a severe case of tonsillitis which showed no signs of relenting. I was actually unable to talk. Great.

Once again, I'd driven home with a phone number in my handbag. But this time it represented something completely different. Last time I had taken a number it had been out of security and comfort. And just in case. There was no just in case about this time: I would ring him for sure. But I felt equally confident that I would have done what I was about to do without that number. I wasn't leaving John because I wanted to be with a 21-year-old body builder from York. I was leaving John because I didn't feel I wanted to be married to him anymore. The muscle was just the catalyst.

Speaking or not, I knew it wouldn't take long for John to recognize the signs. Despite what you might be thinking, I am not a good liar. My face speaks a thousand words. I felt a little depressed, on account not solely of what I knew lay ahead, but also due to my exhaustion and illness, which had me in dire pain and on antibiotics. While delighted to be reunited with Cameron, I quickly became irritated with John, poor sod, and struggled to maintain a cordial atmosphere. It wouldn't do any good to arrive home and start mouthing off straight away, even if I could have done.

We were due to go on holiday with John's brother and family in
France in five days. The plan was that John would drive down to the
South of France and Cameron and I would fly the next day. John
talked with great enthusiasm about the holiday and how we both
needed a break. I attempted to reciprocate but failed miserably. I
wasn't sure whether I should talk to him now, or wait until we came
back. Had it just been the three of us going I probably would have
started a conversation there and then, but I felt I had an obligation
to the others. I didn't want to ruin their holiday by us not turning
up at the last minute. With marvellous hindsight, that is exactly
what I should have done. But being sick had muddied my for-once-
clear head.

So we carried on planning and packing and preparing. I had no
enthusiasm and John could tell. He asked on a number of occasions
if there was anything wrong. 'Yes, I'm going to leave you when we
get back,' I wanted to say, but couldn't. I knew I had to keep up
a front until we got back. A holiday wouldn't change my mind, far
from it. But perhaps I could pick myself up a bit before dropping the
bombshell.

I'm not sure how I struggled through that week. I didn't get any
better, and my mind and heart were without rest. My heart ached
for John; it ached for the pain I was about to inflict, and the
destruction I was about to cause. My head was punishing me for
my dishonesty; my uselessness; my weakness of character and my
ignorance. I detested myself. I came to think I must have always
been this stupid, and my actions were merely confirming it. Here
was another episode to add to my list of mistakes, disasters and
inability to do things right. I was good for nothing. Except perhaps
for being a mother.

I had no extraordinary longing to be with another man. I didn't
feel that James was what I *needed* – but he was certainly something
that I *wanted*. This wasn't about a secure future, or a grand scheme
or a plan for my life. I just knew I couldn't stick with what I had.
Not even for my son's sake. I'd only make both of us unhappy
in the long run, and where would that leave him? No, I wasn't

miserable in my day-to-day life with John, but there was an underlying desire to search out something else and I could no longer deny it. It hadn't disappeared despite a safe, civilized, secure life. There was a real, crazy, wild side of me that wanted so dearly not to be safe and secure, a side of me that didn't want to know what tomorrow would bring. The lamp-post-licking side of me which wanted not to be sensible had been repressed, and I didn't know how long I could go on restraining it. It would remain with me, and us, for ever, and would only fight back unless I unleashed myself and made myself work through it properly.

Another very real possibility was, of course, that I might not find happiness at the end of my pursuit. Perhaps I would end up even more unhappy. That was more than a hypothetical. But I felt I had to go through with it. Regardless. And that was just the word. Regardless. I was doing everything *regardless*. I was living in the world of regardless. Regardless of anyone else; anyone else's feelings and anyone else's life. Regardless – without regard or consideration. That was me.

I questioned and tortured myself from one moment to the next, asking myself questions, challenging my own case, qualifying my argument and sending words flying around in my head in a disorientating fashion. Yet whilst complications reigned in my head, my soul was clear as to what I had to do. When John finally asked what was up I made a request that we have the holiday as planned and discuss any problems upon our return. I actually felt John really needed the rest. How very patronizing, but I knew if I hit him with it there and then he would never get a break. For a long time.

I spoke a little to James that week – not for moral support, for he would have given me none. He did not know I was about to leave my husband. No, I didn't want comfort. I didn't deserve it. But I wanted to hear the voice that had alerted me to my own confusion.

Throughout all this 'confusion' Cameron remained a mummy-and daddy-loving child, just on the brink of taking his first steps at only eleven months old. He was dribbling like mad and constantly smiling. Ironically, he was the one giving me the strength to go on.

I was able to talk by the end of the week, but continued with a temperature, hot flushes and an excruciating throat. The dose of antibiotics was doubled. I sought solace in Cameron: engaging myself with him constantly helped to keep me sane, and I had missed him so. It must have given John encouragement to see me so devoted. Maybe he didn't believe I would do anything that would upset our family unit. Maybe he didn't imagine I had cut out my heart and was about to commit yet another selfish act. Regardless. But he would have been wrong. When he set off on the Friday, it was a relief. For one whole day there would be no need to pretend.

*

On the Saturday morning, just before I was about to set off for the airport with Cameron, the phone rang. It was Michael. A longer, harsher string of abuse I had not heard. The Deborah Ross interview had appeared in the *Daily Mail*'s colour supplement that morning, and he was not a happy man. It would not be fair to recite to you the words which were directed at me, suffice to say that the bottom line was that I was a good for nothing something, which, of course, I had always suspected; that I would never be welcome in his house again; that I wasn't ever to go near his children (my sister and brother); that I was faeces; that I was a female dog; that I was an ungrateful female dog; that I was a stirrer who continued to upset my mother; that I was a fucking idiot; that I was a cow and many, many other such things. I wanted to die! There I stood holding my little son, whom I was about to take away from his father on account of my personality disorder, listening to my stepfather disowning me to the extreme and wishing my life away. Things couldn't be better. He slammed the phone down with the now-familiar words, 'Fuck off!' Well, that was that, then.

I was shaking and I felt sick. My God, what do I do now? I can't go, I panicked. I cannot go to France like this. There is too much to sort out. I cannot take myself away at a time like this, it would be a little like falling from one frying pan into another one. I have to phone John. I can't phone John. I can't tell him over the phone why

I cannot go on holiday for two weeks. I felt on the verge of collapse, but opted instead for a call to Melanie. She had been such a great source of moral, spiritual and emotional support over the past few years, I had grown to depend on her in way beyond a professional capacity. In the absence of confidence in myself and my decisions, my actions, there was always Melanie. She would often guide me, advise me, and in so doing, keep me from insanity's door. So I asked her for help. I had no idea what to do. She knew, of course, where I was heading with my intentions, and sympathized about my step-father. She thought he was out of order, but knew also that she could do nothing to take away my pain or disappointment. She urged me to put it out of my mind and catch the flight. I still had major doubts. Everything felt too heavy. Once more I was faced with a major irregularity in my relationship with my mother, and once more my marriage had run aground. I didn't associate the two. They weren't connected, bar one common denominator – me. It was me. I couldn't feel worse.

At the airport I picked up a copy of the newspaper and read the interview for myself. In my opinion, there was nothing new in there which hadn't been reported on or speculated on before. Ms Ross did claim my mother had 'abandoned' me, a word I had never used, and said I was only five, when in actual fact I was eight. She also claimed I had never been loved or felt loved, something I had never suggested. The interview said my parents had never looked after me, but rather I them. It was a worse indictment of my father and how he had forgotten birthdays and forgotten me for the most part. And how he had suggested when I told him that I was marrying John at twenty-three, that there was plenty of time for divorce and remarriage. But, importantly, I say in the interview how you have to judge your parents and then forgive them, and that is what I felt I had done – 'otherwise you'd go mad'. Worst of all, however, were the words from me about how blissfully happy I was and how John and I had had Cameron because we wanted to stay together. And how much I had grown and learnt since my infidelity. Nothing, of course, could have been further from the truth, but I didn't know that when I had spoken. It had sounded so right then. So right, but so wrong.

I felt desperate about my parents' reaction, but I also felt I hadn't said anything out of order in the interview. I had been frank and honest, but far from sensational. But my mother would be destroyed because her friends would read this. And that was what mattered to her. I did not matter. She felt awkward about the past, but she refused to deal with it with me. She refused to talk to me about it. She refused to entertain the idea that it may have caused me any pain, or confusion. She had done what she wanted. Regardless. The difference between her regardless and mine was I would never leave my child. Regardless.

The short flight was long and painful. Cameron would under normal circumstances have been a welcome distraction, but my burden was too heavy to bear and his loving smiles only brought tears of desperation to my eyes. I hated the trip. I hated where I was going. I hated myself. I wanted to be at home. I *needed* to be at home. John greeted us at the airport with overbearing amounts of enthusiasm, but took one glance at my face and knew immediately something was up. I let him in on the article. He was shocked and held me tightly. Momentarily it was a relief, but then I had to let go. I couldn't break down. Couldn't afford to. He comforted me, as usual. Talked sense to me. Empathized. Criticized my parents' approach. Not in an attempt to make me feel better, but because, in fact, he was right. He said I should try not to let it ruin our holiday. Of course not, I had other things that could do that.

It was a laborious road to the villa we had rented, but on reaching it we were reunited with John's brother's family. It was a relief to see them, but a further strain when we discovered that we hadn't been left a key to the property. We had to go on a wild goose chase for some hours in an attempt to search out the owner or someone of reasonable responsibility. It was not particularly warm and the villa was quite dark and gloomy. The pool was unheated and too cold to bathe in, as well as being covered by a sheet of leaves. The garden was steeply sloped, giving no place for the children to run around. Things felt terrible. I had a pain in my gut so intense, not just because I no longer had a mother and stepfather, and I was about to end my marriage to the most wonderful man in the world, but because the villa had been my choice.

The days were long and dreary. The weather did not improve especially and even insisted on giving us rain, too. Cameron took his first steps and John failed in every attempt at getting closer to me. I couldn't bear him touching me and slunk away like a cat every time he moved towards me. I obsessed myself with Cameron, all the while my health far from good – I continued to feel run down, exhausted, hot and achy. John made attempts to probe further into my mental state, but I refused him access. I lied that I was fine, but that we should talk when we got back. For moral support I would steal away in the car to the local town where there was a payphone, from which I would call Melanie. I would panic to her for minutes on end. Panic, and panic, and more panic. On a couple of occasions I phoned James. I was missing him because I missed someone who wouldn't ask questions. I said I would try to see him when I got back, but no more than that. My personal turmoil was exactly that – mine.

The end of my marriage felt a certainty. The situation with my mother I wished could be less terminal. I felt sure that without me doing something there would be no going back with her. The hostility between us and between myself and Michael was too overwhelming. I loved them, but it seemed I could not get on with them, no matter how hard I tried. And so long as issues remained unacknowledged and unsettled, that would never change. But they weren't going to be the ones that looked at the issues. My mother denied me access on that score, and for Michael sensitivity was not a strong suit. I put pen to paper.

I wrote my mother a letter, which in my opinion was fair and sensitive. I expressed my absolute sadness at the current situation and assured her that despite our inability to resolve any of our issues she would, without hesitation, be welcome to see Cameron at every given opportunity. I would never remove Cameron from her, that wouldn't do anyone any favours. She adored him, and he her. I told her that I had a problem with certain aspects of our relationship, but that it would take the will and desire of two people to resolve it, not one. And as she was reluctant to step forward, the status quo would remain. I felt saddened by what I had to write, but strengthened by the fact that I had done it. I felt that my door would always be open to her, but she would have to do the walking herself. I couldn't make her.

The holiday continued as it had started. My despair was fuelled further by John's brother's announcement that his wife was expecting their third child. I was so happy for them, and wished I would feel happy for myself in the same way. I felt envious of the success of their relationship, in a totally innocent and non-venomous fashion. One night John's parents, who were holidaying in the area, came to babysit so we could all go out for a romantic meal. Naturally, I found it hard to relax. His parents were sympathetic and horrified at the rift with my parents. But I felt I couldn't accept their sympathy, as I too was about to commit a horrible, horrible crime. Towards their son and grandson. Their affection actually frightened me, because I could not accept it in the spirit in which it was meant. I was no longer family.

When we set off home I knew that while one difficult episode was over, another horrific one was about to unfold. On top of which, I had a letter burning a hole in my pocket. On the plane I bumped into Carol Smillie and her family. She was smiley, smiley, smiley and as we chatted and laughed a little I felt a little envious of her happiness and togetherness. Lovely girl. I just sat there falling apart, thinking about the twenty-four hours ahead that lay between marriage and separation.

In all honesty I cannot recall my exact opening words to John. He could probably tell you word for word, but please don't ask him. He deserves better. I told him I was unhappy. That I wasn't totally sure why, but that I didn't want to go on feeling this way. I told him I didn't think it was fair on him. And that was true. He deserved better than someone like me. I explained that I hadn't quite resolved the issues after our first separation and that may partly have been as a result of Renee's unexpected death and my distraction with the issues concerning my relationship with my parents. I told him that I loved him, because I did, but not in the way that I should. And not in the way he deserved. I found it hard to be any more detailed than that.

He was shocked, but had suspected something serious was afoot. He was so, so, sad. He still didn't understand and asked some more. I wouldn't have expected him to understand. I felt so utterly complicated myself that I couldn't expect him to grasp so much so soon. He asked if there was someone else. And I felt I answered him honestly when I said, 'No.' I wasn't leaving him to be with James. James had always been only the catalyst, never a reason. I had made this situation come about as a result of my incompleteness. I had found myself attracted to another man and in my book that was as much as I needed to confirm that I was not with the right person. It was my flaw and my actions that had brought about this situation.

I was comfortable with the idea of being on my own. I had, after all, spent most of my childhood on my own, it was something I was familiar with. And whilst John and I had been a great partnership, there was something about our relationship which made me feel alone – one of the roots of my problems and reminiscent of the premonition I had at the age of ten of having a child but ending up on my own with it. Was it a vision or a self-fulfilling prophecy? And that was maybe my problem and my doing: allowing our relationship to go so far but no further. Cliché or not, I told John I needed to be alone for a while. That I needed space.

With reluctance and further sadness John tried to believe and understand me. He looked at his son longingly and I had to look away. I could not tap into his sadness or I would not go through with it. And I had to. Five days later, on 29 September 1995, our wedding anniversary, John moved out. I don't know if he expected it to be as permanent as I knew it had to be.

To my shock and surprise I received a phone call from my

mother. She said she had received my letter and didn't want to fight, but could we perhaps meet up for lunch? I was pleased, and with great caution invited her over. She didn't want to discuss any issues, and just wanted to make it clear that she didn't want an atmosphere between us. She didn't want to go into details about anything, but was glad to be able to see Cameron as and when. I was relieved, but once again there had been no chance to confront anything. A wasted opportunity. However, I was also well aware that I simply did not have the strength to push the issue right then. I had just separated from my husband, and I was home alone with a nearly one-year-old. And if my mother would not focus on our past, she did at least help me focus on my future. She was devastated when I told her I was leaving John, but understood, perhaps only too well, the emotions of being in a relationship and needing to 'get out'.

John saw Cameron whenever he wanted, and we found a nanny we both liked, who would start the day after Cameron's first birthday. For his big day, 18 October, we met up with Melanie, his unofficial godmother, for lunch. It was going to be a jolly day, despite the cloud hanging over us, but she brought bad news. The press had found out about our separation. We had wanted to go about our business in a private manner.

Now, very few people, if any, knew about our separation. I had told only a close friend and Melanie; my mother knew after a while, as did my family in Sweden. The source of any such leak is always difficult to determine, and inevitably becomes an irrelevance, but it always catches you out. And this would be a sensational story. The wife who was unfaithful was forgiven, had a baby and within a year the marriage was on the rocks again. Knowing what was about to unfold on the breakfast tables of Britain, it became a dark and sad day for us all. When we went over to my mum's to hide out and for her to give her grandson his birthday present, the mood was sombre. But my darling son remained oblivious. Then John left for Kent and later that evening I returned to our once-marital home.

The following day was our nanny's first day. It was a baptism of fire, bless her. She could not get to my front door for press and cars, photographers and hacks. It was a complete surprise for her and despite the shock she remained calm. I had appointments in London, and setting off felt tense. It was her first day with Cameron, and I was being hounded by a beast with a bottomless belly. The shakes had started long before my keys reached the car door. Some of the reporters followed me for a time, but then gave up. I was being chased, once again. I was frightened.

I spoke to James and told him what was going on. He had been shocked when I had told him I had left John. Now John and I were plastered across every newspaper in the land. We'd issued a press release as is the done thing in these circumstances, but the journalists very disconcertingly remained outside my house. The release wasn't enough. There simply had to be more to this story than caught the eye. They were right, of course, but I thought it was none of their business. At the beginning of the following week I received a demand from BT for payment of my phone bill. I told them I hadn't received one, and after further investigation it turned out that someone had phoned them to arrange that *my* bill be sent to a different address. They had no record of who it was, but gave me the address. It was an office in London. There was no doubt in my mind someone was determined to find out who I was speaking to. But I was more cross with BT for allowing it to happen without my authorization in the first place. I became suspicious of everything.

A long-standing engagement to open a supermarket in Manchester meant, once again, pictures in the newspapers the following day. When a few days later I met up with my friend Ross King for lunch to divert myself while Cameron was with John, he laughingly asked if there was anyone else involved. I denied it flatly. I knew of course that as every day passed I wanted more and more to be with James, and that the distraction would mean I wouldn't have to keep thinking about John's pain.

James and I spent Sunday night together. It was proving too irresistible. The following week I escaped with Cameron to Sweden to visit my dad – I needed to get away from everyone, even James, even if we spoke while I was out there. There were no exchanges of romantic promises; more often a silence, which spoke for itself, but James was incredibly sweet. My father had by now a little Jack Russell, called Tutan, who was quite, quite mad and she chased after Cameron as if she was on a hunt in the English countryside. Cameron was happy and content, and his grandfather thrilled to see him. It being November, my country was thick and silent with snow. My dad and I walked and talked a lot. I told him why I couldn't stay married to John, and he remained rather silent. I think it pained him – he loved John intensely, and they had shared so many glorious times. The fact that we would remain in close contact because of Cameron seemed little comfort.

Berit and my sister Linda, who was only eighteen, were equally upset. Berit tried hard to understand what little I could tell her. It is bizarre telling people you have failed and that you are crap. I would have had good reason if John had treated me badly or messed me around, but I was the guilty party. It felt awkward and empty and very lonely. It is hard clutching at words when there seem to be so few words on your side. Especially when the ones you do find are followed by admissions of weakness and the possibility that there is just the shadow of a hint of someone else in another corner.

Two days before I was due to return to England, John phoned in quite a state. He had been contacted by the press who were suggesting there was something going on between the Gladiator Hunter and myself. They were wondering whether this was why we were divorcing. My God! I thought, they clearly don't leave any stones unturned. I wasn't quite sure what to say, but knew that I had been reasonably honest so far, and I couldn't stop now. I acknowledged to him there had been an attraction between us, but that nothing had really happened. Can't remember if I used the word 'really' or not. Maybe something had happened. But I wasn't leaving John for James, that much was true. I was leaving John because I would go on fancying Phils and Jameses for the rest of my life, and he should have someone who could love just him. John was not entirely convinced by my answer.

I left Sweden, bidding a needy farewell to my dad. Strange how

I felt I needed him, despite him never really being there for me
before. But I guess I felt desperate. I knew I was walking a tightrope.
I knew that John might discover that I had already embarked on the
slippery slope of infidelity for the second time. I didn't want tackling
that to be a distraction from my 'main' point. It was almost as if I
told myself that James was a 'by the by' rather than the catalyst he
was. But John would surely put two and two together and quite
rightly get four. With the hungry press on our backs, my time was
running out. And John was running out of patience.

Upon my return he approached me about the number of calls to
York that had appeared on our phone bill. He knew by then that
James was from York, and wanted me to confirm that there was
more to this story than I was prepared to give away. I held my hand
up. I had nowhere else to go. Had I slept with him? Yes, I had. Rare
for us, things got ugly.

I clutched Cameron after John had gone, rewinding and replaying
John's anger time and time again in my head, in the full knowledge
that I had deserved it. Now he knew just what a shit I was. But now
there would also be no going back. It was a relief.

But things became extremely tense between the two of us.
Pick-ups and drop-offs with Cameron were icy cold and without
words. It was unbearable, but there was no alternative – at least, not
yet. What's more, the press continued to hound me, James and
presumably John. I was stifled and nervous; low and fearful. The
press wanted confirmation that James and I were now an item, but
we refused to comment. God knows what they were putting John
through.

In the midst of all this madness, I decided to fulfil a longstanding
desire. I went and had a tattoo. You see, throughout this divorcing
experience I was discovering another person, one who wanted to
undo everything good I had previously done. I now felt like a devil.
I'd committed crime after crime after crime. I was bad, wicked, nasty,
illegal. John had made me feel appreciated and good, but now there
was no more good left inside me. In the world of wicked I was
queen. I had been fascinated by tattoos since I was a child. There

would have been no way dutiful wife Ulrika would have had one. But now I was with no one. Effectively. Petrified, and with my Scottish friend Heather for moral support, I made my way down to my local tattooist. Pain wasn't the issue. Changing-of-the-mind was the issue.

I leafed through sheets and sheets of thorny roses, snakes and broken hearts, but knew I wanted a pig. The only pig the nice man with the long beard and arms covered in tattoos had was Piglet. But Piglet was too friendly. Too nice and too meek. Then I saw it. The one for me. It was a little angry red devil. 'Put it on my arse,' I said, with my head bowed. I asked if there was time for me to have a swig from my hip flask of whisky, but he said I wouldn't need it. He was kind of right. He talked incessantly throughout the procedure in a vague attempt at calming my nerves, but didn't recognize me. I gave him a false name and then his wife coloured the devil in for me. Within half an hour I was walking away with a bit of plastic stuck to my bum and a pain therein. But I was delighted: I had done it.

The following week I was asked to do a photo shoot and interview for *FHM*. They wanted sexy. And I was willing to give it. Although without taking my clothes off – Melanie would see to that. Inevitably whilst getting changed the devil on my arse made an appearance and so did the subject in the interview.

Meantime, James had the press so hot on his heels that he told me he might give an interview to one of the newspapers just to shut them up, and in exchange for money. I suggested this was a bad idea, but his agent didn't want to listen to me and proceeded to play one newspaper off against another in an attempt to get as much money from them as he could. Dangerous game. Don't piss them off. They are cleverer than you and if they smell a rat they will pounce. And they did. One of the papers ran a fabricated interview with James made up of quotes, which in essence confirmed that he had slept with me and that we were an item. And I was a cheat. I was disappointed, but not as distraught as James. He was gutted, apologetic and in fear of losing me. He begged me to meet up with him, which not only I, but Melanie too, thought was a bad idea.

However, after further distraught phone calls from him, I softened and agreed we could meet in the one reasonably 'safe' place I knew. My old flat in Maida Vale, which had remained unsold.

When we met, James cried. He was genuinely sorry for being so misguided, but did not want to lose whatever this thing was that we had. Well, this thing that we had was sex. I didn't particularly want to lose that either, but I was more preoccupied with divorce, the press and my son. Not in that order.

The following weekend I went to Newcastle to stay with James while he was in panto. I was able to do this as John was insisting, in no uncertain terms, on having Cameron almost four days a week. I didn't feel I was in a position to deny him, despite missing Cameron furiously. John had Cameron, and once again no words were exchanged between us when he picked him up. John even refused to cross the threshold. I had to understand.

Fortunately, work was also keeping me busy. We were rehearsing for a *Shooting Stars* Christmas special. Jim, Bob, Mark Lamarr and I were taping sketches. It was something of an extravaganza, and all the fun kept the devils in my head at bay for a bit. On a temporary basis. The 'boys', Jim and Bob, were always able to make me laugh and teased me with jokes about my current status and state, which in turn forced me to joke about it, too. I was game and the boys were wickedly sarcastic. Bob at one stage made a gag about Cameron not knowing who his father was, with the bevy of men crossing my threshold. It was pushing it a little, to say the least, and far, far from the truth – so I gave as good as I got. I knew I had a long way to go, however, before things would get better, when the following Saturday I walked into my newly joined gym to hear a radio ad for 'Ulrika Jonsson's husband John Turnbull's story' to be serialized in the *Mirror* over the following days. 'Read how she cheated on him, not once, but twice,' enticed the sensational radio voice. How lovely, I thought, and walked out. Then I walked straight back in, knowing that I couldn't run away from the reality. Yes, the guilty slut just had to get on that treadmill, with everyone looking at her knowing her business. Needless to say, I didn't read John's story. It was one I was kinda familiar with.

Christmas was fast approaching and the Monday before it, John filed petition for divorce on the grounds of infidelity. Quite rightly – if not with James, which I'd made a grey area, at least I had guaranteed him one infidelity with Phil two years previously. I had no plans for Christmas. All I knew was that I didn't want to be with my parents and I wasn't going to travel to Sweden. My mother suggested it was only fair to let John have Cameron for the duration, as he truly deserved to have him, and I didn't. I agreed. So I resolved to spend Christmas on my own, at home. I didn't want to see anyone, speak to anyone or surround myself with children for fear of missing Cameron too much. I even bought myself a turkey meal-for-one at Marks, in preparation.

Then on 23 December James invited me to spend that 'festive' season with him and his family. Despite feeling it was a little premature, I secretly feared that doing turkey solo wouldn't do much for my sanity, so said yes. I realized I could actually feel myself hurtling into love with James. He was caring, sweet, cute and funny. Physically, despite his ridiculously large body, we were almost made for each other. He was affectionate and playful and we 'fitted' each other. James was six years my junior and we were sometimes childish together, but at times he could seem quite mature for his twenty-two years. I didn't care about the age thing anyway. But it soon became clear that I cared about him. It was confusing: it felt both right and wrong to be with James, but predominantly right, which was wrong. We couldn't talk much about what was going on in my life – it seemed pointless, and I had to sort that all out myself. I certainly was expecting no support from him. I also missed Cameron desperately, but had no expectations that James would understand, so I kept my longing to myself.

On Christmas Eve I asked to borrow his phone to call my sister in Sweden – I knew my father would be spending Christmas with her and Berit. Christmas Eve is the big day in the Swedish Christmas and I was disappointed that my father had not yet arrived so that I could catch him. So I just told her to give him all my love and a big kiss.

On Christmas Day itself I woke up feeling tired and just a little off colour, but not enough to stop me devouring a full Christmas dinner at James's parents, trimmings et al., at least twice. I think James was almost excited by the amount I was eating, and I, a little embarrassed. His parents were kind and sweet, despite me feeling like I shouldn't be there – I was the older, married woman, mother of one child, dating theirs and eating to the point of embarrassment. James, who could devour several chickens in one fell swoop, was left stunned. And impressed. I remember talking about Cameron a lot.

A day or so later I returned home to finally see my wonderful little boy. Once again the exchange of child passed without words. I couldn't get used to it. It hurt me, not because I was the injured party, but because of the pain I had inflicted on John. His face spoke a million words. I felt unable to object when he asked to have him over New Year, too. This bird hadn't a leg to stand on. This ugly, unfaithful bird. So on the morning of the 31st I once again handed my son over to my soon-to-be ex-husband and prepared to go to the airport to pick up my lover. I felt a little strange. My head was aching and I just didn't feel right. I put it down to the stress and strain of thinking too much. I welcomed James with open arms, relieved to see him; relieved for the distraction. On top of which, of course, I wanted to be held and kissed and loved, just a little bit.

When we got back home, I had a message from my sister, asking me to call her. It was important, she said. How strange, I thought. I normally call her. I thought something awful might have happened. Perhaps my grandma had been taken ill or, worse still, died. I called her back, but failed to get hold of her. So I called my father's flat and left a message, urging him to call me back. I made something for James and I to eat, but I was too preoccupied to feel hungry. There was also a photographer hovering around outside who wanted a photo of James and me. I contacted Melanie, who suggested that in order to get him off our backs, we go out, pose quickly for a shot and then let him fuck off. I felt nervous, but James was up for it. We popped out, he took a shot and duly fucked off.

A couple of hours later the phone rang. James and I were about to get 'friendly', and under normal circumstances I wouldn't have picked up. But I was expecting my sister and wanted to take the call. In a rather dishevelled state I went to the phone to find my sister sounding rather breathless on the other end. In the background I heard Berit shout: 'Sit down! Sit down! Sit down!' I didn't understand. 'What?' I shouted back. 'What is it?'

'*Pappa är död!*' bellowed my sister. And with those words I learnt that my father had died.

PAPPA ÄR DÖD

I held the phone firmly in my hand, but my body went into spasm. It was as though it was curling and writhing around in a free and empty space and I had lost control of it. My head bent forwards and was thrown back as I shouted back at the top of my voice, 'No! No! No! No! Don't say that! Don't say that!' Everything had stopped still, and I could see millions of stars and specks. I continued to shout at her, completely bewildered, holding on to my study desk for support before my body vaulted again, 'No! No! No!' Just like when Winnie died, I wanted her to take the words back, to unsay them. I could still hear Berit shouting in the background for me to sit down, but there wasn't a chair that could have contained me and the fit I was having. I knew I had to ask questions, but I didn't know the first word to say – should it be where? should it be when? how? . . . How did he die? But he couldn't have died. What was she talking about?

I knew it was true, but it was just too surreal for me to digest. Linda spoke to me virtually incoherently. 'Dead; found in his flat; no one had seen him for two days; late for a date; dog was with him; don't know what killed him; blood; police had to break in; Örjan found him; flat on his face; in the hallway.' It was too much information too soon, and yet it was so lacking in everything – sanity, comfort, explanation, reason, humanity. Berit and Linda asked if I had someone to be with and I told them James was there. We agreed to speak later.

But I didn't want James. Or anyone else. I wanted my dad. I cried and cried. And James cried, too, for me. I shook and sobbed and my cheeks began to hurt in the way it hurts when you have laughed too much. I couldn't imagine laughing ever again. Images of my father passed through my head and his face flashed a thousand times, and yet I was grasping for an absolutely accurate picture of him. I pictured him younger, older, laughing, sleeping, smoking and whistling. He was so alive, he couldn't be dead. Then I pictured him lying flat on his face in our hallway, but struggled to work out which way he was facing and whether his head was pointing towards the kitchen or the other way. What had killed him? Nothing was clear. Maybe he had had a heart attack – smoking, drinking, overweight. Possibly. But the worst picture for me was that he had been lying there since 29 December. Two whole days. Alone. No one had known, no one had helped. I saw his beloved Tutan pacing around him, incomprehending; anxious; barking; pacing. I felt so guilty I hadn't called. I would have called him that night with it being New Year's Eve. He hadn't got to my sister's by the time I had called on Christmas Eve and after that my thoughts had been preoccupied.

In a moment of madness I went to the phone and started dialling his number. It connected, rang once and then a second time and then I heard his recorded voice. In keeping with his lively, comical nature it was, of course, a humorous message. I rang off, sobbing anew, in the knowledge that I would never hear that voice speak again. I would never see his wrinkled, bearded, saggy face. Or that smile that had won him so many hearts. Or hear the laugh that always disintegrated into a chesty cough. Oh, fuck. Why couldn't my sister undo her cruel words and my father pick up the phone?

Then through my pain and the aching in my heart a vanity inside me told me he was watching me. He was sitting somewhere above my right shoulder. He didn't want me to be sad, but I was helpless. He watched me walk over to the larder and open my single malt. I needed something to stop the shakes and warm my cold, cold body. I wanted to be numbed by whisky, not by pain. Perhaps if I could lose myself in the bottle I'd be closer to my father somehow. He would have loved this single malt – especially as he would never have been able to afford it. So I poured glass after glass after glass and eventually the world became a less painful, but cloudier place.

I was wrapped in a large jumper of James's, wore no trousers and curled myself into a shivering corner of the kitchen against the radiator. After three-quarters of the bottle had found its way into my belly, my lover suggested that I should perhaps end my relationship with the bottle and find some other form of refreshment, but I declined the invitation. Adamantly. James wasn't sure how to deal with me. He kept asking me questions I didn't know the answer to, like what did he die of? I didn't fucking know. My sister didn't know, my father couldn't tell me and the whisky told me the answer lay at the very bottom of the bottle. I resolved to continue drinking.

At some point I realized the body I was occupying had things to do. I had to call John and ask him to hold on to Cameron; I had to book myself a flight to Sweden; I should tell my father's ex-wife, my mother; and I needed to speak to my sister again. John was audibly shocked – he asked if he could help, or if he could come up, but with James there, no matter how irrelevant he was, I wasn't up to a showdown. I booked a flight for 2 January – there was nothing on New Year's Day – and decided to pay for a club-class ticket for the first time in my life. Money was of no relevance and I felt I couldn't sustain a stable personality; in the front of the plane I might be left alone. My mother was due to go skiing, and wanted to cancel her trip, but I urged her to go through with it, saying that I would have more information when she returned. She was saddened and shocked by the news, but a lot more detached than me. She said she didn't want to miss the funeral. Little did I realize that she stood no chance of doing that. I spent the rest of the day with the whisky and the telephone.

My sister had a few crumbs of information when we spoke later. My father's best friend Örjan had found him. My father would go to Örjan's house for breakfast every morning, without fail – evidently a new routine. When he hadn't shown on the 30th or the 31st and failed to respond to phone calls, Örjan drove over and saw the car outside. He knocked on the door and after no response other than the dog's yelping, managed to peek through the window of my old room, where he saw the body, face down, in the hallway. He immediately called the police. I felt for Örjan. He was a broken man. They had been best buddies for a long, long time, and to find your closest friend like this would be a terrible blow.

Örjan also alerted my uncle Pettan, who had called on Berit. At first they had thought my father was still alive, as there had been some mention of hospital, but once the confusion and panic had cleared it became evident there had been no time, or need, for a hospital. He was gone. There was a reference in the story to blood in the flat, and with that I painted my own picture.

The night before I was due to fly I slept not a wink. I sat bolt upright, queasy with shock and whisky. I walked through the airport like a robot, encased in a shell of pain and sorrow, feeling as though I stood out like a sore thumb with my red eyes and swollen face spelling grief. It hurt to speak, and I wanted to be silent and alone. Words were doing a figure of eight in my head – my father's dead, I won't see him again, I miss him, I love him, my father's dead – over and over again. On the plane I defiantly polished off seven Bloody Marys – which, for an 8 a.m. flight, wasn't bad. The hostesses remained dignified even if I did not. I made notes in my diary, scribbling thoughts and the beginnings of funeral arrangements. I felt I had to be in charge, that I was at the helm of his very small family. My sister was about to turn nineteen, and my father had no wife. I had to be the strong one – I had to lead the way.

However, I didn't do much leading the second I embraced my sister at the airport. We stood and sobbed in each other's arms, then fought through the grief to talk about practicalities. I told her and Berit that I felt cold and sick and that I felt hungry. They replied that *they* had not eaten for two days – the very thought of eating left them cold. And boy, was it cold. It was some twenty degrees below and Sweden lay under a duvet of white snow. It felt bizarre to not be picked up at the airport by my father. It felt strange to be in my country without him. It felt wrong to not be staying in his flat. But his flat, my former home, had become in my mind a place of

great fear, anxiety and doom. I didn't sleep well that night, overwhelmed by nausea and an incessant hunger. Berit couldn't sleep
either and watched in amazement as I filled myself with cereal.

*

The next day we had an appointment at the local police station,
where we would be able to reclaim my father's flat keys and one or
two other personal items he had had on him. It was all so foreign
and frightening. I wasn't ready for this; I wanted someone to protect
me. I wanted to ask questions; wanted to talk to the people who had
carried my father's body away; wanted to shake their hands and for
them to tell me what he looked like. I could no longer remember.

The inspector was kind and gentle. He offered us coffee in his
office, which irritated me as I felt it was surplus to requirements. He
must have looked at the three of us and known his job was going to
be a hard one. None of us took him up on the offer. I couldn't stop
the river of tears spilling from my eyes. I struggled to speak to him
and answer his questions. I was at pains to articulate any words,
which seemed to want to slide out of my mouth sideways. My face
felt hard, and there was a relentless stream of secretions from my
nose. It was as if my tongue and cheeks had been anaesthetized by
the dentist and I was battling to keep them mobile.

He explained how the alarm had been raised and in what my
position my father had been found. He described that there was
'blood and mess' left in the flat and that a window had been broken
by the police to gain access. I didn't care about the window, for
God's sake, what about my dad? He was at a mortuary where they
would do an autopsy, we were told, when they had time, but this
was the festive season, so don't be impatient. Not very fucking
festive for us, I thought. But as he took us through descriptions and
practicalities his own eyes filled with tears and I could see he, too,
was feeling for us. I wanted him to hold me, to hug me and tell
me that it had all been a terrible mistake and that it was, in fact,
someone else's father who had died so tragically. But instead he
handed me my father's keys and his silver bracelet, which he had

been wearing when he died. I gave my sister the bracelet, but held onto the keys with a force. And as I looked down at them and felt their rough and smooth edges, my eyes blurred again and soon tears were dropping onto the shiny silver objects in my hands. It was all too much to bear. I didn't want them – I wanted my dad.

As we left the police station and drove reluctantly in the direction of the flat, Berit suggested she go in first, just in case the scene was too traumatic. I was scared, but remained adamant that I would be first to enter. My sister was more reticent, so I said I would check things out and come back to report on what state the flat was in. But as I put the keys in the lock, it became clear that none of us could stay away. Berit stood behind me with Linda behind her as I opened the door. I walked straight in – and stopped. On the hall floor, directly in front of me, was a large pool of dark, dried blood. 'Oh, God, no!' I exclaimed. My eyes welled up once more. I jumped over the dark sea and was immediately overwhelmed by the smell. Despite the chill in the flat, due to the unrepaired broken glass and lack of heating, there was a stench of dried blood and faeces, coupled with the fragrance of the hyacinths my father had grown in a pot for Christmas. The smell was vulgar and sweet. On further inspection the blood had made its way halfway across the hallway and some of it was wiped across the walls in the vicinity. Little paw marks of blood made their way in confusion around the area where my father had lain. The blood marks were thick, dark and heavy. I was so overwhelmed by their smell and my nausea that I immediately turned into the living room. Berit stepped inside, but my sister was so overcome that she let out a yell and turned away. 'It's OK, it's OK,' I called to her, knowing full well that it absolutely wasn't. I wanted to hold her, but wasn't sure I had the strength to cross back over the sea of death to get to her.

Berit was appalled and mumbled and swore in bewilderment. As we looked around the living room we could see the leftovers of my father's last movements – an opened newspaper, a tall half-empty glass and even the impressions left by him on the sofa. In the corner the answering machine was flashing with messages and I knew one of them was mine, left before I knew he was dead. Scared to touch anything, but wanting to touch everything, I tried to move around the flat further, but felt like a stranger in my own father's home. I was also irrationally scared I was going to find him all over again, lying dead on the kitchen floor, or slumped in a permanent sleep at the table, even though I knew his body was somewhere else. But his spirit was still there. I wanted to absorb him; I wanted to wear him. And all the time I knew he was watching me.

After much coaxing and comforting I encouraged my sister to step inside, calling out descriptions to her across the threshold to reduce the shock for her. Eventually, she relented, needing to see things for herself. Berit's immediate reaction was that we had to clean. I knew we had to, but I wanted either that someone would do it for us, or that we could leave all the traces of my father's dying moments as they were. We also had to call a glazier. Within no time darkness fell and we scrubbed the blood and shit from floor and walls still wearing our boots and coats because it was so freezing. Despite the horrendous circumstances, my body was telling me I needed to eat again, but I didn't dare suggest it, as it seemed disrespectful.

Later, I looked through my father's things a little. Touching and smelling his towels, his sheets, and holding the glass he had drunk out of fondly. There was so much 'stuff' in his drawers and cupboard that I became overwhelmed by the thought of having to sort it all out at some stage. A little like Queen Victoria when Prince Albert had died, I wanted to leave his things in their place, only taking out clothes for him to wear each day and keeping the flat clean. I didn't want it tidy. I wanted Tutan's tiny paw marks to be left where they were. I wanted to keep things just so. And at that moment I became overwhelmed by the sudden history of the flat. It would never be the same again. I would never stay there again. I would never pass my father in the hallway again. I would never hug him or speak to him again.

I had just settled myself down next to my sister when the phone rang. We both looked at each other, wondering what to do. I asked her if I should pick it up and she nodded. So I answered the phone as I always had done there, with simply the name 'Jonsson'. To my disbelief, amazement and gall, on the other end of the phone was a reporter from the English press wanting to speak to my father about his daughter's imminent divorce and infidelities. I stood up, my legs tensed, and shouted that my father wasn't there because he was dead, and would he please fuck off and leave us alone. But the journalist was not put off. He didn't see my news as a reason for not speaking about 'Ulrika's failed marriage', until I shouted for respect and shook the receiver so violently it virtually fell out of my hand. He obviously had no idea he was talking to me. I was incensed. We sat on in virtual silence for some three hours before the glazier arrived to make my childhood home secure.

Over the next few days, we visited friends of my father's and wept with them. I also went to visit my disorientated grandma, who had just lost her 53-year-old son. She was confused and had already been showing signs of dementia before this; my father's death was not likely to help her. And I carried on eating for both my father and myself, not to mention Berit and Linda. I was woken in the night several times with my continuing nausea, and the night before I left had severe period pains. Better late than never. I was already four days late.

I had to return to England and was almost as empty of knowledge as I had been when I arrived. We had no date for a funeral. No cause of death. And had had no opportunity to see my father. We had cleaned my father's flat, which would now be put up for rent to someone else. We had also arranged for Tutan to go and stay with Örjan and we knew that we wanted the funeral in the beautiful local church where both Linda and I had been christened, and where Linda had been confirmed. And we had met with the funeral directors to arrange the newspaper announcement of my father's death, and to pick out the nicest wooden box for him to be laid in, whenever we would get his body back. I told my sister I wanted to make our father's funeral a reflection of his life. I didn't want a sombre mood, with coffee and cake. I wanted music, food and drink. She agreed, which filled me with enthusiasm and optimism. I knew he was watching me.

Attending to these things is perhaps something everyone has to deal with at some stage in their lives, but you never expect to actually have to do it. You aren't quite sure what the form is, but somehow you pass from pillar to post and dodge your way to the finish line in an automated if emotional fashion. I couldn't stop weeping wherever we went. I couldn't hold it in. And I trust I wasn't expected to. Then again, even though everyone is so sorry for your bereavement, life goes on, despite your fight to stop it doing so.

When my period had still not come on the day I was due to travel, I needed to confirm that it was due to the shock of my father's death – and nothing else. I knew I couldn't buy a pregnancy test in England without it making the gossip columns of the tabloids, so decided to buy one in Sweden, where I was considerably less likely to be spotted, just in case. I said nothing to my sister. But little did I know that Berit had cottoned on to something already. In the airport lounge I made copious notes about what I thought my father would have wanted for his send-off, whilst downing a third Bloody Mary. The alcohol seemed not to affect me, but the nausea still did. Without thinking about it I took the pregnancy test with me to the toilet and peed on the stick. I was delighted to find a line appear in the second window of the stick. It meant I was in the clear. I *had* just been in shock. But as I looked through the instructions just before I threw it away, I knew immediately I had got it completely wrong. A second line meant just the opposite. I was as pregnant as you could possibly be. Shit.

FIGHTING GOD

Armed and laden with this fresh complication, I arrived back home. For someone so maternal, I was amazed at my nonchalance about the most recent development. There was no way I was going to have a baby right now. By a man I was just getting to know, just a couple of months after my separation and merely a year after my first child. Besides, I had had more sunbeds in the previous months than Judith Chalmers has in a year, and had consumed more whisky and vodka in the past week than George Best has done in twenty. With the preoccupation of my father's death it struck me that there was no other way to deal with it. I had a funeral to arrange and a collection of cells to get rid of.

I refused myself any feeling towards the thing growing inside me. To remain detached I refused to acknowledge it was anything resembling a human being. My focus of attention needed to be on my father, not on another fuck-up in my life. So I became desperately matter-of-fact about it. And desperate. Was I being punished for my infidelity? I wondered. Had God sent my father to his death to serve me right? And had he decided to test me further with an unwanted pregnancy to teach me a lesson about the looseness of my loins and unsafe sex? This was a double whammy. I couldn't do anything about my father's death, except make his passing over to the other side a joyous event, but I could do something about becoming a mother second time around, with a lover of only twenty-two. I maintained the belief that I was being punished, and remained firm that I had to take the punishment standing, come what may.

I phoned Melanie and told her. We had to keep it from the press. They would have a field day with news of 'Ulrika's abortion'. It would add such colour and dimension to my troubled present. I made an appointment with a doctor and made plans to tell James. Melanie thought I shouldn't. I felt James had a right to know: not because I thought he should be allowed to change my mind, but because we had both made 'it' happen and as one half of a whole, he should know.

James had been aware of and slightly concerned about the delay in my period, but was nonetheless floored by the news. I told him I wasn't going to have the child and that, in my opinion and reasoning, he would not want it either. He was having an affair with a 28-year-old mother of one. He was in no position to want a child with me. Besides, I had to tell myself, it wasn't a child. He said he would support me in whatever I had decided, but the look of relief on his face was clear. That night, for just an instant, he put his hand on my belly and said, 'Just think.' I took his hand away with the words, 'No, let's not think. It's too painful.'

My mother phoned the next day to ask how my trip to Sweden had gone, and wondered if there was anything she could do upon her return. 'Yes,' I said, 'you can drive me to the hospital next Monday for my termination.' She became quiet and sympathetic, and asked me how it had happened. I didn't think then was the time to tell her about the birds and the bees, so said simply, 'Because I'm a silly fucking cow, that's how.'

I was booked under a different name and spoke briefly to my unforgiving gynaecologist before the procedure. He gave me a telling-off for playing Russian roulette with my sex life and recommended he fitted a coil once he had removed what needed removing. I agreed. I didn't really have a leg to stand on. Mum also took me home after the operation, which in my mind had to be thought of as the removal of a mole or cyst, or something equally inanimate, otherwise I would have gone over the edge. I wanted to get home and carry on planning my father's funeral.

We were finally given a date – 25 January, almost one month

after his death. I had become fairly obsessed with the arrangements. I was very sure about the elements that needed to be part of the day and set about it like someone organizing a wedding. I wanted bagpipes, which my father had loved; a trumpet; a solo; flowers, food and drink. My father had lived his life to the extreme and I wanted the funeral to reflect that. He would have wanted to see his friends eat, drink and be merry. I also had to try to track people down – old friends, even long-lost ex-girlfriends, and Berit and Linda helped with whatever they could.

I spoke to our lovely vicar and insisted that as my father hadn't been a church-going man, the service needed to reflect that and have an element of lightness about it. I wanted my father to be referred to as 'Bosse', which was his nickname and how everybody knew him. There needed to be lightness and an element of humour about the day, too. He sounded obliging and was actually excited by the thought of the bagpipes in the church. And I knew my dad would be, too.

I was very definite about the flowers, too. I wanted masses of white lilies and ivy trailing the coffin. I love white lilies and thought they would bring class to his wooden box. The church would also be filled with candles. And I knew I wanted to make a personal contribution to the service, and found a verse I wanted to read. In English. Everybody would understand its poignancy, with its words of reassurance that my father's death was not the end of him, but that he was just in the next room. I felt anxious about doing it as I wasn't sure how the day would affect me, but I also knew I didn't want to feel any regrets later about not having said anything. My sister was too shy to read, and that was fine, because it was totally in keeping with her personality.

The biggest issue, apart from the funeral, was if I wanted to go and see my father before he was cremated. I felt confident that I didn't want to go if the lasting memory of my father would be of a corpse in a coffin. My father had been so alive that I was struggling to picture him dead. But I also knew I *needed* to see him. I needed his death to be registered in my head and in my heart and, above all else, I needed to tell him how pissed off I was that he had given us no warning. I had requested he be dressed in one of his ghastly shell suits. I couldn't imagine him in a pretty white frilled robe.

As Linda, Berit, Pettan, my cousin Cecilia and I drove to the chapel of rest, Sweden still lay under in a thick, thick layer of snow, and the three o'clock dusk brought with it an eerie silence and quite a dramatic sense of chill. I knocked on the door and a man opened it, asking me to confirm that we were coming to say farewell to Mr Blomqvist. My heart stopped. No, we were here to see Bo Jonsson. Don't tell me they've lost him, I thought. I need to see him. The man disappeared and returned to confirm that I was absolutely right, and would we like to come in? No, not really, but we must, I felt like saying. As we took our snow clothes off in the anteroom, I felt electrical pulses of fear and sorrow running through my body, petrified, overwhelmed and in absolute disbelief at what I was about to do. There was a counsellor at hand, provided by the funeral director, and I needed him desperately. I told him I wasn't sure. I told him I was scared. He sat me down, took my hand and talked to me calmly. He told me I didn't have to go in and see my father, and that I could take all the time in the world. And he asked me to remember that my father was no longer in pain; it was only those of us he had left behind who felt pain now. It seemed a strange thing to hear, but as it registered with my brain, I knew in my heart that he was absolutely right. Slowly the door was opened to the little chapel and as I reluctantly lifted my head to look inside I clutched the counsellor's hand and dug my nails into it firmly. I couldn't let go and told him he had to come with me. Then as I looked in I turned on my heel and bolted the other way.

'Why have they put different hands on my father? Those are not his hands. What have they done?' I screamed, aghast. What I had seen were two hands on top of my father's body, slender and brown with purple nails, in a 'prayer' grasp. My father wouldn't have put his hands like that – and those were certainly not his hands. Our counsellor tried to explain to me that they had changed a little from when I saw them last. Changed! My God! They were positively inhuman. He suggested he cover them up and that I should maybe try to go back in.

I entered the room at a snail's pace, clutching the counsellor's hand once more. I talked loudly as I approached. I was scared. I was scared he was going to sit bolt upright and start laughing. As I came closer I could see that it was my father. He looked so still and hard and cold. His foundation was all wrong, and they had forced him into a ridiculous choirboy gown, after all. At least, I thought when I got closer and sat myself down next to the coffin, finally letting go of the counsellor's hand, I could see that his nose was intact. He had such a definite nose. But the rest of his face was rather sunken and a strange grey-brown colour. His eyelids had been glued together and his hair combed to one side. All perfect, apart from the right side of his face where he had hit the floor with force. His right eye was a little bruised and damaged. But it was still my father. Attempts had been made to cover up the back of his head where they had had to open him up in order to establish the cause of death, but I could still see the large hole.

My father, we had learned, had had a brain haemorrhage and died instantaneously as the pain had struck him and he the floor. He had been on his way from the living room into the kitchen, with just a towel around his waist, getting himself ready for a date.

I wept and spoke to him gently, like you might to a baby – asking him what he had gone and done and telling him he was so silly. I talked without stopping to catch my breath. I told him how I knew he could hear me and that I loved him so completely. I realized I so wanted to touch him. The thought scared me, but I told myself I wouldn't leave until I had touched him and kissed him. I even told the counsellor to remove the white napkin covering my father's hands, because I wanted to see them. As he did so, I was taken aback at how slender his normally fat, sausage-like fingers had become. They were almost skinny and the nails were dark and long. My father bit his nails and I had never seen them this long. But his nose was still perfect.

I left him briefly to go and get my sister. She, too, was reluctant and sobbed her way into the room, turning to leave on several occasions. Eventually I was able to persuade her to stay and we sat there together. I told him all the things I wanted to tell him and some things he already knew, and then my sister and I were allowed to close and lock the coffin. And that was the last time I saw my father.

*

I had made arrangements for Cameron's nanny to look after him back at home as I feared I would not be able to concentrate on him fully during the trip. John decided to come, but not without a fight. I knew my dad would want him there, and so did I. He *should* be there – he was close to my dad and they loved each other. Tensions were still running high between us. But when he arrived we polished off a decent bottle of single malt together, exchanging stories of my father past and very past.

The effect of the spirit was still with me the following day. I spent the morning rather unattractively on the toilet, but managed to gain control of my stomach in time for my mother's arrival. The limo picked us up at half past two and in silence we made our way to the church. I had decided I didn't want to look dour and plain, but instead wanted to dress myself like my father would have wanted. I wore a leather skirt, high heels and stockings. He would have smirked – maybe he did. As we entered the churchyard I was focused, but not enough to not be distracted by the flashing of a press cameraman running towards me up the path to the church. John ran ahead and 'disposed' of him, as well as two other hacks who had placed themselves in the centre pews of the church, claiming they had a right to be there, because they had come all the way from London. If John hadn't got rid of them, I would have. Grief gives you a strength, or maybe even an anger, which enables you to drive through any wall, climb any mountain and swim any ocean. I was in that state. I would have punched anyone in my way – not terribly Christian I know, but surely God didn't want me to miss the service?

My Christianity, whichever state it was in, failed me a little during the whole mourning period, or maybe I failed it. I was aware that in the Jewish religion a set of practices takes place after a death. You go through a process of events that help you focus on your faith and the person deceased. I feel my Christianity didn't seem to show me the way in that respect. I didn't know how to behave, what to do, what to think. I tried, but found it wanting.

Nonetheless, there we eventually were. In the church saying a last and final farewell to the man whose spirit occupied the most of me. The priest said his piece. I said mine. A soloist sang 'The Road to Mandalay', which my father had loved. A trumpet sounded Last Post and bagpipes led us out to the sound of 'Scotland the Brave'. And that was that. My father's popularity was expressed by the presence of the hundreds of people who showed for the service and the masses and masses of flowers laid on his coffin and pressed against the outside wall of the church. There were messages from companies, sports clubs, football teams, colleagues, close friends, former lovers, boat club members and driving institutions. It was overwhelming and I felt proud. For my part I lay a single red rose on his coffin from me, and a yellow one from his darling grandson, before proceeding to a fabulous local *krog* for food, drink and merriment. And so we all said our final goodbye to Bosse Jonsson.

*

I returned home, but not before I had arranged the shipping of some of my father's belongings back to me. We had sold the furniture in his flat to a house-clearance company, whose representative walked through it with total disregard for our grief and stuck stickers on items with a value of nothing. It was heart-rending to go through, but so essential.

Now I had said goodbye I felt my father no longer sat above my right shoulder looking on. He had truly left me. But now the real grieving took place – now that everyone expected me to be over it. I was nowhere near over it. I wept every day; welled up and sobbed privately. I tried, of course, to give an impression of sanity and well-being, but I was struggling. And my heart, my heart was so, so tired and bruised. It ached immeasurably.

But even if I felt I was losing the fight inside, life had to move on. James suggested a holiday, and whilst I had little enthusiasm I knew I was exhausted and it would be welcome. We went to Guadeloupe and I left Cameron with John. It was a struggle leaving Cameron, but everything was a struggle at that time. I also went to Paris to take part in a live link with David Frost, where Uri Geller would draw a picture of an image in my mind. He got it right, of course. I also went on Radio 4's *Loose Ends* with Ned Sherrin, which was a great honour for such a now-avid Radio 4 listener as myself And this was followed by a pilot with a little-known TV presenter called Johnny Vaughn, who would later invite me on a pilot of his own, where I believe I played ping-pong with David Hamilton. What a life! I also went for my first appointment with darling hairdresser Charles Worthington, Queen of Hairdressing, and have loved him ever since.

I had to get myself a lawyer as the divorce was proving tricky, messy and aggressive. It was to be expected, I guess, but painful nonetheless. The lawyers were soon arguing the toss over money. In the end as we stood, literally, on the threshold of a court appearance I asked him to come and thrash out a deal with me personally. No middlemen. And to my pride and amazement we managed to come to an agreement. After six hours. It was a relief for both of us, and I think we were both satisfied with the outcome. Damage limitation and all that.

*

When just after Easter we did some more live shows of *Gladiators* at Wembley, it was the first time I was both working with James and in a relationship with him. The work side of things was going well, but the relationship side was already showing signs of some foreboding. James became utterly consumed by his job, whereas I could switch off from it during the periods in between. He became

distant – 'focused' or 'locked in', as he would call it – at the expense
of everyone around him. To take second place and a step back was a
little hard when we had grown so close and so emotional. Of this
man who had been so loving throughout my time with him, I was
now seeing another persona emerging. One I didn't like. A life of
pure and unadulterated dedication to the shape and fitness of his
body from the age of thirteen showed commitment, but also a love
of himself that was beginning to go beyond anything I might run
the danger of comprehending. When we went to Mauritius to shoot
later in the year, he was incredibly offhand and dismissive. I was
hurt, and tried time and time again to talk it over with him, but
he was deaf to anything beyond hanging out with his friends, or
improving on his body. Both were to the exclusion of me. But upon
our return, once he was away from work, he became the cute, loving
and affectionate James I had fallen in love with.

With *Shooting Stars* having become such a huge success, the
BBC decided to release a video for Christmas. This involved photo
sessions, rehearsals for sketches and the opening titles and generally
much messing around with the boys. I always had happy times with
them and they always succeeded in distracting me. Their distractions
were always accompanied by a few drinks, and as a result many
fantastic moments remain rather blurred in my memory. The show
had now established itself as rather more than cult, and there was
even talk of a live *Shooting Stars* tour. There was for me a very
clear dichotomy in taking part in two such different programmes.
They each required a certain degree of irony, but for one I had to
hide it somewhat and maintain a respectful front (*Gladis*) while for
the other I was encouraged to air it as regularly as possible. I don't
believe I've ever lost the ability to take things seriously on the one
hand (something which is hard for a true comedian), or to have the
piss taken out of me on the other.

I had by now become very well known for being able to down a
pint of lager in fifteen seconds on the show, but it was, of course,
not without practice. Bob had originally asked me to perform this
prank as he thought it would be the most unlikely thing I could be

seen to do. He was right and wrong. I can take my drink, but it didn't really go with the image of 'the girl next door' created for me some years back by TV-am. But I was as happy to take on the new role as I had been the old one. Because that is exactly what both were. Then, I had been a reassuring and sunny face for family viewing. Now, we were trying to make people laugh with ridiculous actions, words and faces. But it sat uneasy with certain aspects of society who, I suspect, did not like the idea of a woman enjoying a pint. Or two. It was the start of a new celebrity-culture sub-species known as the 'ladette', and apparently I was among the first of its breed.

I was proud to attend my sister's ceremonial end-of-school celebrations in June. She was eighteen, and I needed to be with her and to represent my father. She had done so well in her exams, despite our father's death six months earlier. By the looks of things on the day, she too had been practising drinking. Well done, old girl!

I was cramming a lot in, and hit my limit when I came home for only forty-eight hours after the *Gladiators* shoot in Mauritius before heading off to Hawaii for ITV's *Wish You Were Here*. I didn't know my limits then, but I do now as a result of that quick turnaround. Traumatized by having to leave Cameron so soon, and to go so far away, I knew as I arrived at Gatwick that I was emotionally unstable. I was travelling with a male producer, a cameraman and a sound man. I felt vulnerable and was suffering the most unbearable longing for my darling son – and I was surrounded by men who I thought wouldn't begin to understand. Upon arrival in Hawaii we were met by a female representative. When she asked me how I was, I simply exploded in a fit of tears for Cameron. My God! I missed him beyond belief, and this job hadn't even started yet – it would be another ten days before we would be together again. The only comfort was that the islands of Hawaii were absolutely stunning and I was kept working from dawn until dusk. Don't ever believe those holiday programmes are a holiday. On most days we were shooting from seven in the morning until ten or eleven at night. All for a three and a half minute film! Crazy.

When I finally returned home I couldn't wait to be reunited with the light of my life. It was truly wonderful to smell, touch and kiss Cameron again. I was also to be reunited with my not-so-under-standing boyfriend. I had missed him, too, and had called him every day despite the time difference. But what happened when I was working and became involved in *my* job was a different story to what I had experienced when James worked. I remained close to him verbally, emotionally and psychologically, even if I was on a job halfway across the world. I opened up to him and exposed my longing and my love for him, but what I got in return was nothing short of immature tit for tat. He couldn't handle that I was away. He couldn't handle that there were other men in the world and I would be exposed to them. I went on reassuring him and staying in close touch, but he became cold and distant and was suddenly going out every night I was away. I completely trusted him, and believed he trusted me, but something was lacking. We were, despite all that had gone on between us, not made of the same stuff.

Even when I was back, juggling weeknight shows with the Saturday evening National Lottery draw on the BBC, I began to sense that my boyfriend wasn't thriving on the amount of work and the profile I was getting. I was always grateful for work and never cocky or self-assured, but it seemed to me that there was something in James that wanted to deny me my success. He would never say that, of course. Perhaps it was tough for a man to be less well known than his woman, and a lower earner too – although as far as I was concerned we were equals. We would often clash when discussing work, so I stopped discussing it. He couldn't understand why I might turn a job down, or demand a higher payment, for something he would have done for a quarter of the fee.

James didn't find Cameron an immediate threat, but he did struggle with his young age and found it difficult to communicate with him. Cameron, on the other hand, who was fast growing into a sensitive, bright and well-behaved little person, had an affection for James – as he did for most males – and thought he was fun. But I didn't want to work on their relationship. I felt it was far more important that Cameron had an excellent relationship with his father, rather than with a young man who showed him no real commitment. And James was also faltering in his commitment to me. One night when we were lying next to each other I whispered to him, 'You are losing me!' But he refused to listen.

I celebrated my birthday in August while up in Birmingham for the latest *Gladiators*, as I had done for the past few years, yet it went largely unnoticed by a man with greater priorities – something which brought back unwanted childhood memories. James continued to see his job, his role and his friends as his priority, and refused even to spend a night in my hotel room during the shoot – he felt it would distract him from his 'locking in'. I talked a lot to his mother who tried to give me some insight into her son's behaviour, some-thing she had lived with for a number of years. And she asked me not to take it personally. But I found it hard to switch on and off like he did, and to take his nonchalance on the chin. Instead of taking a step back, I would go the other way and reach out more, only to have my attentions thrown back in my face. So smitten was I by him that I carried on taking it.

The crunch came when I wanted to bank some time with Cameron before the *Shooting Stars* tour. I decided that a holiday was what I wanted. However, my boyfriend had other ideas. He did not see a holiday with Cameron as a holiday. After much thinking and hurting and not understanding I put it to him that if he didn't like it he didn't have to come: Cameron was a priority and that was how it would stay. So he said he didn't want to come. More thinking. More hurt and more not understanding. Then he changed his mind. I felt disappointed, but we all set off for Florida together, me dedicated to my lively nearly two-year-old, but compromised by my 23-year-old. James spent the holiday doing every conceivable sport from dawn to dusk, and asking me to put Cameron in the children's club. I refused: it would have defeated the object of taking him on holiday. I actually like my children, and value my time with them – and I loved Cameron with such ferocious intensity that I even found it hard to be without him. No amount of love from another man could replace that.

We returned just in time for Cameron's second birthday and I threw a party, but James headed straight back up to York. I invited Jim Moir, alias Vic Reeves, to come up from Kent with his beloved daughter Alice. I had grown close to Jim over the past couple of years, but not in an amorous way – I also knew his wife, Sarah. Yet I had a deep respect, affection and admiration for Jim, and he made me laugh tremendously. Things were also not right between him and his wife, as it was becoming evident that she had decided to take the infidelity route I knew so well. Jim was a broken man. He cared so deeply for little Alice and was in real fear of losing her. I wanted to support him and talked at length with him. I almost knew too much about the whole subject – ironically from the other side of the fence, although I knew how it felt to feel so torn about your child. That is how we became close.

One week before we were due to set off on tour, he phoned to say he was calling the tour off. He needed to be with Alice at this difficult time and felt that going off on tour might jeopardize his chances of custody. I sympathized and felt relieved that I, too, could now be spending time with Cameron, instead of leaving him for a couple of nights here and there over the coming month. But it became clear that too many venues had already been booked and too much money would be lost. I was planning on splitting the care of Cameron over the period three ways: between myself, John and the nanny. I would travel on our 'rock and roll' bus for some of the tour, and drive for the rest to enable me to get home to the apple of my eye. I told Jim that he should do the same and that my nanny could mind Alice when she minded Cameron on location. There was just over a year between the children.

The *Shooting Stars* tour kicked off on 1 November in Manchester. Doing a live comedy show on stage is quite, quite different to doing it in a television studio for a recording. We had rehearsed humorous song-and-dance routines, set up gags and learnt certain lines and set-ups. The rest was up to the boys and the audience. So, there was a certain amount that was rehearsed, but one could not rehearse everyone's mood for a show, and sometimes we would all be on top form – other times some of us weren't. And the feedback and reaction from the audiences could easily make or break that fantastic TV atmosphere we were attempting to recreate on stage. It was amazing how important the audience became. I would say our best audiences were up north, where the people know how to have a good time and appreciate the shows coming to their areas. Guests on the teams came in the form of local celebrities who were as a general rule very accomplished. I wouldn't say we were pissed before the shows, but often we would partake in a beer before kick-off – we were, after all, sponsored by Carlsberg. Seemed rude not to.

Just before I departed I had developed the most horrendous eczema around my eyes and lips. It was painful and unsightly. Having to apply make-up every night for the shows didn't help. In fact, nothing helped. Even the mildest dermatological cream seemed to aggravate it. I wasn't sure what to put it down to, but decided to cut out all dairy and wheat products – not the most flexible of diets when you're running around the country and only able to grab a mouthful of anything to eat. It proved incredibly cleansing and slimming, but did nothing for my eczema. I suspect that the condition was a delayed reaction to the emotional trauma of my divorce, the termination and the death of my father. I had got through all these without becoming unwell, but now my body was telling me to slow down and react to what had happened. But did I?

On the first leg of the tour, while we were up in Manchester, I let slip that I was a United fan to our gorgeous Evertonian promoter, Paul Roberts. Paul was the sweetest, kindest man, with a laugh that would drown out even the loudest of noises. I actually thought he was very cute and was very taken with him. But he had a girlfriend, and I supposedly had a boyfriend, so I kept a respectful distance. But he did very kindly arrange for us to go to Old Trafford on the

Saturday to watch Man U play Chelsea. I was dead excited, and Jim insisted on coming too. He hadn't a clue about football, but in the absence of our children and nothing much else to do during the day, he accompanied me enthusiastically and amused me throughout the ninety minutes with his ignorance about the game. He was great company wherever you might be. Thankfully, Paul and I *were* able to talk footie and I cannot tell you what a thrill it was to finally enter the Theatre of Dreams. We were even invited for a drink in the players' lounge after the game. Football, funny men and Old Trafford. What a fucking day!

But no sooner had I left the ground than James was on the phone. He was tense, accusing and not a happy man. He had been contacted by the press to ask if it was over between us, as I had been pictured sitting next to Jim at the footie. I took his concerns seriously, but assured him that there were four of us at the game and I just happened to be sitting next to Jim. The truth was exactly that, but also that Jim was a wonderful companion and great company, as I was fast finding James a selfish, self-orientated, self-serving 'partner'. However, I had absolutely no intentions as far as Jim went, and was just in his company because we were working together.

The following day there was a big article about Jim and me in the *Mail on Sunday*. It claimed that we must be having an affair as Jim's marriage had faltered and we were wearing matching leather trousers. We both laughed and joked about the piece and I spoke to James about how ridiculous it was. He came to Manchester just to be sure, but was already decided in his mind, and we had a somewhat strained lunch.

After that first stint, we went across to Liverpool and I brought my nanny and Cameron with me. On the days off Jim and I took Cameron to Chester Zoo and Tate Liverpool. Jim, being a father, had a totally different attitude towards Cameron than James. He treated him with interest, respect and humour. It was so relaxed between us all. Cameron adored Jim, whom he called 'Bim'. With Bob in tow we also went to Blackpool for a day of donkey rides and fish and chips. The famous double act were now dubbed 'Bim and Bob' by my gorgeous boy.

By contrast, things were going from weakness to weakness on the Hunter front. After Nottingham, and with ever-renewed enthusiasm, I took myself off to see him for a day and a night between Hull and Wolverhampton. My face was still angry with eczema and I felt very down about 'us'. How could things be beyond repair when I still had so much love to give? As tit for tat, James was going out and getting himself photographed with other girls, and at one point he made it impossible to reach him, saying afterwards he'd had a night out with Gladiator friends – 'Nothing important, just like your relationship with Jim.' It was the most hurtful thing he could have said.

At the end of the evening's performance in Brighton a crowd of us gathered in the bar. With Carlsberg running fast through my veins I spent the evening kicking fag ends out of the mouth of a handsome young man, who later reciprocated by throwing prawns at me. That young man was Norman Cook.

In Bournemouth I spent a drunken night in the hotel bar with Mark Lamarr. We had always had a love-hate relationship, with perhaps a bit more hate than love. I knew he didn't like me and I didn't particularly like him either, but we were working together, so I would bite my tongue. Mark never drank very much and was rarely drunk. That night, however, he bought me a drink and we both got quite merry after the show. We talked and I found I didn't dislike him as much as I thought I had. In fact we had a bit of a snog, which must say something about the state of my relationship with James.

By now it was getting on for a year since my father's death, a fact which was brought home to me all the more when news reached us – after Newport, Reading and two nights in Cambridge – that Matt Lucas's father had died suddenly. I really felt for him. There was a side of me that didn't want to come to terms with the passing of my own father for fear of forgetting him. Three nights ended up being cancelled in Glasgow, two in Newcastle and one each in Blackburn and Preston, and the only positive was more time with Cameron.

When our tour kicked off again in York, with a grieving but enthusiastic Matt on board, James had ironically taken up rehearsals in panto in Portsmouth. I felt it was time to start bringing our own curtains down. The daily struggle to maintain lines of communication was proving pointless, as was being part of a relationship that was actually taking a toll on me. Our lines clearly weren't going to meet – they were parallel, and widening if anything. He only had decreasing understanding for my life, my life with Cameron and what I thought we could achieve. I felt his priorities were cosmetic and superficial – his body, his sports and their attendant needs. Nothing was allowed to get in the way of all that. It was certainly no longer enough to have great sex.

On the second night in York, James turned up completely unexpectedly in the bar after the show. I didn't want him there that time. I had spoken to him the day before and told him I found it hard to proceed with whatever we had. But that was why he had rushed up from Portsmouth, in an attempt to rescue the ever-dwindling 'us'. I wasn't flattered, which I would normally have been. I felt compromised. We talked a little more and I explained that despite loving him, I was now not sure that was enough. He left wishing, I'm sure, he hadn't bothered.

After Oxford, Ipswich, Brighton and Bradford we were due to finish off with two nights in Bristol. We were coming close to Christmas, and once again I found myself unenthusiastic about the event. I was scared of the memories it might stir up from the previous year. James would be down in Portsmouth for the duration, and in any event, things weren't going to improve. I was relieved that the tour was coming to an end, but knew I would miss the guys and the team. Jim had by now reunited with Sarah – I was happy for him, but I couldn't help but feel I had lost my friend. Even the gorgeous Paul Roberts was looking forward to a Christmas with his girlfriend. I wasn't convinced Jim's reunion would be long lived.

Perhaps I was biased – his wife had done a piece in the paper blaming Jim's fascination with me for the break-up of her marriage. What-ever happened to putting your own house in order first? Far be it for me to comment, but Jim and I had behaved impeccably throughout, if a little ridiculously.

By now, of course, you should be getting used to the pattern. Despite having told him I believed it was over, I didn't quite let the James thing go. He kept calling and I kept feeling for him, and even that it was wrong to be without him. Not that it felt so right to be with him. We did spend Christmas apart, but shortly after I found myself in Portsmouth, only to have the instant gratification of holding him and loving him disappear the following morning with a repeat of a well-rehearsed argument. It was exhausting and frustrat-ing. I felt I loved him, but didn't understand why any more. But I also no longer felt we were suited.

The anniversary of my father's death hit on 29 December with tears, sorrow and a painful longing. This was the day he had died, although the authorities in Sweden would only recognize New Year's Eve, the day he had been found. I marked the whole period crying and with phone calls to my sister, whom I missed, too. With hindsight it was a mistake that we were apart, but the most wonderful thing was that we had grown so much closer since he had left us, and in a way closer to him in so being.

I guess I had become depressed without really acknowledging it. I felt as if there were a thousand loose ends in my life and I had no means of tying them together. I was regularly overwhelmed by panic attacks, thoughts of my father sandwiched between worries about work, panics about my life – not to mention my being and my outlook – and a general feeling of being lost and out of sorts. When I opened the Boat Show at Earls Court on 2 January, I thought of him as I wandered between the shiny sail and motor boats, wishing he was there by my side.

NAKED

I was asked to shoot a commercial for Walkers Lite crisps with Gary
Lineker. The idea was to further the story of Gary's love of the
crisps not coming between him and anything else – even a beautiful
woman (me, apparently). The commercial was going to be shot as a
classy black-and-white film à la Ingmar Bergman. It was styled as
the 1930s, and we were to conduct the entire commercial in Swedish.
Despite my eczema-ridden face and a depression hanging over me, I
have never laughed so much in my life. Mr Lineker was to blame.
Hearing him speak Swedish with the most hilarious of pronunci-
ations was enough for me to stop production. On the second day,
our wonderful director, Paul Weiland, had to take me to one side
and have a strict word with me. We were running out of time.
Unfortunately, it did nothing but fuel my laughter and panic. On
top of which, Gary and I had to so very, very, very nearly kiss, and
that too made me laugh. Not because he wasn't gorgeous, but
because I would have laughed if any man with that accent had tried
to kiss me. He was a pleasure to work with, not to mention almost
snog. Shooting on film, of course, is far more labour intensive than
shooting for television. Everything takes twenty to thirty takes and
attention to detail becomes quite laborious.

Over Christmas I'd learned that I would be presenting the 1997
Brit Awards, on my own, in February. I was tremendously excited
about this. It was a big show, it was live and it would be the first
time a woman would be trusted to take on the job. At least since
Sam Fox and Mick Fleetwood had made TV history with their

impeccable performances, way back when . . . Perhaps that's why it had been so long? Who knows, but I had a few meetings which all seemed very positive and very definite. However, the day before the press announcement was going to be made, I had a call to say my services would not be required. They had instead secured the talents of Ben Elton. Nice one. I was more than disappointed. I was pissed off. Why could they not have been upfront? Why wouldn't they trust a woman? It was as frustrating as it was to work in television, where a woman would rarely be trusted with her own prime-time show, unless her name was Cilla Black. So often, the powers that be seem to lack courage and insight, foresight or any sight for the talent around them. OK, stick with the safe, old-school bets. Don't stick your necks out. But damn.

Along came another commercial – this time for Kentucky Fried Chicken. I was to fly to the States for this one in which I was to play the role of an Austrian–German waitress on the ski slopes of Europe (or Mammoth, California in our case). Another comical set-up, this time with the talented Ryan Styles. I was particularly excited because I was allowed to bring my hairdresser, Charles Worthington, along with me for the shoot. Charles was great company and, bearing in mind that we were stuck in our Los Angeles hotel for three days with nothing to do because there was a snow blizzard in Mammoth, Charles didn't just sort out my hair, but also tickled my fancy, pulled my leg, and had me in stitches.

Charles is very, very naughty and it was the light relief I desperately needed at the time. He suggested we went shopping. I'm no good at going shopping under the influence of someone else. But the advertising company said we should do whatever we wanted as we were being inconvenienced by having to stay on an extra day or so – they'd pick up the bill for the limo. So, Charles insisted we book the biggest limousine to take us around the shops. We were to pretend that he was Sir Charles Worthington and we would bullshit everyone along the way. The Americans, of course, took every inch of us seriously. We found it hysterical.

We then decided that, as there was very little sun in Los Angeles in January, we would go for a sunbed to make up for it. So we found a dodgy sunbed place. Now, while Charles may be the Queen of Hairdressing, I am most certainly the Queen of Sunbeds. I insisted that I should have fifteen minutes, despite the lady behind the till recommending only ten. As it turned out, I got off the bed after ten, only to find myself completely and utterly scarlet. Charles was no better. This time we were in so much pain, we could hardly laugh. I was bright, bright red, and a mark had even been left by my necklace in the short time. Neither of us could even shower – even cold water burnt us. The only saving grace was that the rest of my face was now the same colour as my eczema, which showed no signs of disappearing.

It turned out that the bad weather simplified things, as the commercial had to be rewritten and relocated to downtown LA instead of mountainous Mammoth. The new storyline had me, dressed in nothing but a towel and sporting long plaits that stood erect on either side of my face, flirting with Ryan in a sauna on a purpose-built set at a fire station. It ended up as a day's work in a six-day trip. But I'm afraid we were far from finished. Because Americans are the way they are – and if you don't know, you don't need to – we couldn't help taking the piss. We messed around the whole time, being rude, funny and even a little disgusting. Someone had left a walkie-talkie in my Winnebago mobile dressing room, and we overheard all the wanky talk that goes on in our world of film and TV. For a laugh we decided to pretend to be American and be talking badly about me, to see if anyone would respond. We swore and called me all the profanities under the LA sun and within no time they picked up on it and threatened 'whoever it was' on the airways that it was a federal offence to swear on the walkies. We promptly switched it off.

Yes, Charles and I took ourselves off to another planet on that trip. It was probably just what I needed, but at the same time not enough. We were forever testing the boundaries of decent behaviour. One one occasion we stood on my hotel-room balcony pouring water over guests arriving below. Amazing how much fun you can have without alcohol. One night in the depths of conversation about American football with fellow hotel guests, I was asked whether I was over there to watch a particular game. 'Watch it, darling? I'm on it!' I replied. So silly were we.

Another night there was a cocktail party at our swanky hotel. Not content with the decadence of a celebratory party, Charles and I stayed chatting to the wee hours with some of the advertising team, then decided to go skinny-dipping in the pool. In our underwear, I hasten to add. But apparently you don't do that in the States. Before we knew it there were guard dogs and hotel staff surrounding us, wrapping us in towels and escorting us to our rooms. Whoops.

And yes, I stayed in constant touch with James, although he seemed rather dismissive. I didn't call him to tell him what a change of atmosphere I was experiencing and what a good time I was having without him. I rang because I missed him and wanted him to be there to share it with me. He remained cool.

When I came home I decided to try and get a grip on a few things. First, my eczema. A dermatologist tested me for everything and came up with nothing new. I was classed as an 'atopic' person, allergic to many common things – pollen, dust, furry animals and so on. Nothing could really 'solve' my problem. On James's recommendation I also went to see a Chinese herbalist. She looked at my tongue, talked of my health and diet and prescribed me some not-so-tasty herbs to take twice a day.

It was painful covering up the eczema when I had to work, but work I needed to. I flew to Belfast to co-host the Hot Press Rock Awards, with one of the nicest, if not *the* nicest guy in the business, Mike Edgar. He had worked as a music journalist for some years and has now reached the dizzy heights of a managerial position with BBC Northern Ireland. Genuine, kind and generous, I like him tremendously. As I found I did Northern Ireland, too, on this first trip back since TV-am days. The people are more than friendly, inviting, welcoming and generous – and what a beautiful place, in spite of its troubled past and present. James was off skiing.

I also decided to sell the marital home – now completely mine thanks to the decree absolute, which had finally come through. Changing surroundings seemed to make sense, if I was going to move forward. Then, on a visit to the surgery with Cameron, the doctor turned his attention to me. It must have been evident that I was unhappy, if not depressed. I told him about my panic attacks, and how lost I felt. He asked me if I would consider going to see a psychiatrist. I was horrified but numbed at the same time. So, not only did I have eczema and depression, but I was now mentally unstable too? Fantastic.

*

But I did as recommended. I went along not knowing what to expect, and not really caring either. I felt so numb all the time. My head was whizzing with thoughts, but my body stood still. My heart was cracking; my soul was unsettled and my eyes saw only bleakness. I didn't want to talk to anyone about me and my life and my fuck-ups. I had done it with Renee and it seemed such a mountain to climb to start all over again. To start from the beginning; to talk about my past; about my parents; about my divorce. I just wanted my father back. And I guess I wanted to be released from this yo-yoing with James. I wanted to feel happy again, not spend the days wondering when I would be overwhelmed by a wave of panic or sorrow or sadness. Right then I didn't want to be me any more. I was still tortured by my betrayal of John; another relationship was failing. Everything felt so heavy, yet I felt so frail and weepy.

I was a nightmare. I didn't understand my role any more – even my role as a mother. I adored my son and I didn't behave differently towards him, yet I couldn't bear to be apart from him. I felt guilty and bad when I had to go away to work. To cut a very long story short, I felt an absolute mess.

At my appointment with the psycho-chap I broke down in tears. I had, as I suspected, to start from way back when. I was bored by my own story, so God knows what was going through his mind. I cried some more. Then he recommended some antidepressants. I declined. I didn't like the sound of drugs – it spelt dependency to me. He assured me I would not become dependent and really persuaded me it was the best thing for me. Well, if it means I don't have to talk, it might be the thing for me, I reasoned. I took one of the tablets he offered me and walked away with my prescription.

By the time James returned from skiing my eczema was improving impressively, but my mood and attitude to him had not. The following day I took off for Kenya with *Wish You Were Here*. Seemingly a regular fix for me when I want to have a really good time! I was on antidepressants, anti-malaria tablets, antibiotics and antihistamines. Plus my herbs for eczema. Great. But the sunshine helped me a little and going on safari to see nature wild and naked was therapy. And this time I didn't miss James. He sensed our end and panicked on the phone to me before I came home, telling me he would move in with me to make things better. There had been a time when I had wanted that. But as often with love, his offer came too late. He had lost me.

When I returned I was predictably doorstepped by the press who wanted me to confirm or deny a split. I confirmed it, if only to get them off my back. In the grand scale of things, it really wasn't that important. I was falling apart, outside and in, and trying to sort that out. James came around that night to try to persuade me otherwise and whilst I found it hard to reject his physical approaches, I knew that the right thing was to not buckle. But buckle I did. I was so utterly weakened by my depression and so fearful of my own decisions that I couldn't bear to cut him out. Amazingly, we resolved to make 'us' work, and I ended up in his arms once again.

The test would be the *Gladiators* Mauritius gig, which was confirmed for a second year. This time we were due to be away for two weeks, which was too long a period for me to leave Cameron, so I got dispensation to bring him with me, nannied by my sister, who was by now living in England for a year's break from studying. But I needn't have worried about James. I should have known it was going to be a nightmare.

From the second we met with the rest of the team and crew at Heathrow, I had lost him. He was like a little schoolboy, going off with his mates and forgetting about his other friend. Yet again, I was brushed aside – and he not only blanked me, but blanked Cameron too. I was in a very delicate state – only kept upright by the antidepressants – and I should never have gone on the trip. It was certainly to be the final nail in our coffin. There was not a single element of us being together or being part of a team about it. I felt like a little puppy running after her master. What was worse was that I wasn't really working out there, but had been asked to come along for publicity purposes – so I wasn't even part of the working team.

Thank heaven, some more 'normal' people came out at the end of the first week. Some of the Gladiators swapped over, and the photographer Brian Moody and his crew joined us. I had worked with Brian before and we got on very well. Shane from the LWT press office came out, too, and she was utterly mad. The scene was set for the Hunter–Jonsson showdown.

After a couple of evenings together, my friends started talking about going late-night skinny-dipping in the sea, which sounded great to me. In Sweden we often go skinny-dipping, even in broad daylight. It's not a big thing. I told them I would come along. James ignored me when I told him I was leaving the bar. Linda had taken Cameron to bed. It was a release to strip off my clothes and run into the ocean. My nudity wasn't an issue. It was dark. And it wouldn't have been if it had been light either: I felt so free and momentarily good about myself. As I left James behind with his 'friends' the words 'fuck you' went through my mind. As I hit the water my depression seemed to lift momentarily. I was bathing in a warm sea of pleasure, comfort and reassurance.

I don't know how long we had been in the water, but as I looked up the beach towards the lights from the resort I could see a small audience had gathered. I could vaguely make out it was some of the Gladiators. The party seemed somehow over. As I lifted myself out of the water, struggling with my feet against the heavy sand and searching in the blackness for my clothes, I could see a large silhouette marching towards me, shouting at me. It was unmistakably the voice of the Yorkshire Hunter, bearing down on me like an infuriated sergeant on patrol. I scrambled for my clothes as Brian and his assistant Charlie tried to appease the oversize sergeant. They asked him to calm down, saying we were only taking a swim, but he pushed them out of the way. I realized he wasn't coming to welcome me out of the water. As I picked up my pile of clothes I was struck to the ground by the force of his hand. As I got up again, he struck once more. I lay, naked and wet, on the sand, pleading with him. He just turned on his heel and made off.

All eyes were on us, and my collaborators took a sharp intake of breath. Throwing on my clothes, crying, the length of my lower arm cut and encrusted in sand, I pleaded with him to wait and to speak to me, but as I wobbled in the sand like a newborn calf, fighting back the pain and more tears, he took off. I managed to regain my balance and started running after him, but I didn't stand a chance against his huge pace and strength. I called out for him a hundred times, but he had gone. Gone deep into the darkness and distance of somewhere I wasn't wanted. As I came to a halt, weeping, I turned to find an entire team of muscle and crew looking on in pity and disgust. Oh, fuck you, I thought.

I spent much of the rest of the night raking the resort for him, but he was nowhere to be found, and a conspiracy of bodies protected him. I eventually returned to the room we shared and waited pathetically just inside the door for any signs of his return. But there weren't any, and the following morning I awoke stiff from a night on a stone floor and in pain from my cut arm. Sand seemed to be everywhere, and I was starting to clear it up as he entered the room. He said nothing, refused to speak and simply started collecting his things together.

Once again I started weeping, pleading with him to at least talk to me about it and I offered apology after apology after apology. But something inside me told me very clearly that the previous night's performance should not have taken place – perhaps not mine, but certainly not his. Despite being at a loss for the right words, I kept talking, begging and appealing to him. He refused to answer me and would not even look at me. I was devastated. It felt that, after spending the past ten days running around him, trying to reach him, he now had a genuine excuse to banish me. It was pathetic. I had allowed him to behave as he wanted, accepting degrading behaviour towards me, and now he couldn't even bear to be in my presence after a night of skinny-dipping. Had I been stronger at the time, I would surely have treated the situation with great incredulity and would have simply let him walk out of my life, if that was what he wished. But I wasn't up to that right then. The antidepressants seemed to have no power to stop me going over the edge.

James finally said he couldn't talk to me right now, and he wasn't sure whether he ever could. I asked him to please remain in the room, rather than check himself into another one, for everyone's sake. I wouldn't understand, and nor would Cameron, if he disappeared, and I didn't think the rest of the team should be privy to another disaster in our relationship. Reluctantly he agreed, but insisted on rules. There would be no affection between us, we would go to meals separately and in general behave like two single people sharing a bedroom. Without hesitation, I agreed. I wanted to do anything to keep him by my side, confident that he would open up to me at some stage. Perhaps the doctor was right: I was of unstable mind.

Needless to say, it became agony. So bad, in fact, that I developed a persistent pain in my solar plexus, generated, presumably, by the anxiety. After another futile attempt to talk to James, I began to lose my breath and eventually collapsed. I can remember coming round and seeing a nurse sitting by my bedside, only to hear James announce that he didn't have time for this and watching him leave. Thankfully, Cameron was being entertained by Linda on the beach at the time.

We didn't speak again for the rest of the trip, despite him asserting his control, manhood and power over me. I allowed him to have sex with me on two occasions. I mistakenly thought this might open things up a bit. But neither that nor pleas from my sister for some leniency had any effect. He had sent me to Coventry, and there I had to stay.

I look back on that trip with great pain and with the benefit of hindsight. What I lacked in self-respect he lacked in humility, and when someone is not concerned when you are in pain, there is no longer a relationship to be had. When someone is unmoved by your tears, devastation and humiliation, you have lost love, respect, integrity and sensibility. I can see now that I had surely lost all those and more. But right then, I didn't know that I could walk away. I could not see that I was better off without it all. These were not circumstances under which any wounds could heal. But I thought I had no other place to look to for everything to be made well.

Besides my wonderful sister Linda, who was shocked by the goings-on, there was one other person who was witnessing my daily degradation from the sidelines. One of our female Gladiators, 'Rebel', better known as Olympic athlete Jennifer Stoute, cornered me one night in the bar with the words, 'Hey, sister, I need to talk to you!' She took me aside and ordered me to find some self-respect. I had to quit this devastating game – I deserved better, and I needed to start behaving like it. She told me to shape up or go down with it. She believed he'd break me, given half a chance, and she, for one, was not about to stand by and let that happen.

Her words came like lightning from the sky and equally unexpected. Granted, they fell on ears that had been somewhat deafened by degradation and the wrong kind of love. But I grasped the essence of what she was telling me. And if I was emotionally unable to behave exactly as she prescribed, I could at least take a step towards it. The task was mammoth though, and I remained shamefully subservient. We left Mauritius with James laughing and joking with his friends and ignoring the wilting flower on the periphery.

IT'S ULRIKA

Before that fateful journey, I had found a house I loved in the same village, had made an offer and had it accepted. The imminent move was therefore something to which I needed to devote my meagre reserves of energy. But there was another project for which I had to muster up some confidence: a show Jim and Bob had written especially for me, to be aired on BBC2 sometime in August. Our *Shooting Stars* collaboration had gone so well that they had long talked about writing a show for me, and had even gone to the lengths of announcing it at the Montreux Television Festival. It was the most publicized show which had yet to happen, so it was with relief that I finally got a schedule and pieces of paper that were beginning to look like scripts. We started having meetings and loose rehearsals, discussing characters and set-ups.

During a break, I was booked to attend a corporate dinner in Blackpool, of all places. I was sure I was in for a boring night, but as I sat at the table and chatted after I had completed my celebrity duties of hosting the evening's sales conference and handing out various awards, I decided to stay on after dinner rather than retreat to my hotel room. I got up and danced, had a couple more glasses of wine, and ended up having a brilliant time with the company girls and guys. It was a release from the tension that had been steadily building up inside of me since Mauritius. One of the guys, who had a cute smile and a wicked sense of humour, was particularly good company – although I made sure to leave him behind on the dance floor. It made a change to be having *fun* with a guy again.

The following morning I was due at a photo shoot for *Gladiators* and knew I was guaranteed to come face to face with the person whose name I didn't even want to hear any more – 'the bastard who had treated me like shit' would suffice. But I found that somehow the night away, and with Jennifer's commandment ringing in my ears, had given me enough confidence to start changing my line of thought. I began to acknowledge that I didn't need this any more. Who was he kidding? I'm not going to fight to have someone by my side; either they want to be there or they can fuck off, I told myself. Go sister! I had finally woken up and smelt the coffee. By the time I saw him I felt as if I had pocketed the little secret of my previous night's harmless flirtation, which he wouldn't know about, some-thing that would ultimately mean we would never be reunited – I'd broken the cycle. He wasn't behaving any differently – his manner was still dismissive and hurtful – but this was par for the course as far as I was concerned. I'd stopped waiting for him to change and stop and notice me. I hoped my different approach was beginning to show. It certainly felt better. But then that wouldn't have been hard – although it was amazing how long it had taken me to get to this point. I had stopped seeing my psychiatrist after only half a dozen sessions. I felt better on the antidepressants and much stronger.

The following week I plunged into the depths of the show's punishing rehearsal schedule. The working title was *It's Ulrika!* – no guesses whose programme it was. It was deeply flattering and an honour to have such a great, dedicated team of people on board – that's guaranteed to make a girl feel better about herself. The director was John Birkin, the costume designer Annie Hardinge and a great make-up department was led by the clever Lisa Cavalli-Green, who made me sit trapped inside a prosthetic mask for at least an hour in order that I might look like Phil Collins. The claustrophobia very nearly killed me. Matt Lucas and his professional partner Dave Walliams were involved on the script and acting front, along with Jim and Bob's imagination and madness. Their generosity knows no bounds and I cannot thank them enough for their enthusiasm and patience. A very young, up-and-coming writer called Rhys Thomas contributed a couple of sketches he had written, where I played a common, peroxided, foul-mouthed, bullying mother and he my medallion-donning husband. Kate Robbins helped me enormously with my impersonations for my opening number and Paul White-house popped his head around the corner a few times during shooting. The Lightning Seeds had accepted the invitation to do a musical number, which was a real thrill as I was a big fan, but I don't think they knew what they had let themselves in for.

Jim and Bob had heard me sing for sketches on *Shooting Stars* and wanted music to be part of the show. The opening number was a tribute to music, with me impersonating Cher, Phil Collins, Dusty Springfield and naturally, it being produced by Jim and Bob, a Smurf. The rest of the show included sketches, such one about GMTV with me as Anthea Turner, and 'Regardez Chien', in which I portrayed the delectable Anne Robinson, together with show-stopping numbers of the Las Vegas kind. Well, the latter is perhaps an exaggeration, but the numbers were amazingly detailed.

The rehearsals were taxing as the spotlight was inescapably on me. I had to take charge and make the show and its characters mine – I had to *own* the show, as the Americans would put it, which required enormous concentration on my part. The boys' confidence in me lifted me immensely and it was the best medicine for a tortured heart. James was by now taking third or fourth place in my head, and he was finding he had to do the chasing – not that I was being that responsive. The antidepressants were at last beginning to kick in – although the problem with them was that while I no longer had moments of absolute despair, I also had no moments of blissful happiness. I was kept suspended above both emotional states by a pill in my mouth every morning. But it felt better than being depressed.

Music rehearsals, recordings, costume fittings and location shoots continued for six weeks, and it felt wonderful to be truly working – this show required something more of me – something more artistic, rather than standing in front of a camera smiling for a couple of hours at a time. My mind was forced to focus on the matter in hand as it never had before and get the rest of life in perspective – something I clearly hadn't had to do enough until then. Moving house in the middle of it all was stressful, to say the least, but true to form for me – it never rains but it pours. Better still, next-to-no support from James actually meant I had to plough ahead without looking for validation – I was unearthing my long-lost, but innate and well-honed, independent qualities. On the last night in the studio I drank more than I should, went back to my new home and collapsed fully clothed on my bed, with exhaustion. I honestly awoke the next day to a more content world.

The show did well. Previews were good in general, but we did not fare so well in reviews. With hindsight there was probably too much Vic and Bob about it and not enough Ulrika.

*

August 1997 found me back in glorious Birmingham for yet another successful series of *Gladiators* – following hot on the heels of still more *Shooting Stars*. And yes, it came in the wake of depression and antidepressants; mismanaged love; anguish and abuse; ongoing mourning of my father, and still coming to terms with my divorce. But somehow I felt slightly excited, perhaps even buoyant. Perhaps turning thirty would signify a fresh start and a new beginning, which I was more than ready for. Could putting a nought to the end of my age also start to put things right?

There was of course the matter of working with James. He'd actually ended up being quite damaged by our break-up, too – the wounds hadn't had enough time to heal and feelings were far from dormant, but we did both know that this time there would be no rematch. We'd confronted our own personal Ultimate Challenge, and both had the sense, at last, to walk away from it.

What I encountered, however, took me somewhat by surprise. Having made some sort of verbal pact with James, acknowledging the difficulties, and vowing to be respectful towards each other, I found my attempts at niceness constantly rebuffed. He would cut me short mid-flow, put the phone down, shut a door in my face or simply walk away. What I should have done, of course, was to walk away or stick my fingers up, but I was hankering after a neat and tidy end. At one stage I remember, rather embarrassingly with hindsight, becoming hysterical after one such encounter, and summoning our most wonderful producer, Kenny Warwick, to my room in the middle of the night to inform him that I couldn't go through with the recording. He sympathetically suggested we should wait to see how I felt in the morning and take it from there. Despite having just come off the antidepressants, the recording did go ahead, with me fronting as planned. I had a new co-host besides. John Fashanu had been replaced by rugby international Jeremy Guscott, a man with a sharp sense of humour, intelligence and a good sense of reality. He was a family man, but was a true rugby-player in his heart of hearts, with all that goes with that.

What James and I both needed was distraction. He had always found this before in his body and his work – known to him as his 'focus'. For me, on the other hand, work like *Gladiators* alone was never quite enough to distract me from personal issues. I knew, before my arrival at the Hyatt, that I would need to dig deep in order to get through the next three or so weeks. But James had some other tricks up his sleeve. Now, the end of an affair is always hard, but what makes it harder is when your former partner takes up with someone right under your nose, just for the hell of it. I feel that on this occasion *I* had at least acted with a degree of subtlety. James, on the other hand, paraded himself with a young dancer with about as much subtlety as a johnny on the Pope's nose.

Knowing I would be working on my thirtieth birthday, and in an attempt to make the passing a little special, I flew my sister and her friend Helene over from Sweden, and invited my close friend Liz – we'd kept in touch ever since secretarial college – up from Cardiff. Together we waved goodbye to my twenties and welcomed my fourth decade with warm, open arms. Some nights later there was a party organized by the technical crew at a local nightclub. The crew are always the hardest and longest working, and their parties tend to be of equal calibre. Before a group of us left the Hyatt, word got around that good old Fash, who still lived locally, had brought along with him some players from Aston Villa. Despite having nothing to do with the production any more, Fash had the power to sniff out a good party, God love him.

With a day off the following day and a tankful of frustrated energy, nothing was going to get in the way of me and a good time. And it didn't. I danced, barefoot, for three hours solid. On my own, and until I was drenched. I even walked back to the hotel on my own, determined to turn my exhaustion into sound sleep – something that had remained elusive ever since my little monkey was born. At the hotel, I found a switchboard message and a number to call at lunch time the following day. The number was a mobile, the name was Stan Collymore.

The name rang a bell, but I dismissed the note with the cynicism of a woman who was presently considering celibacy, and crashed.

*

Coming round the next day, I caught myself fingering the note with a tinge of flattery, and if truth be told, resignation. I called my brother and a colleague to ask about Mr Collymore. Both reactions were positive. My brother informed me that he was a highly skilled footballer who only recently had transferred from Liverpool to Aston Villa for £7 million and that his transfer to Liverpool two years earlier had been for a record £8.5 million. I realize with hindsight that neither of my consultants were women ... But my sister and her friend egged me on. Linda had seen the pain I had gone through with James and thought this was a timely distraction. Eventually, I did phone. What did I have to lose, apart from my sanity some months down the line? And perhaps this one-off returning of a phone call was part of the new thirty-something me.

Calmly and impassively, I agreed to meet him for lunch. I expressed concern about the fact that I had no idea what he looked like, bar possibly the colour of his skin. He told me that he would be in a silver Mercedes, and that was all I needed to know. To be honest, he was right: there was no mistaking Mr C in his Merc.

Although I was going through with it, I'd already decided I wasn't interested, and underdressed appropriately, despite my sister's protestations.

I'd armed myself with a copy of the *Daily Telegraph*'s sports pages, which featured the value of all the players in the Premiership. I was impressed by the price on his head – or his feet, perhaps – and that that was all I knew about him. What I saw sitting before me was a tall man with huge eyes, softly spoken and an incredibly gentle manner. He too seemed apprehensive, and I did everything in my power to put him and myself at ease – by bombarding him with questions. Hearing the story of a young man who has come from a household without a father, and a mother who was holding down three jobs to pay for her son's training, it was hard not to have empathy. When we parted I felt slightly lifted at the thought of a man taking an interest in me again. So much for celibacy. He phoned later to say he had found our lunch 'refreshing'. I was flattered. And distracted at the same time.

After I returned home, Mr C called every day and we met up for lunch. He was always asking me if I thought it was possible to fall for someone so quickly. Our talks were long and wide-ranging. It was clear I was dealing with an intelligent man who had a good grasp of world affairs as well as the world of art and literature. Quite a change, and I felt safe. A week later, we had our first dinner together – at Quaglino's in London. When we were snapped together by several photographers outside, I was surprised and even a little taken aback. I simply couldn't believe this would be of any interest. How wrong I was.

The next day was Sunday, and the world stood still. News had just broken of the death of Diana, Princess of Wales. We walked the streets of London among a sea of shocked faces. It felt as if the world was holding its breath and I with it. It was truly weird. Mr C, however, had other things on his mind. As we strolled along the King's Road in Chelsea holding hands, he suddenly jumped in front of me and stopped me dead in my tracks. 'Marry me!' he exclaimed.

I didn't think I'd heard right. 'What?' He repeated his demand,

and as he came up close to my face, I said, 'Yes!' I told him it was crazy, but I admired his courage and his sense of mad adventure. I meant my reply, but only because I wasn't sure he really meant what he had asked me. The prospect of saying yes didn't scare me: if he meant it, it would happen, and if either of us didn't, it wouldn't. Mad, crazy, nuts. But falling heavily in love seemed the most perfect thing to do to rid myself of the past year or so.

Perhaps this was the way it was meant to happen. You know, like in the films when couples fall in love and know they will marry from the second they clap eyes on each other? Couldn't this be like that? This could almost be a 'licking lamp-post' moment. It had all the right ingredients. It had an element of the forbidden; it would be something your mother wouldn't want you to do; and because it felt like the wrong thing to do, it was something I wanted to do. The hedonist in my father had made its way through to me and everything would be fine.

Everything felt quite mad. Nice mad. I had just accepted the proposal of a man I had had a two-week romance with. I had just moved into a new house. I had just turned thirty and my own show had just been aired, some days before. Maybe this was how it was meant to be after so long in the dark. Whatever, I felt lifted and almost delirious with uncertainty. By my side, the man I had just given the three letter word to persisted in asking again, and again and again if I meant it. I didn't understand him. I kept reassuring him that I had meant it if he had meant it. But he didn't believe me. He must have asked me more than fifty times before we reached my house – surreally passing on the way hundreds of people who had lined the road for miles around RAF Northolt, waiting for the return of the body of the Princess of Wales.

I tended to be busy during the week but catch up with Stan at the weekends. I'd started promoting the Pocket Phone Shop, which would entail me travelling the length and breadth of the country to open their new stores. *Shooting Stars* was also being recorded, and there was the house to sort out. But the excitement and uncertainty of Stan's proposal kept me feeling energetic. I found Stan endearing, romantic, even poetic, but also at times troubled and rather intense. He could turn very serious at the flip of a coin, almost rather unpredictably, but then he would give you a beaming smile and his eyes would temporarily light up.

Melanie had just turned forty, so we had decided to have a joint seventieth birthday party at the Belvedere restaurant in London's Holland Park. My new lover was unable to attend, being otherwise engaged with Aston Villa football club – it was his job, after all. But the party had been arranged, and Melanie and I were going to have a bloody good time, come what may. I brought Cameron along for a couple of hours before we sat down for dinner, because there were people there I wanted him to meet. My schoolteacher Ann-Charlotte had come over, as well a former TV3 colleague, Gunilla. Linda, Berit, Helene and my cousin Micke and his wife made up the rest of the Swedish contingent. My mum and Mike were there, as were my auntie Maureen and uncle Keith. We danced and drank until the wee small hours when the cleaners came in. I felt fantastic until I was woken up by Cameron just a few hours later. A bouquet of roses had arrived from my lover. How sweet.

*

Sometime in among this rebuilding of myself and the acclimatization of having found a new 'love', James called. He sounded quite desperate. I'd managed to largely forget about him, but not the pain he had inflicted. Nonetheless, I felt a good sight stronger now, and no longer feared for my emotions in his presence. He came over to see me one day and he held me. He told me how he was so truly sorry for everything he had done and he explained how he needed me. I saw the tears in his eyes and suddenly he was the malleable little bear I had so loved when we first met. This wasn't a bastard in front of me, it was a defenceless, lost love. I held him tightly and I too welled up, for the pain that had gone on between us and the sadness of our demise, but also because I knew I couldn't go back to him. He had nearly been the end of me and I couldn't allow that again. The warning I had given him when things had started to go wrong for us was ringing loud and clear in my ears. I couldn't even remind him of the warning I had given him halfway through our relationship.

I told Stan that James had been to see me, because I felt that was the honest thing to do. Maybe not the best idea: he went ballistic and for the first time I saw him paranoid. No amount of reassurance about where I knew I stood with James seemed to appease him. But somehow we picked things up again. Then a week or so later he called, saying he wanted to end our relationship. It had nothing to do with anything, he said, it just wasn't what he wanted any more. It was so sudden, and seemed out of place. The man who had proposed to me after two weeks was now ending it after five.

The following morning Mr C was back on the line, saying that he had made a big mistake. He wanted to take back what he had said the night before – he'd only said it because he wanted to gauge my reaction. A rather tortuous way of going about things, I thought. But somehow I accepted his reasoning, if with a little hesitation.

But this sort of thing started to become a pattern. No sooner had I understood one twist or turn in the relationship than I would be presented with another bizarre performance from Mr C. He blew hot and cold, constantly, although it seemed the hot bits were enough to keep me going through the cold spells. And in my mind, surely kindness would be reciprocated with kindness.

Later he was picked to play for England against Italy in a crucial World Cup qualifying game in Rome. I had seen the Collymore in action on TV and knew he was an incredibly talented footballer who could be relied upon to not only convert the ball, but do it with great style. The England training centre at Bisham Abbey isn't far from where I live, nor the Burnham Beeches Hotel where the team stays. One night he made his escape, borrowing Ian Wright's car to sneak away for half an hour of me. It was endearing and I felt flattered, if not a little worried about the consequences for him. His visits down from Birmingham to see me had been getting scarcer, which was odd given his persistence on the phone and his ready expression of emotions. If he did say he'd come and see me, he'd only let me down

– shades of my father all over again – or do it rarely and so begrudgingly it was as if he was doing me a favour. It seemed hardly worth it anyway: throughout his whole stay he'd grumble incessantly.

While he went to Italy with England, I went to Manchester for Granada. I had been asked to do a pilot game show with the working title *Ulrika's Foreign Affairs*. Two days' work was stretched out to a week away, which irritated me because it meant being away from Cameron for longer than necessary. My sidekick was a little-known comedian by the name of Graham Norton. He had an innovative, camp sense of humour rarely aired on mainstream TV, but despite that the show itself was turning out to be pretty weak and it has still not seen the light of day. Graham alone should have been the show.

Mr C called every day and obsessed about what I was doing and whom I was doing it with. No amount of good behaviour and reassurance halted his flow of degrading descriptions of what he thought I might be up to. I tried to ignore his comments for the most part or laugh them off, thinking he didn't mean what he was saying, but there was a nagging corner of my mind that told me that he did. He also called me straight after the game, spitting fire and obscenities. He was furious that Glenn Hoddle had left him on the bench for the entire match. But it's a team game, I retorted, you can't expect to play all the time. Wrong thing to say. Apparently he was one of the best players in the world and this trip had been an insult. He was angry, troubled, bothered and miserable, but attempts at spirit lifting by me didn't go down well.

Weeks passed with more of the same. Eventually came the time for my long-awaited holiday with my girlfriend Liz to Cuba, where we were hoping for some sunshine and sleep. My 'hello, I've got here safely' call to Mr C was greeted with a torrent of abuse. He was fuming because some third-rate tabloid had printed a story along the lines that James had been spotted at my house, and had even sent me flowers. The former was correct, and something which Mr C knew about; the latter I could only put down to the bouquet of flowers sent to me by a company I had recently worked for, thanking me for being my lovely and professional self. The hack who was composing the story must have walked up to my front door and seen the dead flowers on my doorstep, ready for the rubbish. But the explanation cut no ice with Mr C. Incensed, he threatened me, saying I'd better issue a statement to say that we were still together. I told him I couldn't do that, as it would, in my opinion, only give credence to the story. But such was the force of his argument that I came off the phone almost thinking I had courted the press, and that above all else I had left an element of doubt over our relationship. It must all be my fault; I'd just have to work at mending things. Again. How could this possibly be worse than the way things got with James?

What escaped me at that time was that Mr C had a female friend – an ex-girlfriend to boot – who was kind enough to do all his cleaning and shopping for him and even stay over (in the spare room, apparently) to keep him company. When I found out, I was fool enough to buy the story, believing him to be mature enough for female friendships.

Then, as ever, Mr C surprised me. He insisted on picking me up from the airport, drove me home and talked about how much he had missed me. Complete turnaround. He wanted us to go out to dinner that night, and was insistent my sister and Helene – who were living with me while they looked for jobs in London – come with us. The evening was however not without tension, and before I knew it he had got up to leave. I was at a loss as to how to explain things to my sister, but she wasn't stupid and read what was going on. Which was probably more than I could do.

Without wishing to get too intimate, I feel it is necessary to try to articulate just some of the madness that would take place between us. That night, in bed, he had another outburst of vulgarities, this time directed at my sexual behaviour. It was imperative to him that he had absolute control in this department and when he did not feel I reacted or behaved as he thought I should, he ended up pushing me off the bed and storming out. But not before swearing obscenely at me about the various positions other men must have 'fucked' me in and how he 'bet I liked it'. Silly fucking me. I went after him, still firmly believing I could encourage his kind, gentle side to come out.

The following morning he behaved as if nothing had happened and returned to the bedroom as warm and sweet as summer light, full of affection and smiles but inexplicably refusing to consume the full English breakfast he had insisted I cook him. He asked me to go and get the newspapers, which I did, thinking as I headed down the drive that maybe he had seen the errors of his ways and he was just the kind of guy who found it hard to talk about things. Wrong. So fucking wrong.

He skipped through the papers with the disinterest of a five-year-old. We talked about spending the day together and I suggested a few things we could do. I had done an interview with the *Sunday Times*, which he read in deep concentration. It was, in my opinion, a rare, highly positive piece. But as soon as he had finished, he got up, dressed himself and announced that he had changed his mind about the day. He wanted to go and see his mum.

Scenes such as these illustrate the madness that was my relationship with Stan Collymore. He was guilty of behaviour beyond anyone's comprehension and I was guilty of putting up with it in the relationship. He could be kind and sweet and loving for fleeting moments, but for the most part his demands were inexplicable, inappropriate and disassociated from a relationship. And those fleeting moments always served to give me hope. I struggled to understand him and hoped that ultimately he would see the good in me, understand that I was no threat to him, and wanted him no harm. I wanted to be allowed to care for him and truly wanted the best for him. But I was ridiculously naive. In all honesty, I was completely out of my depth.

He ended the relationship again that Sunday, and I took this as my cue to get out.

NOTORIOUS

Children in Need 1997 saw me give the performance of a lifetime. I had been asked to sing 'Making Whoopee' to the most gorgeous partner any girl could wish for – Kermit the Frog. The diehard romantic in me couldn't resist kissing the little green felt amphibian, in the ridiculous hope that he would turn into a handsome prince. Alas!

Despite ending it, Mr C had still been calling. I took his calls, but was cool. That night in the dressing room with Kermit and Melanie, he asked me back. He admitted he was a little troubled, but it was only because he loved me so and he really didn't want to lose me. I declined.

Over the past month I had been developing a good friendship with Paul Roberts, whom I had first met on tour with *Shooting Stars*. We met up a couple of times, talked about life, love and the universe, and drank nothing. I enjoyed his company a lot. He was kind, funny – in fact, hilarious – and deeply genuine. Paul himself had gone through his own personal hell with drink and drugs, but was now clean, and spoke about it with great frankness, sensitivity and honesty – a fantastically fresh breath of air. He knew of my troubles with Stan and we would regularly roll our eyes together at my experiences, or when the phone rang. Paul was always so honest and would often challenge the way I was thinking. I would listen to what he had to say, but sometimes I guess I just didn't hear him, or maybe I wasn't ready to – otherwise I would have shut the door to the crap being thrown at me for good.

I had never, in my television life, asked for a job. Ever. But then the United Kingdom went and won the Eurovision Song Contest, which meant it would be the host the following year. During a meeting at the BBC about some programme idea or another I asked who would present it. They indicated that nothing had quite been decided yet. I said what a huge fan of the show I was and had been since I was a young girl living in Sweden, and that I had a few languages up my sleeve, which would be useful. They didn't seem that interested in my childhood or my CV, but I carried on enthusing overbearingly. I didn't care about any other programme ideas – I was right for this job, and I knew it.

Well, just once in a blue moon things turn out like you want them to. I was in due course offered the job of hosting the 1998 Eurovision Song Contest with the legendary Terry Wogan. I was so chuffed, I was over the moon – blue or not. At the beginning of December I met Terry properly for the first time. He is nothing short of a gentleman, a professional and, quite frankly, an idol. He was amused to hear of my early years in this country, listening to tales of how he would never fail to make my mother laugh. He is like a calm, gentle giant with an experience and knowledge of broadcasting second to none. And there is nothing quite like working with someone you respect and admire to bring out the best in you.

The excitement of my forthcoming job made all otherwise mundane jobs bearable. I carried on opening mobile-phone shops around the country at a rate of knots. Stan carried on calling – either to check on how I was, or to provoke me into an argument about nothing in particular, or because the woman who ran around doing everything for him wasn't answering her phone, and he needed food and the washing doing.

Then our peculiar relationship began another episode. Despite not having seen each other for a month or so, he called late on Christmas Eve. Distressed and his voice shaking, he managed to tell me he had been arrested. He had, according to him, gone over to see his son, whom he had fathered with a girl a couple of years earlier. After an argument he had left. But before he knew it two police cars had pulled up outside his home and he was charged with assault. Scared and angry, he swore to me that he had done nothing wrong. His ex was claiming he had beaten down a door and struck her, and while he admitted that he had left in a fury, he denied he had touched her. I was prepared to believe him: yes, he might have lost his temper, but I figured that if a man of his size and strength had actually hit her, she would have ended up on the ground, which apparently was not the case.

This phone call sparked something inside me. It wasn't love. It was another form of caring, however stupid. I heard the neediness in his voice and the mending woman in me responded to it. I felt for this broken man; perhaps despite the fact that we had been unable to find a romantic way forward, I could be there for him in another capacity. I did not feel, and had not had the chance to feel, that I was in love with him – he'd stifled that with his criticism, bullying, provocation, and the negativity he positively oozed from every pore. But the side of me that thinks it has to make good anything which crosses my path picked up the gauntlet. I told him I would be there for him.

This, in turn, sparked something in him. His spoilt inner child now had what it always wanted, and he could milk this one for all that it was worth.

*

In November 1997 I had attended the glamorous Bond premiere for *Tomorrow Never Dies* and there befriended the great Angus Deayton and his partner Lise. I had become obscenely drunk, but like a good girl had managed to keep the throwing up for the trip home in the car. NB: no drinky neat vodka like wine on empty tummy! Angus and I had revelled in our united love for United, and he promised he would invite me up to Old Trafford the next time he was going.

The chance came in January. I was looking forward to it immensely – there is nothing, nothing quite like football. But to Mr C, the news was like a red rag to a bull. Was I hell bent on destroying him? he asked. Swiftly followed by a torrent of abuse and threats down the phone. For a split second I actually considered cancelling. He was frightening me – the only saving grace was that he was further from me than arm's length. But my sister had had enough: she told me I was going. Come hell or high water. Or Stan. As I left for the airport to fly up to Manchester he pursued me with threatening phone calls. I continued to try to reason with him that I had a right to do what I wanted and that I wasn't in a relationship with him, all to no avail. Finally, I did what I should have done five months before – I switched my phone off.

I continued to meet up with my friend Paul, who was fast becoming a confidant and someone I could turn to for a few moments of sanity every once in a while. I was attracted to him, but unsure if I should risk our strong friendship for a relationship. Besides, I still had the dismembered parts of another one hanging around my neck like a noose. Paul questioned my insistence on taking calls from someone who only brought me misery and unhappiness; I told him that infuriating as it was, I wanted to set the record straight with Stan, and get my point of view heard. Paul asked me outright: 'Do you want to be right, or do you want to be happy?' and I knew what he meant, but figured maybe, just maybe, I could be both. In hindsight, as long as an ounce of me wanted to be 'right' in this mother of relationships, there was no chance I would ever be happy. And I guess it goes without saying that there must have been an underlying emotional attachment.

Shooting Stars went live in London at the Labbatt's Apollo in Hammersmith for a few weeks in February, together with the team from *The Fast Show*. It was a happy reunion for us all, and a chance for us to mess around on stage in the belief that we were actually working, but without having to travel the country. The boys had made a few changes to the routine. It was Jim and Bob's wish that I make my entrance seated on a throne and lowered from fifty feet above the stage, a pair of fake, lit-up breasts attached to my chest. Naturally I agreed, despite suffering the most horrible vertigo – but nothing a couple of beers couldn't calm. I was then to launch into a medley of 'I'm a Cider Drinker', and 'Nuts, Oh Hazelnuts' as I had done before on tour. The madness Jim and Bob can create for you and around you makes you believe you are actually very funny. And I guess in some surreal way we were. We 'worked' six nights a week and for me it was ideal, because I could be home by nine thirty when the show was over.

Being based in town meant I was able to reawaken my long-slumbering social life. My friend Kerry and I would go out on a Friday and sometimes even a Saturday night. I have to say, we had a wild time. Wild, within drug-free parameters and without the constraints of relationships. Cameron, I hasten to add, was having a whale of a time with John. We would, of course, partake in alcohol, in a silly, but non-dangerous way, and it really lifted me to not have to be as serious as the past year or so had been. Kerry had a slightly bumpy relationship track record of her own, and it was a gift to be able to laugh about our disasters and drown our sorrows a little.

One day I arranged to meet Melanie Sykes, the stunning girl from the Boddington's beer ads, whom I had first encountered in Bournemouth on the *Shooting Stars* tour. I think it would be fair to say we hit it off straight away and decided to pursue a friendship. We agreed to meet for lunch in the Harvey Nichols Fifth Floor restaurant. We also agreed to order a bottle of wine, which, by four o'clock, had become two bottles. We laughed and confided in each other, and eventually decided to retreat to the bar next to the restaurant for a bit more of the same.

After another couple of glasses I was quite, quite drunk. But not drunk enough to miss Chris Evans, Paul Gascoigne and friends sitting doing exactly what we were doing. They called us over, and Chris's opening words to me were, rather bizarrely, 'You hate me.' I had no idea where this presumption came from, but told him that I absolutely didn't, responding, 'Of course I don't hate you, I *love* you.' As you would in a drunken state with a former colleague. He then asked me to marry him, and I agreed. This was all playful banter and we were hooting so much I barely heard my mobile phone ring. It was our stage manager at the Apollo. He was wondering where I was, we had a show in an hour and I should get my arse over there. I had almost forgotten, and in panic looked for a knight in shining armour. The lovely Mark Wogan, son of Terry and a friend of Melanie's, appeared as if out of nowhere and obliged with a *Starsky and Hutch*-style chase to get me to the theatre on time.

I went straight to Jim and Bob's dressing room, where we would normally all gather pre-show, to be miked up. I hadn't to worry about costume or make-up, I wore what I wanted and that applied to make-up, too. But I felt embarrassed and shocked by my tardiness and immediately went down on my hands and knees in a completely drunken state, apologizing profusely. The boys were laughing – this was going to be one hell of a show. As I made my way to the stage and travelled my way up to my throne high up above it, I had only the barest inkling of what it was I had to do. As I made my descent and the boys sang the name 'Ulrika' to the tune of 'Jesus Christ Superstar', I could also hear the words, 'she's very, very drunk' – and that finished me off.

Whatever thin veil of seriousness I had assumed was shot to pieces, and I collapsed in giggles. I strained and dug deep to remember the words to my medley, but failed at every juncture, a sack of drunken stupidity. The audience roared. My eyes were focusing, but in two different directions, and my body drifted around of its own accord. Eventually I managed to stumble my way across the stage to my position behind the desk. I had the biggest round of applause I have ever experienced and there were heckles from both on and below the stage. Needless to say, I cannot remember a thing more from the show that night, except that when the show was over and I was still apologizing profusely to the boys for my abuse of alcohol, Bob turned to me and said, 'Don't apologize, Ulrika, it was one of the funniest things I have ever seen. I'd pay to see that again'.

Naturally, it made the papers the following day.

*

My mother turned fifty that April and as a treat I offered to take her on holiday with Cameron and myself. I booked us a luxurious resort on the Caribbean island of Nevis and wanted to pull out all the stops for our ten-day stay. My mother and luxury go together like caviar and champagne.

When I came back I was once again telephonically serenaded by Mr C. He let me know that although he had been seeing someone else over the past month or so – which I thought was nice of him to mention – he wanted us to give things another go. Oh, the ability he had to talk me around. He would become momentarily sensible and, while never admitting responsibility for anything, would talk about how our troubles were all due to our compatibility, not incompatibility. We were apparently two halves of one soul, and if only I stopped provoking him and allowed him to love me in the way he wanted, things would be fine. For some reason, it sounded credible. With the odds against me, with the sign 'sanity' pointing the opposite way, and with a history that was hardly to be cherished, I decided that maybe a little time together was what we needed. Oh, dear.

He told me he was due a few days away from the club and suggested we should go away. Perfect, I thought, this is just what we need. He said he could be away for three days and I became very excited about the prospect. 'You fucking sort out where we are going, but I don't want to go to some dodgy fucking place,' he finished up. This was par for the course – he always spoke and swore at me like that, even if things were going well. And why did I go ahead with it? Well, if I am to be brutally honest now, I was scared of him. There! I've said it. And I still believed I could persuade him with patience, kindness and helpfulness.

So I chased around like a maniac trying to find just the right place for us to get away, in between sorting out Cameron, work and my household, whilst he sat on his arse in Birmingham, moaning. There was no doubt about it, in the world of dogs, I was the underdog here.

The following day, 17 March, I was due to do a photo shoot and interview with *Loaded* magazine. I arrived first thing in the morning at the Park Lane Hotel. As we sat down to talk, tape recorder switched on, I was asked if I wanted a drink. 'Guinness!' I exclaimed. It was Paddy's Day, after all. The journalist asked a series of provocative questions, my answers to which were translated into something entirely different by the time the magazine was published. For example, he claimed I had said I wasn't wearing knickers. Well, I was, and in any event would so most certainly not say that kind of thing. He asked me about women's bodies and I said that the impression I got was that most men preferred women who weren't too skinny – which when the magazine was published came out with a rather different emphasis from that which I had intended! Ho hum! By the time it was time to go upstairs for my shoot with the talented photographer John Stoddart, I was merry, but by no means drunk.

All the while I worked away via mobile on the getting-away-from-it-all front. With flights and accommodation confirmed, I phoned Mr C with the good tidings. But he met my good news with vitriol, abuse and his well-honed negativity. My plan was rejected without hesitation. And he instructed me that things would be done his way and that I had to get to Birmingham that very night, because, out of the blue, he wanted me there for a match. I demurred, on the grounds of my work commitments that day and a son at home, whom I couldn't just leave, which didn't go down well. After seven or eight hours of photo session came another stream of obscenities down the phone. Fazed but focused, I hung up. I wasn't going to him.

I eventually finished at about seven in the evening and was making my way home when my mobile rang again. It was Chris Evans. He wondered where I was. I told him I was enjoying the pleasures of the M40 and he told me to turn around and come for a drink with him and his mates in Notting Hill. I wasn't really in the mood, but it had been a tense day, and this could be a way of letting off some steam. My driver turned around and I asked him to wait outside the pub for an hour while I popped in for a 'swift half'.

When my hour was up, I made attempts to leave, but Chris wouldn't have any of it. He had been drinking since his radio show that morning and was raring to go. He told me quite simply to send my driver away and tell my sister not to wait up, because I was coming home with him. I obliged. I like Chris very much, and whilst we flirted, really nothing went on. I say really, and I do mean nothing. When it got late, he took me back to his place and we talked more. Then he announced that I could stay in his bed or in the guest room, but we were not going to have sex. What a relief, I thought, not because I wasn't attracted to him – on the contrary – but because I, like him, believed sex would complicate things. Friendship was better. So I stayed the night at Chris's house and he told me I could use his car to drive home the following morning, which was also a relief, as I needed to get home to get Cameron ready for school. Linda and Helene were fine babysitting him at night if I couldn't be there, but had to be off to work in the mornings.

As we left Chris's house at just after 5 a.m., neither of us feeling or looking our best, a photographer was waiting outside. For Chris it was water off a duck's back; they followed him around every day, he said, and he didn't mind it in the slightest. He even chatted to the photographer whilst I fumbled my way out of the door, stumbling and growing flustered and red with embarrassment. Chris put the keys in the ignition of his car and told me to hop in. I looked up, horrified. It was a fucking Bentley. I can't drive a Bentley back to my house, I exclaimed. It's easy, he said, jumping out at the next set of lights and leaving the driving to me. I'll call you and come and pick the car up later, he said. And with that he was off.

And so was I. Off to the M40 in a fucking great big £50,000 tank, hung-over and shitting myself.

When I arrived home I called Mr C and left him a message on his mobile saying that I wouldn't be coming to Birmingham, or away with him, on account of his abusive behaviour and recklessness the previous day. I then woke Cameron up and got him ready for school. I knew it wouldn't be long before my mobile would go off. And it did. More abuse from the great man; more degradation and more insults. I told him to leave me alone and told him a few home truths about himself and hung up. As you can imagine, when the next day the pictures ran of me leaving Chris's house, he was not best pleased.

Easter came and with it the sun and my cover shoot for *Loaded*. It was very provocative. I was in leather handcuffs wearing a white coat and a black leather dress, looking at the camera through my fringe. I actually liked it. It was a little hard core in a sense, without me taking my clothes off. The shots were sexually provocative, yet without my naked body splashed across the pages of the magazine. I would not have wanted to do that, and Melanie would certainly never have let me.

I hadn't heard from my Birmingham friend for a while, until that day. He started off gently probing as to how I was. Great, I replied. Then came the insults and the questioning. He questioned me, doubted me, criticized me, hammered me and eventually insulted me. He couldn't bear the thought of other men looking at me like that. I pointed out that I didn't belong to him, or anyone for that matter, and that what I did professionally was really none of his business. There I went again. Justifying myself. Answering back. Rising. I really hadn't moved on at all.

*

Hindsight, experience, knowledge – marvellous things. I realize now that I had been lost for too long in a volatile, abusive relationship, and I'd given over my self-confidence, self-belief and strength. I was a changed person. Linda and Helene tell me they watched helplessly as a relaxed, amusing, fun-loving woman turned into a nervous wreck – impatient, intolerant, unable to make decisions and emotionally unstable. Even John, with whom I was finally having a tolerable relationship, wondered what was the matter with me. I evidently looked like a frightened rabbit every time he saw me. Even my mother had spoken to Melanie to express her concern.

Then after another short period of calm without the attentions of the great man, he re-emerged, like a bad rash that refuses to go away. This time he was calm, friendly, kind, and generally much more together. I was dubious, but he actually said that whilst he may not have done things right in the past, he wanted to start now, and with me. He wanted us to be together, because it had been the being apart which had been our downfall. He wanted to marry me; wanted me to have his children; wanted us to live together and do things properly. We would leave our previous madness behind and be strong together. Well, I was taken aback. And I fell for it hook, line and sanity.

We were back together and now it was going to be so good. He sent me flowers; was kind to me over the phone; as soon as I could sense him falling into frowns and moods I would point them out and he would snap out of them without hesitation. I couldn't believe the change in him and at this rate I was going to start to really like him, if I didn't watch out. He appeared to have developed an overwhelming honesty and requested the same from me. Well, if I am being honest, I could sense he wasn't totally changed, but I felt I owed him the benefit of the doubt. Truth is, I didn't owe him anything, but perhaps it was easier to be back with him, than to take all the hassle and abuse that came with not being with him. I felt I could appease him by being with him and in these circumstances I still felt affection for him, but either way, I couldn't win.

It was the end of April and the altercation with his previous girlfriend, the mother of his son, went to court. He was extremely nervous and fearful, but he was found not guilty of assault and was permitted to carry on seeing his son. At the end of the day in court he drove down to see me, and I was deeply flattered. A couple of reporters hung around outside my house and asked for my reaction. I said I was delighted and relieved for him.

CRAZY TIMES

The Eurovision Song Contest was growing closer. Ironically or coincidentally, it was to be held at the National Indoor Arena, but this was surely much more prestigious than *Gladiators*. It really was going to be a dream come true: being part of this huge technical operation, with audiences across Europe watching an event that had been an annual part of my life as far back as I could remember. And like it or loathe it, as a live international interactive broadcasting phenomenon it remains unmatched anywhere in the world. There had been weeks of preparation, and I took the initiative of stopping drinking alcohol for the duration, so as to guarantee clarity of mind. I had my hands full: an incredible amount of things had to happen like clockwork over the course of four hours, not to mention the ridiculous number of live links to foreign countries. I needed to be sharp as a knife. But I felt confident.

The BBC had put Terry and me up in a hotel in Birmingham, but I knew I would end up staying at Mr C's; he lived right opposite the Arena. I drove up positively bubbling, because not only was I about take part in the job of a lifetime, but I was back with the man I believed I loved. We planned to escape on holiday for a week or so straight after.

Birmingham in May 1998 was suddenly the place to be. It had been taken over by foreign delegations, press and crew. The BBC hosted a dinner at Warwick Castle two nights before the contest, to which I was escorted by Mr C. I was in full view: it was a press night, with all the participating countries attending, and I was representing the BBC. It was a spectacular evening, with everyone talking to everyone, and a lot of interest in me as my idol Terry's co-presenter.

However, none of this went down well with Mr C. The drive there had been bad enough, with him moaning about how far it was, but once he started suspecting, out loud, that everyone wanted to fuck me, the battle was on. In the end he stormed off and I rather embarrassingly had to pretend to not run after him.

The following day meant long rehearsals and press interviews. The buzzy atmosphere was invigorating, and Birmingham itself continued to come up trumps. I never felt exhausted, I was so thrilled to be doing my job and to be doing it with Terry, who was thankfully blissfully unaware of the personal torment I was experiencing. I put on a brave, happy front.

I went back to Mr C's that evening for another round of arguments. I tried to make him understand that I had a big job the following night and that it was important I got some sleep. Eventually, around one in the morning, I told him calmly that if he was going to carry on so negatively, I should leave. And with that he chucked me out. In my T-shirt and knickers. The night before the biggest job of my life. I had nothing more than what I was wearing. Nothing.

I banged on the door for some ten or fifteen minutes. It was May, in England, and keeping myself warm was a challenge. He refused to answer. He actually turned the music up. I didn't know what to do. In the end I started sobbing, begging him to let me in and to forgive me. Yes – I was asking him for forgiveness. Just what he wanted. The door was opened and I shot into the guest room and went to sleep. The next day, he was sweetness and light.

The 9th of May was a sunny, breezy day. I walked over to the National Indoor Arena with excitement, tension, anticipation and a whole host of other long words in my head. I had the same dressing room for Eurovision as I had had for so many years on *Gladiators*, which felt rather bizarre. Nothing was going to be plain sailing –

least of all the live links and the voting – but I knew I was working with the greatest technical television team in the world, and in my opinion with one of its best broadcasters.

I had received phone calls of good luck from friends and family alike and I knew that my relations in Sweden would be tuning in. My sister Linda was coming up from London with Helene and so was Melanie. Stan was going to turn up, too. Some people had sent flowers, but there was one exotic-looking bouquet that arrived with a message which didn't make sense, and actually seemed rather sinister. I thought I must have been the wrong recipient.

As the hour approached I became more and more nervous, but in the confident way that goes with embarking on an experience of a lifetime. The French lines I had to say went round and round in my head, as did the contingency plans. With the number of rehearsals we had done, the transmission deserved to go without a hitch. Which it did. Unless, of course, you count the one where I insinuated that it must have been many, many years since the lady calling in with the Dutch votes had herself taken part in the contest. I hadn't of course, but it sounded like it, with the time delay and hisses from the audience. It was nail into palm time, to stop myself collapsing with laughter. But apart from that, and the fact that our winner from Israel 'disappeared' for several minutes (or hours, in live television time) before her/his reprise of the winning song, everything went swimmingly. Yes, Dana International, as the singer was called, was in fact a transsexual. How very unlike the conventional image of Eurovision! On top of which he/she was representing Israel, which, of course is not in Europe at all.

Immediately after the transmission, apart from hugging Terry hugely and warmly, talk was of which party to attend. The BBC were hosting one and so was the mayor and virtually every visiting country. I thought it would be rude not to pop my head around the corner to thank everyone at the Beeb party, but they wouldn't let me in, because I didn't have an invitation. I found this rather amusing, but decided it was too full of people anyway. Why not return to Mr C's abode with everyone in tow, for a celebratory something. Mr C himself had gone straight back, as he had a game the following morning.

When I opened the door, I saw he had lit candles and left a bottle of champagne out with a note congratulating me on my success. He couldn't believe I had come back so soon – he expected me to be out partying all night. He was touched that I had come back. I wondered if this would make him understand that I did care and that he didn't need to play the obsessive, green-eyed monster. But mostly I was still on such a high from the job that I needed time to come back down to earth. It was one of those rare jobs where you come away from it knowing you have done OK and that, above all else, you have enjoyed every second of it.

*

The following day Mr C's beloved Aston Villa was playing Arsenal in their final fixture of the season. He asked me to come and watch and I brought Linda and Helene along, both avid football fans too. The day before had given the impression summer had arrived, but now there was a chill in the air. Prophetic. Mr C's manager decided to only let him play for the last ten minutes or so, which went down so badly with him that, at the end of the last game of the season when the players normally do a lap of the pitch to thank the fans for their support, Mr C refused to show. I thought it was bad form – after all, his grudge was with the manager, not with the fans. His mother and sister were also at the game, and were both upset by his absence.

When we met up with him in the bar, he angrily declared, in no uncertain terms, that he had put himself on the transfer list. His mother, the dearest, kindest, sweetest lady, became concerned and his sister frustrated with him. We all tried to talk sense into him, but his own self-concern and ego had deafened him. I returned with him to his flat and had a long conversation with him about how he had to try to not fly off the handle so easily. He appeared to listen, but explained once again that he was one of the best players in the world and he didn't need to take this shit. I tried gently to respond by putting my counsellor hat on and saying that he was probably right, but that he would need to prove it – he would need to put the work in. He suggested we call our relationship off again, but when I told him I would certainly let him go if that was what he wanted, he quickly retracted his comments.

Oh, the see-saw of confusions, wrongs and very few rights continued on. The following day I found a card in his car from the ex-ex-girlfriend who did all the running around for him. It confirmed their relationship had been going on and off for some time, but that she now understood he wanted to make a go of things with me. I became hot and angry and jealous and other unattractive things, but, embarrassed about having read it in the first place, didn't mention it.

We went on a holiday together that was truly the worst of my life. In New York he abandoned me in the middle of the street, after deciding I hadn't done things the way he wanted. I became distraught, but was not aware that things were going to get worse and worse. His mood swings intimidated and frightened me and I spent the entire time trying to placate him, but to no avail. Occasionally, he would throw me a crumb of loving, which I would struggle to feed off for as long as possible, but these came few and far between and completely unpredictably. In Jamaica, I was banished to the bar for four of the six evenings while he remained in the room, refusing to talk to me. In between his bullying and dictatorship he would reinforce his desire to marry me and have children, reverting to a former him who had the ability to show affection and love. On one occasion he had taunted me to such an extent and then refused to speak to me that I was beside myself with utter confusion and pain. I approached him and started beating my fists against his chest with frustration. Immediately he grabbed my wrists and told me unequivocally to stop. 'Physical aggression is not the answer,' he said. I stopped dead in my tracks and felt completely embarrassed. And safe. Momentarily. It was a frightening time during which I felt utterly alone.

Upon our return, he left straight away for a *Eurotrash* shoot for

Channel 4 in Paris. I, too, was going on a European expedition. I had been asked by the BBC to do a one-off show about the euro – what it was, how it would work and why we shouldn't be afraid of it. It was a programme to be directed at a wide audience, because, quite frankly, most people didn't seem to have the first idea about the euro. The programme would culminate in an interview with the Chancellor of the Exchequer, the Right Honourable Gordon Brown. But how to make the programme interesting? Well, having confessed that I actually found the aforesaid Mr Brown reasonably attractive, it was concluded that I would have an obsession with the Chancellor, and was using the excuse that I needed to find out everything about the euro in order to obtain an interview with him. I had a great producer and we had a lot of fun making it. But all the hours I was working, I had Mr C on the phone raving about the wild time he was having in Paris. Thankfully he decided to stay on a night.

I had been a little perturbed by some mail I had received while I was away. A man unknown to me had laboriously filled seven or eight A4 pages with his thoughts, feelings and intentions – about and towards me. The sentences were for the most part unpunctuated and ran into each other in a confused fashion. He sent three or four letters of this type, with his name and address. I felt concerned, and told Mr C. He accused me of knowing this person, and to stop lying to him about them. Not the reaction I had anticipated. I kept hold of the letters.

On my second last day I was due at Downing Street for my interview with the Member of Parliament for Dunfermline East and I was really looking forward to it. We were welcomed in by Charlie Whelan and shown around. Mr Brown was charming, playful and dignified and I took to him greatly. For the purposes of the programme I pretended to be overawed and semi-flirtatious. It actually wasn't hard to pretend. I came out on a high. Another fun, successful and challenging job well done.

Being at a complete loss as to what to do when it wasn't the football season – apart from some talk of going into modelling – Mr C decided that we would go to Scotland for the weekend where he had a time share on Loch Lomond. Once again, and probably for the millionth time, I plucked up enthusiasm and showed willing. He was insistent that my sister and Helene come up so we could all have a laugh. Ha! Laugh! I hadn't done that for nearly a year. I also wanted Cameron with me.

Throughout the journey Mr C was as irritable, agitated and unsettled as usual; Miss Jonsson was, as ever, trying to placate, settle and reassure him. It was fucking hard work. Especially with a three-and-a-half-year-old in tow, and my persistence stemmed in part from a genuine feeling that my kindness would eventually be reciprocated, in part from fear; and in part it was justification to myself for being in the relationship in the first place. When we got to the property I left Cameron with the girls and took off with Mr Angry to stock up on supplies for ourselves and for his mother, who was staying later that week. As I walked along picking out items, turning to Mr C for choices, I became aware that he was about to launch into another one of his moods. So, I had learnt something in the past nine months! Yes, yet again he turned on me for no reason. And his verbal abuse did not relent for the trip, with nothing learnt from our trip abroad. He continued to swing with his moods, ignore me and taunt me. And the climax to his performance was to walk out and leave me with my son and nanny at the lodge with two days to go. He literally just buggered off. And that finally, for me, was going to be it. I had had enough madness to last me two lifetimes.

PARIS

In a few days' time I was due to fly to Paris for the night to take part in BBC Scotland's *McCoist and McAulay* programme in anticipation of the World Cup, which was starting on 9 June. I guess I was asked to appear because of my well-known passion for the beautiful game. Originally Mr C had been due to travel with me, but there was no way he was coming now. He was still calling, full of absolute remorse, but I still wasn't interested and remained defiant. I was angry and exhausted by him.

I am now about to take you through an event which virtually every person in the country has read about, but about which not many people really *know*. The events of 8 June 1998 have been much publicized, much talked about, much gossiped about and some facts have been distorted. I will give you an honest and true account of what happened, how I reacted and how I felt. I have never discussed the incident in full with anyone except my closest, closest friends, but feel that I cannot write this book with honesty without writing about it.

*

I told Melanie I would be travelling alone to Paris, as in the light of the latest developments Mr C would now not be coming. We briefly toyed with her coming in his place, but decided against fannying around with the ticket. I would dip into Paris and fly out again the following morning. Then the night before I was due to leave, there was a knock on my front door at about midnight. I disarmed the house alarm and went downstairs. At the door stood Mr C.

I opened the door and there he stood, service station bouquet in hand, needy eyes and rare smile. He asked to come in and I asked him what he was doing here. He told me he had to come to Paris with me. I told him that I thought that was the worst idea he had had since the last one. He came in, handed me the flowers and embarked on a speech of remorse, self-pity and regret. He explained how much he loved me and how we needed to be together. I told him I thought the opposite. Frankly, I was too exhausted to talk. He had taken me on an emotional steeplechase and I was fast running out of oxygen. My head was clear on my rejection of him, but clouded by painful memories and could-have-beens. He persisted. And I insisted. At which point he said that if I didn't let him come to Paris with me, he would follow me, and find me. I thought this was a bizarre thing to say to someone, and dramatic, if not a little frightening. I explained I would be gone twenty-four hours and, whilst I knew we had nothing more to talk about, I reassured him we would talk upon my return. But this was not good enough for him.

After two hours of exhaustive rejection, and with him once again see-sawing from remorse to bullying threats to which I had grown deaf, I told him I was going to bed and that he should leave. I don't think he believed me – and why should he have done? I had let him back so many times, my word was hardly my bond. I asked him to leave again, and he refused. Cameron was at home with me and I didn't want him disturbed. I went to bed. He followed.

Throughout the night he held onto me tightly as I battled to slink out of his grasp time and time again. In the morning I took Cameron to school, while he remained at my house. On my return, I told him once again that he should leave, as I was going to be late for the airport at this rate. He tried pleading with me once more and then he simply stated that he was coming with me. He threatened once again that he would follow me and find me, so I might as well let him come.

I didn't want a scene. I told him in no uncertain terms that if he came, he could not interfere with my job, and that under no circumstances would we be discussing our relationship. I was going to work, not on a bloody Relate trip. He told me he would do anything so long as I let him come with me.

We travelled to the airport in silence. I felt in control, for a change. I thought I was actually holding the reins. He owed me so much after the way he had behaved that I felt sure he would comply with my two demands. But we only got as far as the club-class lounge before he started to put his face in mine and insist I tell him I love him and that we would stay together. He told me I couldn't finish it, after all we had been through. I thought, I have to finish it *because* of everything we have been through, but I said nothing. I reminded him of his pledge, but he persisted. When I got up to get a coffee he followed me like a shadow, refusing to leave my side and not daring to let me out of his sight. I was most definitely not in control, and he was definitely out of it.

The flight carried on much the same. He nuzzled up for reassurances and I kept reminding him I didn't want to talk about it. He didn't let me out of his sight for a split second. We checked into my third-rate hotel and he moaned about how shoddy it was. I didn't care, it was only one night. I really didn't care.

He wanted us to have sex. I didn't. I wanted a vodka. I took one from the minibar and waited for the phone call from someone at the BBC about what time I was needed. In the absence of reassurances from me, Mr C suggested we went to dinner after the programme. I thought that was a good idea and he booked us a table at the notorious Buddha Bar. Eventually, after a suffocating couple of hours in the hotel room with Mr C, a taxi came to pick us up to take us to the Eiffel Tower where they had set up a studio. We arrived, alongside the other interviewees, celebrity Scottish footie fans Ewan McGregor, Richard Wilson and Jimmy Hill, a little early. We were all talked through the programme and then asked to go and wait in the bar next to their 'studio'. It was quite a spectacular venue. The imposing Eiffel Tower overlooking the city of love, which was the place to be on the eve of the World Cup. It was a balmy summer's evening and the place was buzzing in anticipation.

I introduced Stan to everyone and kept checking if he was all right. The BBC's head of entertainment, Paul Jackson, was also in attendance. Ewan McGregor had brought his parents, and Richard Wilson I knew from trips to Old Trafford. We were all heady with excitement, in particular the Scots, who were playing the opening game against Brazil. In the bar I had a couple of beers and so did Mr C, who didn't normally drink much alcohol. We waited and chatted. At one stage Ewan sloped off to get a *croque-monsieur* and at that point they asked us to make our way to the studio. They asked where he was and I told them I thought he had gone to the café across the tower and that I didn't mind going to get him. Stan jumped up and grabbed me, holding me back, and took issue with my plan of action: for some reason he had got it into his head that Ewan wanted to fuck me and I must want it too, because I was running after him (his words). I sat down and told him not to be ridiculous. This was, after all, his regular pattern, accusing me of courting others' intentions towards me. It was nothing new to me, but it was vulgar nonetheless. He then claimed the head of entertainment wanted to fuck me, too, at which point I told him to get a grip. He was unsettled. Unnerved. He wasn't able to get to me and it was provoking him. I stayed calm and professional, bearing in mind I was just about to go on and be interviewed. I asked him to stop talking like that and to just enjoy the moment.

I went on and did my interview. I had had a couple of beers and not much to eat, and I was merry. The audience cheered and whistled when I came on – something I knew Mr C would disapprove of, but I could do nothing about it. Ali McCoist and Fred McAulay were a great double act, and the whole set-up proved very amusing.

When I came off the studio floor, I checked if Mr C was all right and whether he wanted us to go to dinner. He told me he didn't. He wanted to stay and have another drink. He was enjoying himself, but he remained nervous and unstable. We went back to the bar with the others and laughed and chatted. After another beer I told him we should leave for dinner or we would be late. He told me we weren't fucking going to dinner any more, and ended the sentence with another vulgar threat in his normal bullying style. At that stage I thought – right, that's it, I'm not going to ask again; we'll just stay here with the others.

I was starving and suggested we stay there to eat. Other people were also hungry so I asked for some menus. I sat with Ewan McGregor's mum and sister, Fred McAulay's agent Melanie Coupland and a few others. I remember telling Melanie that Mr C was out of order and that I was deeply unhappy. She told me to relax and have a good time. I felt slightly distracted and unnerved by Mr C's comments, when out of the blue he approached me, grabbed me by my left arm and told me that he was leaving and that I had better come with him or he would fucking kill me. I became frightened. And I told him so. I told him I wouldn't go with him while he was like that, and made my way back to the table. He disappeared and came back ten minutes later, giving me another 'opportunity' to leave with him. Once again he threatened to kill me if I didn't go with him. I reiterated my previous reply and asked him to stay with me. He wouldn't and left. I remember thinking about my bag at the hotel, for some reason. I felt secure where I was, but I wondered about the hotel room and my bag – dunno why.

After about half an hour everyone decided to make their way to a Paris Scottish pub, the Auld Alliance in Les Halles, for ongoing celebrations. I felt in no mood to celebrate or party. Flat and anxious, I told Melanie I wanted to go back to the hotel, or find a quiet café somewhere. She spent some time convincing me to go with everyone else and assured me we wouldn't stay long. She would go back to the hotel with me later.

Reluctantly, really reluctantly, I went along. We arrived to a packed pub, full of Scotsmen – inebriated Scotsmen, in good spirits and with good spirits in them. The beer was free and they couldn't get enough of it. Rather than fight our way through, we decided to go in the back way. A BBC Scotland crew was there recording the excited Scots and the rest of us were also warmed by their enthusiasm. There are drunken football fans and there are drunken football fans. The Scots appeared to be of the well-mannered and jolly variety, rather than aggressive and vulgar. As we walked in behind the bar they started chanting our names and it was quite overwhelming.

The staff were unable to keep up with demand and Ewan McGregor started pulling pints. I was asked whether I would mind donning a Scotland shirt. Of course I didn't. I put it on over my black top, much to the delight of the fans. They were funny, kind and incredibly merry. Then they started shouting for me to do my *Shooting Stars* trick of downing a pint of lager in one. I felt certain I couldn't do it, but thought I should give something back in gratitude for their enthusiasm. I succeeded rather unsuccessfully, with much of the pint running onto my Scotland shirt. I then went into the room behind the bar, which was full of barrels of the merry-making liquid. I remember thinking I wouldn't drink any more because I hadn't eaten anything and I asked for a glass of water. After chatting to Ali and Melanie Coupland for a while I went back out behind the bar and started to help pull pints. It was great, because with the beer being free I didn't have to do any adding up – I would be a disastrous barmaid.

Then, out of the corner of my eye, I spotted Stan standing in the doorway of the back room. Good, I thought, he has left his funny mood behind and has come to join in the fun. As his face appeared the crowd started chanted his name in a welcoming manner. I went over to him. Can I have a word? he asked. Of course, I said. I always hate couples arguing in public, so I followed him out.

After that everything happened with lightning speed. As I walked through the doorway I felt him grab me by my forearm and before I knew it I had crashed onto the floor. The next thing I felt was his foot against the left side of my head; then the right side and then the left side again. I remember putting my arms up for protection and the force of his further two blows hitting my arms. A loud, high shriek came from my mouth – I didn't recognize it. I didn't sound like me, and with that I felt myself fall backwards down the stairs into the cellar. I carried on screaming, even though there were no more blows. I could barely look up, but saw two men restraining Stan. I carried on shrieking. I didn't know what had happened.

*

It felt like pandemonium. There were people shouting and people hurrying back and forth. Someone rushed to help me and then tried to lift me down the cellar stairs, out of the way. I carried on shrieking in that voice I didn't recognize. Ewan McGregor's mum sat me down and held me. I was dazed and deeply confused. And I was in pain. My head pounded and my left arm and wrist were in agony. I kept repeating, What happened? What happened? And as I sat there in shock, I knew what had happened. But I couldn't believe it. I thought a fight had broken out and that Stan and I must have been caught in the middle of it. I kept asking if he was all right and then it became clear from the raised voices upstairs that we hadn't been caught in anything. He had tried to kick my head in.

So deeply was I in shock that despite the comforting words from those around me my body refused to stop shaking. I was telling it to, but it wasn't listening. I shook and shook; tried to stand up but failed miserably; kept asking, 'Why?' out loud; and then whimpered like a puppy. Making a noise seemed to distract me from the pain. I felt totally bewildered. I refused to believe what had happened. Despite his verbal threats and his passive aggression, he had told me one time after provoking me to virtual insanity that physical violence was never acceptable. I had grabbed him by his strong, long arms and tried to shake him to try to make him stop bullying me and stop threatening me, but my tears and pain had done nothing to make him want to stop.

I looked down at my clothes – they were caked in dirt and mess from the floor upstairs; one of my sandals had fallen apart and my legs were shaking uncontrollably. Through the hustle and bustle I could hear Stan shouting that he wanted to see me and I felt alarmed. I didn't want to see him. Maybe he wanted to finish me off this time. He was warned off trying to see me down in the cellar, and told to leave. I could hear him remonstrating upstairs, until his voice eventually faded. Melanie Coupland came downstairs and assured me he had gone. She told me I would not be staying in the hotel with him that night, but that I could shack up with her. I wanted my things.

After about an hour down in the cellar, with everyone, from Fred to Ali, coming to check if I was all right, like I was a hospital patient, it was decided we would make our way back towards the hotel. I got up to walk and felt decidedly unsteady. As I emerged from the cellar I could see photographers outside and the staff kindly closed the doors until the taxi was absolutely outside the door. There were crowds outside and my new friends and the staff from the pub protected me as I limped my way to the people carrier. There were a few of us in there and they thought it best that we went to a café across the road from the hotel to assess the situation.

They were talking about me in the taxi; and about Stan; and about what he had done. I sat in silence, unable to comprehend, unable to utter a word, and with my head lost in a sea of flashbacks. I kept going over and over it in my head and I could feel the soreness of my wrist and my head pounding. I didn't cry. I was so deeply in shock that I was almost not even there. All the voices were echoing in my head, but I didn't seem to hear sentences, just disjointed words that didn't seem to make sense. They were talking about me, but I wasn't there – I was somewhere else. I wanted my things. I wanted my bag and I wanted to be home.

We were dropped off at a nearby café and I was asked if I wanted to go back to the hotel. Despite wanting my things, I didn't want to go back. I didn't want to be alone. I wanted to be surrounded by noise and the voices of people. Someone offered to go and get my bag, but I asked them to wait. I needed to go with someone, but not yet. We sat there for ages. The boys carried on drinking beer and I sat on my own or with Melanie as she attempted to comfort me.

Then word came that Stan wanted to see me. I didn't want to see him. He was desperate, said Ali, and he had calmed down, he was crying. No, I don't want to see him, I repeated. But it became apparent that it wasn't my choice. Into the bar walked the great man himself. Everyone rushed forward to tell him to leave, and that they wanted no trouble. He kept calling out to me, asking for me to speak to him. I sat alone at a table for four and looked away, but despite that he was escorted towards me. I didn't feel he was about to go for me again, but there was equally a side of me that didn't care if he did. I was numb, I couldn't feel anything except exhaustion and the pounding in my head. He stood in front of me and pleaded with me to give him two minutes of my time. I refused to answer him. This simply wasn't happening.

He sat himself down, tissue in hand and his eyes red from weeping and with tears rolling down his big cheeks. I felt nothing. He started crying, sobbing unashamedly. He talked about his shame, about his remorse and how he will have broken his mother's heart with his actions. He spoke about his mother a lot. My head kept going in and out of his words, as if someone was turning the volume up and down. In the middle of his soliloquy, Fred McAulay interrupted him and gave him a drunken dressing down about what he had done to me. I feared for Fred in case Stan would turn again, but he simply sat there and wept, and apologized to Fred, too.

I said nothing throughout, except that I didn't think now was a good time for us to talk. But he wanted to talk. Eventually I tried to get up to get away from him, but my body was stiff. He agreed to leave. He begged me to come back to the room. I told him I would pick my bag up shortly.

Then I waited with the others in the café, with nothing but numbness in my head and confusion in my body. I felt no part of myself. I felt as if everything was going on around me, but that I wasn't really there. Ali came back from the hotel where he had been speaking to Stan. He asked me whether I would consider going back to speak to Stan; he seemed desperate, said Ali. No, I don't want to talk to him, but I do want to get my bag. Ali assured me he and Ewan's dad would accompany me and that I would come to no harm. I just wanted my bag.

The three of us walked slowly back to the hotel and Ali knocked on the room door. Stan answered. I looked down. When I looked up he was still clutching his tissue and his eyes were even redder in the light of the hotel. He begged me to come in and talk. I told him once more that I thought this was no time to talk. He told me he wanted to die and pleaded some more. I told him I was coming in to get my bag, nothing more, and as I did so Ali and Ewan's father insisted on standing guard by the door, leaving it slightly ajar, should I need them. I looked into the bathroom, but could see none of my things. I went through into the bathroom, shutting the door behind me. As I sat down – I'd forgotten how desperate I was for a wee – Stan opened it. I asked him to leave me alone, but all he did was toss my holdall in after me. What on earth was he up to? I opened my bag and, on seeing its contents, screamed, 'What have you done???'

For as I looked inside my bag I could see only shreds. My clothes and my belongings, including my toilet bag, had been cut into small, postage-stamp pieces. He had even destroyed everything in my make-up bag and had twisted and broken my hair dryer. I couldn't believe what I was seeing. What have you done? I kept reiterating. He pleaded with me to stay. He said he wanted to kill himself and when I emerged from the bathroom he was sitting on the edge of the bed. He wanted to show me his hand. He told me he was sorry for what he had done, and that he didn't know what had got into him and why he kept doing it. I didn't understand what he meant by 'kept doing it', and he gave me no time to probe further as he showed me the inside of his left hand. It appeared burnt and red. He told me he wanted to hurt himself as penance for what he had done to me, and he had been burning his hand with a cigarette lighter. I told him not to be stupid. He begged me to stay and I realized I had nothing left in me to fight him. I did what I had always done in this relationship, which was to placate him. I never had the fuel to fight and would do almost anything for a quiet life. And I knew in my heart of hearts that he would be no threat to me that night. I didn't want to be near him, but felt too exhausted to worry about him running around trying to find me in the night and causing even more of a drama.

So I told Ali and Ewan's dad that I was all right, and that I would stay in the room that night and leave first thing in the morning as planned. We were booked on the same flight home after all, so I would run into him at the airport anyway.

I had nothing to change into and lay myself down on the very edge of the bed with my painful wrist rested on a pillow for support. I did not move till morning. I didn't sleep for the entire night and neither did Stan. He held on tightly to my other arm and refused to let it go. When I made an attempt to move it he gripped me harder, and I didn't want to fight him any more. I was completely drained, gutted, exhausted and bewildered. The grime from the pub floor had dirtied my legs, and my make-up had left its original location and was now somewhere halfway down my face. But nothing mattered. I wasn't there. This wasn't happening.

The following morning Stan pleaded with me to stay on in Paris so that he could replace all the things he had destroyed. I merely whispered that I wanted to go home and climbed into the awaiting taxi. He came with me, but was flitting between verbal aggression and deep, deep remorse. I couldn't climb aboard his emotional roller coaster any more, I felt numbed by the whole experience. Nothing he said meant anything to me. He meant nothing to me. And I meant nothing to me either. I felt unattached and shell-like; unmoved, but aching; sore, but unemotional. I felt everything and nothing.

Throughout our trip back he would place his face as close to mine as he could whilst grabbing hold of my hands and insist that I confirm my love for him. I said nothing. He wanted me to promise we would marry. I said nothing. I couldn't imagine what he was thinking. Whenever I told him to leave me alone, he would become verbal once again. I would walk away, but had no physical strength. I just wanted to get home.

As we landed at Heathrow and I turned my mobile on there was a message from Stan's agent, Paul Stretford. I had met him a few times, but didn't realize he had my number. He wondered whether Stan was with me, because apparently he had been involved in a fight the night before. The press had been on to him.

Oh, God, the press. I had forgotten about them. I told Stan to phone his agent. My first call was to mine. I told my Melanie, from what I can remember, that something had happened the night before and that Stan had hurt me. She told me she was on her way.

Stan had left his car at my house the day before, and when Mel arrived he was still there. She took one look at me. I could say nothing in his presence, and I was scared. Melanie is just under five foot. Stan is well over six foot, but I would have defied him to mess with her on that day – she virtually lifted him out of my house. She told him he should go. He wanted to stay. So, she lifted him, almost.

I took her through, in detail, the previous night's disastrous events. I relayed both words and actions, and throughout it my body made efforts to cry, but would then contain itself, until the next sentence. Melanie couldn't quite believe what she was hearing, but there was a look of recognizing the inevitable about her face. So, there we sat, on my bed in my bedroom, me talking, her listening, as always. I was dazed and I ached.

Within an hour, Melanie's mobile rang. It was the editor of the *Sun*.

OFFSIDE

What happened next would probably be better told by Melanie, but a veritable circus came to town. Word spread like wildfire through a forest dry of news and sensation. Every conceivable publication, broadcaster and hack stood on my doorstep. The attention was overwhelming. The story had been broken by a journalist from BBC Scotland who had been present in the Auld Alliance on the offending night. He had articulated quite clearly how Mr C had attacked me with ferocity and speed. The attack had appeared unprovoked. Three men had had to restrain him.

I called my mother, my sister and a couple of close friends. My sister came over from London and my mother was soon on her way. My gardeners arrived to do the garden as usual and had no idea what was going on. I told them it was nothing and I chatted with them in an attempt to appear normal. Melanie, quite rightly, felt we needed to issue a press statement to try to appease the starving vultures waiting at the bottom of my drive. Everything felt unreal – I really wanted to wake up.

Melanie felt the most essential thing to project was that my relationship with Stan Collymore was over. Full stop. And she issued a statement with words to that effect. She also added that I was fine and that I had the support of family and friends.

Cameron came home from school. He was only three and a half and I tried in a scattered, disconnected way to tell him what was happening and that I was fine. He had no comprehension of what was going on and I certainly didn't expect him to. So I told him a little white lie about what had happened – I can't remember what exactly. I couldn't understand it, why should he?

Melanie offered to stay the night. I thought it was unnecessary but she insisted, and I'm glad she did. As we watched the evening news together, it became evident that my Paris trip was now a top story.

Then Stan called. He told me that he too was issuing a statement, and he read it to me. It went along the lines of him having been involved in an altercation and that he had reacted without thinking and that he was sorry. I didn't have anything to tell him – I didn't know what to say, and my silence aggravated him. He then proceeded to ask if I was happy that he was taking full responsibility for the incident. What kind of question was that? Fearing public persecution, he was still, in his own mind, expecting me to share the responsibility for his actions. I declined.

The following day the press was still waiting with baited breath for any sign of me. I knew they wanted a sensational picture of me bruised black and blue. But I always took Cameron to nursery school when I was home, and I felt it was important for him and for me that I didn't make an exception at a time like this. I made sure I left my house without sunglasses and with my hair pinned back, as usual. They needed to see that the bruises I had were not on the surface. The blows had been to my head, not my face, and the bruise I had was on my arm and covered by clothing.

I had no intention of sensationalizing this 'story' any more than it needed to be. And a trip to the doctor's would have done just that. However, my vision was blurred from exhaustion and the tears I had finally started to shed the night before. My face was puffy but drawn, and I was still not quite with it – yes, I was walking and occasionally talking, but still felt no part of what was going on around me. As Cameron and I left the house, the photographers went berserk. Cameron again questioned me; I told him it was because mummy worked on the telly. He brought his own camera with him and snapped away at them, from the back of the car. It was unnerving. I was still shaky and unstable on my two legs, but I managed to run the gauntlet.

I had phone calls, messages of support and even flowers from friends, but deep down I failed to register the fuss that was going on. It was like everyone else around me was living the change, the disturbance and the circus, but I wasn't 'living' anything – I was merely surviving.

Another day passed and I ate nothing. Nervy, I wanted to remain locked away, hidden and shielded. But no one could really offer me that. I was due to go back to France to watch England's opening match against Tunisia in Marseilles with my gorgeous friend Paul the following Sunday, but I couldn't for the life of me imagine myself travelling after all this. Paul was generous enough to understand if I had changed my mind, but part of me felt that I didn't want to give in to the devil who had fought me and tried to beat me down so many times. I didn't want Stan to have a hold on my life any more, I wanted to carry on as *I* wanted. So after much deliberation I decided to go – Paul would look after me well, and it was only for twenty-four hours, if that.

That morning the *News of the World* ran a story by Stan's former fiancée who claimed she had been beaten half to death by him on several occasions, and alongside the story ran a diary of his rather chequered inglorious past. I felt sick. He had done it before. This had been no accident: he had wanted to hurt me.

I was shaky for much of the trip, calmed only by a tot of alcohol here and there. Upon our arrival in Cannes, Stan called on my mobile. He deciphered from the ringing tone on my phone that I was abroad. He went crazy, demanding to know where I was and who with. I told him it was no longer his business, but he worked out I had gone to France for the football. This threw him into a deeper fury, but I told him I wasn't interested in what he had to say. Instead, I asked him if he had ever attacked his previous girlfriend. He fell silent. I raised my voice and demanded he tell me the truth. And eventually, after another long silence, he said 'yes', but that it was not what I thought. I put the phone down. He had no idea what I thought.

*

It's wonderful to be the last to know. When you have already been reduced to scraping your self-confidence off the floor only to hear everyone tell you, 'I could have told you so', your dignity and self-belief takes a further nose-dive – if that is possible. Everyone knew of this man's reputation, but no one thought to warn me. But maybe, just maybe, I wouldn't have been able to hear them even if they had. He ended up so conditioning and brainwashing me that I lost all concept of myself, let alone of reality. I realized my own self had been swept away on a tide of psychological abuse over the past ten months or so, a process which had damaged me in a far greater way than anything his feet had done to my skull. I had lost touch with myself, and with everything and everyone around me, as I subjected myself over and over again to someone who was essentially of unsound mind and whose emotions were purely self-serving. I had believed that kindness, generosity and affection would help cure the ailing heart he carried, but my attempts had been rejected at every level. But I'd still I allowed myself to enter the ring, time and time again, in the pathetic belief that he would one day see the light. And in so doing I had been made to believe that I was worthless and that it was I who was mad and out of order and not the situation. My grasp of reason had not only weakened, but had altogether gone.

I discovered that, both to myself and to my close friends, I had become a changed person. I had become nervous, agitated, impatient, aggressive and emotionally exhausted. Any lines marking decent, normal behaviour had become blurred and indistinct. I had lost hindsight, foresight and I was by now squinting. And the squinting restricted my view profoundly. Self-doubt was compounded with shock, but I tried to carry on regardless, I tried to be strong for Cameron and I made few attempts to broach the subject with myself. It was as if my self-confidence had been knocked so severely that I was incapable even of acknowledging that I might be affected by this incident or that I would ever deserve some sympathy – if even just from myself. My head was a mess.

Apart from taking Cameron to school, it was a week before I had the courage to face the world. And rather ridiculously it was because I needed to go clothes shopping for the next series of *Gladiators*. I took a packet of cigarettes with me into London for comfort and wore big, baggy clothes with my hair dirty and pinned back. I was shaking and for a non-smoker I didn't do too badly at smoking that day.

*

A day or so later there was a knock on my front door while I was on the phone to Melanie. I didn't recognize the man on my doorstep, but assumed it was another journalist. I opened the door cautiously. The man started rambling, and I couldn't make out what he was saying. He was upset that I didn't recognize him, and he asked if I had received his letters. Then it clicked. Standing in front of me, on my doorstep, on my property, was the unsound-of-mind man who had by now sent me pages and pages and pages of insanity, provocation and increasingly sexual comments and suggestions. He had even intimated that we would soon meet in death . . . I quickly shut the door and panicked. He left. I didn't know what to do. Melanie strongly advised I phone the police. I did.

Over the next few weeks, he called at my house a couple more times, leaving flowers or a note on my doorstep. The notes always expressed disappointment that he hadn't been able to see me as he had driven all the way from the north of England. And he continued to write letters, too.

The reason I called the police was because the man had actually turned up at my house. I now knew he knew where I lived, and living on my own with a small child, as I had now done for three years since my divorce (Linda and Helene had long since found their own place to live), this was not the most comforting thought. The man was smartly dressed, well-groomed and drove a Lexus – not the stereotypical mac-wearing image. The police spent hours questioning me and were very helpful. They told me that they could charge him straight away, or caution him to let him know his attention was unwanted by me. I wanted him to be warned.

I felt so utterly insecure. I had seen the violent end to one relationship – one which in fact was turning out to not have quite died yet – and I had a stranger pursuing me, making unwanted advances and unnatural suggestions. But overwhelmed or not, I still knew I needed to be allowed to live my life by myself if that was what I had chosen.

So yes, Stan continued to call. And I continued to take the calls. But I also started to realize what had happened over the course of the whole affair. Gradually the tears started and the pain began as the reality of the situation took hold. Soon I wasn't crying about the end of the relationship, if that is what it can be called, but in desperation for the pain he had inflicted on me. Perhaps to reclaim myself and my own thoughts, I began to write down how I felt as the pain turned to anger, but apart from putting pen to paper I had no other outlet to vent my frustration.

Apart from seeing an anger-management therapist, or whatever they are called, *his* life appeared to carry on pretty much as before. He would call and express some form of sensitivity towards me, but then blow it all in anger when I didn't give him the answers he wanted. I prayed so much for *calm*. I wanted to be peaceful, but I knew it was never going to happen with him anywhere near my life. But still he would call. He phoned and told me he had swanned off to the South of France with Davina McCall and that he had gone to a World Cup game. He talked of going away again, and I kept thinking how unaffected by it all he appeared . Of course, I should have cut him off for ever, but deep inside me I felt like a victim needing to speak to her aggressor to try and fathom out what had happened and why. I guess there was some part of me that needed to hear that he was sorry; needed confirmation that the madness he had inflicted on my life came from him and had not been cultivated by me. Yes, I needed to hear that *I* wasn't mad. But he was not the right person to ask.

When I was invited by my lovely friend Paul to go and watch England v Argentina in the World Cup quarter finals, I accepted. It turned out to be a remarkable match, particularly for me as I had consumed a fair amount of cold, cold beer before entering the stadium. But just before I did, Mr C called, cursing me for going to the football. And particularly for going to the football with my friend, who, apparently, was yet another entry on the long list of people who wanted to fuck me. How nice to know. But as he ranted and raved, I actually rang off. And enjoyed the game.

But that wasn't the end of it. By the time I returned, Stan had phoned again to inform me that he was going off to New York on holiday. Whatever. Once there, he sounded more sinister. He told me he was going to kill himself – he was going to go into the subway and throw himself under a train. I felt nothing when he told me this – it just sounded gratuitous and self-serving. I told him he was crazy, but his voice just lowered and lowered until I couldn't hear him any more. I didn't think for one second he would do it – I felt he loved himself too much, and anyway, I understand that people who are really going to commit suicide rarely let you know in advance. But just in case, I called his agent and handed over responsibility to him. Why should I cope with him any more?

Instead, Cameron and I were off to the South of France for a week's break on our own. It was wonderful to be me again, and a boost to soak up some of the strength and power my child gave me.

*

Gladiators that year turned out to be really enjoyable. While I had two weeks or so of being apart from Cameron, on and off, I had two weeks of being with my close friend Jennifer. Here was someone I could truly confide in. She is a bright, strong woman with a heart of gold and a laugh like a hyena. Thankfully, James and I were on better terms by now. Perhaps it goes without saying that when I arrived in Birmingham, home of Mr Collymore, he called to welcome me back to the city and to ask whom I was fucking. Well, I was fucking no one, but that was none of his business. Later, he phoned to let me know that if I ever went for a night out in 'his' city, he would see to it that I would live to regret it. Under no circumstances was I to embarrass him or show him up by going out right under his nose. I put the phone down.

To help me get over it all, Angus Deayton and a group of mutual friends invited me to Tuscany, where they had rented a fabulous villa. I couldn't go for a whole week – I didn't want to leave Cameron for that long – but I managed four blissful days with a crowd of hilarious, kind and sane people. It made a refreshing change.

By the time I came back, Mr C was dancing to a more controlled beat, a calmer drum. Now when he called he told me he wanted to share his new approach with me, and was prepared to accept responsibility for the kind of person he had been and the actions he had taken. He talked about what he had learnt about himself in his therapy time, and he said it was all really making a difference. He could feel it. Well, whatever difference it had made, it had all come a year too late. But, I have to say, it did make me feel calm to hear him calmer. Perhaps now we could both get on with life. Separately. But the calls kept coming. I realized that right from the start this had been largely a telephone relationship, even after just a couple of months. But however much I was keen for it to stop, I was still too weak and shaky to have the final face-off.

The BBC wanted me to host a new midweek Lottery show, to be called *Dreamworld*. I didn't like the idea of the show, and refused more than once. But an offer from Peter Salmon, controller of BBC1 at the time, is hard to turn down, and in the end I relented. I should have trusted my instinct. The show was harmless enough, but the production process was not particularly easy-going, and I didn't have a particularly enigmatic product to sell.

For all my sins, insanities and peculiarities, I was also persuaded to do something else that was against my own innate judgement. Mr C actually managed to convince me that meeting up with him would help us both come to terms with what had happened. He also wanted us to be together, which I didn't, but I agreed strongly with him on the former point. It just seemed sensible. And this from the woman who has just conceded she had long since taken leave of her senses. The best place for me would have been a nunnery, but instead I drove to Birmingham to have lunch with my aggressor.

Needless to say, someone spotted us, and it was subsequently reported that we were back together again. They couldn't have been further from the truth. There had been no joyous reunion, even he would concede that. At last I could see that while I was meeting up with a man who talked a good line in self-analysis, he couldn't walk the walk. I wasn't disappointed. I just knew he would never change, and would never truly accept responsibility for himself. He paid lip service to remorse, but in an utterly self-serving way.

My relationship with Mr C was well and truly over, but the door wasn't closed in terms of 'closure'. I still struggled to come to terms with the past year. And as much as Stan was responsible for psychologically fucking with me, I had allowed him to continue to do so, and to live rent-free in my head for so long. It would take me a long time to appreciate that I might be good for more than nothing.

*

I spent the night in Brixton Prison. For charity. And didn't like it very much, so I hope never to return. The Lottery show continued and I was about to embark on a pilot for ITV, which was cancelled at the eleventh hour. I went with Paul to see England play Bulgaria at Wembley, and I was still opening mobile-phone shops in parts of the country you don't even know about. And instead of having another child, which I had been longing for, I got a puppy, despite my allergies. But the poor thing had to go after four weeks – Cameron was also starting to be snuffly and congested. It was a shame, but imperative. Cameron took it incredibly well.

I started going out a bit more and felt that I was gradually leaving the Stan episode behind. I began to recognize myself a bit better, and so did all my family and friends. Towards the end of

October I hosted a celebrity auction for ITV called *Men for Sale*,
where we quite literally auctioned off time with male celebrities to
an audience of some of London's wealthiest women. Despite their
finery and designer clothes, nothing could stop them rushing upon
the stage to manhandle poor Julio Iglesias. He actually looked as if
he feared for his life. Denise Van Outen was my co-presenter.
Great girl. Can't sing, can't act – won't go far. When in November
I hosted the *New Woman* Beauty Awards, I was rather ironically
the recipient of their Woman of the Year Award. This truly was a
new start – the only other prize I'd won in my life (bar Rear of the
Year and best spectacle wearer) was a yo-yo for solving a crossword
puzzle when I was nine. I also launched the now-defunct digital
channel ON Digital (what does that say?) and was asked to go for an
audition for the musical *Chicago*. Although I had originally been
asked to try for the Roxy Hart role, having seen the show I felt so
big a part might be beyond me, so I sang my heart out for the role
of Big Mama. They were marginally impressed. They said they were
interested, but also suggested I take some lessons to train my voice.

But it was towards the end of 1998 when I was invited, alongside
a whole host of celebrities, to attend a fund-raising evening at the
AIDS charity and home London Lighthouse that a corner was turned.
The evening was hosted by Stephen Fry and I decided to go along
with Angus and a couple of other friends. We met up for drinks
beforehand and we were only due to stay at the reception for the
required hour or so, then head out for dinner. However, we were all
rather merry by the time it came to ten o'clock, and we decided to
stay on.

And there, across the room, I caught the eye of a man who
would inadvertently help me rid myself of the turbulent Mr C for
ever. He was someone I hadn't met before, but whom I knew of
through mutual friends. He was handsome, had an incredible smile,
and the only downside was that he was another footballer.

That aside, we chatted and he made me laugh so much that I
ended up giving him my number at the end of the evening. I must
have been drunk. I never do that. Take a number, but don't give one

out. Crazy lady. When he called, we talked loosely about getting together for a drink later in the week. He called himself 'my new friend'. I liked that. If I was going to like him, he needed to be a friend first and foremost. No one except John had been my friend from the start. And it ended up being a very pleasant evening. He made me laugh – a lot; he didn't take me or himself seriously and it was wonderfully light relief after the heavy year I had been having – just what I needed. It goes without saying that I was deeply attracted to him, too.

The following week I hosted the Royal Variety Show. A broadcasting thrill second only to Eurovision, it did something to boost my flagging self-confidence, too. I also went to Sweden for a long weekend to see my sister and grandmother and to visit my father's grave. And all the while I was excited by my recent sporting encounter. We both wanted to keep it secret as it was early days. And have decided to respect each other's privacy since. Because of this I will only call him 'the footballer'. It felt great because it was not only a pleasant distraction, but it meant I was capable of moving on, something of which I had been increasingly doubtful.

*

In January 1999 I had to call the police again. The letters from my 'stranger' had started to reappear on a biweekly basis, and the tone was increasingly frustrated. This time I gave the police the go-ahead to charge him. I discovered that by the time they had brought him in for questioning, they already knew he was a family man with his own business and a property in Spain. He seemed, on the face of things, quite normal, but when they delved deeper, a darker side emerged. He seemed slightly manic and would often not make sense in his answers. He also failed to understand that his advances towards me were unwanted. In fact, he rejected this fervently – and said other things, too. They decided he should be analysed by a police psychologist.

Following up on the *Chicago* verdict, I started singing lessons with a wonderful lady in Camden who told me that everyone could sing, but some voices just needed a little guidance. She told me I could *definitely* sing, but that I'd benefit from a few facial and vocal exercises. And while Old Trafford was an entertaining enough diversion for me, I thought my beautiful son Cameron deserved a holiday on sunnier shores. Having already experienced the Caribbean I plumped this time for the East – the Indonesian island of Bintan, just an hour's boat ride from Singapore. I was excited by the prospect of a new experience and the luxury of the sun on our bare skins, whilst everyone back home would be cramped by damp and cold on those dark February nights.

Before we left, the police called to ask if they could come around to talk to me. Of course they could. They seemed rather reserved and quiet as they came in. They sat down and told me slowly that although a court date had been set for next week to prosecute the stranger who had persisted in sending me unwanted mail and turning up on my doorstep, it would now have to be cancelled. Why? I enquired cautiously. Because, they replied, the man had committed suicide, fuming himself to death in his garage. I gasped. I couldn't believe it. And the immediate emotion, overriding any sense of relief, was that of guilt. In my pursuit of a private life, I had driven a man to death. A man with children and a wife. The police tried to convince me not to think like that – they urged me to realize that he must have had other woes in life than the prospect of my court case. But I felt devastated. Well, devastated and slightly relieved. But also confused. And guilty.

STEAM HEAT

My dear friend Jennifer had had a traumatic break-up from her long-term boyfriend, on top of which she was working incredibly hard to get herself back into the athletics domain after a break of a few years. My relationship with the footballer was going well, but I was hesitant to mention my planned ten-day holiday. Yet I was looking forward to it and felt, deep down, that a little time apart wouldn't be a bad thing. On the other hand, would whatever we had stand the test of time? However, I stiffened my resolve and, to keep Cameron and me company and give her a break, I suggested Jen come with us, and to my delight and surprise she said she would.

After a twelve-and-a-half-hour flight, a six-hour time difference and a sickly ferry ride, we arrived – in a cloudy Indonesia. We were pale – well, Cameron and I at least, Jennifer was 'as black as the lead in the pencil', as Cameron put it. And next to her Olympically athletic body, I looked like a fading doughnut.

No sooner had we installed ourselves by the pool, me studying nimbus patterns intensely and wondering why the hell I had spent all this money to travel to warm cloud, and Jen feeling homesick, than a tall, tanned, barefoot European man passed by us with his short, bald French colleague, asking if we were here 'for the seminar'. 'No,' I replied tersely. I would have thought two young women and a four-and-a-half-year-old would quite obviously not belong to any business seminar. 'Where's the bloody sun?' I bellowed, irritated. 'You will still get brown in the cloud,' replied the tall European kindly. Yeah right, I thought. But within twenty-four hours of this unpromising start we found our groove. Jen thought less and less of home; the sun came out to kiss our skins; and the jet lag faded rapidly.

The European chap made a fuss of Cameron whenever he saw him. I however kept my beady eye on my son, and my distance from the man. Jen, on the other hand, who has an inability to stop talking – to anyone, at any time – kept up a running conversation with him. And everyone else around us. One evening a toy watch was delivered to our room for Cameron, with a compliment slip signed 'From the Captain'. This was the tall European – he had been dressed in a waistcoat with gilded buttons one night, and from then on Cameron had likened him to a captain on a ship. The watch went down well – Cameron was watch-mad. I was rather taken aback by the gesture, and made sure Cameron thanked him properly. Other than that, I had few conversations with the Captain, but I always felt his eyes on me. Wherever I looked, he was there. When I wasn't looking, he would appear. His eyes were burning holes in my back, but not uncomfortably so. I didn't think he had his sights set on me – I already had him married with children, although the presence of a wedding ring, a wife and two children would probably have been a better indication.

Halfway through our holiday, word came from Jen that he really liked me and that he would love to talk to me. But I only wanted to talk to my footballer, whom I had only reached on the phone a couple of times. I missed him – and I made the mistake of telling him.

This tall European turned out to be German, and not a captain at all. He was the resort manager. We eventually exchanged the odd word, in company, in crowds or with Cameron running around my ankles. But the German wanted more. He wanted us to talk alone. I saw no need and resisted. He, on the other hand, persisted. He sat at our table for the odd lunch and dinner, whilst gently trying to persuade me to join him for a drink at his house overlooking the resort. Still I resisted. One night he didn't come down for dinner. His short, bald colleague told us he was in a sulk. Something to do with me ... And, ironically, there was something really lacking about that evening. Somehow.

This wouldn't have been a story if I hadn't relented. But rest assured, I did. Jen had borrowed his minidisc player one day, and I offered to return it to his office – choosing a time when I thought plenty of people would be around.

He sat behind his desk like an emperor in a large leather chair. I commented on his office, not knowing quite what to say. He asked me again to join him for a drink up at his house – watch the sunset, that kind of stuff. By now I was feeling some kind of pull, some kind of attraction. But I didn't want to go there. He was tall and bronzed with shoulder-length light brown hair, glasses and a deep husky voice that betrayed a long history of smoking. His chest was hairy and was inviting my hands and face to stroke it under his white linen shirt.

Warming to his theme, he actually suggested, laughingly, a night together in another resort. I smiled, embarrassed, flattered, and saying I was too old for those kinds of jaunts. I shook my head and got up to leave. However, he reached the door before me, and totally unexpectedly our lips attacked each other with such fervour that I almost forgot myself. I felt the excitement in me and the excitement in his trousers. 'This is no good,' I said, 'I have to go.' Truth was, even as I left, I knew it was very good.

I was actually electrified by our encounter and had to admit to myself that I wanted him. But it was purely physical. I was pretty sure I was falling in love with the footballer, and I really did miss him. I'm not a believer in what you don't know doesn't hurt you; I felt committed, and comfortably so.

That night, the German, whose name was Markus, insisted we join him for dinner in the resort's Italian restaurant. He placed himself opposite me at the table, next to Jen. The poor short bald Frenchman was dragged along too. He had a soft spot for Jen. She laughed at the prospect. All night the German looked at me sug-gestively, and toyed tantalizingly with my legs under the table. He pretended to forget my name constantly, in order, presumably, to appear to slow down his sense of urgency. Again his persistence won through that night: I found myself asking him what the hell it was he wanted from me. 'I want you,' he replied, simply. Well, I may have wanted him too, but there was no way I was going there. To the place of infidelity, lust, passion beyond the realms of humanity and an aching frustration at the end of the holiday? No way. I was *too old*. I wanted the footballer. But my lips, at that precise moment, wanted to meet the German's again.

The next time I passed by his office, and was forced to make my rejection clear to him, our lips found each other again with renewed hunger and even more consuming electricity. Divine intervention must have brought me to my senses after the few seconds, which seemed to last minutes. My mouth was dry, my head was spinning and my legs felt like I had just completed a marathon. Damn temptation! I was determined to resist. And resist I did. Whilst my body truly ached for him, my head thankfully guided me to safer, calmer shores.

And that was the end of it. Nothing more happened between us, even though he did ask me to spend the last night with him up at his house. Nothing would happen, he assured me. Yeah right, and I'm Julie Andrews, I thought.

On the morning of our departure, he called down to reception to wish me a safe journey and told me to take care of myself. I said I might call him one day. And that, as they say, was that, even if I spent a huge part of my return flight thinking about the tall, tanned European who had somehow made such an impression on me. But I concluded that I had been right to reject his sexual advances. It was the sensible and mature thing to do. And what's more, I had the safe arms of the footballer to look forward to.

Dreaming of what lay ahead, I leafed through the previous day's *Telegraph* – only to read that *Gladiators* had been axed. 'We're unemployed,' I shouted across the aisle to Jen. My exclamation was met with dismay and concern.

No sooner had we landed in the early hours of Saturday 13 February than I was on the phone, announcing my arrival to my footballing friend and my wish to see him as soon as possible. My conversation was with his mobile's voicemail. He knew when I was returning, so I was sure, despite him playing that day, that I would hear something before or immediately after the match. But by half past ten that night – nothing.

Gradually inside me grew the realization that all was not as it should be. On that account, at least, I was right. I began to feel terrible – uncertain, unsure and extremely disappointed. It is amazing how someone can have the power, albeit unbeknown to them, to send your confidence into a nosedive. Jennifer immediately kicked into action – sensing, too, the potential of bad news on the way. In an attempt to boost my rapidly diminishing self-worth, she suggested giving the German a call in Indonesia – if only in order to have at least have an air of confidence about me when, or if, I did next hear from the footballer.

Expecting I wouldn't get through, and largely unsure of my reason for calling, I dialled. But I got lucky and was put through immediately. (He must take every call that comes through, I thought.) After over an hour's conversation about life, work and the beauty of the world, Jennifer pointed out by means of sign language that this was an hour longer than I had spoken to him during my entire stay in Bintan. The conversation ended positively – although he did say he didn't want to take my number, for fear of wanting to phone me all the time. Smooth operator, I thought, you just want it to be my bloody phone bill. But Jen's trick worked. I came off the phone feeling great.

The footballer, unfortunately, did not feel so great when I got hold of him a few moments later, requesting some form of explanation for his Lord Lucan act the previous night. I told him that he'd best get his arse over here that evening and talk to me face to face. And cut the bullshit. He obeyed.

He explained that he did not feel the same way as he figured I did. He wasn't after the same thing as I wanted – yet. I admired and respected his honesty, but knew that I didn't want to wait. I wanted to seize the day. My eyes heated and welled with disappointment – because I knew he was lying. He was running scared. But no matter how convinced I was, far was it for me to try to sway him from his belief. Yet I had heard from him, during the previous three months, things he hadn't, by his own admission, wanted to impart to anyone before. He hadn't ever felt this way, he had said. And that was only a couple of weeks prior to this showdown, and a game of cat and mouse. Still, I reflected, I was tired of only being able to meet at his place or mine; tired of not being able to talk about him to anyone. In short, tired – again, I just felt too old for this sort of thing. Above all else, I guess what I really wanted was to be with someone who wanted to be with me. There was no point in compromise. So I let him go that night, filled with disappointment and a strong feeling of having been let down. He, too, felt disappointed – that I was taking such a final decision.

Perhaps fuelled by rejection, I embarked on a rejuvenated approach to life. It was time for changes and new challenges. And as if on cue, along one came. A month or so before, Melanie had been asked if I would be interested in taking on a musical to be directed by the great Simon Callow at the Birmingham Repertory Theatre. Naturally, I had declined. I say naturally, because I now didn't believe my singing was up to a musical, and certainly not one hoping to transfer to the West End, via Toronto; on top of which, despite my love for Birmingham, it didn't seem possible or practical to be based there for weeks on end given I had a four-year-old son in tow. That very week however, the enquiry resurfaced. This time I decided I might be interested.

The morning I was due to meet up with Simon, the musical supervisor and the producer, I had for my sins woken up with swollen tonsils – a regular for me whenever I'm run down. This seemed just ideal for a musical audition. Nonetheless, after chatting and listening to their plans for the musical – a revival of the 1950s Broadway hit, *The Pajama Game* – I asked if they would like to hear me sing. 'We know you can sing,' they said, practically in unison.

Well, I didn't. So I insisted, and let rip on Mama's opening number from *Chicago*, with tonsils the size of tennis balls and hot flushes running through my veins. They liked it.

As Melanie and I left, climbing into a cab, we both squealed with delight and excitement. I was about to be directed by Simon Callow in a musical! Mr Callow wanted to make *The Pajama Game* sexy; it was to be an ensemble production and it would be a massive new departure for me. It was a chance not just to stretch myself professionally, but to really sink my teeth into a serious project.

At around the same time as I had fronted ITV's sports awards alongside ITN's Dermot Murnaghan in November 1997, I had also been invited by ITV's Network Centre to host a few seminars for their advertisers, showing off what ITV had lined up for future seasons. ITV's then new man at the helm, David Liddiment, promised a fresh, direct and more instantaneous approach to the commissioning of programmes. I had felt honoured to take on such a role, and positive about the forthcoming changes. Television can be such a slow, frustrating business. Often programme ideas come to nothing because the people at the top refuse to take calculated risks, or want simply to stick with what they know. I had over the years been asked to put my name to hundreds of programme ideas, and it goes without saying that the best ones were never commissioned. It became impossible, because it seemed only the safe, boring ideas ended up on screen. I was also hoping to try to get away from the most obviously commercial genres, like game shows and quiz shows, but apparently no one else wanted me to. I was still offered show after show that I felt wasn't right for me. But I refused to give up hope for something more live, something more people-orientated, maybe even something more in-your-face. With class. I have always believed I am a 'people person' – I am interested in people and how they tick, and in interacting with them. I found myself itching for something where I would go out to them, rather than them being sent to me in a studio.

With the *Pajama Game* proposal, perhaps I could find something of this. I'd be leaving far behind the TV world I was fast losing faith

in. Here was a new world, totally unrelated, with new people and
new attitudes. And what a chance to work hard and channel my
energy into work, instead of doomed relationships. I agreed to take
on the huge task of the show's rehearsal period and four-week run
in Birmingham, but to opt out of the Toronto run in order to spend
some time with Cameron during the summer months. I'd then rejoin
the cast for what would hopefully be a victorious run in the West
End in the autumn, when I could be based at home. For the initial
period, Cameron would be cared for two nights of the week by my
nanny or John, but I would make a point of being there for the other
five – as well as getting to know the M40 on an intimate level. The
deal was, I could only do Birmingham if I signed for the West End.
Despite personal concerns about my ability to cut a West End run,
I was assured that they wouldn't take me if I wasn't good enough. It
seemed to make sense . . . and I was only weeks away from starting.

That night I called the German in Indonesia and told him my
exciting news. Again we talked long and intimately. It felt nice to
have a friend at the other end of the world, and such an exciting job
on my doorstep. I blotted out any thoughts of the footballer,
resigning myself to the fact that I had lost that battle.

In the coming days I started to receive my schedule for the
musical – rehearsal times; costume fittings; singing practice and a list
of fellow cast members. I was going to have to clear the decks of any
other commitments before plunging into this major new project.
After a night out with a friend, I spoke to the German once again.
During our conversation, he asked when I might come out and visit
him. Don't be ridiculous, I retorted, if we are ever meeting again we
will meet halfway. At which juncture he promptly suggested the
Maldives. With the contents of a bottle of wine running through my
veins, I thought that sounded fair. We even played with dates.

The following day I didn't need to look at a map to know that
the Maldives was as halfway for him as the South of France was for
me. But hey, it sounded exciting – and I was in a 'fuck it!' kind of a
mood. On top of this, I should mention that I had been asked by
Comic Relief to go to Barbados with the fabulous Richard 'I don't

believe it' Wilson, to shoot a promo for their holiday competition. They didn't need to ask twice. It was a good cause, great company, and a five-day trip: with miserable February weather outside – very welcome. So I was looking into flights to the Indian Ocean whilst packing and preparing for my trip to the Caribbean – if I were to go ahead with this blind date, I would have to leave only a week after returning from Barbados, before knuckling down to my job of a lifetime.

The night before my departure for Comic Relief, I was invited to attend the Brit Awards by the head of Radio 1, Matthew Bannister. It seemed appropriate to go out and celebrate my new job in style, *and* stick two fingers up at the demise of another brief relationship. Make-up was applied accordingly. Hair was styled wild. As I boarded my plane to the Caribbean next day, I texted the footballer that I was taking a job away from it all. I meant away from him.

I hated the fact that all this flying around limited my time with Cameron. I did feel I could fully justify a trip on behalf of Comic Relief, but not one on behalf of a whim with a stranger. However, Cameron was still, thankfully, at the age when time bore no relevance; he didn't know twenty-four hours from seventy-two hours – or at least that is what I believed. He was a secure, happy child with a lively personality and a strong bond with both his mother and his father. And without that bond, a great nanny and a fabulous ex-husband, I wouldn't have left him under any circumstances.

Barbados was hot. And so was my phone line to Indonesia. I was instructed to pack lightly for my blind-date trip – I would only need a bikini and a sarong, he said, no high heels. How little he knew me. High heels had never been on my list. The days between the two trips were spent rehearsing and laying down tracks for the musical in order that musical arrangements could be made and singing keys could be established. I was embarrassed to hear my voice, but it was met with relative encouragement from the management. I could sing, there was no doubt about that, but just how well was the question.

What the hell was I doing, I thought – not about the show, but as I set off to spend five days with a stranger. I had felt secure enough in our phone calls, but I had no idea what to expect. I arrived, as you do, somewhat dishevelled in Singapore, where I was met by a tall, tanned, handsome man in linen trousers and a slightly exposed chest. I felt embarrassed by my own presence there and behaved accordingly. We went to a nearby hotel to wait a couple of hours until our connecting flight. I sat on the bed, and he in a chair, and we talked a little. He just stared at me, which was slightly unnerving, and rejected point blank that this was a crazy thing to do. He was a gentleman and we both maintained our dignity. But as we left the room to return to the airport, he kissed me with such passion that I found it hard to keep myself upright.

We didn't say much on the flight and arrived to a black and balmy Indian Ocean. Our accommodation, which I had been made to believe was a tent, was a short boat ride away. I didn't care where we stayed, I was just happy to be there. As it turned out, we had a villa built out over the sea. It was unbelievable. We talked into the early hours and then went to bed.

The next five days were lazy and passionate, interesting and peaceful. I *liked* this man. I told him a bit about me, who I thought I was, what I was like and my various relationship disasters. He seemed to me confident, worldly, charming, caring, sensitive, forthright, vain, and very tall. We exchanged tales of life experiences. His appeared to be predominantly successful ones, filled with beautiful girls and a great time, in sharp contrast to my tales. He had lived within the holiday business for some twelve years, and in that time had never had to go to Sainsbury's, cook a meal, or pay a bill. His life sounded charmed, if not a little unreal. We soon behaved around each other as if we had been lovers for some time, and I felt completely at ease.

One day he spotted someone pointing a large telephoto lens in our direction and wondered what was going on. I told him reluctantly that I suspected it might have something to do with the job

I had. And then I explained what I did. He didn't seem particularly impressed, which to me was a good sign.

The wonderful thing for me during those days was that I was being taken for who I was, not what I was. I was with someone without preconceived ideas of who I might be. He had no history of me. I could have told him anything about me and he wouldn't have known if I was lying or not. He took me at face value. And it was appreciated. The long-term disaster of Stan aside, I had just spent three months with someone who would ask me if this thing he'd heard about me was true, or if that rumour going round about me was right. It had been exhausting trying to paint a picture of myself onto an already blackened canvas. With my new encounter I could just be straight, and not have to justify myself constantly.

I returned to England both happy and sad – I had so much to look forward to at home, but it would have been nice for those days to never end. We kissed each other goodbye and said we would stay in touch. At home there were three messages from the footballer. He was sorry. He thought he might have made a great mistake. He now thought he knew what he wanted, and it was me – would I call him? Typical.

*

The weekend before *The Pajama Game* kicked off, a journalist appeared in my drive. She asked me about a Mr Markus Kempen, a German I had met in the Maldives, she said. We have pictures of a reasonably intimate nature of the two of you, so would it be fair to say you are a couple? she inquired. No comment, I replied. But that weekend the *Sunday Mirror* printed pictures of myself and the German kissing in the Indian Ocean, and dubbed them with a caption that said I was in love. How nice to be told these things. I warned Markus, and it wasn't long before he had a journalist visiting his resort undercover. It was a little unusual for him, but nothing he couldn't handle and, I fear, something he rather enjoyed.

Rehearsals for *The Pajama Game* began on 15 March, five weeks before we were due to open. It was the first time I met the entire cast and I was humbled by their kindness and professionalism. Anyone who devotes their life to the theatre for next to no money at all is truly dedicated to their calling. They generously welcomed me with warm, open arms, which was more than I could have hoped for. I had anticipated some deep-seated animosity towards a person who, with no previous experience except for Cinderella in panto, swans in like there is no tomorrow and tops the bill in a musical directed by Simon Callow.

There was no shortage of talent in the cast. I felt vulnerable at first, but then figured that I had to overcome that in order to achieve whatever it was I was hoping to achieve. Besides, it was hard to feel scared for long around such friendly, loving and hilarious people – if there was any animosity, it was a credit to their acting abilities that they didn't show it. But, in all honesty, thank God I am the first to laugh at myself, and as a result I don't believe I set myself up for any frostiness. I immediately hit it off with several of the members of the company, and I appreciated and valued their friendship and laughter.

I met Anita Dobson for the first time in rehearsal. She played the part of Mabel, a middle-aged secretary to the boss of the pyjama factory. She was not only stupendously good at her job, and comedy in particular, but also real and lovely in the flesh. She is a very real person, deeply honest and emphatic. Many a post-show glass of champagne was consumed in her company. I was to play Babe Williams, originally played by the one and only Doris Day in the film version. Babe was a spunky character, and the shop steward for the union about to lead the factory out on strike. The musical, written by Richard Adler and Jerry Ross, was based on the novel by George Abbott and Richard Bissel called 7½ Cents and centred on the relationship between my character and the male lead (played by Graham Bickley), who was the new work supervisor in the factory. The two characters were deeply attracted to one another, but one worked for the management (Bickley), the other stood firmly by the unions (Jonsson), and therein lay the love story. I have to say it is one of the gutsiest musical storylines I have ever come across. It is deeply passionate, sassy, political, hilarious, vibrant and independent. The poet and comedian John Hegley played Vernon J. Hines, previously played by Max Wall, a pivotal character also known as 'The Timekeeper', and it was his first musical, too. The set was designed by the Canadian modern artist Frank Stella, and David Bintley, director of Birmingham Royal Ballet, had been appointed choreographer. Frank and David had never done musicals either, which was a comforting thought. But one of the people I would be working very closely with was our musical director, Nick Barnard, and he was used to working with the West End's biggest names.

The acting and singing rehearsal schedule was nothing short of punishing, but I wanted to – and knew that I would need to – work hard to get on that stage and sing. And one thing I have never been scared of is hard work. I spent much of the days singing and trying to improve on and understand my voice. The rest of our time was taken up with choreography, dialect coaching (the musical was set in the American Midwest), and being directed by the great Mr Callow. Simon was charming, intelligent and generous. He was kind to me and always had time and ears for me. He helped me greatly, and it helped me that I had such a deep respect for him. He was sexy, emotional, alive, a very physical being, intense and captivating. Oh, and he insisted on sucking Olbas pastilles, so it was important not to get too close. He said he had become quite addicted to them.

This was more than I could say about my feelings for my male lead. Graham was kind and handsome and a marvellous singer, but for me he lacked that spark. I had to snog him several times in the show, but I apparently didn't tickle his fancy. There was something slightly unsexual about our scenes, despite me tickling his throat delectably with my tongue. Basically, I think he couldn't bear to work opposite a trainee, such as myself; he would have preferred Elaine Paige. Which was a shame. Nonetheless, I believe we made the scenes work. I believed my lines and I believed him when he told me his. Wouldn't be the first time I've had the wool pulled over my eyes, though, would it?

We worked a five- or six-day week and, Cameron aside, I didn't want to be doing anything else. I wasn't being paid anywhere near what I would get in television, or on a corporate gig, but it didn't mean a thing to me – I was able to do something I really wanted, and money can't buy that. I also relished being away from London and TV and all that showbiz bollocks. I was safely tucked away in good old Birmingham, with a new crowd of friends and colleagues, who had nothing to do with anything I had known before. It was like being a student again, although for the first time that actually felt good. Yes I raced home as often as I could to see Cameron, but even when I was away I was humming tunes and reciting lines.

I found the singing hard, it has to be said. I could do it, I just lacked confidence in my voice and knowledge of it. Singing lessons and practice amount to nothing when you cannot quite understand the mechanics of your own instrument. It was a tough call and a couple of times I ended up in tears, as I could no longer hear the difference in my voice between this and that. Nonetheless, giving up was not an option.

Racing alongside the musical was a relationship that was fast blossoming into a romance. The German and I spoke at least twice a day and faxed each other too. It wasn't hard work, like some other affairs of mine. We were both very positive towards each other and encouraging. It quickly became clear we had both fallen in love. He was utterly open about his feelings and completely caring. He knew what I was doing in Birmingham and what a challenge it was for me, but he was also desperate to see me – and I him. As it turned out, the only time he could come over was the week running up to the opening night. It wasn't ideal. I needed to work hard and would be very preoccupied, but he was not to be put off. In the end, I thought it might actually be quite nice to have him around for support.

As we headed for opening night, Cameron developed chicken pox and I developed nerves. My mind racing, I had nightmares about forgetting lines, my voice failing – you know, the usual stuff. I really began to doubt myself and the only thing that kept me going was the support from the fantastic cast and my director.

When Markus arrived, I was more tense than I'd imagined I would be. I felt different around him to how I had been before. I was still deeply attracted to him and we had by now both confessed to being in love with each other, but I felt preoccupied. When I picked him up in London and took him up to Birmingham with me, he insisted he didn't mind that I would be busy, but I felt bad that it had turned out this way. He spent the days working on his computer whilst I ran from rehearsal to rehearsal and dashed back to the hotel for lunch and dinner. I actually found it difficult to have him around me. He was virtually silent and wouldn't open up to me, which meant I found myself expending energy on trying to work him out, rather than us just having a nice time. I hadn't experienced this intensity or introversion from him before. I concluded he felt out of place in my silly little world, and could not come to terms with me running around like a woman possessed. It's not like I wasn't caring and loving towards him too, and I kept checking in with him, but I couldn't get any deeper than the fake smile he would give me in the morning as I skipped off to work. When I expressed my insecurities and worries, he said he was all right, but things clearly weren't great. Then he came to our dress rehearsal, despite me asking him not to, and decided to give me 'notes' afterwards. Perhaps his way of being thoughtful, but a little out of place from a man who, by his own admission, was uninterested in the arts and entertainment. His words were actually quite harsh, and without the benefit of experience sounded naive. In any event, they were pretty superfluous: it was by then a bit too close to opening night for anyone's liking. It was a hard pill to swallow, and I told him so.

On the morning of the press night I had a phone call from Melanie to tell me that the *Daily Mail* had vox-popped the audience after the previous night's dress rehearsal, and had run a piece about how good I was and that I could actually sing. They had also complimented me on coping with a rather tricky scene, where I balanced an apple on my head, allowing it to roll off before John Hegley had a chance to throw a knife at it. I had apparently managed to maintain some dignity. It was encouraging, but I knew the critics would not be as kind.

Opening night came and so did much of my family. I felt tense, but knew there was no going back. The ancient and nigh-on-dying lyricist, Richard Adler, had flown over from New York, as he was still entitled to some kind of input. He loved me, predominantly because I was female, but also because he thought there was a lot of Babe about me. He made comments to everyone about their performances – wanting us to change virtually everything about the way we had been doing things for the last few weeks. We felt it was all rather negative and everyone, including the producers and our beloved director, merely rolled their eyes and humoured the old man.

The morning we were due to open, I had a phone call from the said Mr Adler, summoning me to an audience in his hotel room, some floors above mine. He asked me to sit down, then proceeded to completely tear into my solo performance of the new ballad that had been composed for our production. Word by word he told me how I had ruined the song – which, incidentally, he had complimented me on at great length two nights previously. I felt demolished inside, but gave nothing away – I knew I had to hold my nerve for that night's performance. He told me to talk the song, then he told me to sing it. I couldn't make out from his ranting what he really wanted. And then he criticized my costumes, which really were not my responsibility, but which I defended to the hilt. We had an extremely talented costume designer. Still, Mr Adler continued to express his disappointment, and then finished off by wishing me good luck for the night's performance. I left the room, scraping my dignity off the floor.

I therefore made my way to the theatre shortly after feeling confused, bewildered and a little distressed – to say the least. But I knew I couldn't let the tears in my eyes actually fall. I had to stay strong. Anita took this flagging Swede in hand, and everyone chimed in that I should take no notice. Simon was furious and said Adler had no right to approach me like that. I just knew I mustn't let my disorientation over it all show on stage or the whole thing would fall apart, and I with it.

I set about preparing myself for the performance, applying make-up, pinning my hair in a French pleat and warming up my voice. I began to notice the inescapable electricity running up and down the corridor outside my dressing room. Once again I felt fuelled. Fuelled by correction, energized by criticism and elated by the support I had received from my new colleagues, I duly went on stage and gave it some. I felt slightly self-conscious during my rendition of the song in question, 'If You Win You Lose', but decided to do it the way I had the night before. I tried to own the song, but I suspect I only rented it. Nonetheless, the girl did good.

As we all piled on stage for the finale and curtain call, I felt an amazing buzz of achievement I hadn't felt in forever. I was a part of something truly amazing, something which would truly be nothing without everybody being somebody, and in which we all shared the appreciation of the audience. I had succeeded in something. Succeeded in getting there on that night and doing it. Succeeded in truly feeling that teamwork had got us all where we were. There was no star of this musical. The musical was the star and we were grateful to be standing in its glow.

I rushed to my dressing room, predominantly to crack open the champagne, but also because I knew Markus would be meeting me backstage as soon as possible, alongside some other members of my family. He was congratulatory, but rather hesitantly so. He took a step back and became the observer of the circus that surrounded me. I tried to bring him into the hubbub but he preferred the periphery. This was rather distancing, but I couldn't really allow anything to come between the celebrations and me. I had, after all, alongside everyone else, worked my balls off to get this far. I had had to battle with faith, self-confidence, self-awareness, emotion, criticism – the list was endless – and I'd pretty much won out. There was a party, and I wanted Markus to share the joy of it all with me, but again he refused to leave his zone. Even when I begged him to dance with me, he steadfastly refused. He wanted to leave; I asked him not to. but I told him if he left, I would go with him. He chose to go.

The next couple of days were tense, with him irritating the hell out of me. There was now an air of arrogance about him, and his never-ending silences drove me to frustration. He wouldn't, or couldn't, speak to me. Stranger? In front of me was a man I had never met before. He was nothing like the man I had met in Indonesia, or the Maldives, or anything like the man I had so intimately developed a telephone relationship with. He confused me – and annoyed me. I just didn't get it. I think he felt I too was different. But while I was admittedly a tad more manic than when we'd been on holiday, he was a different animal altogether. Gone was the charmer, the confident man in charge of himself and everything around him. I began to wonder if he was nothing without his surroundings. He felt foreign in 'everyday' life, and didn't know where to place himself. I, on the other hand, was equally comfortable in both. But I was decidedly uncomfortable with him like this, and I couldn't hide it.

So we argued a fair bit over the next few days, and I felt a great relief when he left. I had felt suffocated by his presence, and didn't understand what it was I was in love with. He told me he didn't believe we would see each other again. I feared he might be right, and when we next spoke on the phone told him I thought this relationship was over: all things considered, we were best to put it to bed. But he disagreed. He insisted we kept in touch, because he felt there was something special going on between us. Well, I thought, there could be no harm in staying in touch . . .

While the groundwork for the show was complete, there remained work to be done. There were still rehearsals during the day, as well as performances in the evening. Changes were being made on a daily basis, in order to tweak, perfect and improve the piece. And every day I battled with my head and the comments of our musical director, who would come into my dressing room every night before the performances and comment on any number of aspects of my singing. He was right about a huge element of everything he had to tell me in his notes, but I felt that there was a small element of him taking advantage of the fact that I was, undeniably, a musical virgin. He would tell me I was 'sliding' my notes again; or that I was 'popping', or anything else you care to think of. Gradually, a sense of complete disbelief in myself and my abilities to sing began to grow inside. I began admitting to the devils in my head that told me I wasn't really up to the job that they might be right. I sincerely and genuinely could no longer tell when I had sung a reasonable performance or when it had been a blighter, and this only muddied the waters. I couldn't see what he was talking about and I couldn't hear it when I sang. The rest of the cast were enormously supportive, but it wasn't enough to convince me. I battled night in and night out with my solos, in particularly the ballad, and it was beginning to affect my attitude towards my entire performance.

Up until this point I had hugely enjoyed the acting, and actually felt I could do it. I knew I could. But soon I began to doubt my acting performance too – it was all beautifully and intrinsically linked. Gone was the joy of being liberated from my usual work routine: I had never felt such professional confusion in my life. By this stage, no amount of singing practice would cure me of this psychological hang-up. It was tattooed in my head. It was not only uncomfortable, but also depressing and debilitating. I began to cross off the number of performances we had left, and almost began resenting going to work. All rather different from how I had felt at the very beginning of the experience. Who'd have thought then that what I had to do in my two days off from the musical – the final five shows of *Gladiators* – would prove to be a blessed relief. I didn't have to sing, after all. And our recording took place, as always, around the corner from the Rep, at the National Indoor Arena.

Cutting it in the West End would require something other than just the spirit and will to work hard. It required a stupendous voice. Mine was only all right. And on that score the issue was not so much hard work, but genes. I couldn't possibly have worked harder over the past two and a half months if I had tried.

I spent the rest of that week thinking and knowing. Knowing I was not meant for the West End. Not without a brilliant singing voice, at least. And the ability to dance and sing at the same time – something I didn't hesitate to do on a dance floor after a huge consumption of alcohol, but this was somewhat different. I didn't need to step onto a West End stage to feel professional credibility. I didn't need to feel that sense of achievement. Instead, that Saturday I went with Paul to watch England be beaten by Sweden at Wembley. Hoorah!

At the end of the Birmingham run I requested to be released from my contract, as I really felt I wasn't good enough. And I started looking forward to my summer. When *The Pajama Game* opened in London with Lesley Ash playing Babe, I sent her a bouquet of flowers and wished her all the luck in the world.

TREACHERY

Markus and I successfully rekindled the flame that had been put out by his visit to Birmingham, and we were soon back to talking twice a day. He really was romancing me like crazy and, by now, I him. But this was 'Cameron's summer', and I was intent on having a holiday with him on my own. The German, however, wanted me to return to Indonesia. I wanted quality time with my son without the distraction of a needy man. But Markus convinced me that he would be working every day so I would have all the time I wanted with Cameron. Before setting off however, and on one of Cameron's weekends with John, I took my friend Paul to Barcelona for a soak in culture, Rioja and Gaudí. We were photographed together on the trip and were labelled a couple. Which we weren't. We had a better time than most couples would.

During our three weeks in Bintan, Cameron got on so well with Markus that it was truly a holiday for me, too. They played well together and they both liked each other. So much so that after about a week Cameron was suggesting the German return to live with us. Markus and I looked at each other with shock and prospect. I spent the days with Cameron, who in turn spent the days with all the other children in the pool, and it was a wonderful time. And I fell in love.

Yes, Markus and I declared our love for each other and he started talking about us having children. He was right on target. Having wanted another child for the past few years, but not having been in a relationship which could sustain one, and having just fallen for what seemed to be a wonderful man, I felt inclined to agree. We talked and talked and talked and planned. He had never wanted children with anyone else, he said; he based his desire for breeding with me on the fact that I was a wonderful mother and his great love. I was flattered, his argument seemed a good one, and I was deeply taken with this man. He was affectionate, romantic, not particularly funny at all, but confident, kind and caring. Still, five out of six ain't bad. He was German after all.

So, far, far away, in the distant East, I fell in love with a man who I felt I could be with endlessly. We were surrounded only by beauty, and it was the perfect setting for planning a future together. That future would have to be in the country I was living in, as Cameron would have to be near his father. But this was fine: the German wanted a change of direction, and a change of lifestyle from the holiday business, which he'd been in ad nauseam. I was over the moon. And so was Cameron.

A month later when I celebrated my thirty-second birthday, Cameron was on holiday with John, so I snuck back out to Indonesia. The man I was so deeply in love with treated me like a princess – a far cry from my Stan Collymore days. Knowing that I was something of a porcinophile, he had even gone to great lengths to find me a pet piglet – quite something in a Muslim country. I called her Molly. I don't know what happened to Molly when I left at the end of the week, but I know Markus was delighted not to be sharing the bedroom with her any longer. Our time together in 'his' territory went largely without problems. It was an easy life, with few complications or distractions, and not only was I relaxed, but he was in control – of his life, his actions and his moods. We decided we would try for a baby. I knew by then that he would be joining me in England at some stage that autumn, where he hoped to be given a post in London by his present employers. Everything sounded wonderful. Then in September, shortly after Cameron had been put into his shirt and tie and headed for his first day at lower school, I was asked to choose a favourite holiday location for the BBC's *Holiday* programme. I chose Tuscany and invited the German to come with me, flying him over from the Far East. And that's when things started to go wrong, again.

We had a terrible time. When I wasn't arguing with him, there were stone-cold silences that sent a chill down my spine. Once again, it seemed that as soon as he set foot in 'my' world, he became a changed man – silent and intense. He couldn't tell me what it was that made him retreat into his shell. And he wouldn't accept my help and concern. I felt at the time, and to this day, that it was all to do with being a fish out of water: he was unfamiliar and uncomfortable in the 'real' world and in a world where he had no authority; where he had no 'role' to play professionally, other than that of lover, friend and companion. I suspected I was with a man who measured his worth in professional terms only. He seemed to me to be a man used to having his own way; lacking in compromise and flexibility; and a man lost without his crown in a land where he was not king. His life, hitherto, had been filled with work and beautiful girls – who had wanted him more than he wanted them, and who had been with him on his terms, not on theirs. He was used to being the centre of attention, something that I know he would disagree with. A single man. A single man, with a single-parent family.

Halfway through our trip, against the most stunning scenic backdrop, he announced that he was going to leave. Just like he had threatened in Birmingham. I went crazy. How could he just want to take off leaving behind him only traces of cowardice and immaturity for me to hold on to? I told him if he was going to leave, to just do so. But he stayed. Why, I don't know. He made no effort to join in with or fit in with the rest of the crew – a jolly bunch of four. We were having a laugh, despite me rather disappointingly getting my period. There was no sign of the social skills he so readily displayed on his own territory. It wasn't that I was the centre of attention: we were all in it together, except for the brooding presence in the corner of the room. I felt this wasn't going to work. And I also felt I didn't like him, but could not fathom how I could think that I loved someone I didn't actually like. Perhaps it was the idea of romance I was in love with, and the very real physical attraction that sustained us.

We returned, I to England and he to Indonesia, under a some-what darkened cloud. We both agreed a little thinking time was in order. So we thought and eventually we talked. We discussed how we felt and despite having two disastrous trips under our belt, we could only conclude that we still wanted to be together, live together and start a family together. How does *that* work? I tried not to ignore the issues and the recurring themes of our relationship so far – and indeed, of so many of my relationships to date – but I suspect they got lost in a sea of romance; of affirmations and positivity, not realism. And it was a relief, no doubt, to feel that we could allow ourselves to be in love, despite being totally incompatible. A relief which is immeasurable after a period when you thought you might lose whatever it was you had. Relief that you wouldn't have to face up to the pain and longing of loss.

When I went to Dublin for a press call to promote the Hot Press Rock Awards, which I was due to host the following month – once more with the delectable Mike Edgar – Markus called. (My mum came with me and we had a hoot together, and got very, very drunk. We were actually pretty terrible.) He was about to resign. I was overjoyed: this meant that he was finally going to come and live with me. I was looking forward to sharing my life with someone properly – for the first time since my marriage to John.

*

The plan was for Cameron and I to go to Indonesia during his half-term in October and bring the German back with us for our new life together. Both Cameron and I were really excited, and felt ready for a different home life.

I had also prepared the way a little by popping over to Germany while he was there on a business trip to 'meet the family'. They were very pleasant people, and although I could tell from the way his dear mother behaved around him that he had been spoilt as a child, it didn't matter. It's always reassuring to like the parents.

We arrived in Bintan to discover Markus had given up his heavy smoking and attendant coffee drinking. I told him he should do it only if he wanted to; not for me. It was an important affirmation – I didn't want him to resent me for denying him his addictions. It did mean that I encountered a slightly more nervous, preoccupied man, but I was there to support and help him as best I could.

While there, I rather miraculously bumped into a photographer friend who was staying at the resort with his family. Richard McLaren is a right cockney. He always has me in fits and is constantly taking the piss out of everything, but he is a kind-hearted man and his partner Hedda is someone I've always got on with. One night we all decided to play boules, or pétanque, children in tow. Richard as usual was messing around, on a court on which Markus was normally king, and I thought we were all having a laugh. It turned out Markus wasn't. This was the first time we were really socializing with people I knew; out here it had always been his social arena. Now, Richard has the archetypal English toilet humour, with bums and tits and all their associated suggestions and connotations – never offensive, just silly and funny. But not funny for the German. We ended up having a fight about how I had lowered myself with all this nudge, nudge, wink, wink hilarity. Nothing had been overtly suggestive, and Richard was no flirt, but it had gone down like a lead balloon with the Führer. It was uncomfortable: I stood my ground, but did begin to wonder where the line was between being yourself and not offending the other party.

Soon I was told I was taking the piss too much; I was too sarcastic and too ironic. I told him I only did it because I felt we were all strong enough to take it, and that I had never before encountered criticism for my sense of humour. I didn't understand him, but was prepared to listen. After a third night of arguments, I suggested that he didn't actually like me and that he would be more comfortable around someone who let *him* be funny or be in control. I don't think I was ever hungry for control or the limelight, but if my partner isn't making funny remarks or being amusing, the chances are I will be. And I do actually think I can be rather witty. But it had become apparent that we absolutely did not share the same sense of humour. At all. I wanted a partnership with equal respect, but we were wide

One of the Playtex photos
that caused such a stir.
(Jordan, eat your heart
out.) (David Anthony)

With my hero Terry Wogan before the Eurovision Song Contest, 1998.

Meeting Gordon Brown at No. 11.

With the jolly, lighthearted,
fun-to-be-with
David Bailey, March 2000.

My on-screen family (Osbournes, eat your heart out). (© BBC Picture Archive)

On location with Grattan in Arizona. (Not my ciggy, Mum.)

FHM shoot. The minx look. (Dean Freeman)

On location with my dear friend David Ginola, October 1999.

Chelsea v Utd, Stamford Bridge, 20 April 2002.
The man in front of Angus was obviously devastated by the news of
Sven and me. (My brother Kristian, far right.) ('News of the World')

Photo shoot with Rankin for Charles Worthington.

Me and my little man at my thirtieth birthday party. (Brian Moody)

Bo's birthday party, November 2001. (John Turnbull)

Me and the most gorgeous woman in the world, my Mel, May 2001.

My family, August 2002. (John Turnbull)

off the mark there – there was no doubt about who felt he had to be in control. He'd disagree, but the tension between us could be seen and heard. I remember thinking one night that he shouldn't come back to England after all. But I knew I owed it to us to see this through. And I wanted to.

On the other hand, I knew that I didn't want to be back in a relationship where I was suppressed. I knew my spirit needed to be allowed to run free and my hard work and dedication to the relationship to be equally valued. I would have to make sure I stood my ground. Richard McLaren told me he thought it would all be over by Christmas. I told him he was much mistaken. Besides, it was October already. Our new life together began with Cameron ill, new jobs waiting for me, the onset of winter, jet lag, and Markus taking up exercising to complement his denial of nicotine and caffeine. Talk about putting pressure on yourself. As we walked into my house, I could sense the tension growing. Or maybe just being reawakened from the lightest of sleeps.

Markus immediately closed himself off. Retreated into his shell and withdrew into the living room on his own on a regular basis. I was running around nursing Cameron, tending to the house, and working. He made no effort to join in. I'd check in on him and ask after him, but he didn't talk. After four days I said I'd had enough of things being like this; but he still didn't want to talk. When I eventually cried and said that I thought we needed help, he stead-fastly referred to my comments as ridiculous. As ever, he knew best.

By Saturday morning the atmosphere was too heavy for me to remain in the house. I went over to see John, and asked him what the hell I was doing. He listened, which was more than I could have hoped for. I came back and told Markus where I had been, and asked him if he had packed his overnight bag as we had been invited to a bonfire party at my dear friends Charles and Allan's place. I hoped that by going to the country for the night, things between us might ease off. After a long pause he told me to go on my own. He was leaving. For good.

I was shocked by his words, horrified by his intentions and

saddened by his attitude. He would say nothing but that he was disgusted by the way he had been treated. He had been largely ignored, he said, or treated like an exchange student on a visit abroad, and he wasn't sure which was worse. And there I was thinking he was a big boy and that he wanted to exercise the independence he was so proud of. It might have been nice, he said, if I had arranged a mobile and a car for him, so as to give him a little bit of status. What? I told him that of course all these things might be on the cards, but we had barely been back a week – a week during which I had been working, had been wiped out and had nursed my sick child. He also complained that I hadn't undersood that he wanted to have some input into my career. But he had no time for my explanations, he said. It was too late. He was packing his bag. Oh, and by the way, could I give him a lift to the airport in the morning?

I cried and asked him to stay and to talk this through, and not to run away every time he couldn't deal with something. Like he had wanted to in Birmingham. Like he had threatened to do in Tuscany. A pattern had emerged and this time he was following through. I asked him time and time again to stay, but he said my pleas came too late. Too late for what, I thought. We were not long ago planning a life together – for ever, I had thought. I asked him one more time, before we set off for the airport. But he took his flight.

I returned home with mixed emotions: there was sorrow that he had left, but also joy to be on my own again, as if a weight had been lifted. Yet my heart ached, nonetheless. The next day and the day after that I went on the defensive and bucked my ideas up. I certainly wasn't going to go chasing after him. I had to presume he had gone back to his mum and dad's in Dusseldorf, but I wasn't going to phone. By Tuesday night, he texted me from his best friend Dirk's mobile, in Germany. He asked me to call him. I thought twice about it, but knew that there was little point standing on ceremony: at some stage we were bound to have contact again. So I called. He was at his parents'. And he wanted to come back.

Well, no surprises there then. Predictable, shallow, transparent and immature, just a few of the thousands of negative words which went around in my head. Oh, and bloody cheeky. So I told him he couldn't. I told him you don't make a dramatic exit out of someone's life like that and change your mind. He pleaded. No, came my response. I may have sounded strong, but inside I was hurting and cracking. I felt severely damaged by his actions: I'd trusted someone whimsical, self-serving and thoughtless; I'd also had to explain to Cameron why the German had suddenly disappeared. Markus had had to go to Germany to work, I'd said. Is he coming back? came the inevitable reply. I'm sure, I just don't quite know when. No one else I told could believe what I was saying as easily as Cameron had. My mother was shocked; Melanie surprised, but said his actions had kind of spoken for themselves previously. My friends found it incomprehensible.

The following week he continued to phone to try to re-establish himself in my affections. He did not succeed. He was beginning to sound weak to me by now. He wanted to pick up the things he had left behind. I told him I could send them to him. But that was not what he wanted. One night he caught me on my way to Wembley to watch England play Scotland. He wasn't getting the response he wanted, and started to become abusive and rude. He suggested I go and fuck the footballers. Which was a lovely thought, but there's only so many hours in one night and twenty-two was pushing it. Just. The more he showed his true colours, the more I was glad he was gone, if hurting at the way and the speed with which it had all happened. It's like thinking you are home and dry only to discover that you are actually still all out at sea.

He continued to call me the following week and he wanted to make arrangements for someone else to pick up his belongings. I was keen to get things sorted out before I went to Sweden for four days to host an AIDS charity fashion show in Stockholm, but suddenly he disappeared. I couldn't get hold of him at his parents', who also didn't know where he was. Nor was he traceable the next day. Or the day after. Something was up.

*

I returned from my trip and still there was no word. Then on the Thursday, as I was rehearsing for the Miss World competition, which I was presenting for Channel 5, he called and asked me one last time if he could come back to me. He sounded calm and slightly different. I told him that it might be better if we had some space for a period of time, before we rushed into another disaster. I still felt this contradiction: I did somehow still feel for him, but I didn't understand him, and increasingly found more and more about him that I didn't like very much. And I could hear the pain and distance in his voice, so decided to handle him with care. Which was to prove more than he deserved.

Miss World was to be broadcast live across the world from London's Olympia. My sidekick was the most beautiful Melanie Sykes, who had once led me astray during a lunch in London, I vaguely remembered. John was covering the event too, so we planned to travel into London together. I was beginning to get myself ready when, at about nine thirty in the morning, there was a knock on my front door. I opened it, hair wet, naked of face and barely dressed. It was a reporter from a Sunday tabloid, asking me how I felt about Markus Kempen selling the story of his life with me to the *News of the World*. Did I have any comment?

What???

I became hot and I could feel my cheeks redden with shock and embarrassment. But deep inside me ran a calm, solid river of comprehension and reality. It kept telling me that what the woman was saying was true, and told me to hurry up and register it with my brain. I stuttered and faltered but managed somehow to ask her what the content of the story was. She whispered it was about how we had met, and how he had left me and how we had made love, you know, that kind of thing . . . Do you have anything to say? Plenty, I thought, but not to you. Thank you for bringing it to my attention, but no thank you, I'm just on my way to work, so if you don't mind . . .

I closed the door and felt like collapsing, but knew I couldn't break now. Had he lost his mind? If he had, I wasn't about to lose mine. I had to bloody work tonight. And he would have known that, too. I sounded off to John, who was himself in disbelief. The only thing I could do was to put pen to fax. 'I hope you have a slow death, you mercenary cunt', I believe were my exact words. Then I packed for work. I could feel nothing but anger. Not sadness. Feeling like shit, I had my make-up applied and my hair styled. Just you wait, Henry Higgins, just you wait. I got through the broadcast with the support of those around me – Melanie S, my Mel and a wonderful ex-husband working on camera one, but Robert Palmer and Enrique Iglesias's performance helped too.

I stayed for a swift half after the show and then returned home. But not before making my driver stop at every petrol station in search of a copy of the offending article. And there it eventually was: 'In bed with Ulrika, by the man who really knows', plus sultry pose from the *FHM* shoot, featuring aforementioned celebrity. Great!

Inside was our brief history detailed across a spread, with photos of him and me taken by us; a photo of him looking like a fat bastard; and a copy of one of the letters I had faxed him. The story ran along the lines of how we had met and had had the most amazing sex in every conceivable location and position (detailed) and how he had come to England to live with me, but had to walk out after six days because he couldn't compete with my career (what?) and my demanding lifestyle (like the school run, presumably). The fax they featured, some months old, was of an intimate, sexual nature, which I thought was cutting it a bit fine. I was truly horrified by the whole thing, and knew I had to track him down. If his nice parents answer, I said to myself, I'll just tell them, in my best German, what their beloved son had been up to. But I didn't need to. He answered.

'Markus, what have you done?' I asked him calmly and with a civility he absolutely didn't deserve, but somehow I felt I had the upper hand. He had shown his true colours and I had done nothing wrong. He refused to answer. I carried on talking to him gently, asking him if he was out of his mind; what was he thinking? how much did he get paid? did he think of Cameron? did his parents know? He never answered and on two occasions put the phone down, which only served to increase the level of my voice and my fury. He told me simply that he knew I wanted him to die, and that was all he needed to know.

Eventually I let him go. But I hadn't finished with him yet. I was still so amazed by his actions that the following morning I contacted his best friend, Dirk, because I feared he might have been in on the whole thing. Poor Dirk had had nothing to do with it, and was almost more shocked than me. Disgusted, he offered to help with anything if he could. He telephoned Markus, who admitted it and said he 'didn't know which devil rode him'. The money devil, I suspect. He had always known how sensitive a subject the press was for me. How what they said affected me and how powerless I felt against them. And he had now gone to bed with them. It was more than unforgivable. It was . . . treachery.

The following Monday I contacted my lawyers and asked if there was anything we could do, especially as the newspaper had printed a letter in which I had copyright. There was. We could sue him or the paper for breach of copyright. Let's sue him, I said. I was fed up with being fucked with; taken the piss out of; taken advantage of. They wasted no time in proceeding. Within an hour of the writ being served on Markus by fax at his parents' house he was on the phone. He begged me not to sue him. He said it would kill his mother. Should have thought of that before, you selfish bastard. No, I'm afraid this lady was not for turning. Not any more. This one was not getting away.

He begged and pleaded, but my resolve was unshakeable. I left him to speak to my lawyers. He made arrangements to come over to Britain to negotiate a financial settlement in order to avoid a visit to the unaffordable courts. In the meantime, I had drafted a confidentiality agreement I was going to make him sign. He was never going to be allowed to whisper another word about me, good, bad or indifferent, for eternity.

To cut a long story short, we met at my lawyers' office and my lawyer explained to the man in front of him, who was unbelievably thick about it all, that this was not a nice thing to do. In return for the invasion into my private life, we wanted the money he had made from the newspaper (some £23,500, it turned out), after which he should sign on the dotted line and go away. Very far away. But he was so undignified. He admitted his stupidity. He showed his fear and panic. He blathered on and on about his new job in Turkey – mistaking us for people who gave a fuck. And spent the rest of the time trying to convince me how sorry he was. Arse. It took six or seven expensive hours to get what we wanted. Although, it has to be said, I hadn't wanted the situation in the first place. I was deeply hurt.

It was so bitter. There in front of me sat a man whom I had fallen deeply in love with and who had fallen deeply in love with me. Not with 'TV's Ulrika Jonsson', but Eva Ulrika Jonsson herself. Whoever she might be. We had developed an intimate relationship in a relatively short time, but I thought that I had finally met a mature man, who a) wouldn't take any shit from me, and b) was grown up enough to cope with all the rest of the emotional and public baggage that came with me. With whom there would be the security to bring a new life into the world. And above all else he had always vowed that he would never allow the press to come between us. I had thought that would be the least of our worries. He had seemed so ... so *right*. My love for him had seen the best in his confidence, self-belief and experience, overlooking his arrogance, his inability to cope in a 'normal' world and his inexperience thereof. Perhaps I had once again allowed my heart to rule my head, but presented with the package I thought I was getting it would have been ridiculous to do anything else. And isn't trust and belief what love is all about? But he had made a mockery of everything.

*

Once the German had left, my anger turned to sadness. Not sad that he had left, but sad that he had wanted to injure me in such a cold-blooded and vulgar way. He had known exactly where to aim. His motives will remain known only to him. Thankfully the bullet hadn't quite killed me, but it did leave me severely injured. But this time I managed to box my emotions into a corner of my heart and head, where they would not be accessed readily, and planned a great Christmas. Ironically it turned out to be one of the best in years.

After it, the German was back on the phone, pleading for forgiveness and offering to do anything to make my life easier. Well, his disappearance would have been a great start. I was cold and sharp, and when I had said whatever needed to be said, I would simply put the phone down. But then he would fax, long letters asking for mercy, extending his good will to help me get over the travesty he had brought about. Then he was off to Turkey. Running away again.

*

After a very pleasant seeing-in of the year 2000 with my parents and Cameron, I hit a trough. Well, more of a pit of snakes, complete with venom and writhing self-loathing. What was it about me that had deserved this last bullet? What attracted me to vicious fools? How could I keep on missing the signs? And why did I choose to ignore them when they did rear their ugly heads? Who was 'I', anyway? It seemed I was something to everyone else and nothing to myself.

On deeper inspection I began to realize I had lost so much of 'me' to a public persona. I found I didn't know the person the papers were writing about; she bore no resemblance to the woman I thought I was. I was, according to them, highly driven, ambitious; an often thoughtless mother, a socialite, a heavy drinker, a bit of a lad, an incorrigible sexy thing. And it was during this time that I decided I needed to chart my life, somehow. The only way I could think of doing it was to write everything down. Everything which had happened to me since birth, as part of a process of analysis and catharsis. I wanted to find out what it was that made me who I am. Because the simple truth was that I just didn't know any more. I had been battling for years to reconcile what I wanted to do with what I thought I ought to do. And never the twain appeared to meet. Yes,

Melanie would guide me, and sometimes tell me what I needed to do in my personal life for the benefit of both my private and public lives. But often I ended up doing the 'right' thing long before I was ready to do it. And I figured you should only do things when you are ready, otherwise you spend your time looking back and wishing. Besides, you need to truly understand and believe in whatever you have to do, or the action becomes mechanical and ultimately pointless and maybe even regrettable.

Take Stan, for example. Melanie quite rightly told me that relationship had to end as soon as he physically abused me. Without question, she was right. But I found myself with unresolved emotions and unable to understand what had gone on at all. I hadn't wanted to take up with him again, but I maintain that there was a part of me that needed to face up to him, in order for me to be ready to close that door. Who are others, least of all the press, to judge what I need to do, and the speed at which I need to do it?

James and I finished a couple of times before we finished properly. Is that not often the normal course a relationship can take – some coming and going before you are able to go properly? Yet all through that time I felt I was being forced to justify what I was doing and who I was with. And I was being made to feel stupid, rightly or not.

And now here I was facing probably the most heartbreaking situation yet. No physical abuse, but disappointment and deception of the highest degree. Even with the passage of time I could not comprehend it. Maybe you are not supposed to understand everything; but it's hard to stop asking yourself 'why?' It was also hard not to start hating myself. For someone who already had little self-respect, I was fast losing even that. No, I didn't blame myself for what Markus had done to me, but I did take responsibility for attracting such a prick. Perhaps it was an attempt to take responsibility that made me start writing this book. Not initially for publication, but for my own good and in order to reclaim some sanity from, hopefully, a clearer mind.

I also began to question the job I was doing. If I could not cope with the accompanying press attention, perhaps I'd just have to give it up. The past few years had affected me so profoundly that I no longer felt fit to do my job. If I couldn't deal with it, I really was in the wrong profession – it wasn't going to go away.

To top it all, I fell out with my mother, heavily, again. So there I was, feeling rejected and unwanted and very, very angry.

As my depression intensified, so did the German's focus of attention on me. After having spent the past month or so telling me he loved me still, and me telling him that he absolutely didn't, he began to want to prove it. Our conversations became more amicable by the day; he was actually listening to me, and wanted to support me in whatever capacity he could. He knew he couldn't undo what he had done, and wasn't looking for forgiveness (unusual for a Catholic), but he said he wanted to make the future better. Did a part of me still love this person after all? I didn't know. I knew I hated him for what he had done, and I knew I was in a great deal of pain as a result. Then came the big question. Could I ever forgive him for what he had done? Did I need to? Should it be part of my recovery? Could I just walk away and leave this potential future behind me?

Well, here comes another truth. With hindsight, I'm not sure if what I felt for him was love at that time. What I felt was a deep desire to have a baby, and by fucking things up the way he had he had taken away that prospect. But he had said he wanted one too – in fact, he'd encouraged the idea. Little did I know then that he didn't understand what having a baby was all about. One aspect of my depression was a grieving for the loss of my longed-for maternity. On top of which, the easiest route out of heartache, though not necessarily the best, is the route that leads back to the person who caused it.

Long term it would have been easier for me to stay away, but short term it was proving hard. And I was, at the time, finding it impossible to find strength from or in anything. A bit like the wolf in Little Red Riding Hood, my former lover was now wearing grandma's clothes to convince me that he would be the person to help me out of the sorry state he had put me in. And in turn, I began donning kamikaze gear.

I stumbled and crawled reluctantly through the next month or so, battling with myself, my life, myself, my past, myself and my fear of tomorrow. Then I accepted an invitation to visit the German in Turkey, where he now worked. No strings attached. Well, despite supposedly being violently severed our strings were still somehow attached. And we both knew that. He'd suggested I go out there for a few days to mend; to get some fresh mountain air and sleep. I told only my mother I was going because I knew the objections would have been intolerable. How could I spend all the time thinking about what it would look like in the papers if I did this or that? One of the lessons I had learned was that I needed to do things because they felt right for me, not abstain because it might look wrong to others. Why be an adult and still be answerable to another? I took the flight.

REUNIFICATION

Arriving in an uninhabited part of mountainous Turkey and being greeted by the German, I rejected his warmth and proceeded with a chill in my demeanour, which shocked even him. I passed the three days there wrapped up against the bracing air and spending most of my time alone, just looking out over a clean, clean sea. In the evenings we would engage in heavy conversations about what had passed. We both talked and we both listened. He cried when he spoke of what he had done, and it seemed to me that he was able to acknowledge his weaknesses and label them accordingly. He spoke of his feelings and how he hadn't dealt with them at the time and how I had never deserved what he had driven himself to do. He also told me how he felt I had contributed to certain aspects of his downfall, but didn't blame me in any way. I took responsibility for the things I knew I hadn't acknowledged properly, and with that he declared he was still deeply in love with me and wanted only the best for me. Whatever that might be.

I began to think not only about what he had done to me, but about the whole picture and how I fitted into life itself. How I had been over the past few years and how I wanted things to be. How I wanted a change of direction, a new attitude and new experiences, but above all else, how I wanted another child.

As I travelled home I reflected that I had got to know a different and better side to the man I called the German. I had now encountered a man not afraid of his weaknesses. We'd had the worst; could we not now achieve much, much more? I felt closer to him than I ever had. Or maybe it was just my hormones talking.

We continued our telephone relationship. I began to take pride in having turned this situation around. It felt right that he was part of my life again. It had eased the long road of pain I didn't have the strength to walk along, and it had proved that we hadn't come to the end of 'our' road just yet. There was more travelling to be done.

In the middle of a conversation on 15 February that year, Markus asked me outright to marry him. My heart agreed. But I'd be lying if I didn't admit that in my head I didn't really believe it would happen.

Later that month I took Cameron out to Turkey for his half-term holiday. Unofficially reunited, the German and I began to talk again of starting a family. He was desperately keen; I was so aware of my keenness that I held back a little, to make sure it wasn't me driving the situation. During our short stay, I conceived.

I returned to England none the wiser. By now Melanie knew I had gone back into the lion's den. She made no comment, but I could read the ones in her head. Instead, she got me three days of *Techno Games 2000* for BBC2 at the lovely Dome, a place I had sworn I would never set foot in – so much for my conviction. To recover, I went up to Old Trafford to watch United play Derby.

My third pregnancy came to my attention on 17 March 2000. Although my period was by then four days late and I had been the premenstrual bitch from hell, I really felt Mother Nature was just playing her monthly game of delayed disappointment with me. The thing to do was a test, but having spent the past year pissing on sticks in search of positives and ovulations, there was a natural reluctance. At the back of my knicker draw was a small Boots packet, and in there, I knew, lurked a pregnancy kit. I looked at the faint pink line with a mixture of excitement and doubt. Excitement because there was a line; and doubt because it was faint. I quickly calculated my due date and immediately phoned Markus to find out if he was free around 21 November. He was overwhelmed and truly excited.

This pregnancy felt different to the others. I wasn't nauseous yet and somehow I didn't *feel* pregnant. The pink line on the test was faint enough to make me retest some days later, by which time it was positively fluorescent. But I kept not feeling as pregnant as I should. Armed with more knowledge than is good for me, I knew that women who suffer nausea in pregnancy stand less chance of miscarriage, and that miscarriages are as high as one in three. No, I simply didn't feel sick enough.

At five weeks pregnant and with my stomach just a little swollen, I actually had to do a press call for Slendertone, which I had been employed to endorse long before I fell pregnant. It makes your stomach flatter. Thankfully, no one was looking at mine. I got away with it, but only because my breasts were so large they took all the attention. At that time I had told nobody. The following day I told three people. My good friend Lisa, my mother and my agent Melanie. In that order. There were no flowers, no champagne and no warm congratulations until I expressed my own delight and happiness. All three approached the news with caution and trepidation, not being aware of what stage of my European reunification I was at. My mother was not surprised, she knew I wanted another child; Melanie, however, was shocked and slightly panicked until she remembered that I always shock and panic her.

After a fairly hefty dose of diarrhoea at seven weeks, I had a bit of bleeding. I panicked and started to mourn, but a sympathetic obstetrician and one ultrasound later I was reassured by the sign of a (and I quote) 'good, strong heartbeat'.

Maintaining my hormonal mood, I progressed in my pregnancy, becoming more nauseous by the day. I ate everything that came into sight, including the forbidden, such as wheat and dairy products, much to the confusion of my stomach and bowel. I worried more this time, figuring that the six years since the first time around would have somehow changed things, and having spent those years talking predominantly to fellow mothers I was even more aware of risks and problems. I wasn't yet ready to shout this from the rooftops.

For our Easter holidays I went back out to Turkey, with Cameron, my mum and my sister Kelly. I felt foul and was an emotional time bomb. I still felt premenstrual and desperately needy. I don't suppose it helped that I was having a child with a man who had injured me so badly not that long ago. But looking to him was not a good move: during our stay of fourteen nights, Markus took one day off work. He could barely manage to meet us for lunch, and in the evenings I felt abominable. When I tried to express myself it only came out as screams and tears. I attempted to talk sensibly to him about our future, however. He wanted to resign straight away and come back to England. I, however, felt it was imperative not to make the same mistakes as before. I pointed out that there was no rush – I wanted us to see how the pregnancy progressed before he threw in the towel. He said all he needed was a job, and he'd be over. Then, more than ever, I wished he had been able to listen. But he had a job to do, rushing around the resort.

Some days after we returned there was a knock on my front door and a journalist congratulated me on the good news. I feigned ignorance and thanked him for his visit. But it meant Melanie had to confirm the pregnancy, and it was front-page news. As we refused to confirm the identity of the father, the press embarked on several days of investigation, speculation and confusion. I refused to name the father because I felt it was my right to keep it to myself. I had not wanted it to be public knowledge yet that I was pregnant, anyway – they were lucky to get that much. I was only ten weeks. Having embraced the absolute miracle of conception and childbirth so early on in my life, and having established a healthy and genuine respect for the whole process, I knew I still had a long way to go. I had never been a believer in the premature announcement of pregnancy.

But my twelve-week nuchal-fold scan was a delight. I even videoed it for the German delegation (albeit with the power off for the first five minutes). My obstetrician measured what he had to, fed the details into the machine, which then pronounced that my chances of my baby having Down's syndrome were one in three thousand.

It doesn't get any better than that, said Mr Eustace. The chances of chromosomal abnormalities increase with age, but my result was the equivalent to that a fifteen-year-old would hope for. Any lower and someone would have to be arrested, he quipped. He asked if I was interested in a blood test too, but I declined, singing 'Que sera, sera'.

So, not unlike Doris Day, I skipped out of the unit with my video recording and a tremendous sense of relief. We had seen hands, feet, toes, ears, eyes and a heartbeat; we had even seen a stomach. Every day that my son has lain sleeping or sat talking next to me, I have wondered in absolute awe at the miracle of his creation. Touching his toes, looking at the twists and turns in his ears, feeling the skin at the back of his neck, all the time thinking, I helped make that. The sensation that runs through me is not just one of achievement, but absolute wonderment and even disbelief at nature's powers and imagination. The maternal fire that's been burning ever since the age of ten when I beheld sister Linda still shows no signs of extinguishing.

As I'm sure most mothers would agree, pregnancy is one long wait, divided only into a series of shorter waits between ultrasound scans, when we finally get the opportunity to see what Nature has blessed us with, and to somehow make that first human-to-human connection. As is expected with a second pregnancy, I started to feel the flutters of movements much earlier on, and I knew then that this little monkey was the opposite flavour to my first. My partner's instinct told him this was a boy, so this further fuelled my conviction that it wasn't – even when we got on, he tended to be wrong more often than he was ever right.

Yes, as far as my relationship with the German went, it was a mixture of frustration and what could be. As long as we were apart from each other, we could engage in sensible, meaningful conversations of an extremely loving nature. I was pleased that I could now acknowledge my love for him and that we were intending to make some kind of future together. But doubts niggled about *life* together. Things had always gone so awry when he had come over, but now he was once again talking about dropping his job and coming to live with me. I wanted us to learn from our mistakes, and aired my concerns constantly, but he seemed to be prepared to rush headlong back into the same situation. I pointed out that it would be best, at the very least this time, to find himself a job in England before he came over, in order to avoid revisiting the same problems and atmosphere. He agreed to try. With a baby due in November, we had at least five months on our side.

The German came to visit me towards the end of May. I don't know what it was, but before he even came, I wasn't looking forward to it. I had the sinking feeling in my stomach that you get when you sense that something just isn't going to go right. Sure enough, by the second day, those familiar feelings were returning. Those feelings of irritation and frustration with a man who thinks the world owes him something. He was in dispute with his previous employers – the ones he had left in order to come and live with me originally – and was heading for the same with his present ones. It turned out that he would be leaving Turkey in a few weeks. This surely spelled trouble. We absolutely had not been able to resolve any of the issues that had plagued us before. Had anything changed at all? I had been so pleased and so hopeful when I had spoken with him and spent time with him in the early months; there now seemed to be nothing but uncertainty. Apart from the certainty of our child, for whom I had longed so desperately, and whom both of us had hurried to make.

*

This child may have been more wanted than many brought into this world, but its parents could not find any common ground to work from. Markus's impatience with the future was as strong as my fear of it. In truth I was discovering that I had not forgiven him properly for what he had done in going to the papers. And every time I thought about it I failed to understand how he could have done it and why. He must really have hated me then. How did we get from there to the supposed love we were now sharing? I still needed to be able to talk about it. But all he wanted to talk about was getting himself a job. With a little babe in my tummy, though, it was a little late for confusion. By the middle of June, I had a word with myself: I needed to forgive him properly or not be with him. I chose forgiveness.

He said he was delighted I was pregnant, but seemed relatively unenthusiastic at times. I had to ask him several times if he wanted to see the video of the first scan. When the time came for my twenty-week scan, I was adamant that Markus should accompany me, so that he could grasp the wonder of nature and share this miracle. For a man who had seen most things, I knew this would top it all. And I think it did. Andrew, our sonographer, saw all the bits he needed to see, and asked if we wanted to know the sex of the 'fetus'. We declined. Then he paused for some time over the chest. He couldn't make out all the chambers of the heart. We heard a healthy, regular heartbeat; the absence of the statutory four must simply be due to the way the baby was lying, we told ourselves. But he suggested I come back in a week or so to see if the baby had moved to a more convenient position. As we left, I asked him to write down the sex of the baby and put it in an envelope, just in case I would one day be seized by an insatiable desire to know.

The following ten days or so passed quite quickly. Cameron was by now on his summer holidays and I thought it would be a good idea to bring him along to the follow-up scan. I had not anticipated a problem, otherwise Cameron would have stayed at home. Upon arrival at the hospital it was Andrew scanning again. And once again, he struggled to distinguish the four chambers of the heart, as did his colleague Yvonne, and so indeed did Mr Eustace, my obstetrician. Poor Cameron was by now well put off the prospect of a little sibling – it was all so boring. The only thing that excited him was when I showed him a pair of stirrups and told him that women's legs were placed in them when the doctors needed to look in their nunnies. His eyes lit up – I think he was hoping for a demonstration.

The only conclusion that could be drawn was that no conclusion could be drawn. I was referred to the fetal cardiology unit at Oxford's John Radcliffe Hospital. The appointment needed to be for the following day. Fear led to tears and a desperate need for reassurances, of which there were none. What's more, there could be a chromosomal link with a heart defect which would indicate a fault in the genetic make-up causing some form of disability. Bear that in mind, they said. And with that I left, maintaining a confident front for the sake of my adorable son.

I phoned Markus immediately, throwing at him a chronological series of events, facts and possibilities. The tears streamed and my voice was becoming shaky as I ran through the various prospects, or lack of them. Without hesitation, he volunteered to come over from Germany, something I hadn't expected or counted on. But by the time he arrived I was already drowning in my own fears and the impossible task of removing the negative thoughts from my head and allowing positive ones into my heart.

For some reason I felt that I could probably find it within myself to deal with a heart defect, without any knowledge as to what that would entail. But I somehow refused to accept the possibility of a chromosomal link – based on nothing but intuition and perhaps denial. As the hours slowly passed until morning, I closed the emotional doors around me, shutting out my partner for fear of sharing my fears, for fear of collapsing, and for fear of dependency – where would I be if he then decided to reject me if there was to be no baby?

When we arrived at the hospital we were put in an anteroom. There was something about it that shouted bereavement and exclusion to me, and I remember trying to focus on objects in the room to take my mind off that and the fact that I was beginning to lose control. It was littered with year-old magazines and decorated with depressing furniture, as if to complement the imminent bad news. In traditional British manner we were offered tea. My soul was crying out for whisky, but I made do with water. We didn't speak to each other; the constant ups and downs in our relationship meant that somehow I was not sure how much I could lean on him, depend on him, break down in front of him. The state of our relationship spoke for itself.

A doctor and a colleague took us through to the scanning room. As the doctor started work, Markus massaged my hand – a little too hard. After ten minutes they thought it was only fair to say that the heart did not look normal. The tears started again, Markus gripped my hand and I wanted to let go and run out screaming loudly. The scan continued for another thirty-five minutes, during which there was much whispering from them and silence from us. At one stage I remember feeling so exhausted I wanted to fall asleep . . . and not wake up again. When the procedure was over we were redirected to the plastic 'bereavement' room, to await the return of the doctor, who in my mind had now become Dr Death. We sat again in silence. It was an unbearably hot July evening and people's voices outside irritated me, the sight of fellow pregnant women angered me and my helplessness frustrated me.

Dr Death drew us a diagram of what a normal heart should look like, then, just below, our baby's heart, showing the double inlet left ventricle defect they had diagnosed. There really was no similarity between the two. Our baby's heart was a mess. This, however, was contradicted by the fact that we had heard it beat so healthily in the past. But that wasn't all. The foetus doesn't look right, we were told. The hands are in 'flexion' (fists pointing inwards), the knees are knocking together and the legs are pointing out. I immediately felt I had a monster growing inside me – and I could no longer stem the tears. As the doctor continued, each sentence seemed to compound the last. I was only able to pick up certain words – chromosomal link, Trisome 18, Edward's syndrome, incompatible with life, need to move quickly, fetal blood sampling . . .

Reality did not set in. How could this be true? My baby was moving inside me, I'd seen it move so freely. I'd looked at its face. Its heart is beating, I've heard it, I've seen it, I've felt it . . . Stop calling it a fetus, I wanted to scream, it's my baby.

An appointment was made for the next day to sample the baby's blood from the umbilical cord in order to test for chromosomal abnormality. Fetal blood sampling carries a thirty-three per cent chance of miscarriage, and I was deeply unhappy to have what felt like no choice in the matter. As we drove home silence continued to reign. I cried continuously, much as I wanted to stop. When Markus did open his mouth, it was only to talk about his hunger. It seemed trivial and unnecessary. I hadn't eaten for hours, but any signs of hunger had long since left me. Besides, I didn't want to continue to feed the monster I had growing inside me. Now I wished it would somehow just go away.

I cried some more when we got home. I remember standing by the Aga, holding on to the handrail for support, sobbing with despair. I was unable to give Markus the greatest gift in the world and, with our relationship so apparently volatile, rightly or wrongly I felt sure he wouldn't want me if there was no baby. I felt very strongly, too, that I was letting Cameron down. He had wanted nothing more than to welcome this little sibling into the world. How could he be expected to understand, when his mother certainly couldn't? I slept little, but dreamt plenty that night.

*

The following day I awoke numb and irritable. Numb because I was emotionally drained, and irritable because Markus was going about his business as if nothing else was happening. He wasn't giving me the slightest inkling that he was in any way concerned, let alone involved. I felt I was taking it all myself. Still devastated by the previous day's barrage of painful information, I nonetheless wanted to speak with my obstetrician. After a long conversation he told me that he didn't see the need for blood sampling just yet, and that he didn't understand the hurry. I felt slightly eased by his comments. I would go back to Oxford, but only for another scan.

I couldn't bear to see the face of the fetal cardiologist we had met the night before, but I reasoned it wasn't his fault. The doctor brought another colleague this time, whom I recognized from the hospital where I had given birth to Cameron. Together they scanned in silence. The colleague confirmed the heart was not right, but struggled to identify the other deformities his colleague had associated with the fatal Edward's syndrome (or Trisome 18). But not wishing to undermine another doctor's diagnosis, he suggested further investigation. If the baby has this Edward's syndrome, what happens then? I asked. They explained that they would give the baby a fatal injection and then induce my labour. Or alternatively, they could induce me and then simply not resuscitate the baby on birth.

My God, I thought, I can't do this. This can't be meant for me. I can't bring a dead child into the world. Or watch it die in front of me. What are they talking about? Thoughts were racing around my head at a thousand miles per hour. I fired off more questions, trying desperately to clutch at positive straws. What about the heart defect? What did you call it – double inlet left ventricle – could the baby survive that? Well, as long as the fetus is inside you it will be supported by breathing through you, they said, but when it is born it will need an operation to correct the defect.

My God, an operation. My baby, my baby, my baby, what are they saying about you? You are moving away inside me, I can hear your heartbeat on the monitor, but they are telling me you might die.

The doctors stayed behind to talk as Markus and I left the room. He talked about food again and carried on as if we hadn't just been told what we had. I hated him for it. And then, out of the blue, he commented on how beautiful my feet looked. They are fucking irrelevant at this precise moment, you arse, I thought. It wasn't as if this was his way of dealing with it. He wasn't dealing with it at all. He was also chatting away with the staff, being the resort manager all over again. Charming the women, joking with the men, and all the while I felt I sat there with this fucking great burden on my shoulders, a monster inside me . . . and beautiful feet. I didn't want to be there. And I especially didn't want to be there with a man whose only way of dealing with it was pretending nothing was going on. And above all else, who was still able to have an appetite.

My obstetrician called later that night and suggested I come and see him the following day to discuss how to proceed. He was one of the few people I could talk to lucidly. When I spoke to everyone else

– my mother, Melanie who was on holiday, or my friend Lisa – I just cried and cried and cried and I was unable to get the important words out. I also spoke to John. I missed him so much. He took everything seriously and profoundly and understood totally the implications. He had some words of comfort, and I clung to them.

After my appointment the following day I was asked to make the decision about a chromosomal test. The choice was whether to go through the pregnancy blind and hope there was no chromosomal connection, or have a test now and risk a miscarriage. It was up to me. Markus was adamant I should have a test. The thought of a disabled child, I could tell, absolutely horrified him. If the baby had Edward's syndrome it wouldn't survive, but with Down's it probably would. I had never had to consider having a baby with Down's syndrome, but with my child growing inside me, I felt I couldn't give up on it yet. With a heart defect and Down's the baby would have an even shorter life expectancy, as a baby with Down's would not cope with surgery as well as another child. Oh, God, it was so complicated.

I didn't want to risk my baby's life, but I knew that uncertainty for the rest of the pregnancy would take its toll on me dramatically. I already worried for Britain. So the following Monday, 24 July, at twenty-three weeks pregnant and precisely one week after my follow-up scan, I went in for a CVS – chorionic villus sampling. They remove a small piece of tissue from the chorionic villi, part of the placenta, which has the same chromosomal composition as the fetus. More cells are generally obtained by this method than by amniocentesis and the results may be obtained slightly quicker. I realized that I might be saying goodbye to my baby, if I was now to lose her through miscarriage. And yes, she was a girl, I had opened the envelope.

Afterwards I was told not to bother resting, because if I was going to miscarry it would happen regardless. Cheery news. I'd be contacted with the results within a week.

I waited and tried to forget what I was waiting for. After four days I had not miscarried and it was evidently now unlikely I would

– that, at least, gave me tremendous hope. I kept flitting from despair to great hope and confidence. I started to love my baby again, after feeling she was a monster. Now she had a face, somehow, and she had a sex. She was my little girl. Cameron was briefly disappointed by this, but then we talked about the advantages of having a sister, such as all the pretty friends she would bring home, and his inevitable protective role, and he soon came around. However, I constantly had to remind him that the baby was very ill and that we would have to see how things went. He remained naively positive.

After nearly a week, Mr Eustace called to impart the good and the bad news. The good news was that the fetus didn't have Down's. The bad news was that that was all they knew. I was so far gone in my pregnancy that analysing the sample was taking longer than they had anticipated. I would have to wait another six days. Once again, my emotions were mixed. I was relieved my baby didn't have Down's, but ignorant of what she did have, if anything.

The next days were automatic somehow. I was on automatic pilot. The tension between Markus and I had reached such a high that he decided to go back to Germany for a while. I was relieved he had gone. We had just kept arguing and failed to reach each other. Following one row when I was immersed in tears, he turned to me and asked, 'Why is this all about you?' What he was implying was that I was behaving self-indulgently and that I was expecting all the attention in this terrible, terrible situation. I thought it was a most bizarre thing to suggest, and explained that with him behaving as if nothing was going on, I was in fact the only one of us facing up to the prospect of giving birth to a dead baby, or to watching the baby die in front of me. Further, I was naturally bonded to my baby in a way in which he had no possibility of being, but in the absence of any empathy from him, I was also being forced to come to the conclusion that he wasn't as involved as he could be.

He was happy to return to Germany. Leaving was something he was used to doing. Every time we hit a wall, he turned on his heel, instead of staying to learn how to get over it. His matter-of-factness and complete absence of understanding was infuriating. I knew that he hadn't had to worry about much in his life, except which girl to go with every night, or making sure the parasols were upright, but I had hoped for a little more than this in such dire circumstances.

On 3 August I called the hospital for the results. I was tense beyond belief. The person I was due to speak to had gone on holiday. Eventually someone else called me back. There were no chromosomal abnormalities, and the test also confirmed I was definitely carrying a little girl.

Finally the sun was shining. I was over the moon. Overjoyed, delirious – and above all, relieved. I caressed my growing tummy and spoke to my daughter, telling her it was going to be all right. We would mend her broken heart with an operation, and then she would be fine. I phoned those closest to me with the good news and sensed the relief in everyone. I asked Mr Eustace if I could go away on holiday, as God only knew when we would next be able to get away. He recommended it. I also asked for a second referral. I didn't want to go back to Oxford – it had not been a positive experience for me. I knew the diagnosis was right. I knew my baby had double inlet left ventricle and would need an operation, but I didn't want to go back to an environment with all those bad memories. Mr Eustace made an appointment for me at Guy's Hospital with a Dr Sharland.

Cameron, Markus and I went off to Sardinia with my good friend Lisa, her husband David and their two sons. Away from the realities of home, I was more able to pretend that I was a healthy pregnant woman carrying a healthy child. I knew that on my return it would be back to hospitals for scans and appointments, and then eventually a birth. Of some kind. Predictably, the German and I got on well away from the 'real' world, too. This was as good as 'his' territory, to boot. The resort was managed by a former colleague of his, and he ran around as if he ran it himself. On a couple of occasions people even came up to him and asked him for help, directions or assistance. He also discussed job prospects. All of them were abroad.

SECOND OPINION

After the holiday, I returned to England and the German to Germany. The following day I had an appointment with Dr Sharland at Guy's. In the absence of the father of my child I had asked my friend Lisa to accompany me. She is very sensible, has had two premature babies herself and was guaranteed to be able to listen to what the doctors would have to say, should I blub through the whole experience.

Dr Sharland couldn't have looked less like a doctor. When she smiled at me as I walked into an office full of people I presumed it was because she recognized me from the telly, and I looked away after smiling back, impatiently waiting for the doctor. When it turned out to be her, I felt relieved. She was a petite, elegantly dressed lady of Far Eastern origin with the most beautiful face. Not very doctor in my experience thus far. She told me she needed to scan me again to confirm the diagnosis, which I had anticipated, but it hadn't stopped me dreading the thought of yet another ultrasound. Within seconds she confirmed my baby indeed had a double inlet left ventricle.

But what she told me next didn't make me feel as relieved as doubtless intended, but rather angry. 'There is very rarely a link with a chromosomal abnormality with this kind of heart defect,' she pronounced confidently. I shuddered at the memory of what they had made me think I might have to go through in Oxford. I wished I had been spared all that worry. But I knew that time and energy were now both precious commodities, and I needed to concentrate on the future rather then become frustrated about the past.

After the scan she invited me into her office, together with a counsellor and her colleague, the cardiologist Dr Qureshi. She asked me what I had been told and asked if I had any questions before she started. I couldn't think of any, except for 'Can you save my baby?' Gently she explained that the defect my baby had was a serious one. They deal with all sorts of defects at the hospital, and this was one of the major ones. My baby would require a series of three operations, of which two would be open-heart. Open-heart, she explained, entailed stopping the heart and putting it on a bypass machine. During a closed-heart operation, the heart keeps pumping and the surgeons work around it.

They drew me diagrams of what each operation would entail. My baby's first operation would be within a couple of weeks or so of birth, but nothing was guaranteed time-wise. The second would be between nine and twelve months; the third might happen between the ages of two and four, and preferably before school age. Then after patient explanations, diagrams, descriptions, and a flood of tears from me, they started to discuss risks. I decided I preferred to stress the 'survival' element – I knew I needed to feel positive in order to proceed with the pregnancy. I was reassured that every operation had a very high survival rate.

I asked if many women had terminations at this stage. 'Some,' they answered. For me it was not an option. Whatever chance my baby had, I wanted to take. But then came the question of whether this was a lot to put my baby through. Yes, it was, they conceded in unison, but with all the expertise and will in the world, she should go on to have a good quality of life. What about after the third operation? After the third operation there is nothing more we can do at the moment, they said. And as far as they knew children were so far living up to fifteen or twenty years old.

Strange when you suddenly have to put figures on life, whether it be survival rates or length of life. I didn't want to think about her living only to fifteen or twenty. I needed her to get through this first bit first. A lot of first bits, in fact.

I also needed to ask about the birth. According to them there was no reason why she couldn't have a normal birth. And it was up to me to choose where she should be treated – there were a number of choices. I didn't want choices, I felt secure at Guy's. I didn't want to take the chance of her being born where they wouldn't know what to do with her. I wanted to be here, with these kind, gentle doctors. Yes, Guy's was in the wrong part of London for me: it would take me an hour and a half to get there. But I didn't care. I wanted to be with the kind doctors who talked about my baby as a 'baby', not a fetus. She wasn't a fetus. She was my baby. As we prepared to leave, I was asked if I wanted a tour of the SCBU, or Special Care Baby Unit, and if I'd like some books and leaflets to read. Sherida, the kind-faced counsellor, also talked about Cameron, and how he would need to be informed and cared for. God! I hadn't thought of that. I think we had a little tour of the Special Care Unit, familiar territory for Lisa, and visited a couple of cardiac babies and their mums.

That night at home I realized that despite all the explanations in the world, I still didn't understand. Why was this my destiny, and the fate awaiting my baby? If I was honest with myself, I had wanted to give up. I was too exhausted to carry on. Yet seeing the other mums and the pictures of other babies, I knew I could and had to carry on. But I was sore and sensitive, vulnerable and bloated. And I felt as if I might collapse or disappear from view at any moment. I certainly wanted to. And despite all the stories of hope and pictures of possibilities it was all too depressing. What if we aren't that lucky? What if I'm in the percentage of negative outcomes, if my baby is in the fatalities? I couldn't presume everything would be fine, no one could offer me guarantees. Fuck the statistics. Just hold me and give me your word.

When I told Markus about the unexpected three operations, I could sense him falter and hesitate at the other end. The assurances that I wanted from him just weren't forthcoming. And I thought I heard a man sigh at the inconvenience and disappointment rather than with sadness. When he came over the following weekend we discussed things in detail. I thought it would be a good idea for him to come up to the hospital to see and meet everyone for himself, so that he would have an idea of what I was talking about. During our visit he irritated me intensely. He was cocksure and confident; he appeared to me to be asking questions about the impact this would all have on his life, rather than on our baby's. I had never thought to question how this would affect my life – my primary concern was my daughter. He laughed and joked throughout his banter with the doctors, which I felt was inappropriate. I didn't believe things could get more serious than the situation we were in.

At home he turned silent. I worried that the vulnerable side of him was suffering. But it turned out that he was smarting because he felt he had not been asked his opinion about where the baby would be born. I was flabbergasted. We had discussed it. He knew this was, for me, the only secure option, short of being transferred by ambulance from my local hospital to Guy's or wherever immediately after the birth. And I didn't want to risk that. His experience and knowledge of childbirth and babies was limited, and I had involved him at every stage, even when he had appeared bored and uninterested. Suddenly the ego had spoken and it was about the authority of a decision, not about what was best. I raised my hands in disbelief and walked away.

Two weeks later he left me once again. The atmosphere between us was, seemingly, irreconcilable. I had, this time around, set him up with a bank account, organized a mobile phone for his sole use and given him a car to drive. He said he didn't want the money, but I said he needn't pay me back. I just wanted him to have a feeling of independence and the 'status' he felt was important. If it was important to him, it was important to me. I asked him not to go, to dig deep and find some space inside him where there might be a place for him and me. A foundation on which we could build. I told him that if he left, it was his choice, not mine. He replied that he was going back to Germany for a few days to get some space to apply for jobs and to give us both a break.

The period that followed was to be the most harrowing in my life.

*

Just before Markus left for his few days in Germany, I was contacted by a *Sun* journalist and alerted to the death of my first and most precious boss, Bruce Gyngell. He had been sick for some time and had passed away at the age of seventy-one. He left five children and a bevy of mourners. I wept and wept. I couldn't believe such a great man was no longer with us, and that I would never see him again. We'd stayed in touch long after I left TV-am. Bruce would not accept death, surely. He was so alive – more than all of us put together. And my thoughts turned to his wife Kathy and his two youngest sons. The funeral was appropriately sombre, but it was joyous to spend time in the company of Mike Morris, Richard Keys and Lorraine Kelly, my old TV-am colleagues, reminiscing about the old codger. He would have loved that.

On one phone call with Markus, he suddenly announced that he was due to undergo tests for cancer. This came totally out of the blue – he had never mentioned it before. With the amount of cigarettes he smoked he was certainly a candidate for cancer, but he had shown no symptoms of any ill health. While naturally I was prepared to be sympathetic, knowing him as well as I did by then, I had a sneaking suspicion that this could be an attempt at attention-seeking behaviour, and challenged him. I told him to go ahead if he felt he really had to, but pleaded with him not to forget about the serious situation that we knew for sure already existed. He then became uncontactable for two whole days, which seemed to last a week. On the third day I got hold of him. He told me he didn't know if he was ever going to come back. I became hysterical – I was beside myself with fear, insecurity, fear and fear. I was being deserted at seven and a half months pregnant. Pregnant with a severely sick child, anticipating a motherhood that I had begun to dread. The future was more than just uncertain, my volatile relationship with a man on another planet aside. He made me feel as if I had forced him to this conclusion. Actually, I had been pushing for an amnesty between us so we could both take control of our situation and stop it slipping into the hole it was now, thanks to him, so obviously in.

But there was to be no reasoning. He was resolute. He was in Germany for his cancer tests, indefinitely. He was disappointed that our child's defect had not brought us closer together. It should have done, he said. Well, it can't with you in another part of Europe, I fought back. I asked him if he was scared of the baby and the possible outcomes. He told me, categorically no. What then? What could be so terrible that you are unable to support me in the condition you got me in? I asked. He didn't answer. He needed space, he had said. What about *my* fucking space, then? He wasn't the one with the parasite living off him, a parasite we didn't even know would survive, a parasite which wouldn't give me the evening off to get completely blathered in the circumstances . . . I couldn't run away. I pleaded with him to come back, because I was scared. I was scared of this baby, but above all else I was scared of myself.

The phone call ended, but not my hysteria. I panicked, sobbed, threw myself around the empty rooms in the house, dying inside. I was out of control, but I managed to call Melanie, who said she would come straight over. She was deeply concerned. I couldn't catch my breath. When she arrived I was still unable to stop crying and start breathing. I was supposed to go to a script reading that evening and she strongly recommended I went. She thought it would distract me. 'I can't, I can't, I can't,' I said. 'You have to help me.' But I knew she could not. I knew that no one could help me, least of all the man in the foreign country. However, she did phone Markus and spoke to him for over an hour, at the end of which he told her to look after me for him. She told him that was now his job, not hers.

He didn't want to help me. He had heard my desperation and chose to pass on it. If he didn't want to help me, who would? But I went to the script meeting, heavy of heart and swollen of face. My eyes were vaguely visible in a reddened, blotchy, puffy face and I could feel a pain inside me so intense that I wanted to scream and cut it out. I wanted to cut my baby away from me and drink myself to death. I wanted to die, such was the intensity of my pain and desperation.

The German had requested we did not speak. But for me the uncertainty and volatility of every hour that passed rendered me more desperate than I thought humanly possible. It was worse than ever before. And as before, I began to punish myself in my head. Telling myself that it was my fault, that I had done something to drive him away and that I had been wrong from the start. I was on my knees. Physically and psychologically. I didn't understand why he was doing this, but I understood that I hated myself. I also understood that I had to go to the doctor's.

I learned I could take antidepressants quite safely, or maybe speak to a psychotherapist. The idea of being drugged away from the pain of the spear in my heart, the pain in my stomach, which refused to go away, and the aching in my head which persisted through the death of one minute and the birth of the next was tempting. But in the end I refused the antidepressants and sought counselling with a local therapist. She was kind and listened, but she, too, was unable to take my pain away.

After ten days of no word from the German, I had to call. But as I opened my mouth to beg for help, sobs muffled my words and tears interrupted my breathing. He remained cool. He repeated he would not be returning. I had driven him away. When my desperation became uncontrollable hysteria, he simply threatened to end the call. He was doing what he wanted and that was that. It was clear that our child and I were not even secondary.

Towards the middle of October, some three weeks after he had left, I had an appointment with my obstetrician at Guy's, the choice of hospital on which I had 'failed' to consult the Führer. But he did agree to fly over. At my check-up, a date was set for my induction, three weeks before the baby was due. So desperate was I when he came over that I knew I would go all out to persuade him to stay. The first thing he did was make love to me, despite my heavy belly. I wanted to weep, so scared was I of losing this man. But despite our physical closeness during those couple of days, he refused to stay. He explained that he didn't know where work might take him in the world, but that he would be back for the birth.

A week later I started to get Braxton Hicks contractions. My anxiety mounted. Markus just has to be here, I thought. I was sure that when he saw his baby he would embark on the greatest love affair of his life, and one that would give him purpose. She would matter more than I would, but that was how it should be. But she would also matter more than him. Instinct would make him lead his child to a safe harbour where sickness and death would not touch her. Where he would be her mountain; her bridge; her warmth and her light. Where he would know that nothing he had seen before would compare, and where he would start living for real. One smell of her and he would be smitten.

The Sunday night after Cameron's sixth birthday party, two days after Markus had returned once again to Germany, I called him. Exhausted by emotion, I was quiet and calm. I had had some more practice contractions and a bit of spotting. I was careful not to embellish these facts, for fear of him believing I was making him come over sooner than he was ready. He said that as he had now had the results from his cancer tests, which were rather unsurprisingly negative, he was ready to come over.

His arrival was accompanied by luggage. Not the kind of luggage for a two-week visit, but the sort which indicates an indefinite stay. I felt relief. He treated me warmly, affectionately and caringly. I breathed. He made love to me as soon as he arrived and we attended a celebrity dinner promoting Bulgari that night like two smitten lovebirds. Things had never been as good as this. I was too scared to ask any questions and knew that I had to be content with his presence. But he was surely staying this time.

We got on well. Extremely well. There were no arguments, just kind words. I took time out for affection at times when I would normally have been running around. We soon started discussing things, and each expressed ourselves whenever we needed something to be heard, not least about our baby's welfare. I occupied myself with preparations for a long stay in hospital and spent time with Cameron whilst Markus beavered away at job applications, often sending off ten or fifteen in a day. I felt something would definitely turn up, but we agreed that our priority was our baby and that if he didn't find anything until January, that was absolutely fine. It was November.

Markus's best friend, Dirk, came to stay a week or so before I was due to go into hospital. It gave Markus and him a chance to catch up, and me a chance to cook for company. I remember vividly Markus coming up to me in my study that Saturday morning, cupping my chin in his hand, looking into my eyes and kissing me with the words, 'I'm so in love with you.' I thought we had it made. Our troubles were gone, and here he was to support me and his child. Despite our volatile past, we were again captivated by our love for one another, and would never let it go. He then proceeded to tell Dirk that evening how wonderful things were between us and that if we didn't work out, nothing would. What a memory to have now!

I was due into Guy's on Tuesday 7 November, in the evening. I prepared my large bag – who knew how long the whole process would take. I selected a few things for the baby, but felt unable to pack too much just in case. I took all those things that make you feel special, like comfortable slippers and nightgowns worn only by your grandmother. I packed thick sanitary towels for after, and a little pig to put in my baby's cot. But I was sad and tense throughout. I didn't want to leave Cameron, and I knew that the arrival of a sibling would somehow alter our relationship for ever. I was desperately close to him. I didn't want anything or anyone to take that away. But it was inevitable. I wanted a last photograph of us before I left, and he sweetly obliged, stuffing a balloon up his school jumper and standing himself belly to belly with me while John took a Polaroid. And with that Markus and I were taken off into the depths of a dark, cold London, dreading something most people spend their lives looking forward to. We were both losing our nerve.

*

We arrived at the hospital and were put in a cheerless NHS room on the antenatal ward. I unpacked a little and awaited my standard checks – baby monitoring, blood pressure and temperature. Later that night a midwife inserted a gorgeous dose of inducing gel up my honeymoon passage and I lay once more waiting for the fireworks to start. Markus fell asleep on a mattress on the floor but I stayed awake for much of the night with contractions coming and going at regular intervals. By early morning, however, they were diminishing.

Contractions had started but once again my cervix refused to respond. My body had no intention of giving birth for at least a couple of weeks, it seemed. Later that morning I was examined for the hundredth time and it was decided another dose of the gel would be inserted. Glorious. Melanie arrived with magazines, cheer and travel Scrabble. My contractions resumed, once again, causing me discomfort, but nothing much else. I recommended Markus and Melanie go out to lunch.

By five o'clock that afternoon, after a round of Scrabble – which would not have been my strength under normal circumstances, but was even less so with contractions tugging away at my nether regions – Melanie took on the role of breathing fascist. She was insistent on me breathing rhythmically, which I found impossible to do with contractions coming every couple of minutes and with increasing force. She would shout at me and mimicked a breathing routine, which frightened me half to death. Her intention had not been to stay, but soon things were progressing with next to no respite. Markus, too, was encouraging, in between his coffee and fag breaks outside. I asked him to massage my back and my feet. I wanted to get up and move around, even though it felt like the contractions were breaking my back and despite the inescapable rotting feeling in my stomach. We wandered around the ward, shuffle by shuffle, until by nine or ten o'clock they suggested I head down to the labour ward. On floor bloody thirteen.

My cervix wasn't taking great strides in the dilating department, but my male midwife hoped things might improve. However, after about six or seven hours of intense contractions I was becoming weary. I felt drained. I hadn't slept the previous night and had eaten nothing. I was running on empty. I didn't want to go for the epidural just yet and I was recommended a bottle of gas. Not quite as tempting as a bottle of whisky, which was what I really wanted, but impressive nonetheless.

Yes, as I sucked on my tube of gas, drawing in the wonder fuel with deep breaths, I simply couldn't stop laughing. I felt completely pissed. Melanie thought it would make a great photo to add to my collection. I laughed and laughed and laughed until I started to feel nauseous. One of the side effects, I was told. Well, get it out of my sight then, I requested, kindly. The pain was intensifying. I wanted to remain on my feet, but found I was severely lacking in strength and conviction. I requested the epidural.

Markus popped in and out of the labour room, looking disorientated and concerned. Talking about food, as he was hungry. I was starving, but allowed nothing, so asked him to eat far away from me. By midnight, or just after, a female anaesthetist bounced into the room, proclaiming, 'I never miss.' How encouraging, I thought, as I offered up my spine for injection. The pain was more intense than I had remembered from my Cameron's birth. I was asked to sit still, which seemed an impossibility with contractions of such magnitude. But the needle and the drugs went in. Phew! I thought.

But an hour later I was still only anaesthetized down my right side. My left side was still in the grips of the pains, as they shot up and down my body. My patient midwife suggested we needed to resite the epidural. Oh, good, I thought. Could we ask Eric Bristow to do it this time? But following another excruciating attempt I was eventually virtually free of pain on both sides and in my general undercarriage area. Hoorah!

It was the middle of the night and Melanie dozed off in a chair while Markus lay spreadeagled and snoring on his mattress. I certainly did not sleep. I chose to vomit my way through the night, but not without taking photos of my labour buddies. Markus had remained quiet throughout the experience, whilst Melanie and I laughed in between contractions and examinations. He had popped out more than he had popped in, but I forgave him on account of the fact that it must be bizarre being so helpless in a situation like this. Whenever he popped in, he stank of fags and strong coffee, smells I could ill bear.

A change of midwife was accompanied by further vomiting, to which there is an art when you are lying on your back with nothing in your tummy. But I was also gasping for something to drink – I have never known such thirst. But no sooner had I consumed a thimble of water than it made a reappearance in the paper bowl strapped to my mouth. I was actually ready to kill for a Coca-Cola, but sensibly I wasn't allowed more than an ice cube, despite my attempts to bribe anyone who came into the room to get me a can of the stuff. By nine or ten o'clock in the morning I was examined again, but my cervix was virtually on strike, and had only made feeble attempts to dilate. It was too depressing for words.

By midday, my lovely obstetrician, Mr Maxwell, entered – the room, not me – and made his own little check. He reassured me that my baby, throughout the almost forty-hour ordeal, was showing no signs of distress. He also announced that my cervix was now reluctantly heading for dilation, so he would leave me to it for an hour or so. Nice to be kept informed of progress. When he returned, my midwife had decided it was time for me to start pushing. Melanie and Markus looked on in amazement at the little head of black hair attempting to exit my nunnie area. I pushed and pushed for a good half an hour or more, but to little avail. When Mr Maxwell came back, he became concerned that the baby was actually positioned with her face up, rather than down. Without hesitation he called for reinforcements and informed me I would be going into theatre. A Caesar, I thought. I was given a boost of anaesthesia, at which point my midwife informed me confidently, 'We will still have this baby vaginally!' We will, will we? It all sounded very familiar. God, I hope she's helping, I thought, because I'm too disorientated.

Markus was going to come into theatre with me and was made to scrub and be gowned up. They plastered a sticker with the word

'Dad' on it to the left side of his chest. Just in case there would be any confusion. As if.

Theatre was busy. It was a small stage, with a packed audience. In the corner were a little cot and two paediatricians on standby. I looked at them with trepidation, and resumed throwing up. I was then laid flat on my back and asked to push like a bastard, but she wasn't coming out. 'We are going to use the ventouse,' announced another doctor. Sounds appealing, I thought, before yocking up even more. 'When I say push, push!' he ordered. And I did. I pushed twice. Hard, hard, hard, as if my blood vessels would burst. And shortly after I heard the cry of my newborn baby girl. Markus kissed my cheek and told me he loved me. I returned the compliment and told him to go to her. He was armed with a Polaroid and an Instamatic and flashed away. After a couple of minutes I was handed my baby, as the doctors tried to patch up my nunnie.

And there she was. My baby girl. My baby girl I had been so frightened of. She was reddish-blue in colour; her face was swollen and puffy – or maybe just fat – and she squinted at me angrily, as if she had been woken up before she was ready. She voiced her complaints without hesitation and tried repeatedly to focus on me. Her eyes were like lines in a face chubby with cheeks and her lips were luscious. Tears filled my eyes and I turned my attention to her feet and saw immediately she had her father's. Her fingers were long and her thumbs double-jointed. Her voice calmed itself, but her face maintained her demonstration. I held her in my arms and repeated to her how I loved her. I kissed her and smelt the elixir of life – the smell of a newborn, which is incomparable. She wore a knitted hat to protect her little head after the ventouse and I thought she didn't look dissimilar to Bob Marley. She was my baby, my flower. I knew I would shortly have to hand her back. Sure enough – one of the paediatricians asked for her to be returned. As much as I wanted to keep her in my arms I was equally anxious that she be handed over to those who would monitor her condition. I had been prepared, but although I knew it was clinically right, it felt morally, emotionally, psychologically and naturally wrong. She belonged with me. But if I held on to her for too long, it might be detrimental to her health. As they took her from me, I kissed her. I kissed her and kissed her and wept. And I asked them not to wash her. Her smell was fundamental to me.

BO JONSSON, MARK II

As my baby was wheeled away by two doctors, I asked her father to go with her. I wanted him to go with her. Besides, I was about to have my nether regions tended to and hopefully, ever so hopefully, I would be allowed a Coca-Cola.

As it happened, by the time I was taken out of theatre and back into the delivery room I had changed my mind. What I wanted above all else was a cup of NHS tea and a slice of toast. There is simply nothing better. Melanie joined me. There wasn't a celebratory atmosphere. I had given birth to a baby with a serious heart defect, but that moment with Melanie immediately after the birth was probably as good as it was going to get. I felt a little buoyant. I'd done my bit. I couldn't think about where she was now. I had to trust that the professionals would do everything to examine and stabilize her. Melanie and I quipped about how ridiculously useless I was at getting babies out. I was good at making them, but I couldn't get the little buggers out.

I cannot remember at what stage Markus and I had decided on her name. I know we had toyed with a selection of names, foreign and romantically linked with us. But I do know that 'Bo' was Markus's suggestion. Even though she was a girl, she was to be named after my father. He knew how much my father had meant to me and had he not made the brave suggestion, I guess I wouldn't. Her second name was Eva which was my great-grandmother's name and my first name. It was a family name and Bo deserved to carry it on. Her last name would be 'Coeur' – the French for heart. It has a romantic connotation and, with her defect, a very real medical implication. So it seemed appropriate. And to top it all she would be a 'Jonsson'. Therein lies the explanation behind my beautiful Bo Eva Coeur Jonsson's name.

After a couple of hours a paediatrician and a cardiologist came in. They seemed positive. My mood was a jovial one, in the hope that I might drown out any bad news. But there was no 'bad' news as such. They had done an echo (an ultrasound scan) of her heart to confirm her diagnosis, and she was now settled. Her oxygen saturations were such and such; her temperature this; and her heart was beating nicely. Oh, and she's hungry, said the paediatrician, you can go down and start feeding her. It was the best thing I could hear. I was to be reunited with my baby. I would be allowed to smell her again.

When Markus eventually returned, he was enthusiastic. I think it had meant a lot for him to go with her. It had given him a role in it all. He talked about what she looked like, where she was and how good she smelt. Told you, I taunted. My legs were still drunk from the epidural, so I was wheeled down to the paediatric intensive-care unit – the ward I had been shown before. It was host to dozens of little birds who had flown their nest too soon. I was pointed to a cot in a room with eight or nine others, but Bo was easy to tell apart from the others: she was virtually twice their size. But I felt uncomfortable in the room. Whilst the other babies were mostly the result of premature births and were in the unit waiting for improvement and growth, I was going in to watch my daughter deteriorate gradually. I felt like a foreigner and as if I didn't belong. The staff went about their business and the other parents just sat and stared at their little monkeys. Staff sister Eve showed me Bo and all the equipment she was attached to, explaining everything to me clearly, but matter-of-factly.

My baby angel looked fat and almost tanned in her plastic cot, and something else that set her apart from all the others was her thick mop of spiky black hair – so black it was almost blue. Her eyes remained closed and slitty, and her cheeks the wrong size for her face. She stirred as I stroked her, but she didn't know me. I asked if I could hold her and maybe put her to my breast. I could. With confidence and care I lifted her out of her cot and fought a little with the wires attached to her chest, feet and hands. But it wasn't long before her lips were chomping away at my breast and for the first time in many, many hours I felt like a mother. Markus was by my side and Melanie, too, got a glance at her little god-daughter.

I smiled through the tears at her and willed her to live. I whispered to her softly, stroking her as I did so, telling her how much I loved her. I needed to do this partly to calm myself and also to try to rid myself of the fear I had of her. I feared her life and I feared her death. I feared myself – my movements and my emotions and the enormous depression that I could sense looming over my shoulders, springing from being so unnaturally separated from my newborn. I wept. Markus looked on, emotionless, it seemed. I wondered if he wanted to hold her and he said yes. But as soon as she came away from me, she objected.

I was shown the sad little room with two milking machines ready to be attached to the breasts of the mothers whose children weren't quite theirs yet. There were sterile bottles, labels, freezers and age-old magazines for our distraction and entertainment. I couldn't wait to get back to my seven-pounder and stroke and talk to her again. Markus went out for a cigarette and to make more birth announcements. When he came back it was late in the evening and time for the night shift. I was told I should go and get some sleep. But how could I? I belonged with my daughter. I wanted to stay with her and be nowhere else. I lingered and loitered and lingered some more. When she seemed settled I went to attach myself to the milking machine and made a somewhat pathetic, but surprising nonetheless, deposit into one of the sterile bottles. I placed it in the fridge and kissed my darling goodnight one final time. Wake me as soon as she wakes, I pleaded. They nodded at me, like they had at so many mothers whose instinct had dictated that they should stay with their little birds, but who were in fact desperately in need of sleep themselves.

Markus came with me and we spoke little. All I could feel was heaviness and darkness. I couldn't stop weeping. I needed to be held and to be holding, but neither was forthcoming. He chatted away as if everything was just fine, and probably found me a pitiful sight. At least that is how it felt. As ever, I couldn't bear the fact that he could behave with such nonchalance. He repeated over and over again the names of the people he had called to announce our daughter's birth. But the truth was, I didn't care. I cared about nothing but the child from whom I had been separated and whose future was always going to be rather uncertain.

Sometime in the early hours before dawn, someone came in to tell me my baby was hungry. Again, it was the best news in the world. I had had a disastrous night's sleep – wakeful and disturbed by the German's loud snoring. I hurried as fast as my shaky legs would carry me, and entered the world of motherhood, daughterdom and temporary satisfaction. She wasn't pretty, my girl. But, by God, she was beautiful. She wasn't refined and petite, but thank God she was solid and butch. I was in awe of her and hoped and prayed she would not remember I had been forced to leave her for those hours in the night.

And so the next few days continued. We stayed another three nights in my antenatal room, with me down on Bo's ward for probably eighteen hours or more each day. I saw no reason to leave her. I expressed milk for her, sat and talked to her, changed her and tended to her daily needs. In between, she was constantly monitored and scanned, blood tested and poked. Rounds and rounds of doctors would visit her bedside and wake her from her sleep, prod her and then leave her to be soothed by her mother's growing breasts.

I was in pain down below and in my breasts, and the tears that kept falling involuntarily, sporadically and without warning hurt my head. I felt awkward within myself and incapable of ridding myself of the cloud over me. It didn't help matters that Markus and I hardly spoke. As of old, I couldn't reach him, and it wasn't from lack of trying. He ran around the place, busying himself with phone calls, cigarettes, drinks and food for me, and buying newspapers. He would come onto the ward a few times a day. After Bo had been on my breasts I would hand her to him and he would breathe his smoky breath over her, whispering to her in German and patting her on the bum in a throwaway fashion. Other than that, we had little communication. I wanted to talk about her, about how fucking scared I was and maybe even about him and me. He point blank refused. I asked him to open up to me, to share with me this terrifying, anxious time, but he only said, 'I have to be the strong one.' But truth was, he wasn't being the strong one. He was holding onto whatever he was feeling and not letting it out.

At one stage, we bickered and I said, 'This has got to stop,' meaning the wall he had built around himself. He said simply, 'Yes, it has,' and there was something about the tone of his voice and the fact that he stormed out of the room without another word which made me think he meant 'the whole thing', not just what we were experiencing. Already, we were a million miles away from the positive intimacy of only a few days ago.

Another time, I begged him to stay in the room with me and he didn't answer me, but left the room and went to find his peace in the foul communal TV room. He would moan about the standard of the NHS; the poor hygiene and the inefficiencies, and maybe he was right, but I failed to see that that was the time to be doing it. I wanted the NHS to save my daughter's life; I couldn't be worrying about the fact that bins weren't emptied. Yes, the food was pants, but I wasn't expecting room service. But that was where we differed. He noted everything, and wanted to discuss the fact that the US had failed to democratically elect a new president, and oh, wasn't that funny, when all I could think of was the next hours with my daughter. It was truly as if we were living two different scenarios.

On our third day, I suggested Markus went back to my house for a good night's sleep and to pick up and drop off one or two things. I was alone when he had gone, but not lonely. I felt I was as good as in this on my own. When we spoke that night on the phone, as he soaked in a hot bath, he gave me the customary 'I love you' at the end. But I didn't feel convinced.

Friends and family came to visit and it was equally emotional every time. Bo's birth didn't generate the same amount of celebratory generosity as Cameron's had. We received some flowers and some gifts from close friends, but others didn't know whether to express delight at her birth or wariness about her survival. It was a peculiar situation, and I understood people's awkwardness.

As the days passed my darling daughter started to show signs of deterioration. These were the signs we were anticipating and would eventually dictate the timing of her first operation. This would be closed-heart surgery to put a piece of banding around her pulmonary artery to stem the flow of blood which would otherwise have flooded her lungs. With every day that passed she was becoming more and more breathless. It became increasingly difficult for me to breastfeed her as she lacked the energy to suckle for long. It was horrible to watch her struggle, but I kept firmly in the back of my mind that she was in the best place and she was showing all the signs she was supposed to, albeit detrimental.

Markus understood less and less my growing anxiety. He behaved as he always had, with nonchalance. We became intolerable to each other. He would march into the ward and go to pick Bo up in the middle of a sleep. I would express my disapproval. My breasts were by now red with aching soreness and I knew the second she woke up I would have to feed her, and she would struggle for milk before becoming exhausted and upset. He took my disapproval personally and would walk out of the ward in silence. As ever, he refused to accept that someone else might know better. At first I had thought that his refusal to acknowledge our daughter's situation was taking its toll on him emotionally and psychologically, but soon I found myself wondering if maybe it wasn't taking its toll at all . . .

*

On Bo's fourth day, the doctors began to talk of her operation as imminent. It would take place on the coming Wednesday, when she would be just six days old. Added to the anxiety of the operation itself came the grave concern for the conditions to be just right. She must be fit enough for it, and we had to hope an emergency case would not take her slot. All the possibilities were entirely out of our control and therefore twice as frustrating.

As soon as the cardiologists started talking about her operation, I would weep openly and uncontrollably, although quietly. They would sympathize, but had to carry on talking, otherwise nothing would have been said. Markus would miss some of these encounters. I think he found it hard to be in the hospital all the time; it made him feel claustrophobic and there was so little he could do. We had been given a room across the road at the hospital's charitable hostel for the parents of sick children, for which I would leave the hospital at eleven or twelve every night and return by six in the morning. Markus would increasingly try to make me limit my visits, but I couldn't bear the thought of being apart from her.

Bo was by now being fed my breast milk through a nasal-gastric tube, which was also slightly distressing – more for me than for her. I was expressing milk to keep her allocated shelf in the fridge fully stocked. My breasts couldn't take much more, but I knew I had to persist. My milk was the best thing for her, and quite frankly she needed all the help she could get.

Both Markus and I made friends with other parents on the ward, me with the mothers and he with the fathers. One couple in the corner who also had a cardiac baby were always jolly and united. They could think of no name for their daughter, so decided to call her 'Doris', because had it been a boy, he would have been a Boris. She was a gorgeous little thing. Another couple had had their son dramatically early at only twenty-five weeks or so, which had come as a complete shock for them. Not to say that the situations we were in were not a shock to us all. I found it a massive comfort to swap notes with them, cry with them and occasionally find something trivial to smile about. We all looked out for each other and confided in one another and became mutually indispensable.

The day before Bo's operation, the surgeon, the marvellous Mr David Anderson, came to speak to us. He explained exactly what he would be doing, which at a time like that was almost too much information. He asked us if we had any questions and I came up with some trivial ones. While I'm sure Markus took the talk seriously, he continued to make light of the situation, presumably to help him cope. Then Mr Anderson handed me a form. On it were explanations, no guarantees, but specific requirements for consent. He told me I could return it to him in the morning if I wanted, but I felt very strongly I had no option but to sign it there and then. Nothing would change overnight. We couldn't change our minds – my daughter wasn't having plastic surgery, she was about to undergo one of three life-saving operations. I read it and read it again, the words, 'risks' and other negative words ringing out to me.

Wednesday came. My daughter was scheduled to go down to theatre at eleven o'clock. She had not been allowed any milk since midnight and was positively starving by six when I came in. I tried to comfort her but it was a struggle. From time to time she would tire herself out with her crying and simply doze off to sleep again, until the next wakeful moment. To prepare her for theatre she had a line put into her foot for her intravenous drip and was dressed in the appropriate clothing. I was tense and weepy throughout the morning. She screamed blue murder when they stuck yet another needle in her precious little body, and her pain became my pain. Markus came in at about ten and together we tried to soothe her. I was allowed to hold her throughout, and I realized it was essential for me.

Time passed. Eleven o'clock came and went. Twelve o'clock came and went and she was becoming more and more fractious and so was I. They were running slightly behind schedule, we were told, but the waiting was becoming almost unbearable. Eventually at about twenty past twelve a porter came up with an empty hospital bed, calling out the name, 'Bo Jonsson'. It was hard for me to hear. Firstly, it meant it was time. Secondly, it was my father's name. At that stage I remember getting a hot flush and tears rushing to my eyes with renewed vigour. I clutched my baby and held her tight. By now she was happy to suck away at my index finger for comfort. I looked at her innocent face, which told me she had no idea what was about to happen. I asked if I could carry her down, despite her being attached to her oxygen saturation monitor. The nurse agreed and the porter looked on as if with complete disinterest. I sobbed as we waved goodbye to our friends and the staff on the ward, and their wishes of good luck only fuelled my floods. One of the mothers handed me a good luck charm and I clutched it as if it was the key to life itself.

Only one person was allowed to accompany Bo into theatre. I walked into a small archaic-looking room with a large table in the middle. The gowned nurse on duty was jolly and enthusiastic – rather out of place, I felt, it wasn't hitting the spot. Eventually the anaesthetist came in. I had met him the day before and it was comforting to see a familiar face. He asked if I wanted to hold Bo while he sedated her. I managed a weak 'yes', in among the tears and secretions dripping from my nose. As I took my finger out of her mouth, she called out to me in objection and started to cry. As the analgesic entered her blood stream, I could feel her wilting and fading from my grasp. And before too long she lay still in my arms. I didn't want to let her go. The absence of her voice comforted and perturbed me at the same time.

I was asked to place her on the operating table. The anaesthetist told me to kiss her goodbye. His words were heavy with foreboding, but I knew he didn't mean for them to sound so final. But was this my last farewell to my daughter? I couldn't bear it. I buried my head in her still body and told her I loved her.

*

As Markus and I walked down the corridor to the exit he took my hand and I held his firmly, then sobbed into his arm. There was no other option but to go and have a drink. I was emotionally drained and the next few hours could be impossible. The operation itself would only take from forty-five minutes to an hour, but preparing my little baby for the op would take a couple of hours at least. She had to be ventilated, as she would not be breathing on her own, and she needed to be connected up to every piece of machinery imaginable. So we went to lunch at a bar around the corner and I ordered a pint of Guinness. Despite the tension, the sadness and all that was hanging over us I did feel somewhat lifted by knowing I'd spent every minute with her over the last few hours that I possibly could. I had loved the way she had suckled at my finger and it had given me a chance of bonding with her and feeling like a mother should with her newborn. Now I knew there was nothing more I could do. Her little life was in their hands.

I could eat nothing but consumed my Guinness with speed and displaced hunger. The atmosphere between me and my daughter's biological father was artificial and stilted, and it stumbled through the next few hours like a vagrant on crutches. Eye contact was avoided somehow and we chose to talk about the less contentious things in life. Now was not the time for an argument.

Almost before I knew it there was a phone call from the intensive care unit to say that Bo had come out and she would be ready for us to visit in about twenty minutes. This was followed shortly after by a phone call from Mr Anderson, who said all had gone well and that he felt happy with the tightness of the banding he had applied to her pulmonary artery. Overjoyed, I wept as he spoke to me and I couldn't thank him enough. But he was a modest man and refused to take any credit.

At the very end of a long room lay my little princess, on her back, naked and clothed only in wires and tubes. Across her face and mouth was the ventilator, which was aiding her breathing. Her eyes were firmly shut and she looked not only peaceful but grown up. As I approached her I spoke to her softly and stroked her skin. She didn't feel as cold as I had been told she might. Across her chest, covering her scar, was a piece of clear plastic, protecting it from the outside world. I didn't care about her scar. I was only interested that she had come back to me in one piece. She remained motionless and I watched her attentively and listened to the information being fed me by the nurse tending to her. My daughter's strength humbled me, as did the expertise of those looking after her. I felt, despite knowing we had a long way to go yet, content. I thanked God for his patience and generosity and hoped he had more put aside for later.

Markus looked at his daughter for some time, stroked her feet as he always did, and went out to make phone calls to spread the good news. I was happy to be left alone with her. As before, there was something about the circumstances that made me feel it was her and me, alone together. Just as I felt excluded by him he, no doubt, now did by me, but it was inescapable. When he returned with a hot drink he rubbed my shoulders for a while, as they had become stiff from the constant sitting and lack of movement. I carried on watching my baby girl and prayed that she would continue on the steady road to recovery.

I left her at about midnight, exhausted and utterly void of everything except gratitude. Despite sleeping and dreaming dreams of madness, I could not resist waking early and crossing over to the ward before it was even six o'clock. She had come round at about two in the morning, but had had a good night. She was not ready to be extubated, or to come off the ventilator just yet; her breathing wasn't quite good enough. But she would be transferred to another ward later that day. All I could do in the meantime was sit beside her on a hard plastic chair and watch her, occasionally talking, caressing or cleaning her.

Gradually, she began to rejoin the land of the living. Parents are asked to leave the ward when babies are taken off the ventilator to see if they can breathe on their own, as it can be quite distressing to watch. If they aren't ready, they have to be ventilated all over again. I had found it distressing enough watching her fight with the tubes as she was regaining consciousness, so did not need persuading to leave.

We were lucky. Once extubated, she coped with the breathing herself, but as a direct result of having had a tube down her throat for so long, she was unable to make a noise as she cried. It was horrible to witness. Also, she was on restricted fluids, which frustrated her no end. I was still expressing, but she was only allowed

limited amounts – yet she was hungry! It is hard when you know
how to comfort your baby, when you know what she wants, and
you simply cannot give it.

Friends and relations came to visit, and Markus's brother even
came over from Germany. I felt I had more in common with him
and it was a relief to watch him handle Bo with such ease and
explain to Markus the dos and don'ts of newborns. It also gave
Markus a chance for a boys' night out, which I felt he would benefit
from. By the Monday following Bo's operation the doctors started
talking about an imminent discharge. I felt apprehensive about it,
remembering how nervous and weepy I had been when I had taken
my perfectly healthy son home six years prior. Now I was about to
take a sick child home, but I knew I had to put my faith in the
doctors and my beautiful girl. She was able to resume breastfeeding,
and although she would still become quite breathless, it was evidently not a problem. It just meant she took longer to feed and
probably didn't get as much as she wanted. Her scar was impressive
and appeared to be healing well.

It was recommended, but not obligatory, that I spend a night
with Bo at the hospital with medical staff nearby before I took her
home, to help put me at ease. There is what is known as a 'mother's
suite', which is nothing like a suite, but where you can sleep the
night with your baby. It's basically a room with a bed and a window,
and, oh, a storage heater in the middle. I asked whether I might stay
the two nights before we were due to go home – one night with her
saturation monitor attached, and one with it switched off. They
kindly agreed and made the necessary arrangements. I was excited.

That first night, however, was an absolute nightmare. Every time
Bo moved her foot the monitor would blare loudly at us, as it failed
to pick up a trace. I didn't sleep at all. On top of which, twice when
it happened Bo refused to settle again and insisted on crying. I called
in the nurses on those two occasions, believing that she perhaps had
some difficulty. It emerged that she had developed regular hiccups
as part of her routine, and these caused her a lot of pain. And every
time she was picked up the soreness of her scar caused her pain

enough to cry. She was also suffering from oral thrush, quite common in newborns, but especially uncomfortable for her and me since her mouth was in such regular contact with my breasts.

I couldn't put my finger on it, but felt deep down that Markus's attentiveness was waning. We didn't see much of each other as he was more out of the hospital than in it. And I knew he spent much of his time on the phone. To whom, I wasn't sure. On the last night in hospital he managed to persuade me to go out to eat before I locked myself away with my baby girl for another sleepless night.

I was truly exhausted, to the point of feeling dizzy and weak – physically and mentally – but I indulged in a glass of red wine to relax me and also as a small celebration before taking my girl home. We sat in the same bar around the corner. Then came the bombshell.

'I've got to think about my career and getting myself a job,' said Markus out of the blue.

'What do you mean?' I asked. 'And why now?' I heard myself adding.

He explained that he couldn't be unemployed for ever and that he needed to find himself a job. He had been offered something that he was considering. Abroad. A burning sensation consumed my insides and a thousand questions flew into my head. I couldn't understand why he would be telling me this now, when we were about to take our daughter home to the first signs of normality for any of us. Why would he mention this now, when finally we had an opportunity to start to worry just a bit less and develop a life and a relationship with the little person who had so far spent most of her time out of our arms and occupied by an attentive medical profession? What was he saying? What was he *really* saying?

I had no choice but to ask him outright: 'You're leaving us, aren't you?' He looked away and did not reply.

The night before had been wakeful because of Bo. That night I also had his silence festering with me. I had no monitor waking me up every ten minutes, but instead the terrifying fact that my daughter's father was indeed abandoning her and me. I couldn't believe it and refused to do so. It was insane. I cried and cried, but became increasingly aware that what he was saying was the most horrid reality I could ever have imagined. His silence had meant 'yes'. Had he always just intended to stay for the birth, so affirming to himself and the rest of the world that he had done the decent thing and 'been there'? Whilst he had been my communicator with the outside world during my imprisonment in hospital life, now, when we would come home, was when I would need him. This was when life was supposed to begin. With her. I felt cheated. The wool had been well and truly pulled over my eyes. And he had also cheated Bo. With this, I felt he was openly, publicly and very personally rejecting and banishing her. He was giving her life away, because his feelings towards her were clearly not strong enough to keep him here.

The night brought no answers. When Markus arrived to pick us up in the morning, he looked at my dishevelled, well-watered face and asked what was wrong with me. 'You are leaving us,' I kept repeating. He asked me not to make such a fuss. 'Don't be so dramatic and hasty,' he said. Well, if this didn't deserve drama and haste, what did? No, he wasn't going to change his mind, he said, but he thought we should still be civil and pleasant. How on earth could I be? I wanted to feel happy and excited about taking my little girl home, but I could feel nothing but the slow descent of the depression that had been hanging over me. It enveloped me like a dark and heavy coat – one too heavy for my shoulders and too big not to touch my baby angel.

As I bade my farewells to the sensational staff on the ward, who had cared for and saved my daughter and kept me afloat when I had been sure I would drown, all he could do was skip out with the enthusiastic spring in his step of a man excited by the prospect of a much better life. I hated him then, and I never hate. No, the birth of his daughter hadn't touched him. It hadn't moved him, or else he couldn't behave like this. And in nearly two weeks in this institution not once had he opened the doors to his vulnerability or pain.

I called my mother to tell her we were heading home, to screams of delight from her, and only tears from me. She could not believe the rest of my news. The house didn't welcome me, it was simply there. The champagne my mother brought round felt wholly inappropriate. Markus laughed and joked his way around the place, which only added to my sense of outrage. As I pushed some food my mother had kindly prepared around on my plate – my appetite halted in its tracks by a fullness in my belly and by the tears falling so furiously into the food – he looked at me and once more told me to stop making such a fuss. I couldn't contain myself any more. I raised my voice and swore at him with venom. He noted that we certainly didn't seem to make each other happy. He was right, to go by the past few months, but I had thought we had been too overwhelmed by our tragic times to be able to find common ground. Truth was, I had been too overwhelmed. He had kept a steady head and a closed heart throughout, just in case he too would experience this terrible trauma.

And now he would be off. Escaping unscarred. It wasn't just cowardice that immediately sprung to mind, but the most abhorrent selfishness. When he needed something, he made sure he got it. As for everyone else, well, we didn't feature, all of a sudden. He felt he had done his duty and now he was free to go.

*

What became evident that night was that I had brought home a near-nocturnal baby. Bo didn't sleep much during the day, but even less at night. Her feeds would take me on average two and a half hours, then she might sleep for and hour or two and then the same pattern would restart. She slept next to me in bed. Somehow, Markus felt it acceptable that he should do so too. I slept not at all. Amazingly, he asked me the following morning when he finally emerged whether the baby had woken up in the night. He started talking with enthusiasm of his parents coming over to visit their new grandchild. This didn't tally. Was he now expecting us to play happy families, as well? I asked him if they knew he was leaving us. He wasn't leaving us, he said, he was simply considering a job in the Canary Islands. With good prospects. And good weather presumably.

So this was his idea of fatherhood. He said he would like our relationship to carry on – he didn't want 'us' to end, he still loved me and was, as he put it, still *in* love with me. 'What about your daughter?' I asked. 'I cannot give a commitment to the baby, when I do not know where this job might take me,' was his answer. I couldn't believe my ears.

You see, my anger and heartbreak weren't for me. They were for this most beautiful being in my arms who had fought so hard to stay alive, and who was now being deserted by one of her parents. I couldn't abide his rejection of her; it cut me like a blunt knife, right down the middle and then into a thousand pieces. I couldn't think what I would have to tell her when she grew up. *If* she grew up. I couldn't bear to look down at her and for her to feel unwanted in any way, shape or form. It killed me. It absolutely killed me.

So I told him I didn't want a relationship with him under those circumstances. You know, the circumstances where I stay at home and bring up baby and we fuck once every three months when I go and visit him. Uh, uh. That is not the life for me, or her. Was he seriously suggesting this was a good compromise, a viable suggestion and something I would be enthusiastic about?

'When are you planning to leave?' I asked. I was brave. I needed to hear his words in the hope it would make this cruel situation into the reality it inevitably was.

'I am not planning to leave,' he said.

'When?' I pushed.

'Perhaps after my parents have been to visit . . .'

Well, if that wasn't planning a leaving date I do not know what is. Over the coming few days, I kept asking him to think about what he was doing. I knew there would be no turning back once he left. I had run out of forgiveness. I didn't sleep, I couldn't eat and he was of no help to me. When he asked to hold Bo once or twice, I felt reluctant. When challenged, he admitted that he was leaving so soon in order to ensure he didn't bond – that would only tie him to us. I replied that in that case there was no point in him holding her – it wouldn't do her any good, and it would only feed his ego.

That weekend, four days after we had brought our little baby angel home, I told him that if he was going to leave I would prefer he left sooner rather than later. He seemed relieved. I have never seen anyone head for the phone with such enthusiasm as he did when he went to book his ticket.

*

On Tuesday 28 November, with my daughter just under three weeks old, her father left her for a better life. He walked out of her life, with not so much as a tear in his eye, and with one simple request: a Polaroid of the two of them together. I didn't deny it to him. I also told him I would never stop him seeing her. As he was about to shut the door behind him, I cried out pathetically, 'We love you.' And he was gone.

DESPAIR, HOPELESSNESS
AND DESOLATION

I had no idea there could be such unhappiness. I was overwhelmed by the task before me, and still afraid of my own child. I was tired and exhausted to the point of insanity and I was now in this alone. Completely alone. I was capable of seeing only darkness; I didn't think the future was bleak, I knew it. I hadn't wanted to have another child in order to could bring it up alone. I had wanted the unit. I had wanted to go out into the world holding my lover's hand and looking at the miracle of our child. This was not to be. And I would struggle for ever, I knew, to reconcile myself to that.

As ever, I blamed myself. My choices, and especially my choice of father. My eagerness to have a child had made me completely overlook his quality and potential as a parent. I had thought I was right. I thought he would make a caring father, at the very least, but he had failed his daughter at the very first hurdle. Whatever sadness I had felt before in my life was simply dwarfed by what I was feeling now. And it dwarfed me too.

Bo wasn't as well as she should have been. Her scar didn't look too clever any more, and I worried it was infected. I took her down to the doctor's, depressed to be seeing a member of the medical profession so soon after our discharge. A second visit resulted in antibiotics, which slowly healed her scar, but only worsened her thrush.

No word from the father of my baby.

After three days I called him and asked if he cared. His reply was that *he* thought we needed a few days of not talking. Which was considerate of him. Only I didn't have that luxury. I was closer to the edge than I had ever been. I told him that if he wanted to be involved with his daughter, which he conceded he did, then he must maintain a reasonable and regular level of communication. When he started talking about us, I cut him off, saying that this no longer was about 'us', 'we' were over.

As if to further endear himself to me he called the next day to ask if I had slept well, and to explain how I must sleep properly in order to care for the baby, and that avocados were good to eat. Fuck avocados. I couldn't even eat chocolate. My appetite had gone without a trace. Any food put in my mouth had the texture and flavour of rubber – I couldn't bring myself to even chew. I knew I had to feed myself to feed my daughter, but I simply couldn't.

Another time, feeling at breaking point, I called him. He didn't pick up, so I left him a message saying I needed to talk to him. He called back late that evening and said he had just finished eating with his brother and they were now going out for a drink – and, oh, what did I want? I irritated him with more tears and desperation. He told me he didn't want to talk.

All the while I kept thinking – what if I had wanted to give her up and walk away as well, what would have happened to her then? Why was he taking for granted that I could cope and that I would? What if the selfish bastard in me decided to rear its ugly head and tell the world to stop, I want to get off? It wasn't as if he was having a nervous breakdown and simply couldn't face things. He was fine. He sounded fine, acted fine and carried on his life as if Bo hadn't happened. I kept anticipating hearing him sob, or break down or wake up to the fate he had dealt her, but it wasn't forthcoming.

My close circle of friends rallied around me with words of astonishment at his actions, wonderment at my little girl and encouragement to keep me breastfeeding. And all I could do was cry in their presence. They all gave me licence to call at any time, day or night, but how could I? I couldn't pick up the phone at two thirty in the morning when Bo had just sicked up an entire feed and my nipples were scarlet with soreness.

Every new day was a burden. There was always the very first three or four seconds when you wake up, before your mind is in gear, and the world seems an OK place, but then BANG! it hits you. Or in my case, your destiny and heartache knock you over and gag you.

My poor, poor, darling son had to grow up overnight. I couldn't cope with the routines that had previously been second nature. Cameron did everything I asked and obliged sincerely when I shouted. I raised my voice unnecessarily and scolded him at the slightest thing. I would nag and nag and then shout some more. And he took it all on the chin. He behaved impeccably. And all the while he never, ever once took it out on the person who was indirectly the cause of his mother's misery, his sister. He played and cooed with her, and every day he brought renewed enthusiasm to my door, even if I answered him only with negativity. I want to thank him for his patience during that period. I would not have lasted if it hadn't been for him.

I would also not have lasted without the generous, selfless and unfailing support of my ex-husband. John came to me without me needing to ask. He saw in me a broken woman and he wanted to help, for the welfare of my children, but also for the welfare of me. He suggested he stayed over at the house a little, in an attempt to give me the chance to go to the toilet at least once without the company of a one-month-old. He shacked up in the guest room and held Bo for me every evening to enable me to shower on my own. He brought home food as I didn't even have the strength to venture out of the house. He forced me to eat, even when the food was making me gag. He talked to me for hours about the situation, with the disbelief of a father who lives for his own child. He never tried to counter me or make comments that would fuel my anger; he simply listened and attempted to find positives in my words of anger, sadness and disappointment. And then he would take Cameron to school for me.

But even John's presence had to stop at some stage, and after a week or two we both knew that I would have to go back to coping on my own. He maintained his offer of delivering Cameron to school every morning, which was a huge weight off my broken shoulders.

The health visitor came. And I lied through my teeth on the form that tests you for post-natal depression. If I had answered the questions honestly, they would have taken me away in a strait-jacket. I did, however, feel it was appropriate that I tell her my partner had gone, just in case she had a miracle cure. She looked at me with disbelief and pity, and I knew then that, of course, she hadn't. She did, however, recommend a visit to my GP.

I talked to every professional I could think of. I couldn't pretend everything in my garden was rosy, especially as it turned out I didn't even have any roses. The doctors at Guy's kept a close an eye on me as well as on Bo, despite me finding it in me to joke myself through my tragic tale of desertion. How else was I to tell people? If I broke down again, I wouldn't know what to do with the sympathy. Bo's doctors understood that I needed to be healthy in order to look after my monkey. But I wasn't, was I? At least, not in my head.

Melanie, needless to say, was my iron support and took more than a dozen calls of desperation, depression, anguish and panic, every day. Once Cameron had left for school in the morning, all that was left was me and my little codependent and the heaviest and eeriest of silences. The silence petrified me and the long hours felt dangerous.

Within six weeks of birth, the law states that a child has to be registered with the local authority. With the length of our hospital stay and of my depression, I was fast running out of time. When I called to make an appointment at our local town hall, I was forced to explain that the father was no longer present, and it was made clear to me that I would not be able to register the father's name on the birth certificate as we were not married and he would not be present. It was something I hadn't considered, and I told Markus immedi-ately. He was perturbed by the news but had to understand. So when I went down the following day and registered Bo's birth, the column under 'Father's name' was left blank.

*

As we headed towards the middle of December, I had been asked to present an award at the British Comedy Awards. Despite not coping personally, I felt I should show my face professionally, just in case people thought I had disappeared off the face of the earth – even if that was exactly what I wanted to do. So I attended, squeezing into a pair of old jeans and with my breasts leaking enough milk to feed a ward of babies. I rushed home immediately afterwards feeling that I no longer belonged in that world either. I wasn't fit for my personal, maternal world, but I felt equally uneasy back in the world of showbiz bollocks. I belonged nowhere any more. I peeled myself out of my tight jeans and resumed my daily uniform of baggy trousers and black M&S top, and continued as I had for the best part of six months: breastfeeding, sobbing and staring blankly at bare walls.

Then came Cameron's Christmas concert at school and I knew I had to venture out and support him. There I sat, on a hard plastic chair in the school hall, with my baby in the car seat at my feet, surrounded by friendly faces who cooed and aaahed at the newborn, and all I could do was weep uncontrollably at the sight of all the families and fathers.

Apart from that, Christmas was cancelled in my house. For someone who is so utterly committed to the Christmas festivities under normal circumstances, my home resembled a morgue. No decorations, no spirit, no warmth. I acted enthused towards my son when he described his wish list, but wondered how on earth I would be able to make his dreams a reality. I bought presents for no one except Cameron. Neither John nor I had plans, and we were very kindly invited by a friend of mine, whose son is in Cameron's class, to partake of Christmas dinner with them. But I was unsure how good company I would really be.

On Christmas Eve, Melanie came to visit, and we cracked a bottle of champagne, but the bubbles did little to lift my spirits. John had a cold, and Bo, too, seemed rather under the weather. She was sleeping a little more than usual, which was normally not at all. I had heard nothing from the German for a couple of days. Bo continued the next day in a sleepy, fevered state, which was only stabilized with regular doses of Calpol. Everyone commented on how good she was, sleeping so much, but all I could think was how unlike her it was. Then I found a message on my mobile from her father, who sounded slightly down, but who wished us a 'Merry Christmas'. How thoughtful of him.

By the time we returned home at about seven o'clock, my instincts told me to be more than a little concerned about my daughter. I became alarmed when I changed her nappy and saw that with every breath she was attempting to take her stomach sank in deeply and her chest became protruded. The previous morning the doctor had given her chest the all-clear, but I now felt something was wrong. Guy's recommended I take her straight up to my local A & E department. By this stage she was barely awake and not even interested in feeding. Limp and listless, I cradled her in the back of the car as I tried to placate her concerned brother while John drove for England to get us there as soon as possible.

Accident and Emergency departments are not at their best on Christmas Day. The waiting room was full of drunks, broken arms and legs, cut heads and bleeding limbs. I rushed straight up to the reception. The lady behind the counter wanted to take my details. I had no patience in me: I knew my daughter was seriously ill and raised my voice accordingly. I ignored the reception desk and ran straight onto the ward calling for help for my sick baby. A doctor wearing a Father Christmas hat ushered me into a side room and started to question me. Through the tears and panic I managed to get the words out – cardiac baby, not feeding, listless, fever, difficulty breathing. He seemed too relaxed for my liking and I became irritated by his wealth of Christmas spirit. I tried to enforce a sense of urgency about the situation and eventually they put me on a bed with her as we awaited the arrival of a paediatrician. My heart was racing, my tears were relentless and all the time I looked down on this little being with the oxygen mask attached to her face.

After minutes that seemed like hours, the paediatrician came along. He didn't examine her with the amount of urgency I felt she deserved. He looked at her, listened to her, wanted to take blood, but like all doctors with small babies, failed to do so at least a couple of times. He didn't say very much, and when he did speak, his heavy accent forced me to ask 'Pardon?' repeatedly. She was X-rayed, then with her tiny blood sample in his hand he left us to it. I was left sitting there with my tiny babe in arms, thinking once again that this could be the last I would see of her. I had given birth to my son in this hospital, but this was where I could lose my daughter. I prayed to God to spare her and that he could do what he wanted with me, but please, just spare her.

A kind nurse took time out for me. She could see the sheer panic in my face. She offered me a cup of tea, and made me one despite my refusal. I didn't want to be there. I wanted to be at Guy's where her own doctors could mend her; I didn't feel they understood what was going on here. After some time the doctor came back. He explained that it was 'more likely than not' bronchiolitis – a condition quite common in babies and whilst some get through it others 'don't do very well'. What the fuck did that mean? Had I lost something in the translation? What did he mean, 'more likely than not', how fucking imprecise is that?

I felt more panicked by his verdict than I had been before. The question I really longed to ask, the question on the tip of my tongue, the question tearing at my heart and burning in my soul was – is she going to die?

But I couldn't ask it, because I was to fearful of the answer. We were transferred up to the children's ward, which was quiet and largely empty. The nurse on duty, Julia, was upbeat and welcoming, but I didn't want her welcome, I wanted my baby home. We were put in our own cubicle as the virus my daughter 'probably' had is airborne. Bo was laid in a cot and they put a line in her vein and a perspex cubicle over her upper body to supply her with much-needed oxygen. She wriggled and remonstrated as her saturations, temperature and more blood samples were taken. When it was all done, I had to give personal details and her health history.

John had tried to reach the German, but had only got his mother, who said he was away for the night. There was no response on his mobile.

I sat that night, on the bed assigned to me, watching my little baby as she woke and slept fitfully. The exhaustion of the day gripped a tight hold of me. But although I became glazed and confused I continued to pray. My question still remained unasked and unanswered. The trauma of the previous hours had taken their toll on my breast milk, which was by now drying up, despite attempts to extract the ivory nectar from my sore breasts throughout the night.

In the morning the kind nurses offered me a cup of NHS tea, which, as I have said already, is the best cup of tea you will ever have – presumably because of what has preceded it. Bo remained under hourly checks and I could see little improvement. I requested that Guy's be informed of her condition, just in case they would suggest she would be better off there. But as it was the airborne RSV or common cold virus that was attacking Bo's bronchial tubes and making her struggle for oxygen, I learned that Guy's would not, for once, be happy to welcome her. She was better off staying put.

I spoke to an elderly, kind-faced doctor who was jolly and positive and told me that he had seen worse cases, but she would have to fight it alone as there was nothing anyone could do. Her cardiac condition was of obvious concern, but at the moment her heart was coping well. He reckoned she would be unwell for three to five days but then she should be able to go home. Providing . . .

In the middle of the day I eventually got hold of the biological father of my baby. I trusted he'd had a pleasant night away. I told him his daughter was sick. 'Do you think I should come over?' he asked. 'That's your decision,' was all I could reply. He never failed to surprise me.

He did turn up, and I managed to be more than civil. He arrived all swanky and tanned – if looking like a man who may have had too many sunbeds, a few too many drinks and a few too many late nights. I for my part looked pants, like a woman who has not long since given birth, hasn't slept for a month and has recently been deserted by her partner.

I spent the days caring for my little one, as he looked on. I nursed her, or tried to; I expressed for her, or tried to; and I kissed and loved her. Gradually she needed less and less oxygen and I began to see some light at the end of one of my very dark tunnels. Although he'd made the effort to come, the German's abhorrence of hospitals kept him out of this one a lot of the time, smoking, calling or shopping nearby. One time he even came back with a sexy bra and knickers. Just what I felt like, and an honour to receive them from him. He tried to get me to leave the hospital for the evening for a meal out, but I refused. My place was with Bo – always had been, always will be.

I slept on a bed beside Bo's cot and he on a mattress on the floor. One night he came over to kiss me, and whilst my physical needs might have wanted to be met, I certainly wasn't going to reciprocate. He then told me he was scared to kiss me, just in case I got the wrong idea and thought he was coming back to stay. I told him I wasn't some kid waiting impatiently for the return of a distant lover, and that I knew he wasn't coming back – I wasn't going to have him back. The following day we sat and spoke while my daughter slept. He told me he wanted his quality of life back and that was what he was in search of. I was flabbergasted that he refused to believe his own daughter couldn't offer him that. He wanted to drive an old-fashioned sports car, he told me; he wanted to be the master of his own destiny. I questioned his ability to reason that work was more important than life – Bo's life. He failed to answer, as he had done so many times before. I kept asking what he thought the future would hold for her and him, but he didn't want to contemplate it. Rather, he had to get back to Germany for New Year's Eve as his friend Mattias had invited him to a party down in Munich. How charming, I thought.

After further sleepless nights and anxiety Bo was finally discharged on 30 December. Two hours after arriving to a cold house set deep in snow, the German had booked his return flight. He couldn't bear to stay around his daughter. Or me.

That day I made a decision: to stop breastfeeding. I had struggled for eight weeks with sore breasts and one largely unsatisfied customer, and the challenge had become one burden too many. I resolved not to feel guilty about it, and set to mixing some formula to satisfy her more completely. And she liked it.

When John and Cameron came by on New Year's Eve there seemed more cause to open a bottle of champagne. Once they'd left I tucked myself into bed with two large cannonballs for breasts and one baby daughter, and turned out the light by nine o'clock, hoping the next year would be more worth remembering.

ENLIGHTENMENT

Early 2001 still saw me unstable and depressed, but I now had the bonus of a little help with my baby. A previous nanny of mine had agreed to come back and help me out from time to time and I was glad of the relief. Bo had another check-up at Guy's and she appeared to be progressing well, and the virus in hindsight began to look like more of a hiccup. She had her first inoculation, which she coped with equally well.

When I had fallen pregnant, Melanie and I knew there would be another maddening media circus unless I made clear how I was going to manage the information, and we had entered into an arrangement with *OK!* magazine in order to get the story across on my terms. It was to be a two-parter, and in the New Year I was due to have a follow-up interview to talk about the life of my little daughter, and then some. Little did they know the story they were about to get. I had told no one outside my inner circle about Markus's departure.

I was interviewed by the then-editor, Martin Townsend, himself – a lovely man who lets you unfold things at your own pace. I began to talk of the trauma of discovering I was carrying a child with a heart defect, her birth and first surgery and then, obviously, about her desertion by her father. He was gobsmacked and couldn't believe what he was hearing. A dedicated father himself, he was appalled. It was the right time to talk about it publicly – it was inevitable that I would have to – because I was that much less emotional about it than I had been a month before. I simply laid my cards out on the table and spoke of the facts. I also spoke of my emotions, but not anything that sensationalized the immediate departure of Bo's father in any way. His actions spoke for themselves; I didn't think they needed spicing up from me.

The following day, Sven Arnstein, a lovely man too, came to my house to take the photos that would accompany the piece. My new little monkey proved to have a mind of her own throughout the shoot. My sister, Linda, came down from Sweden that weekend and it was wonderful to see her, talk to her and be around her. She is such a stable, honest, real, wonderful person – I appreciated her presence more than words can describe.

Bo's German's grandmother, Christa, had been dying to see her new grandchild since the birth. She had called me on a number of occasions and together we had wept over the phone about the subsequent situation. She was stunned by her son's departure from his daughter and she feared she would have no contact with her grandchild. I reassured her that the door was always open for her, and that I looked on the situation with equal doom. Markus ended up accompanying her, but only very reluctantly, on a weekend visit. As luck would have it, 'my' edition of OK! came out the very day they arrived.

I picked them up from the airport and from that moment on Markus was besieged by phone calls from journalists who had read the story. He knew in advance I was doing the interview and I had even had the decency to tell him what was in it, although I believed everything I had said was fair and harmless. But while his mother doted on her new grandchild, he paced my kitchen with anxiety over the implications of the interview for him. That night when his mother had gone to bed, he offered me a glass of my own single malt and sat me down to talk. He sounded hesitant and verging on regretful, but not quite. He was bothered that I had talked so publicly about him leaving us. He thought it would damage him as he looked for a job. Aha! So therein lay the rub. He was concerned about his reputation, not the welfare of his daughter. I told him in very plain language that the piece could have included my heavy, heavy depression, my desire not to live, my inability even to walk from one end of the kitchen to the other without feeling I would collapse, but I had chosen not to go there. He agreed, and shut up. But not before he asked if he couldn't sleep in bed with me that night. You don't need to guess what my reply was.

The day after they left I had a meeting at the BBC about a new show. I couldn't have cared less – I didn't want to go back to work, I had a little monkey who needed me at home. But apparently my name wasn't the only one in the hat, anyway. When the following week Melanie told me with absurd delight that the job was mine, and the show was called *Dog Eat Dog*, I still wasn't keen and began to think of ways of getting out of it. Until it dawned on me that as the only breadwinner in the house, maybe, just maybe, I should work while I could, as this next year was sure to bring my daughter more surgery.

A weekend or so later, Markus's brother, Martin, came to visit Bo and me. If only her own father had shown the same level of interest.

*

So my first job after Bo's birth was hosting the prime-time game show *Dog Eat Dog* for the BBC. The show centred around six members of the public who didn't know each other but would try to use their talents to outwit each other in an attempt to win £10,000. There was to be a huge element of cunning and cruel elimination to the show. Leaving my daughter was a worry, but knew I wasn't really in a position of choice and perhaps that's why it went so well. I found a new attitude to work. An attitude that told me it wasn't the be-all and end-all. I cared about it, but I didn't over-analyse it. I was much more relaxed and content. I wasn't half as highly-strung as I might have been. My children's health was all that mattered – everything else would just be a bonus. On top of all this I was also sent one of the kindest, most brilliant producers I have ever worked with: Mike Agnew. He was funny, talented and caring. He cared for the whole production and the whole team. It was a team effort. No one was more valuable than anybody else. Everybody was working for a common goal and it seemed that his kindness, professionalism and enthusiasm paid off. I had a lovely time on the series and felt humbled and honoured to be working alongside such a dedicated team of researchers, technicians and production staff. They made what I had anticipated would be another trauma of angst and tension from leaving my newborn into an enjoyable trip and a pleasure to go to work.

I had started to lose weight, too. Not because I wanted to, but because of the stress of my situation. I now ate well, but just not enough. All the while, Bo's father was sitting unemployed in Germany when he could have been enjoying the delights of watching his daughter grow and develop. It seemed as if I had to ram it down his throat that he needed to see her regularly if he wanted her to be part of his life. Ironically, he began to take issue over the birth certificate. I told him it was more important that he knew his daughter than that his name was on a piece of paper. I would always tell her who her father was – Cameron, I said, had never seen his birth certificate, but he bloody well knew who his father was.

Berit came to visit, and I found it a massive comfort to have her around. She, too, has been dealt a few hard blows by life, and carries with her a realism that is sometimes hard to swallow, but is ultimately right. We talked and talked and talked and I unburdened myself as she guided me through opinions, emotions and the rights and wrongs of everything. She is a deeply honest person and I appreciate her in my life tremendously.

Bo had her second inoculation and after much persuading I managed to convince the German to visit his daughter again. We had a stilted couple of days together while I tried to enthuse her father with the joys of his baby daughter, and in between the civility there was a colourful scattering of heavy conversations about the future, which got us nowhere. When he left, I felt the devastation once again. Not that he was leaving me, but that the situation was what it was and that my daughter would never really know her father. I guess I was familiar with a kind of rejection by my own mother, which I didn't acknowledge until adulthood, and I couldn't bear the thought of Bo feeling the same. She deserved better.

There were a few things about my own person I had to attend to. After having my lower regions checked to ensure they were back in full working order, I had my gynaecologist insert a jolly nice coil to stop me reproducing, should I ever have sex again. While he was down there, I asked if he could recommend a good corrective surgeon to do something about my horrendous varicose veins. He obliged, and two weeks later I was under the knife. Good riddance to bad veins! Having said that, that would be as far as I would go with cosmetic surgery.

I'd long before adopted the sensible policy of not reading newspapers, to save myself from inadvertently stumbling across some hitherto unknown aspect of my private life, holiday photos or personal comment, so I tend only to come across them when at work. But whilst recording *Dog Eat Dog* in February I came across an article concerning the plight of a little cardiac baby called Margaux Bride. She desperately needed a heart transplant, and after being subjected to countless surgical interventions since birth was on the verge of losing her fight for life. But with such scandals as the organ removals at Alder Hey, it seemed people were more and more reluctant to donate organs for transplantation. This little baby's life hung in the balance, and I shed a tear as I read her mother's story in the otherwise no-go *Daily Mail*. With the plight of my own daughter, who had been more fortunate, so recent an experience, I wanted to do something. In my mind, we need organs for transplantation *and* research. Without organs for research, Bo's second-stage operation would never have come about. Perhaps I was in a slightly better position than most to do something.

I contacted *Tonight with Trevor McDonald* and told them I wanted to do a story to raise awareness about the dwindling numbers of organ donations. They agreed. By the time we came to shoot the story, little Margaux had just been given a transplant. She'd made it through by the skin of her teeth, twice going into cardiac arrest as her parents sat and watched. By a miracle, a heart had become available abroad. When I went to visit her she was still in hospital and being barrier nursed, so we were only able to film this amazing little creature from behind glass. But her parents' strength, faith, optimism and enthusiasm did nothing but inspire me. As I sat and interviewed Margaux's mother we both wept, because the story she was telling me started as mine had, with a diagnosis in the womb. We had no doubt lived through the same fears and anxieties, but what they went on to experience in terms of being so close to losing their daughter was my absolute worst nightmare. However, through their faith, friends and more than a little help from the medical profession, they could soon look forward to their daughter coming home from hospital properly for the first time in her year-long life.

*

I had always known I wanted Bo christened. I had wanted Cameron christened when he was little, too, but instead I decided to get a divorce, which kind of put a damper on things. I wanted Bo christened for all sorts of reasons. Firstly, I was christened, and have faith. This does not necessarily mean I will be at church every Sunday, but it does mean I believe in something. Quite what it is, is very personal to me, but so far Christianity is the religion which speaks to me the loudest. I do not swallow everything the church throws at me, but there are aspects of its teaching which I feel are of absolute relevance – whether to life in yesteryear or today. Secondly, with Bo's condition, I wanted her to be welcomed into the church as early as possible, because I felt it would give her an added strength when fighting all the trials life will put her way. Thirdly, I had found myself questioning my faith over the past traumatic months, asking all sorts of 'what now?' and 'how?' questions in search of clarity – for my own situation as well as Bo's. I had never asked God, 'Why me?', opting instead for 'Why not me?', acknowledging that there should be no discrimination in my favour. I had fought with God a lot over the past few months as I battled to reconcile what he wanted me to believe with my fears for how things would turn out, but I did think that I had begun to find a peace, and not just with God, but with myself and my life. And the church would be a good place for Bo to have, and Bo a good girl for the church to have.

The Swedish Church is by definition Lutheran, or extremely Protestant. I had had contact with the vicar of the Swedish church in London, Lennart Sjöström, on a number of occasions in the past and decided I wanted to go to him for the children's christening. I had never felt that much at home in the Church of England; in Sweden the church remains an integral part of the community – and even more so in London, where young and old meet on a daily basis. Lennart's welcome was as warm as I had hoped, and he thought nothing of me sitting there in front of him with my ex-husband planning the christening of my two children by two different fathers, one of whom was about to become godfather to the child of the other.

Bo was finally, at twenty weeks, beginning to sleep slightly better. I still had to go to bed with her at eight or nine in the evening in order to hope for even a half-decent night's sleep. I was still completely and utterly exhausted, but my hard work and wakefulness were now rewarded with smiles and gurgles. I was also able to behave and react more decently towards my wonderful son, whose patience had been tried on every level. I became increasingly aware of the growing closeness between him and his father, which I found encouraging, but of which I was also slightly envious. But I couldn't seem to split myself completely in half for my children: Bo needed me on a more physical level, while Cameron's demands were now more emotional ones. I'm sure it's a dilemma for every mother with a second or third child, and I tried hard not to beat myself up about it.

My communication with Bo's biological father had not improved. I was tired of constantly trying to coax and encourage the paternal side of him. It was hard work but I still believed that she needed a father figure and I wanted to do everything in my power to fight her corner for her. I wanted to be able to look her in the eye when she was older and tell her I did everything to encourage her father's involvement. Eventually, however, I threw in the towel. It was getting neither me nor Bo anywhere, and I decided to break the self-defeating cycle.

I told him that, regretfully, fed up with things blowing hot and cold, I didn't want to hear from him or anyone in his family for at least a month. It saved me – at last a sense of getting things under control kicked in. It gave me the mental space to finally start reasoning with myself, and to step forward again in my own right after crawling in the dark for so long. I could now see that the situation was about me and Bo and not about a reluctant, immature, selfish father who was never likely to come up with the goods.

I still struggle to comprehend – and will never accept – that a person who had been as keen on having a family together as I was, and who had given up his career to achieve that, was also capable of walking away from his daughter, his sick daughter, with such ease. Also he had made no financial contribution to his daughter's upbringing. I didn't want his money and maybe don't even need it, but I felt very strongly that there was a principle at stake here. He had wanted this child very much and now he was going to be able to walk away without a care in the world. I told him I had set up an account in Bo's name and I wanted him to contribute. He said he wouldn't until his name was on the birth certificate. I told him that would not now happen.

He broke our silence after a couple of weeks by sending me a fax to tell me he had accepted a job in Turkey, to start at the beginning of March. To me, choosing to live halfway to Asia was further evidence that becoming a father had made no impact on his life whatsoever. When I asked him outright what difference Bo had made to his life, thinking what a huge difference she had made to mine, he did not answer. Because he could not.

*

I continued to pick up the pieces of normality in a struggle to move forward. I did a photographic shoot to promote *Dog Eat Dog*, managing to conceal the blood-encrusted surgical stockings my wonderful surgeon had dressed me in whilst I was under anaesthetic and in no position to object. They were charming and certainly enhanced my femininity. The only downside was not being able to wash properly. Thankfully they were crotchless, which enabled me to spend two weeks splashing water at my nether regions even if I couldn't shower properly. It was an awkward and painful two-week recuperation and not something I would relish doing again, but the results were worth it. Needless to say, the press got hold of the story and asked for a pic. Strangely enough I declined.

At Easter I went to visit friends down in Kent and it was nice to almost feel normal again. Everyone is concerned when they talk to you. Concerned about the baby and then cautiously come the questions about the reluctant father, at which stage I would normally laugh it off with a joke about how much I love the Germans. It was my only way of getting through it. The situation was too tragic to take seriously with any but my closest confidants; it required humour and lots of it. The front you put up impresses people, which is not the reason you do it. You do it because there is no other way. I felt myself dishing out the same lines all the time, almost like issuing a statement. And this allowed me to not think about what I was saying, as that would have set me back too much. Thinking was something I had been doing too much of; it had become tiring, obsessive and relentless. Being alone with your head is not always healthy.

I was deeply flattered to be asked to go on *Parkinson*, as it is simply the mother of all talk shows. Besides, I quite admire Parky himself. He is an excellent journalist and I like his basic, direct approach. However, I was extremely nervous. I decided to wear a cheap black dress I had bought at Gap, which was simple and unfussy. My legs had only been out of the stockings for a week or so and I was only just getting used to seeing them again. I couldn't have been more surprised when Parky's opening question was about my recent surgery. He caught me off guard and after that I kept talking, but in constant anticipation of the next question. I talked a little about having started to write my book too, and as a result received enquiries from several publishers. It felt as though I handled the interview reasonably well, and I was overwhelmed by the comments I received from friends and unknowns afterwards.

I think my image had overshadowed my 'self'; it was time people began to see a different side to me. Their impression was of a blonde, exhibitionist, beer-swilling ladette with a penchant for racy, dangerous men; a publicity-seeking, ambitious, late-nighter who bed-hopped her way from wrong 'un to wrong 'un. Now I was coming across as reflective, intelligent, articulate, thoughtful and contemplative. I'd never been the former, but I certainly believe that the previous six months or so had brought about in me a maturity and seriousness that made me closer to the latter. I had been knocked down so hard by the experiences of the past year and a half that it had taken me a long time to get back to my feet. And in that time, I had been forced to look at myself and the things around me, and generally sort the wheat from the chaff. It had been a bitter lesson, but I believe I became a better person for it.

With a general election looming, I had an idea for a TV project that I felt better used my talents than some of the 'fronting' I'd been known for. I arranged a meeting with Alastair Campbell, Tony's right-hand man, to request a pre-ballot interview with the Prime Minister. I had done one with John Major before his last election. This time I also wanted to accompany them on the campaign trail. I had made enquiries with the two other major parties and they had agreed. All we needed was the approval of the BBC. But in the end the Beeb decided to opt for soulless, plain, uninspired, un-thought-provoking coverage. Still, it was excellent to meet the hugely handsome Mr Campbell. I'll get Tony another time.

I also planned to take Bo to see Markus's mother in Germany, something she deeply desired. With her son in Turkey, I knew the coast was clear. Unfortunately, two days before I was due to leave, Bo became very ill with a stomach virus. She developed a temperature and diarrhoea. Distressed, I took her into hospital and they decided to keep her in while they ran tests. Laboratory testing is frustratingly slow and we would have to wait forty-eight hours for any results. The doctors were, in the meantime, working on the theory that it was a virus known as Rota, which affects the stomach. But just to make sure they wanted a urine sample as well, to make sure she didn't have a urinary infection. You try getting a urine sample from a nappy-wearing reluctant baby girl. It is nigh on impossible. Oh, how I tried! Sadly for Markus's mother, we had to abandon the German trip. All I could think about was getting back home. Being in hospital once again felt like a massive step back. We were in exactly the same cubicle as when Bo had had bronchiolitis. Was this going to be the pattern for the rest of my life? But something deep inside told me to remain positive and grateful that my little darling was not afflicted by something graver. And this time I felt less stricken by heartache and abandonment. I *was* becoming a different person.

I had had the pleasure of my darling daughter for an additional few months and she was clearly becoming one of life's delightful creatures. I knew her better, feared her less and was allowing more positivity into our lives. Even in hospital, little things which some-how have no life-changing meaning came to have enormous value – a cup of tea; the kind, open face of a professional on duty; a silly joke; a solo visit to the toilet; even a lukewarm shower. I surprised myself at how optimistic I began to feel after a day or so there; the time passing meant we were closer to going home again.

As soon as Bo was safely on the road to recovery – and leaving behind the foulest-smelling nappies I had ever experienced – I threw myself back into making the arrangements for her and Cameron's christening. I wanted it to be a massive celebration, and already had half of Sweden coming over for the merriment. I decided to invite *OK!* magazine to cover it because I felt it was important for people to see how well Bo was developing and how much hope she carried. But I wouldn't have cared if the magazine hadn't been there: I didn't get the kids christened for them, I was doing it for the kids and me.

The day of the christening, Sunday 20 May, was gloriously sunny and warm and I was feeling excitement – an emotion that had long lain dormant in my heart. With life and death staring me in the face for so long, it had seemed like a guilty extravagance and rather superfluous.

Cameron had Melanie, John's brother Dave and his wife Sharon as godparents; Bo had John, Melanie and my sister Linda for hers. It was a beautiful service with lessons read, candles lit, water poured and hymns sung by all. Bo screamed furiously as Lennart doused her head. I think it is meant to be a good sign – something about crying the devil out. Cameron was more dignified and smiled politely through the service, before narrowly avoiding burning the church down with his candle. After the service we went to the London restaurant Monte's for a fantastic lunch and fun for the kids.

The service was a deeply moving and emotional experience for me – it galvanized something deep inside. Perhaps it was God and me; God and my children; me with life; me with defiance; my desire for life after all. Perhaps. I'm not sure which, but maybe a perfect blend of all of the above. I also felt so much love in my heart on that day: for my children, my amazing ex-husband and my family – of which all my friends are members. After having felt troubled and awkward, wrong and wronged for so long, I finally felt good. I felt right, not in action but in spirit – I suspect I was beginning to feel at one with myself. Finally.

There wasn't a German in sight on the day of the children's christening. I had done the right thing, and invited the father of my daughter to her baptism. His reply had been, 'I'm sure my mother will come.' I hadn't expected him to turn up. For a second. Unfortunately, his track record had forced his mother away, too. Despite showing great willing, she ultimately felt too embarrassed to come, and she was also scared of the English press. Understandable. And it had to be her choice.

The greatest thing I can feel in my heart is love for others. It does not come naturally for me to accept the love others have for me. I have often rejected it on the basis of my independence, my fear of dependence and my tendency to reason that someone loving me must be faulty. I love to feel love, give it and show it. Friendship warms me greatly and often overwhelms me. I am open and trusting. I instinctively want to give, offer and share of myself. I do not give to absolutely everyone, but to people I think 'get me'. And when it comes to friendships I am normally instinctively right. In love, however, this has not proved to be the case.

The friendships I have made over the years have been solid, reliable and caring. Friends had rallied around me over the past impossible year or so and I felt indebted for their generosity, kindness and warmth. So the day of the christening was a celebration of that, too. I felt so proud of my friends, and finally of myself for having got this far, whilst knowing I still had a long road to travel. I had been inspired by thoughts of wisdom; by reasoning; by the non-judgemental attitude of others; by the sheer fortitude of emotions expressed by some; and by good common sense. I had been living in a world of emotional darkness and still found it hard to shed any light on my predicament. I was too close to myself and my situation to take a step back and look on with objective eyes. And it was a relief, in some ways, after so many years of self-reliance, finally to have the ability to depend on those that could take it. I am so grateful to those few, close friends who allowed me to tap into their honesty, knowledge and foresight. None of us had hindsight. None of us had lived the trauma of the past year, and so in some genuine, responsible way we managed to fumble our way forward together from week to week. Although for myself, alone, it was more from hour to hour.

FIGHTING SPIRIT

At six months, Bo was still sleeping in bed with me, as she had done since I had first brought her home from hospital. I think our need for each other was mutual, but I was also plagued with thoughts of cot death and her serious condition. I wanted to have her close to me and as she was still having two or three bottles a night, I figured there was an element of practicality behind my thinking, too. This meant that for six months, not counting the months before she was born, I had been surviving on about six hours of broken sleep a night. Some nights Cameron crept in with us, too – my only close physical time with him, which I felt was extremely important.

I was informed that my recent acquaintances, the Bride family, were expecting their little champion Margaux home finally, some weeks after her transplant, and I was invited to visit her at home on her first day. It was an honour. She was still on medication that she would have to take for the rest of her life, so that she wouldn't reject her new heart. But she looked fantastic and it was heart-warming to see her excitement at her new surroundings. Her mother, Claude, dealt with her homecoming with a mixture of efficiency and affection. I admired both her parents tremendously and felt so proud to have been allowed to be a part of their lives, if only briefly. I felt, more strongly than ever, the importance of organ donations, even if it meant asking myself if I could perform such a selfless, inspired act should anything happen to one of my loved ones.

As a direct result of Bo's condition and my profile I also came into contact with a truly remarkable man, Professor Sir Magdi

Yacoub. This surgeon extraordinaire has been performing cardiac operations for more years than he would choose to remember, and has also set up his own charity, Chain of Hope, which takes teams of doctors and nurses from this country, as volunteers, to perform operations and care for children in countries that do not have the expertise. Sir Magdi asked me if I would be willing to consider a position of patronage with the charity, which was something I didn't have to think twice about. The man and his work are both inspirational; he is kind, thoughtful, gentle and much revered. And if my ridiculously superficial job as a TV presenter meant I could help raise funds and the profile of the charity, then I was more than happy to oblige.

I have always been careful with charity work; I get an average of ten to twenty requests a week for various worthy causes, and am wary of spreading myself too thin. So I have always opted to help smaller outfits that lack the profile of the larger charities. I have always tried to find a personal affinity with the causes, and if that doesn't exist then I decline. Every cause is worthy, of course, but some are worthier than others, in my opinion. Here there was not just an affinity, but a deep understanding, a medical connection, and above all else a will on my part that I had never felt before. Chain of Hope spends as much time as it can on its missions in order to mend as many broken hearts as possible, and I hope one day to go on one, when Bo is a little older and I feel more comfortable about leaving her behind.

*

By June, Bo was sitting up on her own and able to say 'bababa'. Most babies' first word is 'dada', but I thought it unlikely she would ever say that, the way things were going. There had been no input from the paternal end of things since February.

My part-time nanny went away on holiday for a couple of weeks and decided when she returned that she didn't want to work for me any more. I found myself completely nanny-less, and it was incredibly hard to scrape together suitable childcare and babysitting for when I was working, but we managed it somehow. In the meantime, Bo and I did everything together, 24/7.

Her condition was good, but there would come a time when she would need to be admitted to hospital once again for cardiac catheterization. This meant sending a fine tube up from her groin to assess how her heart was coping with the pulmonary banding and when she would require her next surgery. She was due to be admitted on 11 July for two nights. I was nervous about the procedure – as with everything, there is a risk – but knew that it was essential in order to move forward with her treatment.

I thought I should try to get away for a while, as Cameron was on holiday with John in Italy, so I decided to travel with Bo and my sister Linda to the south of France for a week's break. I'm not sure how much of a break it was with an eight-month-old baby, sterilizing kit, bottles, baby food and a suitcase-full of nappies, but my sister and I laughed and laughed until we cried. The holiday was something I never thought I would achieve. The past eight months had been so utterly tense, draining and emotionally taxing, but I was determined that we should have some normality in our lives, despite the wait for surgery.

When I took Bo in for her catheterization I didn't feel as depressed at the sight of the hospital as I had thought I would. To be honest, I think it felt better to be there alone, rather than having a heavy German weight around my neck. The procedure went well, despite me weeping through my meeting with the anaesthetist, the whole process bringing back so many memories. Bo was allowed home two days later. I would be informed of their findings in a week or so, and a date would eventually be set for her next surgery.

I found it agonizing trying to anticipate when it might be. I knew I would need time to build up for it; prepare myself for it, mentally and emotionally; and plan around it. And I was also well aware that the conditions for it needed to be just right. A fortnight later I heard that it was to be on 10 September. My heart raced, my eyes filled and my stomach churned. Would this be the date I would lose my daughter? I spent the next couple of weeks panicking, worrying, welling up and going a little loco. I couldn't get the date out of my head and every time I looked at Bo I couldn't bear the thought of her being cut open again. Eventually, however, I managed to reason that I needed to enjoy the time with her now, and put off worrying until closer to the time.

After a silence of a month or so from her father, he sent me a fax asking if he could see her at the end of August. I agreed, but told him he would not be welcome to stay at my house. Which shocked him. He asked me to recommend him some hotels. I told him of some local B&Bs and left it at that.

In the meantime, work was getting busy. There were plans for another series of *Dog Eat Dog* and I was just completing a pilot for ITV, on top of which *Shooting Stars* was coming back. We were required for filming on location over a number of days, before starting the series proper in the studio on 13 September. When I got the dates for *Dog Eat Dog* they were around the same time, but there was a week's window directly around Bo's op. Nothing mattered to me more than my daughter, so a contingency plan had to be put into place for both shows, should I not make it. Everyone was terribly understanding, and I am grateful for that.

On the evening of Thursday 23 August, the father of my daughter dropped in at our house. He'd just arrived at Heathrow. He had not seen his daughter for six months, almost exactly to the day. I wasn't sure how I would feel when I saw him again, and more to the point what she would feel when she saw him. He came through the door, dressed smartly, like the businessman he isn't, wearing sunglasses. We shook hands. I didn't even want to do that. I found I couldn't bear to touch him.

He greeted Bo with warmth and enthusiasm. I showed her off like the proud, loving, affectionate mother I am, and hoped he would be astonished, impressed and in awe. Eventually he took his sunglasses off. I offered him a glass of wine, like the decent, polite, mature ex-lover I am. He declined and proceeded to play with Bo on the floor, as if he was visiting a favourite niece. He even brought her a cuddly dolphin, something I know he always gives his favourite niece. To Bo I called the stranger 'man' or 'Markus'. I could not bring myself to call him 'daddy'; he simply didn't deserve the title.

We spoke cautiously and with civility in quiet tones, but I continued to feel uneasy. I had allowed this stranger back into my heart once too often, only for him to crush it with callous brutality. This stranger had slunk away from the wonderful little creature in front of me, who had battled so hard to stay alive. I couldn't help but feel he had qualities that were inhuman and alien. I felt quite naturally, without provocation, that he didn't belong here. With us. With her. He didn't *know* her. How could he? You can't walk into a baby's life at six-monthly intervals and expect to pick up the pieces. In any event, he made no impact with Bo. But then, why should he? Yet I also realized there and then the complexities of one day having to introduce him to her as her biological father. Thank God, she wasn't speaking yet. But they played well together. He looked at her a lot and responded to her pointing and waving; he kissed her a lot and smelt her skin. And I felt uncomfortable with it – as if I was allowing a complete stranger to be intimate with my daughter. I actually had to look away.

I asked about his trip and where he was staying. Rather surprisingly for a man who hasn't any money, he had taken up residence in one of the finest local hotels, on the river. He had brought me a bag of nuts from Turkey, which I thanked him for and placed out of sight. It was not until after he had left that I realized he had said not one word about his daughter during the time he had spent playing with her. I was stunned: she was nearly nine and a half months old, compared to three months when he had last seen her. Back then she was a baby with dark hair and capable of relatively little. By now, she had blossomed into a blonde, crawling toddler with long eyelashes and a winning smile. She was stunning. And she had become a little person who responded, initiated and communicated, in her own little way. She had changed so dramatically since he had seen her last that she was virtually a different child. And yet, he had said nothing. No 'isn't she gorgeous?' or 'isn't she beautiful?' or 'look how clever she is!' Not a word.

The following day we met in the park for a walk. He gently asked about my life. I gave short, reluctant, simplified answers. He also asked to take the pram. I wanted to say 'no', but managed to reason with myself before the word came out. I just couldn't bear him pushing her and pretending to be the proud father he so definitely wasn't. This was only the third time he had seen her in her life. He didn't deserve any part of her. But I relented and allowed him to push, as he puffed nonchalantly on his cigarette.

It was a warm day, and I had planned to take Bo over to my mother's for a swim in her pool. I invited him along, suggesting he would enjoy seeing her in the water, but he didn't want to come. He was scared, I could tell – of seeing my family again. I knew he had no reason, because no matter what my mother thinks of him, she would avoid a bad atmosphere and maintain civility. I told him it would be his loss, and that he would need to face up to real life if he wanted to be with his daughter. As I packed the car, he reluctantly climbed on board.

At my mother's, Bo and I got into the pool. He took some photos and attempted some enthusiasm. My mother made coffee and polite conversation. Later he pulled me to one side and asked if I would consider coming out to Turkey to visit him on holiday, so as to allow him to see Bo more often. He'd even put us up. In responding I made every attempt not to be sarcastic, tempting as it was, explaining that I would not be travelling anywhere with my daughter for his sake. I would not spend my money, take up my time or risk taking her to a country with health considerations at this early stage. In fact, I didn't care if he lived in France. I wasn't about to make life easy for him when he had made my life, my motherhood, my sanity, my health and my head so impossible to reconcile. I told him I had no desire to see him in his natural environment, it was all that I could do to spend these hours with him for the sake of Bo without trying to punch his lights out. He thought he was being generous, kind and helpful. I thought he was being an immature arsehole. And that really set the tone for the rest of his stay.

When I would try to coax out of him some reaction towards her, by saying, 'Isn't she cute?' he would simply look away. Well, either he didn't think she was, or he thought she was but wasn't going to let me in on it. Eventually my frustration brimmed over. It was actually insulting – to both her and me. I asked him if he realized that in the forty-eight hours since he had arrived he had not mentioned or given one compliment about his daughter. He retorted, 'I will never tell you what I think of her. I can never tell you anything, you just shoot down whatever I say!' Well, with that I did decide to shoot him down – well, I didn't decide, it just happened. I explained, in no uncertain terms, that this 'situation' we were in was no longer about him and me, it was about what was right for Bo. Which was why I had made an effort with him when he arrived, despite my deep-seated, personal reluctance. All the time he had been there I had had to put Bo in the forefront of my mind, not my repulsion of this stranger who walked into our home and played at being daddy for a few hours. This stranger who thought it acceptable to pick up where he thought he had left off. This bloody stranger who had rid himself of any responsibilities, paternal, emotional or even psychological. Because, as I have said before, whatever was going on in his head or heart, in terms of turmoil over the whole affair, he had never given away. If he was suffering from this terrible, terrible situation he certainly wasn't letting it show.

Within no time at all our conversation had disintegrated, descending into a war of words. When he told me he had never had any problem with any other woman, and that it was all my fault, I could take no more – and I knew I didn't have to. I picked Bo up from the floor, for comfort and defence, and physically drove him out of the house.

*

So, off he went once more, out of our lives. And once more it was a huge relief when he had gone. But I remained impossibly tense, thinking about Bo's next op, only a couple of weeks away. I had long since started preparing for our stay in hospital, packing for a minimum two-week stay for us both. I labelled everything with care, packed a couple of favourite toys, a Swedish song book, the singing lamb her German grandma sent when she was born and a stone for good luck sent to me by a member of the public.

I became obsessive about Bo's health as the date grew closer. It was imperative she was in perfect health if the operation was going to go ahead as planned. With Cameron exposing himself to a hundred or so kids every day, it would be a miracle if he didn't bring something home. But Bo was quite fit enough to go up to Guy's for a day of pre-op tests on Friday 7 September, and we were given the go-ahead to come back on the Sunday for admission. But we were asked to phone in the morning to make sure they still had a bed for her – it seemed as if everything had a 'but' attached.

John and I had decided he would drive us up to the hospital and that Cameron would go to friends. Neither of us thought we could cope with the distraction of our lovely boy at a time like this, good, bad or indifferent. As we dropped him off and I kissed him goodbye, I kept wondering if I would come back a changed person; whether, if something happened to Bo during our stay, I would ever be able to be a normal mother to him again. I kissed him goodbye with all the dread and anticipation of a mother who didn't truly know when she would return. It was painful. Thankfully, he was none the wiser.

I was tense in the car up to the hospital but Bo kept me occupied. I made the mistake of putting on a tape of Swedish nursery rhymes an old friend had kindly sent me, which made me emotional and brought on tears. Thankfully, Bo was none the wiser either.

Once we were installed in our 'cubicle', one of the six or so rooms furnished with a cot for patient and bed for fraught parent, a number of staff came in to introduce themselves. Most of them I was familiar with and was able to keep up the banter. Eventually in came a counsellor-type nurse, who is there with information, pictures of children who had emerged from previous ops and a long chat about what will actually happen on operation day, logistically. I wasn't interested in the photos – I had seen them before, and I had also seen Bo cut up and hooked up to drains, machines and wires. I thought it might be good to prepare John, however. As she flicked through her photo album, I heard a loud 'thud' as John fainted. Seeing children in such a condition is distressing enough for anyone, without thinking it is going to be your loved one. And Bo was, by now, his loved one.

I spent the night with Bo in the bed with me, and not in the cot allocated for her. She was to be allowed no milk after six a.m., and after that only a few millilitres of water two hours before she was due in theatre. She ate a small breakfast and consumed her last drops of white elixir just after six. She had always been a contented, happy, loving baby and that day was no exception. She was second on the operating list and we were hoping to go down at eleven. The wait was to prove emotionally and physically exhausting. At ten months old Bo could crawl and stand, but was not quite walking. However, so inquisitive was her character that she would remain sitting in the cot playing with toys for only a few minutes at a time before she wanted to get out and explore. I couldn't put her down on the floor, for obvious hygiene reasons, so I had to walk her up and down the ward, time and time again.

By twelve o'clock I decided to dress her in her little theatre gown. Melanie and John were present and we took it in turn to entertain my little angel, who had no idea what was about to happen to her. We all knew and we tried to joke and laugh away the anticipation, anguish and fear. By a quarter to one, emotions were running high with me and Bo was becoming hungrier by the second. It was hard to keep her occupied but we had no other option. I knew that once she went down to theatre, I would somehow have to let go. Her life would no longer be in my hands.

Time kept ticking by. And ticking. And ticking. And still no word. Then suddenly, without warning, along came a hospital porter who called out Bo's name. I rushed back into the room where John and Melanie were waiting. I became flustered and emotional and again chose to carry Bo down in my arms, rather than put her in the porter's bed. Melanie and John followed. I talked incessantly all the way down in the lift, so as to stem the tears, but it was impossible.

We were accompanied by a caring nurse, and I tried in vain to avoid eye contact with anyone for fear of breaking down.

Only two of us were allowed into theatre with Bo, so John stayed in the doorway. The theatre was cold and foreboding and so was my mood. Eventually the anaesthetist walked in and I was reassured to see he had an older, comforting face. Everything counted. I wanted everything to feel right. He asked me to place Bo on the operating table as we had agreed to put her intravenous line into her veins down here, once she was 'under the gas'. Trying to find veins in little ones is as impossible as looking for needles in a haystack, and incredibly distressing for both parent and patient.

Bo was unhappy about being laid down and as she started crying the doctor gently placed a mask over her face to sedate her, I tried to hush her with calming tones. But she was having none of it. She was having none of the gas either, it seemed. For minutes we tried to hold her down, the nurse, the doctor and I, but she did not relent. It was good that she cried, I was told, as it meant she would take in more of the gas. But if she did, it was having no effect. The anaesthetist couldn't believe what a little fighter she was – at one stage he even had to check if there was any gas coming out of the mask! It was as though Bo was proving to us she wasn't going to do anything she didn't want to. Thankfully, eventually I could feel her little limbs weaken in their fight and her eyes began to close, until gradually she became completely still. The only movement was her breathing. I was asked to kiss her and leave.

The wait was not as painful as I had anticipated. Once again I found myself across the road from the hospital with a plate of food in front of me and a glass of wine in my hand. I now had to put out of my mind, as much as possible, what was happening to my baby and concentrate on my reunion with her. I put in a call to Bo's biological father, who was lounging around in Turkey, but his assurances that everything would be just fine irritated and aggravated me – his voice alone did that now. I swore at him and slammed the phone down. I couldn't bear that he should feel so fucking complacent when I was living the nightmare he had chosen to walk away from.

We sat on for a couple of hours, at least, and waited further back at the hospital. When I heard a voice saying Bo was out of theatre and she would be ready for me in forty-five minutes I breathed relief through every pore of my body. As we walked into the now-familiar intensive care room, my initial instinct was that she looked remarkably well. My little miracle lay there, still, beautiful and all grown up. I went over to her and kissed and caressed her as much as I could in between the wires, leads and drips. I was overwhelmed by her presence and I talked to her as I always had done, certain she could hear me, despite her deep, drug-induced sleep. I even felt at peace with a world which had dealt my lovely daughter such a cruel blow.

I stayed with Bo until midnight that night, leaving with a promise I would be back in a matter of hours. And with that I ran across the road to the hostel room I was sharing with my bags. Monday was over.

The following morning, Tuesday 11 September, I was over at the hospital, as usual, by just after six. I was delighted with her progress. They had taken her off the morphine and she was no longer ventilated. I sat and studied her for hours, playing with her toes, her fingers and her little nose. As the day progressed she became more and more independent of hospital intervention: tubes and lines came out, and medication was reduced. I kept on worshipping at the temple of a truly remarkable creature. She was blessed with a recovery, and I was blessed with her. I thanked God for helping us both through this, especially as I understood he was a busy man. But not as busy as he was about to be . . .

Later that day, sometime in the afternoon, the staff nurse walked onto the ward and announced that a plane had just crashed into one of the World Trade Center's twin towers in New York. Everyone gasped in disbelief and horror. The tragedy of such an accident almost eclipsed what had been going on in my own life over the past twenty-four hours and I began to almost feel guilty that Bo had progressed so well, when I knew full well that a vast number of people would be suffering the loss of their loved ones.

Within half an hour the staff nurse returned to announce that a second plane had gone into the other tower, at which point we all knew this was no accident. I immediately became terrified of what was going on beyond the doors and corridors of the hospital and the first thought that crossed my mind was that we might lose electricity in the hospital if there was another attack. What then would happen to all those so dependent on it here?

The hospital did not lose electricity, and with the blip of a minor febrile hiccup, which could have suggested an infection, Bo made a full recovery over the next few days. In fact, she progressed so well that five days after her open-heart surgery she was discharged. Armed only with the remnants of a bottle of antibiotics, aspirin, and two types of diuretics we headed home; John, Cameron – who had come to visit his brave sister – Bo and I, like a bunch of kids who had been allowed home early from school.

Within three hours of being home from the hospital, I kissed my children goodbye, climbed into a car and headed for Pinewood Studios to complete the second series of *Dog Eat Dog*. Life was good.

SVEN, SVEN, SVEN-GÖRAN ERIKSSON

Bo progressed well through the autumn, and I threw a big party for her birthday. Our existence was beginning to take on a more settled pace and feel, which was long, long overdue. My social life was still fairly non-existent, but by December there was one do I knew I had to attend. Newspaper and magazine king Richard Desmond was celebrating his fiftieth, and was throwing a lavish party in London. Having made several contributions to his publications, and liking the man and his wife Janet a great deal, I knew I should be there to pay my respects. However, I was still not in great party mood, suffering more than a little from sleep deprivation *à cause de mon petit ange* – not the greatest incentive for a night on the tiles. But attend I did.

Melanie, by now single, was my date for the night and we were in good spirits by the time we arrived. Everyone was there, from Alastair Campbell to the most famous faces from TV, theatre and sport. Shortly after we arrived, in walked the one and only England Manager, Sven-Göran Eriksson, with his partner Nancy on his arm. As a major football fan I was thrilled to be at the same function as my fellow Swede, and as he walked past the aforementioned Mr Campbell introduced us. I shook his hand and told him it was a pleasure to meet him, and he congratulated me in Swedish on my success in this country. I wanted to congratulate him back, but thought it was funnier that, just then, I was standing between the two most powerful men in the country, and saw fit to say so. I also shook the hand of Miss Dell'Olio, who reciprocated with a false, hard smile.

I thought nothing more of it, other than jumping up and down with excitement at finally meeting a man I had read so much about and about whom I had even written an article for a national newspaper, to mark his arrival in this country. I would get his autograph for John later. That was for sure.

The party was in full swing when I plucked up the courage to approach him with a pen and scrap of paper. I apologized for disturbing his evening, but explained my ex-husband had kindly agreed to babysit for me that night and I wanted to thank him with this special gift. Mr Eriksson's partner looked daggers at me, but lightened up temporarily when she heard the half-word 'husband'. Perhaps she hoped I was still married. As Sven signed my dog-eared napkin, he once again complimented me on my success and asked, in Swedish, if he could obtain my number so that we might meet up. Of course you can, I replied. I walked away thinking how pleasant he was and that it was nice that he wanted to touch base with a fellow Swede. That is genuinely how it felt. I thought that maybe he was looking forward to a bit of Swedish conversation. Nothing more. He was engaged to be married, as far as I was aware.

Immediately after dinner the Eriksson/Dell'Olio contingent departed. I stayed on and had a bit of a boogie, then headed home for a short night's sleep.

The following Monday Melanie mentioned she had had a call from Mr Eriksson's agent, requesting my phone number. I was impressed by the haste of the request, and delighted to oblige. What with being a diehard football fan and all that.

A few days later my mobile rang with a number I didn't recognize. I anticipated it might be him, and for once I was right. We talked in Swedish, I rather nervously, like any fan would. He complimented me on several occasions on my beauty and further on my success. I didn't quite know how to respond to either observation. I felt shy and deeply embarrassed. At the end of a conversation that spanned Sweden, England, football and Italy, he asked if he could call me again. I said he could, but not content with that, he asked if I was sure. I was sure. I thought he was very pleasant and it could never be a bad idea having the England coach as one of your acquaintances. I jokingly felt I was finally one up on Angus Deayton, whose contacts had so far reached only to Manchester United. It was all very flattering and exciting – not to say unexpected – but felt no more than that. Call me naive, but that's how I took it.

A few days later he called again, and we continued our previous conversation. It was nearing Christmas, and I talked about my relations coming over to spend the festive season with me. He didn't sound too excited about his forthcoming Christmas, which I understood he was spending with his partner. I whimsically suggested he should come over for some Swedish food on the twenty-fourth, presuming he would understand that invitation to extend to his partner too. He turned the invitation down in muted tones, with a sigh of 'if only'. At that stage it became clear to me that this was not a happy man. I, on the other hand, was incredibly happy. Bo was home, my family was coming over and Christmas was upon us.

Further conversations every day for the next few days, and suggestions about meeting up, signalled to me the possible motive for his attention. When he asked whether I was able to go about my personal business without the press at my heels, I told him that for the most part I could, these days. He said we should think about where and when we could meet up and we would speak later. It all sounds rather cloak and dagger, but I still maintained that until I had irrefutable evidence to the contrary, this was a man in a foreign country who simply wanted to hook up with a fellow ex-pat. The fact that I was of the opposite sex and twenty years younger didn't immediately convey to me that there were ulterior intentions.

I had an idea. I was due to take my relations into London to see *Mamma Mia!* on one of the days between Christmas and New Year. I would suggest we meet for lunch at a discreet Italian restaurant in Knightsbridge, which I have patronized since I was nineteen. I texted my suggestion to his phone and he agreed it would be lovely.

I was nervous in anticipation of our rendezvous. I had my

relations telling me he was interested, but I steadfastly refused to believe it. Besides, I certainly had no agenda other than lunch with a charming man. And possibly some England tickets, at some stage.

We met at Signor Sassi. I was late – a woman's prerogative. But he was not lonely. He was being serenaded and attended to by the entire Italian, Portuguese and Spanish staff of the restaurant. Only my arrival forced them to disperse and assume their normal duties.

We sipped champagne and talked calmly about life, football and a little more about life. He was calm, gentle and had the most fantastic sparkle in his eye. His face was kind and he was softly spoken. Our food remained fairly untouched, as it does when the company is more captivating. Just as I started to ask him if he was getting married soon, my relations arrived at the restaurant to take me away for the matinee. There was just enough time for him to roll his eyes, shake his head and protest, 'No, no, no, no, no – quite the opposite.' And on that note, sadly, it was time for me to shoot off.

I texted him a thank you and said it would be my treat should there be a second time. He phoned immediately to say that there absolutely would.

*

I was charmed by my new acquaintance, because the man was just that. Having emerged from a series of erratic, volatile and highly emotional relationships, what I had encountered within myself on 28 December 2001 was an inner calm in the presence of someone respectful and respectable. I had absorbed the gentleness with which this man carried himself and the kindness he extended to others. He also had a sense of humour, and a philosophical approach that I had never encountered in any of the men in my life. He was measured, but had a passion inside him that was hidden under his considered exterior. He also had lovely eyes. And I felt comfortable about myself in his company.

I saw in the New Year with friends, then, at the request of Svennis – his Swedish nickname – agreed to see him at my house on 2 January. He said he would pop by for a cup of tea on his way to a football game up north. When he arrived he presented a gift for the children and a bottle of Veuve Clicquot for mum. I put the kettle on as he befriended Cameron and Bo. Again he was calm, kind and gentle.

After I had shown him around the house, we sat down for a cup of tea. I had spent the morning working on the book – which had now become a reality – and was as scruffy as they come. Svennis was in a suit and tie, as usual. We talked loosely for a while and then out of the blue he announced he was going on holiday in a couple of days. When he told me the destination I told him it sounded lovely. He disagreed. He was going away to fight, he said. I didn't understand. And then he explained.

He told me without hesitation or interruption that he was in a relationship he was desperately trying to get out of. There was too much arguing for his liking and it was sapping him of his energy. When he had finished his speech, I not only understood why he was here, but I also wanted to know if his partner knew that was how he felt. He said he had made his feelings clear to her. I imagined myself in her shoes for a moment and thought how I would have left before he had the chance to finish his sentence of rejection. I've been in negative relationships, but if someone waved me goodbye, I'd be off. It was just that mine kept coming back.

I was shocked by what he was saying, because I couldn't imagine that kind of situation for myself, but it was not for me to judge. And I was very surprised at his openness, directness and honesty. This was only the third time we had met. When it was time for him to leave, he brushed his hand across my cheek affectionately and asked if he could call me while he was away. I nodded. Again, he asked if I was sure; he said I didn't have to say yes. I know, I said.

He called me every day from the sunshine of the Indian Ocean, while I was being entertained by the shelves in Waitrose and the torrential rain of a January England. He asked me to text him messages, which I did only once. Bizarrely, I found that I missed him. But instead of feeding that emotion, I chose to simply acknowledge it and put it away to the back of my mind.

For the last three days of his holiday, Svennis contracted amnesia and forgot to call. I didn't mind. But when someone tells you they will phone tomorrow and tomorrow becomes the day after and then the day after that, you worry. Needless to say, he was fine. When he did call, I told him frankly that he didn't have to call me every day, but if he says he will, he should. He was amused by my directness, but took my comment on board. He was keen to meet up and suggested the following Friday, for lunch, as he was on his way to a football game up north. (Just the merest whiff of a pattern emerging here.)

I made lunch, but felt slightly nervous about the impending meeting. He had been away. To myself, I had acknowledged some form of emotion for him and this would be the first time we would meet up since then. On top of which, my children were out. Once again, he turned up with a bottle of champagne and looking tanned. I welcomed him with a kiss on the cheek and a warm hug. It was good to see him. He looked at me and continued to comment that I was so beautiful, which unnerved me hugely. I brushed his compliments aside and continued with my preparations for lunch. And as I turned to open the fridge in search of help and security, I felt his hand on my neck as he turned me around and kissed me.

To say that I was taken aback would be an understatement. I was shocked and pleasantly surprised and excited by his boldness. I reciprocated without needing to think about it. We sat down for lunch and once again played with the food on our plates. Eventually we gave up and resumed our affection for each other. Impulsively he asked me to come away with him for twenty-four hours – he had a meeting in Portugal and wanted me to come with him for the night. He had a villa there. He was a dark horse, truly! I hesitated as I processed the information. My initial reaction was to decline, so I said nothing. He told me to think about it. And seeing the look of doubt on my face he further suggested that maybe I would wish to wait until the 'third party' was out of the picture to be part of this 'something' which was happening. That sounded more appealing to me, but I also felt that I didn't really know yet what this 'something' was. It felt a little wrong to turn down what I didn't know. When he left he said he would call. And this time he did.

I thought about his suggestion, and so many things went through my mind. A little adventure was something I hadn't had for some years, I thought. Then I thought how dangerous it was both publicly and privately – how frightening it was to feel something for someone I had only just met, and someone I wouldn't have pictured myself with until that moment. I wondered how we would be able to get away with it without anyone knowing, but most of all I had to consider leaving the children for a night.

I agonized, but time was not on my side. His trip was only four days away. I shared my conundrum with a close friend, who suggested I go for it. Still doubtful, I waited for divine intervention to guide me in the right direction. Once again I was going to have to trust how I felt, and that was the most terrifying prospect of all. I felt in control of how I felt, which was a first. I wasn't allowing myself to run away with my feelings, and felt equally that I wouldn't mind a short adventure without having to contemplate a future.

The day before his trip I told him yes, I would come. I'd give it a go, as he had told me his relationship was as good as over. I had made my domestic arrangements and my travel arrangements too. I was to fly to Lisbon on the same flight as him and return without him the following morning, as he headed off for his meeting in Porto. We would pretend to meet on the flight, which could be feasible. This did not hinder my nerves. The acting would not come naturally to me – this was no play, this was real life. However, I did feel confident about the reason for the trip, if not about the public performance upon which I was about to engage.

We 'bumped into' each other in the airport lounge and sat there chatting like two good friends who hadn't seen each other for some time. We walked separately to the plane, but had conveniently been assigned seats together. Outwardly I felt this could look exactly like we wanted it to. Two fellow Swedes, coincidentally on the same flight to another country. But in reality I was still nervous, cautious and full of butterflies, concealed only by huge smiling exchanges and his hand grabbing mine whenever the hostesses were out of sight. It felt sweet, romantic and totally ridiculous.

When we arrived, we were met by an old acquaintance of Mr Eriksson (as he called him), who drove us to his villa, 'Joli', in the hills overlooking the sea. Named using the first two letters of his children's names, it was spacious, gracious and beautifully situated. His housekeepers, an old married couple, were eagerly awaiting his arrival. I was introduced and felt momentarily like a young floozy he had picked up in a nightclub the night before. If only they knew I was a mother of two and had long since given up on the prospect of romance. I kept joking to myself and with him about how crazy the situation was, and he laughed and smiled in response, kissing my hand and cheek affectionately. He was so relaxed he almost convinced me this was perfectly normal and natural. The only thing I felt was normal and natural was my affection for him.

We talked and rested that afternoon, and later on dinner was prepared for us before the couple disappeared to their quarters. Our conversation was comfortable, interesting and wide-ranging. We shared many similar opinions. I don't know if that was the ex-patriotism in us or just luck, but I felt hugely at ease in his presence. He was generous with his affection and extremely tactile – there was no sense of hesitation about him, just a calm gentle loving.

When I woke up the following morning he was holding me in his arms and was gazing at me. I wondered how long he had been lying like that, and thrilled at the comfort and ease of it all. When later that morning we parted ways he insisted that he wanted to pay for my flight. Being a woman of means, I steadfastly refused. He became very serious about it and handed me a blank cheque, telling me to fill in the blanks. My protestations were silenced by him placing the cheque in my handbag. I had no intention of filling in any blanks. And still have not.

I returned on the Thursday, he on the Friday, whereupon he told

me that his fifteen-year-old daughter was coming to visit him from
Florence. Miss Dell'Olio had been asked to go away, for as long as
possible, and had apparently, if reluctantly, agreed. Svennis phoned
me and asked whether I would like to have dinner with him and his
daughter on the Saturday night. With memories of time wasted in
the presence of my dad's girlfriends, I suggested he spend the
weekend alone with his daughter. He didn't agree, and said that he
would love to see me. He asked if I wanted to come to his house, or
if it would be easier for them to come out to me for dinner locally.
I felt reticent about meeting his daughter, when I was only just
starting to get to know her father. I juggled babysitting and downed
a glass of champagne before welcoming them into the house on our
way to my favourite local Indian restaurant, Malik's.

As it turned out, we had a great evening. His daughter was not
just utterly charming but maturer than her fifteen years. Svennis
and I resumed our acting roles at the table, but below it there were
feet fighting for affection and the occasional meeting of hands. I
didn't feel that the evening out was a risk – for me. It was for him.
As far as the world was concerned, he was spoken for – although in
my world that was turning out not to be the case. The risk for him
was being seen with another woman – famous at that. People talk
and someone always knows someone who knows someone at a
newspaper. On the other hand, this was not an intimate meal. There
were three at the table and I was grateful his daughter would deflect
any unnecessary attention we might attract. I guess most people
wouldn't raise an eyebrow anyway, as we were both Swedish and
were perhaps not the most likely coupling. I liked the idea of the
latter, because he truly was different from any of the previous men
to whom I have been attached.

They dropped me off at my house after the meal and Svennis
came up to the house for an affectionate farewell. It was not how he
had wanted the evening to end, he said, and I took that as a
compliment and kissed him goodbye.

The following day he phoned, and once again I was able to detect
disappointment in his voice. His partner had announced she was

returning: she hadn't stayed away as long as he had hoped. I remember feeling the disappointment in my stomach too, which surely was a sign that this man was making an impression on me. I had not inquired about his personal circumstances more than he had told me, both because I didn't want to get too involved, and because I didn't want to make a negative feature of Miss Dell'Olio in our conversations.

I hadn't lost my heart to this man – thankfully I found I had finally learnt to hold back – but I could feel myself starting to like him enormously. And with that feeling of disappointment weighing heavy in my belly and with a reluctance to be part of a triangle going around and around in my head, I knew I had to talk to him properly.

He was eager to see me soon after that weekend and suggested the Wednesday afternoon (as he was again on his way to a game). That suited me fine. I was working on my book at home and could do with the hour or so's distraction. As soon as he arrived, with champagne once again, I sat him down and told him I just wanted to get a few things straight in my mind. What exactly is going on at home? I asked him. He reiterated to me the present state of his relationship and that he was in the process of ending it, but it was rather complex. He wanted to do the right thing by Nancy, and wasn't sure how long the procedure of ending it would take, but he was positive and explained that in the meantime he would like to continue to see me. I was and probably sounded doubtful. But in some respects this relationship suited me. I enjoyed being with him. Despite being uncomfortable in the role of 'mistress', there was no serious commitment on either side and we would see each other once a week or so, as it suited us. So far it remained a private affair, and that is how we both wanted to keep it.

I didn't want to be seen to be in another relationship, let alone necessarily be in one. I was cautious. I owed it to myself, and of course those dependent on me, to tread carefully. I wasn't going to give my heart away easily this time, and therein lay my reluctance. I believed him; I saw him as deeply honest. He seemed straight, direct and genuine. He knew I could take the truth, so there was no reason for him to lie to me. Besides, I had never known such keenness. He phoned two or three times a day and wanted to see me as often as possible. When we did see each other, his affection and warmth were overwhelming. Pleasantly so. And I was happy for him to do the running. I never phoned him. Very occasionally I would send him a text, but that was it.

A few days later I was due up at Old Trafford with Angus to watch United play Sunderland and Mr Eriksson was also going. By genuine coincidence we were on the same flight up to Manchester and I pretended to Angus that I had met the England coach for lunch as a fellow Swede some weeks back, and introduced them. Angus suspected nothing – why should he have done? We both played our roles admirably, though mildly nervously on my part. I couldn't bear to make eye contact with Svennis and looked away at every opportunity. I could say my lines, but I found it hard to make my body behave as if I had never kissed this man, let alone touched him.

The days before I saw him again, he phoned several times a day. I now quite looked forward to our conversations. They were brief, but kind, gentle and flattering. I was invariably sitting at my laptop typing away and he would call to wish me a good morning, a pleasant afternoon or a good night's sleep or to tell me how diligent and hard-working I was. He'd tell me what he was up to in his day.

Our meetings were now becoming a habit and a few days later he graced my doorstep (he was on his way to a game up north) the day after his birthday. I had bought him a few personal gifts and a couple of humorous ones. We made love again and briefly fell asleep in each other's arms, before he reluctantly took himself off. The calmness and affection this man brought me was being reciprocated with a deep caring from my side. But I couldn't deny that deep down I was also uncomfortable about the situation.

The following day when he called I told him this. I was unnerved by the way I was starting to feel, which was intensified by the presence of the third party, regardless of the fact that their relationship was supposedly over. I believe he had answered me honestly when I asked him whether they still made love. He seemed utterly resolute about his situation. Nonetheless, I told him I wanted out. I did not feel brave enough to risk my emotions in this situation – despite feeling reassured his relationship was over.

He was disappointed, he said, and it was not what he wanted to hear. I was due to go to Paris for a girls' weekend with Melanie, and he asked me to think about it while I was away. I told him quite bluntly that it was he who needed to do the thinking, but we resolved to not speak over the weekend, in order that I might put things into perspective.

I had a wonderful break and discovered I didn't miss his phone calls, which I told myself was my defence mechanism kicking in. But already on the Saturday my mother phoned me to tell me he had been pictured with Miss Dell'Olio at the British Open tennis in Birmingham. I felt a little slighted by the news and confused, too. Why was he parading her around so publicly if their relationship was over? I knew they were still together, but I would have thought a low profile would have been the order of the day, considering the circumstances.

We spoke the day after I got back. He told me he had been missing me and I joked that the tennis must have kept him busy and we laughed a little. I told him that I had come to the conclusion that I would go on seeing him as long as I could feel in control of my feelings and as long as he would be honest with me. He assured me he would and we made arrangements to meet up upon his return from the forthcoming England game in Holland.

He always showed a great interest in my work, and would often ask when I would next be on telly or whether he could come along and watch me in action. I thought at first that he was joking, but I believe he was serious. At which point I asked him to attend a charity evening for the Chain of Hope, with or without Miss Dell'Olio. His wallet would be as welcome as he would be! He was unable to attend. My escort for the evening was Mick Hucknall, whom I'd worked with. Sven, Mick and I were equally bemused next day when the press labelled Mick and I an item. I should be so lucky. Imagine if they'd known the *real* truth.

When I hosted the 'Miss Sweden' competition for Swedish TV he even asked his mother to tape the show. It was flattering; he was always hugely complimentary and said he was impressed. This in itself was a refreshing change from many of the men I have been with, who have either been envious of my work or envious of the distractions in my life. This man actually applauded me for them. In that respect I felt he was good for me. He also noticed little things about me, whether it was my picture and an interview in the paper, or a mark on my hand which might have faded every time we met. It gave me the impression I occupied his thoughts more often than not, and in that way I didn't feel I was taking second place to someone else. With the high level of honesty between us, I did not feel these thoughts were the product of an overexcited imagination on my part.

For me, what was special, too, apart from his treatment of and behaviour towards me, was the fact that whatever we had was private. And in a way I guess I already knew that if the press got hold of the story, things would not only change, but it might even bring about our demise.

Two days after Valentine's Day, which is a day I choose to ignore, I received a huge bouquet of dark red long-stemmed roses from my admirer. He had asked for my full address the day before and told me what a fuss his partner had made about being ignored on the aforementioned day. From this I assumed he felt nothing for her and was concentrating his attention on me.

After Svennis had been on a business trip to Japan, we met up at my house in the early hours when I was alone. He crept into bed with me and he told me how much he had missed me. I said nothing in return. I still felt reluctant to give anything away; besides my actions spoke louder than words. I was weary of words. That was a Sunday.

The following Tuesday I went into London for a haircut. He phoned and suggested I come by his office at the FA for a coffee, which I told him was a terrible idea. He then suggested lunch. I thought that sounded mildly preferable. Nothing wrong with two people being seen out to lunch together. We chose Signor Sassi again and sat full of affection for each other, but unable to touch each other except under the table.

I had a job the following morning. I was due to meet my mate Paul Roberts for lunch afterwards, but he cancelled at the last minute. Svennis called as usual, and he suggested we meet for lunch again. I recommended the presence of another body at our table in order to avoid attracting raised eyebrows two days in a row, and my darling brother Kristian kindly obliged. So the three of us had lunch together as Svennis and I played footsie under the table. He also managed the briefest affectionate compliment in Swedish in between courses. My brother knew about us, of course, but Svennis didn't know that. And the rest of the world knew nothing, either.

The following weekend was to bring about another change of heart for me. Melanie phoned me on the Sunday to warn me that Svennis had been pictured kissing his partner in Italy. I was not only disappointed, but angry. I didn't wait for him to call on this one occasion, but left a terse message on his mobile asking him to call me back. Eventually he did. Protecting my heart with an iron shield, I told him about the picture and exactly how I felt. I explained that I was willing to believe him as long as I didn't have evidence to the contrary. Which I now believed I did. I was angry and forceful and insistent. He tried to interrupt me but failed on several occasions – I was damned if I was going to hear one thing from him, whilst being exposed to something completely different. I wasn't about to be his fool.

Gradually though, he got his words heard. He asked if he was kissing her or she him. 'You were there, for fuck's sake, you should know! Besides, it doesn't make a difference,' I told him. 'It does,' he said. 'She will often put on a performance if she knows there might be cameras around.'

I knew he had gone to Italy, I knew he was with her, and I made it clear that if he was having his cake and thought he could bloody eat it as well, he'd picked the wrong woman. He tried, time and time again, to explain that he was telling the truth and that *he* hadn't shown *her* any affection. But I'm afraid his words fell on deaf, injured ears. Despite his pleas, I resolved once more to call the relationship off until she was out of the picture.

When he phoned me the next day, I was still feeling a little injured, but not sorry for myself. He asked me if he could carry on calling me. It was as if he didn't want to let go. He told me he was disappointed with my decision; so, I said, was I. He told me it was now up to him now to sort out his private life as soon as possible. He could continue to call, I said; besides, two days later we were both due up at Old Trafford again for European game, and this time we were both staying over.

But I failed miserably at finding hotel rooms in Manchester for Angus and me for the night of the game. With no flights back, it was imperative we found somewhere to stay. We were becoming desperate – but everywhere, absolutely everywhere was full. When Svennis called I asked if his powers extended as far as the Manchester hospitality industry. Well, hooray, for the FA! Rather conveniently they found us two rooms in the very hotel Sven was staying in.

After the game, once in my room, the phone rang. It was him. The man I knew I would spend the night with. The man I knew I would take from, as long as I had the power to hold my own. And I did. I stayed the night in his suite and tiptoed my way back to my room in the wee small hours of the morning after a night of no sleep.

That morning, after settling our bills, Angus and I had been asked to attend a question-and-answer breakfast hosted by Sven in aid of the Prince's Trust, for which I am an ambassador. It was a hall decked with hundreds of businessmen, who had paid to have breakfast with the Sven. I had been placed on the top table, one seat away from Mr Eriksson, and it felt bizarre and wonderful at the same time that none of the people in that room knew we had spent the previous night together. As the Q and A ended with questions from the floor, one person stood up to ask him whether Nancy Dell'Olio would be accompanying him to Japan for the World Cup. He replied in front of them and me that he wasn't sure. I knew to the contrary.

*

I knew that Miss Dell'Olio would not be making her exit before the World Cup – I told him I didn't believe he would get around to it beforehand, and he replied that he simply didn't have the energy or time to achieve it – but he reassured me that he would be cutting ties straight afterwards. By then, his time in England was short before he would be heading east. I also knew that I wanted to be able to share that time with him. What was there to gain by stopping seeing him for a few weeks? I could tell he wasn't keen on the idea either. But first I asked him to clarify a few things for me. Firstly, why was he prepared to take this massive public risk with me during the biggest year of his professional life? He answered that 'some risks are worth taking'. He continued that there surely was no capital punishment for carrying on as we were – 'what will they do, hang me?' I tried to let him know that this would be of significant interest to the press and one should never underestimate them.

No matter how I tried to turn it in his mind, he was adamant that this was how he wanted to proceed. On top of which he suggested he rented an apartment in the North London area at which we could rendezvous with greater ease. I explained that I thought it would be very risky and declined the suggestion on the grounds that I would then permanently become the mistress – nothing might ever get sorted out. He took my points on board. And with that he stayed on in my life.

However, circumstances beyond our control meant we were unable to see each other for the next two weeks – Svennis had a trip to Sweden, on which he asked me to join him but I declined, and England had another international friendly. I had my hands full recording a new series for ITV, *Home on Their Own*. On 30 March

I set off for Barbados on holiday with my two beautiful children. Both had been ill with fevers and colds the day before, but I decided to brave it, knowing that the sunshine would do us all good.

It felt wonderful to be away from it all, and gradually over the first few days the children's health improved and Bo even began to like the sand under her feet, and her fear of the sea diminished. Cameron was a dolphin in the sea and an artist under cover when it rained. The holiday was something I would never have dared dream of a year ago and I felt we all deserved it.

Svennis had left several messages on my mobile and I left one for him telling him we had arrived safely. Then, time difference permitting, we would speak once or twice a day. He commented on the fact that there was a picture of me in my bikini in one of the dailies already, and complimented me over and over again. I still hadn't learnt how to accept this attention from him, and chose instead a quick change of subject. He even phoned me early the morning after Beckham's foot break to share with me his surprise at finding the press outside his door awaiting his comment. He told me, 'People are dying in Palestine, and they want my comment on his foot injury . . .'. I think he was overwhelmed by the media's need to know. We exchanged terms of endearment and the fact that we missed each other, but I could not have been happier than I was, alone with my children. Perhaps because he didn't threaten my time with them did it suit me so well. And this relationship was far from volatile, aggressive or contentious. It felt comfortable, affectionate and warm.

*

I returned bronzed from Barbados on the morning of 12 April. It was not long before the phone rang. Svennis was well aware that I was about to embark on two weeks' intensive work on the fourth series of *Dog Eat Dog*, and he had his own busy schedule. He wanted to see me, he said, and asked if I was free the following night. With great excitement he phoned me that Saturday morning to announce that he had managed to dispose of his partner and that he would be free from six o'clock that evening. He invited me over to stay.

I felt uncomfortable once again, but curious at the same time. I wondered where in the street I should leave my car, just in case it would be spotted, or if indeed, I would be, upon entering his Regent's Park abode. We hadn't seen each other for some weeks and I was looking forward to being with him again. I brought a jar of caviar I had bought some months before I met him, and strawberries and cream. He welcomed me warmly, but had to remain on the phone as he was negotiating a team for the England game the following week. I had a little look around the most beautifully, tastefully decorated house I had seen in a long time. It definitely had a woman's touch. There were a few photos of the Swede and the Italian in the same pose on various beaches around the world, which made me feel vaguely criminal to be there.

But when he got off the phone we made love. He told me that despite sending the Italian away she had tried to make her excuses to come back early, but he had refused to let her. Just then, for a fleeting moment I had visions of her walking through the door and an almighty scene erupting. But he reassured me she was abroad. On that note he led me upstairs.

As he entered their bedroom I told him that I hoped he didn't think I was sleeping in there. He paused and conceded that maybe it wasn't the best idea. We took up residence in the guest room and in the morning he brought me breakfast in bed.

I drove home early, full of the joys of spring, and I had no sooner arrived than the phone went. It was him. I was just about to text him, I told him. Then do, he exclaimed excitedly, and put the phone down.

We didn't have a chance to make arrangements to see each other again, because on Thursday 18 April, four months after our first meeting, Melanie called. The story of Sven and Ulrika was about to break.

*

Inevitable as this was, I was physically and emotionally shaken. I simply hadn't been expecting it. I had always known it was a possibility, but I had cocooned myself with this man in a world where no one knew about us, and now that world was about to be blown apart. I felt uncertain, unsure, but most of all very, very sad.

I was told that Piers Morgan, editor of the *Mirror*, had got whiff from a very excited *News of the World*, who were about to break the story that coming Sunday. Instead, he now had the chance to break it in his newspaper the following day. I knew, and Melanie knew, that we could not deny it. If we denied it now – and we had no idea what the *Mirror*'s source was – the papers would only pursue it and persecute me if they found that I had lied. We had absolutely no choice. But, equally, we refused to confirm it. By doing that, it meant we had not done anything to contribute towards the making of the story. But it goes without saying that Piers Morgan knew that we would have denied it had it been untrue.

For the second time in my life, I had to phone Svennis. And swiftly. And once more he wasn't there. I had to leave a message, but he phoned back within half an hour. I broke the news to a silent man. He stayed quiet for a while, and then calmly let out, 'OK, I see.' He kept asking me what they knew, what evidence they had. I couldn't answer any questions. I had no answers. He then asked what my agent's response had been. I told him that she had insisted on not confirming it, but she had also refused to deny it. I was hoping he could read between the lines, but his mind was elsewhere. All I kept thinking was, Shit! Shit! Shit!

Mr Morgan, of *Mirror* fame, had decided, in his infinite wisdom, that there was no scandal to the story as neither party was married. I think he thought it was a rather amusing coupling, which is more or less how the story ran the following morning. I had thought so too, until then. But that was before the world around me went mad, once again.

On the morning of Friday 19 April, my mother's birthday, some twenty journalists and photographers were gathered outside my house gate. Occasionally the phone would ring, when one would decide to ask me directly what was going on, as opposed to going through my agent, but for the most part they were bombarding her. Cameron was very perturbed by their presence at the gate, and vaguely remembered that the last time this had happened, when he was three and a half, Stan had done something nasty to Mummy. This time, however, surpassed even that. By my return from the school run, there was even a camera crew outside.

Apart from the *Mirror*, many of the rest of the newspapers were in disbelief and thought perhaps it was a hoax. Was it really so strange? It is hard to explain how you feel when this circus comes to town, especially as this was the biggest one my village had ever entertained – even for me! Things began to feel bizarre, unreal – maybe even surreal. I become tense, bordering on hyper. I find it hard to concentrate, eat or even be normal at times like that. It is as if a madness takes you over. Apart from the madness outside my world, inside it relations and friends are calling to ask if it is true and can they be of any help. But sadly, for me and them, there is no one who can help. You have to ride it yourself. I think the feeling is best described as being out of control, which is perhaps why it frightens me so. My sadness, of course, stemmed from my deep affection for the Swede, whom I now knew I wouldn't be able to see for a very long time. It would be far too great a risk to take. And still we didn't know the source of the outbreak.

Later that morning he phoned. I asked if he was all right and he sounded shocked. He said he couldn't believe the number of journalists and photographers outside his house – he was flabbergasted. I asked him how things were at home and he replied that the Italian wanted to call a press conference to deny it. I said nothing. The story was breaking in Sweden, too.

That day and the next were spent trying to work out who was the source of the story, and the *News of the World* would give nothing away. They were holding on tight until they ran on Sunday. Svennis had an emergency meeting at the FA, where they thankfully told him he could deal with it as he wished – it was a personal matter, not a matter for them. I had to go to Pinewood to record

ULRIKA JONSSON

Dog Eat Dog and as I walked on set a silence swept across it as if I was German and everyone had been told not to mention the war. I decided to break the ice and put everyone at ease by making a little quip about the newspapers. One could almost hear the audible sigh of relief from a crew and team who wanted to get on with the job in hand.

Before we actually started recording, Svennis called. I was worried about him. He sounded exhausted and rather quiet. He insisted that he would never comment on his private life, which I respected, and that he would never confirm his affair with me, but he said things had gone too far for him to deny it. He said he had three choices: confirm, deny or bite his tongue. I told him only two of those were viable options. If he denied it they would go after him, come hell or high water. He said he was going to think about it until Monday. I knew then he didn't have a clue what machine he was dealing with. Monday was a lifetime away.

The following day I woke up to headlines quoting Miss Dell'Olio, who had called me a wretched girl in search of publicity, someone whom Sven didn't even know. Despite this I pursued my trip to Chelsea to watch them take on United, with my brother and Angus. The trip had been arranged a while back, and I did not want to cancel it and disappoint my brother. Svennis had not told me he was going. Normally he would always tell me where he was going to be. As fate would have it he was attending the same match. We sat at opposite sides of the pitch and the press went bananas for pictures of us at the same game, apart. I think it was seen as provocative of me to be there. Had I known for sure that he was going, perhaps I would not have attended. He didn't mind me going, I knew that. He phoned me immediately after the game to ask me if I'd enjoyed it. I asked him how things were at home. And he laughed and said that he was still alive. He also sounded slightly jovial. He commented again on his disbelief at what was going on, but equally tried to convince me that it would soon be over. He still has no idea, I thought.

With everyone still second-guessing the source of the story and convinced the press had no photographic evidence, it was suggested by the Sven camp that mobile phone calls and messages were being bugged or traced. I felt sure that wasn't impossible, but wondered if there was a contribution from somewhere else. But what? Or indeed, whom?

*

I was soon to be put out of my misery: early that Sunday morning it emerged that my nanny had let slip to someone who had told someone else who had then sold their story about Sven coming to my house. It was now open season. There were no photographs, but as I was put out of one misery, another one kicked in. There before my eyes, in one of the papers, was a picture of Sven and Nancy at dinner very publicly in London the night before. She had confirmed they were engaged and still 'very much together'. I didn't believe that for a second – that was not the reason for my misery. Mine was with him. For a man who wished to keep his private life private and had no intention of making any contribution to the story, he was now very naively parading his 'partner' out in front of everyone. I was angry and hurt. Did he not realize that a picture speaks a thousand words? He looked like a man who was completely ignoring my existence and snubbing the very thought of 'us'. I had never for one second thought he would leave Miss Dell'Olio before the World Cup, not even under these circumstances, but the absence of a comment from him to the press and the presence of a very indicative picture was, in my books, naive, ignorant and showed a disregard for me.

I comforted my distraught nanny, who was on the verge of a nervous breakdown, and assured her that, whilst the mistake was hers and she was in breach of her terms of employment, I couldn't bear to see her in such a state and she still had a job at my house. Continuity was very important for the children, and more importantly this was a very out-of-character thing for a normally incomparable nanny to have done. She was not about to be sacked. She was relieved and joined me and my family and friends, who were rallying around me, for Sunday lunch. No word from Sven.

By early evening I called him and told him I was confused and hurt by his behaviour. He suggested we should all go about our business as normally as possible. Despite the circus surrounding us? I wondered. I suggested she had made him go out to dinner. He denied it. But not without hesitation. I also challenged him on something rather unpleasant. It had been put to me, by a source who shall remain nameless, that he had had other lovers. If they were before my time, they were none of my business, but what if he had us running concurrently? He confirmed there had been other women during his time with the Italian, but before me. Some relief, but I was angry with him. Angry for not protecting me somehow. For not acknowledging me in some way and for showing complete disregard for me by parading about town as if the circus was my problem. And I was pissed off with him that this all now meant the press were pitting me against Miss Dell'Olio. It was as if he wasn't part of this problem. He had left me to battle without protection, when in fact he was the one 'playing away'. He was leaving everything open to question. I told him very aggressively and in no uncertain terms that I would fight, fight for me, but never over him. His voice became nervous and he pleaded with me to allow him to phone me back. I put the phone down.

He did call back, ten minutes later. He sounded considerably more unnerved than the last time we had spoken. He pleaded with me to give him until the next day and then he quickly added that two members of the FA were on their way to his house. He thought they were coming to fire him. In that brief conversation I went from anger at him to concern. Surely they wouldn't *fire* him? This whole thing was getting out of control.

The Monday brought more comparisons and supposed 'battles' between myself and Miss Dell'Olio. They gave us each marks out of ten, for compatibility with the Swede and our own merit. I wasn't coming out of it particularly well. I have, of course, fucked every man I've clapped eyes on and she was far more dignified, what with being a lawyer. But the comparisons themselves didn't bother me. What bothered me that he was out of the picture all of a sudden and that this issue was now between Miss Dell'Olio and myself. I had no feelings for her, negative or positive, but the triangle, it seemed, had lost its third corner overnight.

The newspapers in Sweden were also going crazy. My low-level fame there was now replaced by absolute notoriety. Friends and relations were very concerned about how I was coping. I was coping well, but I struggled with Svennis's approach and lack of conviction. He had to host a press conference to reveal the England players' new Burton suits, and naturally was bombarded with questions. The only one to achieve anything was the first, from a female journalist, who asked whether he felt there had been any inaccuracies in the press reporting over the last few days. He said no, there hadn't been, and if there had, he would have complained. And that was the sum of his confirmation of his affair with me. Silence.

But the press reports of the affair had their inaccuracies – as historically they always have and presumably always will. One rumour was that the whole affair – if it had even happened – was a publicity stunt to publicize my forthcoming book. My initial reaction was dismissive, but the rumour refused to go away and in some quarters gathered momentum. Well, firstly, the plan at that time was that my book would not be out for another year. In which case this 'stunt' could only be as premature as they come. Secondly, yes, the affair had actually taken place. Thirdly, if anyone *doesn't* want publicity of this kind, it's me. I don't believe I need it. I was a single woman engaging in an affair with an unmarried but attached man. I had neither sought him out nor hunted him down – he had done the running. With my history of wrong men and complicated situations, I hardly think it would have been in my best interest to want this 'relationship' to go public. The joy for me had been the privacy of it all. And I doubt Mr Eriksson would have gone this far for publicity either, as he seemed to be so uncomfortable with it.

So there it was. Svennis said nothing at his press conference. No denial and no admission. Not even an acknowledgement of some kind. I didn't necessarily agree with his tight-lipped approach, when he had so readily gone through with a very visible show of 'unity' at the weekend, but that was how he wanted to play it. *We* both knew the truth. I felt that people read between the lines and the press knew what was really going on, but I knew that he would be pursued for a quote nonetheless. However, he offered none and neither would I.

My parents were being inundated with journalists, stories were running galore about my past and how I was supposedly behaving in the present – I was heartbroken, apparently, and I had evidently issued Svennis with an ultimatum. According to the papers, he simply HAD to choose between Nancy and me. What rubbish! In the absence of quotes or comments the press spins into its own orbit. They were desperate for a conclusion. Who would Svennis select?

It was extremely perturbing – that was simply not the situation at all. Had the papers not found out about the affair, the Italian and the Swede would have gone to Japan as planned, without anyone being any the wiser. It wasn't a question, there and then, of some-one being 'chosen'. And in any event I had understood he had made a choice – there was not going to be a future with Nancy. As for a long-term future with me, we had both agreed to just enjoy the moment. Now that the press knew something was afoot, however, they were not going to leave any of us alone until there was some sort of ending.

He didn't understand that. But I did. And I wasn't about to hang around for the next two months while my family and I were bombarded, accosted and confronted with questions about this affair. The story would go on and on as long as the papers could breathe life into it, and with no conclusion, they could make up their own fairy-tale ending.

I have to say, I felt deeply uncomfortable with the way Svennis simply turned a blind eye to the stories, pretending, ostrich-like, that they did not exist. I realized then how unaware he was about the realities of British public life. He was practically the most important man in England at that moment. My previous experiences with the press had led me to impress upon him just how serious the situation was – I knew he could not afford a distraction on this scale. Besides what had become of the famous quiet, calm confidence of the man, which had been so appealing? He had now begun to become reluctant to talk over the phone, for fear of us being bugged, and consequently changed his mobile number three times in as many days. It now hurt me that he was incapable of protecting me better and that he was simply leaving me to face my battles alone. He seemed to carry on with his job as normal – but this, for me, was not normal. Yes, things had broken publicly before, but it was never *normal*. It was not how I wanted normal to be for me or my family.

My mother was deeply hurt by some of the reporting which painted me as a man-eating slapper and serial affairist. *Tonight with Trevor McDonald* was planning a feature on the 'affair' and asked her to appear. To my dismay she agreed – I say dismay not because of what she might say, but for fear of this opening the floodgates to her every time a story about me broke. But how else, she felt, could she express a reasoned point of view? I actually understood her helplessness. I felt the same. On both sides of the fence – my family's and the press's – the size of the story seemed to have surpassed everyone's experiences, and it now qualified for prime time television.

By Wednesday morning, despite being asked by someone in Svennis's camp – who shall remain nameless – whether I would wait for him until he came back, because it was evidently me he wanted, I still felt very strongly that his own personal reluctance to protect or reassure me spoke volumes. Everyone seemed to think there was a decision for Svennis to make, yet in reality I knew there was none: he had said to me already that he wanted out of the relationship he was in. Yet to the world that remained unexpressed. I decided I was not about to sit back and wait for him to make some kind of public choice. I would make one for myself and for my family.

I told Melanie that I could take no more invasion, disruption and persecution. My position had become untenable – I could not, knowing the truth and holding onto it very tightly, go on witnessing this public speculation. *I* needed to make a public statement. For the good of me and my family, but I also knew it would be to Svennis's advantage. They would have their long-awaited 'conclusion'. And

Sven would be free to concentrate on the challenge he was to about to face.

Melanie asked me to think about it. Not to cut the cord, unless I was really sure. Together we went through every possible 'what if' scenario but none changed the way I felt. On Wednesday 24 April I issued the following press statement:

> In the hope of dispelling any further rumours about my relationship with Sven-Goran Eriksson, I would like to make it clear that I have never issued him with an ultimatum. Like everybody else, I wish Sven the very best for the World Cup. But I also have a job to do, both as a mother and professionally, and would like to be allowed to continue to do my job without further speculation involving me in this relationship. I am no longer a part of this relationship.

Beforehand, I phoned Sven to tell him what I was doing, in the hope he would understand *and* understand that it could bring the circus to an end. He was unavailable, but I left a message. He did not call back that night, instead escorting the Italian to a football game up north (without visiting me first this time, needless to say).

The papers the following day interpreted my statement as defeat. 'Nancy 1, Ulrika 0', read one headline. There were pictures galore of the happy couple at the football game and commentary running alongside. According to them, I had met my Waterloo.

I myself couldn't have felt more differently about the situation. The next morning brought only a sense of enormous relief: I had gone ahead and made the right decision for *me*. However, I still subjected myself to watching the *Tonight* programme, which was more or less dedicated to the affair that had supposedly spent seven days shaking the world. I had to watch the likes of Vanessa Feltz proclaiming inexplicably close knowledge of the situation and retelling the story of the evening of Mr Desmond's party with all the glamour and fiction of a bad Barbara Cartland novel. Her appearing on the show was disturbing if not a little self-serving, in my opinion. But the programme did attempt to explore Svennis's part in the whole affair, rather than facetiously pick apart the two women in his orbit and what was supposedly one of the most imaginative 'publicity stunts' of all time. My mother did appear and she attempted to defend my reputation. She did well. But there was even less conclusion to the programme than there was in real life for me and Svennis.

The journalists hung around my house the following day, desperate for a photograph of me looking sad, lost and forlorn, but they were disappointed. I felt none of those things. Then that afternoon Svennis did call. I asked him if he had heard my press statement, and he told me someone had mentioned something to him. I took it upon myself to read it to him, in order that there would be absolute clarity between us. I also asked him if he knew why I had done it. He replied reluctantly that yes, he thought so. Once again I clarified that I had done it because I felt the way that things had been dealt with and turned out was not something I wanted to be part of. I told him I couldn't bear for it to look as if I was waiting for him to make a decision between me and another, even if he promised that was not the truth. What's more, he had offered me precious little support when the whole thing blew up. Circus time was over; there was too much at stake for it to continue. Cameron was now being teased at school, which was a step too far for a story such as this to take. I also pointed out that he had a very important job to do. With this conclusion handed to them on a plate, the press attention on this aspect of his life ought to peter out and he would be able to get on with it.

He listened intently and repeated that his feelings and situation hadn't changed. Gratifying and, in other circumstances, reassuring as this might seem, on this occasion that was not going to be enough. He asked if he could carry on calling me. I replied that I didn't think there would be much point. He said he understood and would see how things went.

After that he did not call for ten days. I had my hands full picking up the pieces after a manic few weeks and trying to come to terms with the untidy end to yet another relationship – the end itself and its untidiness. When he did call we were both subdued. He told me most of the press had left him alone, so I told him wryly that he had me to thank for that. He suddenly exclaimed that, contrary to what might have been printed in the papers, he was *not* engaged and was absolutely *not* getting married. I know, I said. It was the conversation between two people who had somehow been forced to quit something which might have been, but which was now simply an 'if only'.

He did confirm that his plans were still the same – go to Asia for the tournament and sort out his private life upon his return. He said he would call again when he got there, because he was still nervous of potential bugging in Britain. He also wanted me to have his mobile number in Japan; he'd feel more at ease communicating once there.

Then he called again the Friday before he departed for the England team's recreational week in Dubai. He asked me whether I would make any plans to go to Japan. Absolutely not, I replied. He sounded regretful. He said he would call again as soon as he could.

When a week later he called from South Korea, we had what seemed by comparison a long conversation. Then he called on the day of the England–Sweden game and left a good-luck message (I, of course, would be supporting Sweden) on my mobile.

And that was that. They thought it was all over – it is now.

*

As I write this I don't know what I feel about it all. I can't deny that there are still 'what ifs' hanging in the air some days. But I know it was the right decision for me. I was, and to some extent still am, deeply fond of a man who promised me something he never quite had the chance to fulfil. I had only the brief beginnings of a relationship that was never allowed to run its natural course. But on the other hand, I did have three and a half months of blissful privacy and the affection and generosity of a man I respected. I will hold onto those things as I move forward and feel proud that I did not lose my heart and subsequently my head. And it was the first relationship I had achieved in a long time. With all that I have on my plate, what with children, work and a house to clean (I've finally found a cleaner), I did not need further complications. I chose to protect myself and my family. Perhaps for the very first time.

SELF-ASSEMBLY

Shortly after my father's death I discovered, tucked at the back of one of his kitchen drawers, fifty or so letters and postcards from my mother to both him and me, forced together in a wide, overstretched elastic band. I read them with great interest. The first few seemed to be answers to questions from my father about how my mother was living her new life in Holland and even about her new daily routine. Others referred to letters in which my father had struggled with the heartbreak of a pending divorce. It is clear from my mother's replies that while my father may have remained deeply in love with her, she had moved on. More often than not, her notes also contained contributions to our non-existent household funds. Her letters to me were filled with longing and affection.

In many respects these letters enabled me to understand her more fully. These were not the communications of an uncaring mother, but of a woman who, although having made a commitment to a new life, retained one to the subjects of her old one. I realized from reading them that she had indeed, deep down, wanted me to be part of her new world, but that she had felt at the time that it would offer me greater continuity to remain with my father and my friends. It was as though she needed to find her own feet first, before inviting me to join her. She did not perhaps know exactly how permanent her move would be, either. She probably thought that further instability would have been an even more negative experience for me. Yes, my mother *had* cared. And she had strived to maintain a good relationship with me, and my father too.

As a child I had understood that she left my father because she had fallen in love with someone else. As an adult, I could never understand how the mother in her could have brought herself to leave her eight-year-old daughter. But I *did* understand the woman in her wanting to get out of a dysfunctional relationship she had grown out of. Yet I still cannot imagine leaving one of my own children in such a way, and my contention with her has always been that she has been so reluctant to discuss this with me. It may have damaged me as a child, but I didn't experience the consequences until I was much older.

But having spent many years questioning our relationship – never quite understanding my inner anger towards her, coupled with an incessant desire to please her – I have finally reached a point where I can put most of those issues to bed. I am quite different to my mother and my character displays traits closer to my father (which may even bring back unfavourable memories for her), but despite our sometimes volatile relationship, she has been a rock for me at times when I have really needed her – my rape; my divorce; the demise of my relationships; the sickness of my daughter, and the departure of Bo's father. She worries about me, I know, and she doesn't always know how to express herself emotionally, but her intentions are good. And where both of us have made an effort, we have made great headway. We do not always agree and we still have the ability for heated exchanges, but equally are able to show each other generosity and laugh like drains. I love her very much and have grown to accept things a little better.

*

My relationship with my father has been equally frustrating, but for different reasons. I am still hurt by his lack of responsibility when I was a child, and I am still hurt by his absence from my life today, when I feel our relationship would have finally achieved some maturity. I acknowledge his death, but still find it hard to accept that I will not see him again. I have been more forgiving in my attitude towards him because he had such ridiculously redeeming features –

his humour, his face, his practicality, his naivety, his hedonism and his endless joie de vivre. And I'd like to believe I will carry those characteristics with me until my dying day.

But it is perhaps those characteristics that have led me into some of the relationships I have forged with the men in my life. I certainly haven't been scared to dip my toe in the water or to test the proverb that variety is the spice of life. But, needless to say, this has led me into some disastrous situations. Naivety has at times made me believe the best of people, and has also meant I have failed to acknowledge that pain inflicted on me by another person, whether physical or emotional, is the beginning of the end. More often than not, it is not advisable to persist.

I've come to learn that selfishness has no place in a relationship. I'd like to think that I have longed for and contributed towards solidarity and teamwork in most of my mine, but it has rarely been reciprocated. I have also learnt not only that the sexual forces at play can be as damaging as they are heavenly, but also that on their own they are never enough. Insecurity and lack of self-respect in the past have meant I have not followed my instincts, which could have shown me a quicker way out of some pretty dreadful situations. The romantic in me has mistakenly believed that it is words that count, when in fact it is deeds. Deeds have also proven to me that parenthood is a privilege that is earned, it is not just a title. Yet, ironically, the only relationship I do not consider a disaster is the one which I seemingly grew out of, but which is still standing – the one with my ex-husband John Turnbull. Perhaps it was right for me, but at the wrong time. And I have come to realize that it is no good saying that I am a shit person, thereby excusing shit behaviour. If I am prepared to accept myself as a decent person, then I have to behave accordingly.

I started out with a slightly confused interpretation of what the relationship between a man and a woman was all about. I was mostly brought up a boy, but have always had the highest regard for womankind. Other early influences led me to have a confused attitude to sex for many years. I did not see it as an act of love – it was something I feared and did not respect. I think it was this, coupled with low self-esteem, that has often made me settle for less than second best.

There are times when in not daring to trust myself I've managed to thoroughly confuse myself. Despite being utterly comfortable with my independence, I've gone on – both as a child and an adult – to spend too much time inside my head, beating myself up with guilt, a sense of failed responsibility and even self-hatred.

Perhaps that's why I have often questioned myself as to why I do the job I do, with all the public scrutiny and speculation that goes alongside it. It seems foolish as an already-unresolved person to put yourself in a situation where you can potentially be unsettled even further. So why have I stuck with it? Because I guess I've found something I believe I am good at.

I thoroughly enjoy what I do, but have never felt that ambition has got the better of me. On the contrary, I feel I have almost stumbled into this career. There wasn't a defined career plan, but there was a strategy to survive and succeed. Fortunately, one job has led to another. And while fame has put so many aspects of my life into the spotlight, I have also managed to keep private more than you might have imagined. I don't spend my time going to the press with titbits about my life, but I do have to spend some time trying to manage the things that get kicked around about me. Particularly when I live in a country where the attitude to women is bordering on schizophrenic.

Women here are sexy objects and can be appreciated for that alone, but they are rarely respected like men. Equality for women is fought for on a daily basis, but then fought against by some women themselves. This country appears to struggle to come to terms with the headway women are making. The thought that a woman is financially or spiritually independent can still breed not only contempt, but also confusion. Infidelity committed on the part of the woman – as in my case – is considered sluttish and loose, whereas a male perpetrator is largely seen as not only manly, but also stud-like. Indeed, I had never really considered the divide between men and women until it was thrown in my face.

In Sweden, society is such that you ignore egalitarianism of any kind at your peril. It is so second nature to me that I have never weighed up my power or lack of it in relation to the opposite sex. Perhaps this has proved to be a challenge in many of my relationships; it certainly has been in the public perception of me. It is a totally different approach to mind and body. We have even been known to sunbathe topless without it being misconstrued as a sexual display!

I love women. I respect and appreciate them. Contrary to popular opinion, I'm not a 'geezer bird'. I have always known that enjoying the company of men doesn't have to be at the expense of other women. I value my female relationships more highly than I do those with the opposite sex. Ironically, women have turned out to be less threatened by my professional successes and have identified greatly with my personal failures. After all, many women experience the kind of relationships I have had; it's just that I tend to experience mine publicly.

This is not to say that I don't genuinely enjoy the company of men. God bless them! Many have become great, close friends, who too carry personal failures as part of their baggage. Some of the men with whom I have had relationships have become friends. But others were never friends in the first place – another lesson learnt. Needless to say, it is the friendships that I now value most. Perhaps I will eventually find the two together in a lasting way, but I am not, contrary to overwhelming popular opinion, currently recruiting. I am bemused to read that any contact with the opposite sex is seen as public affirmation of 'the new man' in my life. I don't need a man to define me or to complete my life. Yes, there was a time when I very much saw a man as the missing piece in my puzzle. And, yes, I can't deny it would be nice to have, but it is not something I cannot live without.

What I cannot live without is what I have already been blessed with: my children; my strength; the loving care and support of Cameron's father who has now generously extended fatherhood to my daughter; friends. Oh, and football.

*

Writing this book has been cathartic, which was what I original hoped it would be when I set out to do it. At that time, it was for my eyes only. But it has also at times been a humiliating experience as I have had to look at situations, moments and emotions in the cold light of day, and it has fortunately taught me some important lessons about others, but foremost about myself. And what started out as a quest for self-discovery became a process of self-assembly. Some way down the line it became clear that I'd lost the instructions to my own personal flat-pack; a series of attempts – some of which ended in chaos – have now, finally, resulted in the pieces being assembled in something approaching the correct order.

It's not a crime to make mistakes, but it is a crime not to learn from them. And the most recent and final blow for me a year or two ago knocked me down so forcefully that the lengthy recovery period served to wake me up and make me rethink my approach to life. Having a chronically sick child has also made me less patient with the superfluous aspects of life and more patient with where I am at myself – you find your way to the fundamentals much more quickly. For me, life has been hard to grasp at times, but now that I have accepted that change is inevitable it has somehow become a little easier to deal with.

Honest.